The Passing of American Neutrality *1937-1941*

DONALD F. DRUMMOND

GREENWOOD PRESS, PUBLISHERS
NEW YORK   1968

66522

Copyright 1955 by The University of Michigan

Reprinted with the permission of
The University of Michigan Press.

First Greenwood reprinting, 1968

Library of Congress catalogue card number: 68-54416

PRINTED IN THE UNITED STATES OF AMERICA

Preface

THE AVOWED RELATIONSHIP OF THE UNITED STATES WITH THOSE PARTS
of the world which lie outside the Western Hemisphere changed pro-
foundly between 1937 and 1941. As diplomatic aggression, and war
itself, laid bare the security problem of the twentieth century, the
United States broke from the isolationist tradition of American
thought: neutrality ceased to be the expression of its attitude toward
disturbances in Europe and Asia, and the nation assumed a major responsibility in the guidance of world affairs. If this role becomes as
permanent as now seems likely, its acceptance constitutes the weightiest
development in the external relations of the United States since the
adoption of the Constitution. My objectives are to examine American
foreign policy during the most crucial years of change, to show its
connections with the policies and actions of other governments, and
to align the whole with such imponderables as the growth of public
opinion and the force of executive resolve.

An extensively revised doctoral dissertation, this study owes much
to the perceptive criticism of friends and colleagues at the University
of Michigan. I am greatly indebted to Professors Arthur E. R. Boak,
Dwight L. Dumond, and Lawrence Preuss, who read the original
manuscript in its entirety, and to Professor Marshall M. Knappen, who
labored especially hard to keep me from going astray on matters of
style and questions of fact. My deepest gratitude goes to Professor
Howard M. Ehrmann, under whose supervision the study was planned
and whose wise counsel has been of inestimable value at all times.

By their grant of a fellowship, the Dean and the Executive Board
of the Horace H. Rackham School of Graduate Studies, University of
Michigan, afforded me several months of leisure to complete the work.
The perceptive criticism of Miss Ethel E. Tuttle, Assistant Editor of
Scholarly Publications, University of Michigan Press, has improved

the quality of the manuscript in every way. I wish also to acknowledge the many courtesies extended by the staff of the University of Michigan General Library; by Mr. Herman Kahn, Director of the Franklin D. Roosevelt Library, Hyde Park, New York; and by those very able officials of the Department of State—Dr. G. Bernard Noble, Chief of the Division of Historical Policy Research, and Dr. E. Taylor Parks, Chief of the Historical Advisory Staff—who did everything possible to facilitate my examination of unpublished diplomatic correspondence and memoranda.

Finally, I must record my obligation to The Macmillan Company for its generosity in permitting me to quote numerous passages of copyrighted material from *The Memoirs of Cordell Hull* (1948).

Donald F. Drummond

Table of Contents

66522

Historical Introduction: The Isolationist Tradition and American Foreign Policy

I

THE DISTINCTIVE AMERICAN FAITH IN THE VIRTUES OF ISOLATION WHICH WAS shattered by events leading to American participation in the Second World War enjoyed a long and vigorous history before December 7, 1941. It was, in some respects, as old as the first English settlements on the North American continent. It was already a genuine creed when the United States achieved independence. And it wielded a self-conscious ascendancy over the nation's thought from that time onward.

While none could doubt its general meaning, this isolationism, viewed in detail, was somewhat amorphous. It had so many different facets representing so many different points of view that no person or group could effectively embrace every one. Some aspects of the belief consistently received great emphasis, others less emphasis, and still others almost none at all. It was always susceptible, moreover, to the pressure of outside forces; both its strength and its direction varied regularly with the intensity of other native ideals and with changing international conditions. As a result, its main objective—to steer clear of wars that did not originate in America—was now and then completely ignored at significant moments in the nation's life. Nevertheless, its basic assumptions were always persuasive enough to confine the American outlook within a recognizable framework of easy precept and deep conviction.

II

History and geography together supplied one foundation of the isolationist belief. Owing to the circumstances of their discovery and to their distance from the closely joined land masses which had been the environment of ancient and medieval man, the Americas were originally conceived of as a new world; and the sheer physical difficulty of reaching their shores helped perpetuate the idea that they belonged to a distinct geographical sphere. Isolation, in short, appeared to have been ordained by nature.

A second reason for the early growth of isolationism, at least in British North America, was based in the satisfaction of those who settled there. That area, above all others, was peopled by discontented Europeans—men and women who left their homelands to escape from living conditions that were demonstrably bad—and in America they found, or thought they found, the principal material, moral, and social benefits that they were seeking. At the very least, each westbound immigrant put his former troubles a whole ocean behind him; and while America offered a full quota of new difficulties, these were mainly problems of underdevelopment whose solutions fell ultimately within the grasp of the average man. By an entirely natural process, therefore, inevitable comparisons led to foregone conclusions. America was a new world because it was a better world, and from the early colonial period most Americans habitually viewed their country as a land of special destiny, with opportunities and interests fundamentally different from those of European nations.

Glimmerings of this attitude could be observed even when conditions were most unfavorable. Whatever their intangible gains, the original colonists of Virginia enjoyed no material betterment in their way of life for some time after reaching America. With respect to food supplies and creature comforts, indeed, they were much worse off during their first few years in the new world than during their last years in the old one. Yet, the land held a promise which dulled the pain of immediate hardships. That ebullient soldier, Captain John Smith, struck a characteristic note of optimism when he wrote, in 1612, that "heaven and earth never agreed better to frame a place for mans [*sic*] habitation . . . . The vesture of the earth in most places doeth manifestly prove the nature of the soile to be lusty and very rich. . . . The country is not mounta[i]nous nor yet low but such pleasant plaine hills and fert[i]le valleyes, one prettily crossing an other, and watered so conveniently with their sweete brookes and christall springs, as if art it selfe had devised them." [1]

Self-congratulation was likewise apparent in early New England.

[1] John Smith, *Travels and Works of Captain John Smith, 1580–1631*, ed. Edward Arber (Edinburgh: John Grant, 1910), I, 48–49.

Take, for example, the views of the Reverend Francis Higginson. Living at Plymouth, where the rocky soil and harsh climate did not encourage such optimistic descriptions, Higginson, as an honest expounder of God's Word, could not ignore the bleakness of his surroundings. But he was not slow to find atmospheric compensations for what the neighborhood lacked otherwise, and recorded his belief in 1630, only a decade after the colony's establishment, that "a sup of New England air is worth a whole flagon of old English ale." [2]

Within a generation or two the horizons of American life broadened considerably, and its votaries no longer had to rely upon topographical appreciations and such nebulous encomia as the one just quoted. Thus a somewhat different, if equally favorable, comparison between Europe and America was drawn toward the end of the century by the German immigrant, Francis Daniel Pastorius, who in 1683 set down the reasons which impelled him to quit the land of his birth. "After examining to my satisfaction the European provinces and countries, and the impending *motus belli*," [3] he wrote, "and taking apprehensively to heart the vicissitudes and troubles of my native country arising therefrom, I have suffered myself to be moved by the special direction of the Most High to journey over to Pennsylvania, . . . especially as the audacity and sin of the European world are accumulating more and more from day to day, and therefore the just judgment of God cannot be long withheld." [4] That he did not repent his decision was made clear ten years later, when, with due emphasis for the practical as well as the spiritual endowments of his new situation, he took a moment to rejoice at God's having "so graciously sheltered this province under the wings of His mercy . . . that no unfriendly clamor, whether of trumpet or musketry, has broken in upon our daily toil and nightly rest"—and finished his picture of well-being with the happy reflection that "in all these years, we have not been obliged to pay a farthing for war . . . ." [5] So Pastorius indicted Europe for war and wickedness together, and Pennsylvania gave him the relief he demanded.

Nor were other solid advantages found wanting as time went on. Virtually everyone acknowledged that the land was extremely well-equipped to satisfy the physical needs of humankind and agreed that the common man enjoyed almost unlimited opportunity for self-im-

[2] Francis Higginson, *New-England's Plantation* (London, 1630), p. 11.
[3] "Tumults of war."
[4] Albert C. Myers, ed., *Narratives of Early Pennsylvania, West New Jersey, and Delaware, 1630–1707* (New York: Charles Scribner's Sons, 1912), p. 411.
[5] *Ibid.*, pp. 416–417.

provement. Writing about conditions in Pennsylvania in 1698, Gabriel Thomas, a Welshman, pointed the moral by explaining that the wages of servants were "much higher here than there" for the reason that "if these large Stipends were refused them, they would quickly set up for themselves, for they can have Provision very cheap, and Land for a very small matter." [6] A much later but distinctly parallel estimate of life's goodness in a neighboring colony was given by William Eddis, surveyor of customs for Maryland, who in 1770 wrote his considered opinion that "by prudent management, a respectable appearance may be supported in Maryland, on terms infinitely more reasonable than in most parts of the mother country; and that greater opportunities are offered to the industrious and enterprising to lay the foundation of a comfortable provision for a succeeding generation." [7]

The writings of colonists, native-born and immigrant alike, fairly bloomed with such commendations of their material environment; and nothing—not even the gradual hardening of institutions in the older colonies—was able to reverse this trend. If religious, economic, or other freedoms became too narrowly circumscribed in the quasi-European societies on the Atlantic seaboard, a man could create his own opportunities through the simple expedient of continuing the westward movement which had brought his ancestors or himself to America in the first place. A Roger Williams could establish a new haven for dissenters in the wilds of Rhode Island; a Thomas Hooker could lead a band of determined men to a better life in the Connecticut Valley; or anyone, if he were hardy enough, could strike out independently and settle where he liked. Armed with a kind of guarantee that America would retain its pristine advantages so long as there was no undue interference with the natural order of things, the average colonist permitted himself few doubts on the score of America's future. It was even assumed that culture, like freedom and prosperity, would quickly find a new axis on this side of the Atlantic. Indeed, an enthusiastic almanac writer stripped the old world of its final claim to preëminence as early as 1730, when he hailed Philadelphia as the new abode of art and wisdom:

> 'Tis here Apollo does erect his throne;
> This his Parnassus, this his Helicon.

---

[6] Myers, ed., *Narratives*, p. 328.
[7] William Eddis, *Letters from America* (London, 1792), pp. 34–35.

Here solid sense does every bosom warm;
Here noise and nonsense have forgot to charm.[8]

Guarded by distance from the worst tribulations of the European scene, this complacency became an essential part of the American tradition; and since the axiomatic benefits of American life were usually presented in terms of contrast with the manifest shortcomings of life in Europe, it was only natural that attempts to make the colonies serve distinctly European interests should eventually be regarded as likely to saddle America with those very practices and disabilities which had already brought Europe so low. Thus the psychological rift between the continents grew wider throughout the colonial period.

The logical culmination of this growth was political independence, but colonial isolationism did not become of political importance until the third quarter of the eighteenth century. The deep affinities of blood and culture existing between colonies and mother country offered one hindrance to its rapid development. Down to the Revolutionary era at least 75 per cent of the colonial population traced their origins, immediate or remote, to the British Isles [9] and did not, generally speaking, find it easy to slough off an inherited love for things British. Another reason for keeping the Imperial connection, a reason both close and practical, was found in the problem of security.

Notwithstanding their physical separation from Europe, the colonies lived in the main current of European power politics until the very eve of the Revolution. Both Canada and the Mississippi Valley were still ruled from Paris; Great Britain and France were still natural enemies; and from the time this rivalry took definite shape, every major war in Europe had its counterpart in America, giving the lie to Pastorius and others like him almost as soon as their rejoicings were committed to paper. From 1689 to 1763 the colonies faced a nearly constant threat—and sometimes the reality—of invasion from the north and west; and while their response to military direction from London was often grudging in the extreme, the necessities of self-defense would not permit them to stand aloof from this long series of wars. Until the American continent was freed of the Anglo-French struggle for empire by the overwhelming victory of British arms in the Seven Years' War, the

[8] Quoted in Moses Coit Tyler, *A History of American Literature* (New York: G. P. Putnam's Sons, 1878), II, 239.

[9] Merle E. Curti, *The Roots of American Loyalty* (New York: Columbia Univ. Press, 1946), p. 7.

colonists were unable to think seriously of cutting a political relationship which guaranteed them the protection of the British Army and
Fleet. Despite the separatism which was implicit in so much of the
colonial attitude, therefore, traditional loyalty to the British Crown
remained strong, and a marked Anglo-American nationalism was evident in some circles as late as the beginning of the Seven Years' War.[10]
Only when British authority was solidly established at Quebec and in
the trans-Appalachian West did the colonists gain that confidence in
their immunity to foreign aggression which became the third major
element of the isolationist gospel.[11]

After the Peace of Paris, however, when it became evident that the
colonies were not to receive the coördinate status within the Empire
which they regarded as their due, American isolationism crystallized
rapidly, gained new impetus and direction from such specific irritants
as the British mercantile system and British policies of taxation, and
was channeled into a demand for independence. Considering the
record of the past and the promise of the future, it was not easy to deny
the logic of Thomas Paine when he wrote in 1776 that

> any submission to, or dependance [*sic*] on Great Britain, tends directly
> to involve this Continent in European wars and quarrels, and set us at
> variance with nations, who would otherwise seek our friendship, and
> against whom we have neither anger nor complaint. As Europe is
> our market for trade, we ought to form no partial connection with any
> part of it. It is the true interest of America to steer clear of European
> contentions, which she can never do, while by her dependance on Britain,
> she is made the make-weight in the scales of British politics.[12]

III

That American isolation had been ordained by self-interest as well
as by geography was a clearly defined article of national faith when
the Revolution started. Particularly in official circles, isolationism was

[10] Max H. Savelle, "The Appearance of an American Attitude toward External
Affairs, 1750–1775," *American Historical Review*, LII (July 1947), 656–662; Charles M.
Andrews, *The Colonial Background of the American Revolution* (New Haven: Yale
Univ. Press, 1924), p. 125.

[11] Cf. Ralph H. Gabriel, *Main Currents in American History* (New York: D. Appleton–Century Co., 1942), p. 22.

[12] "Common Sense," in Thomas Paine, *The Writings of Thomas Paine*, ed. Moncure D. Conway (New York: G. P. Putnam's Sons, 1906), I, 88–89.

almost unbounded during the first year of the war. Practically none of the colonial leaders favored political engagements with European states. Many also distrusted the effect of overseas commercial relations.[13] But independence meant that such questions could no longer be discussed solely in terms of academic preferences. A conscious national faith now had to be translated into a workable national policy, and the relatively inchoate ideas of colonial isolationism lost some of their force as this policy took shape.

The initial decision of the Continental Congress related to foreign trade. That vigorous commercial activity might produce serious commercial rivalry was obvious. But the need for European goods and European markets was just as clear, and in its Treaty Plan of 1776 the new government embraced the doctrine of freedom of the seas as well as a program of making formal commercial agreements with as many European countries as possible. Since it was stronger, the American antipathy for political understandings with European governments yielded more slowly. Even when reverses forced the Congress to seek military help abroad, that body acted grudgingly and with perfectly evident misgivings which seem to have been widely shared by public opinion.[14] But the old entanglement with Britain was not to be thrown off without submitting to a new one, and the French alliance of 1778 included provisions that drew America much nearer the orbit of European statecraft than most Americans liked.

Since it meant, to them, the difference between success and probable failure, the treaty was hailed in the colonies with an enthusiasm which hardened readily into permanent gratitude. But neither gratitude nor enthusiasm could undermine the isolationist conviction. American leaders knew that both France and its Spanish ally had entered the war for purposes of their own—Spain to retrieve Gibraltar, France to revenge past humiliations and to secure a measure of compensation for its losses in the Seven Years' War by detaching the colonies from Great Britain and making them permanently dependent on itself. They realized that either country would cheerfully sacrifice American interests to gain its primary objective. As a result, France was trusted only in part, while Spain was not trusted at all. Fear of seeing their

[13] See especially John Adams' notes on debates in the Continental Congress during October 1775, in John Adams, *The Works of John Adams*, ed. Charles Francis Adams (Boston: Little, Brown, and Co., 1850–1856), II, 473–484.

[14] J. Fred Rippy and Angie Debo, "The Historical Background of the American Policy of Isolation," *Smith College Studies in History*, IX (Apr.–June 1934), 75, 93–94.

country used as a pawn led the American peace commissioners to accept, without consulting France, the very favorable preliminary terms offered by Great Britain.in November 1782.[15] In effect, if not in form, this constituted a separate peace. And the speed with which Congress approved the act reflected the eagerness of the American people to draw away from a disturbing relationship which necessity had thrust upon them. Vague though its meaning had become, however, the French alliance still existed.

Some breaches in the isolationist façade were gradually closed during the years that followed. No longer confused by the immediate necessities of war, American opinion subscribed to the doctrines of political isolation more vehemently than ever; and most of the old reasons for this attitude were given new currency by the leaders of the young republic. Benjamin Franklin evoked a familiar theme of colonial times as he wrote:

> Whoever has travelled through the various parts of Europe, and observed how small is the proportion of people in affluence or easy circumstances there, compared with those in poverty and misery; the few rich and haughty landlords, the multitude of poor, abject, rack-rented, tithe-paying tenants and half-paid and half-starved ragged laborers; and views here the happy mediocrity that so generally prevails throughout the States, where the cultivator works for himself and supports his family in decent plenty, will, methinks, see abundant reason to bless Divine Providence for the evident and great difference in our favor, and be convinced that no nation known to us enjoys a greater share of human felicity.[16]

Elucidating a similar view, Thomas Jefferson suggested that *any* traffic with the old continent might be dangerous to American institutions. In 1785, for example, he uttered the wish that the nation could "stand with respect to Europe precisely on the footing of China . . . ." [17] "If all the sovereigns of Europe," he mused on another occasion,

> were to set themselves to work to emancipate the minds of their subjects from their present ignorance & prejudices, & that as zealously as they

---

[15] See Samuel Flagg Bemis, *The Diplomacy of the American Revolution* (New York: D. Appleton–Century Co., 1935), p. 255; also chaps. viii and xvi.

[16] Benjamin Franklin, *The Works of Benjamin Franklin,* ed. John Bigelow (New York: G. P. Putnam's Sons, 1904), X, 398.

[17] Jefferson to Hogendorp, Oct. 13, 1785, Thomas Jefferson, *The Works of Thomas Jefferson,* ed. Paul Leicester Ford (New York: G. P. Putnam's Sons, 1904–1905), IV, 469.

now endeavor the contrary, a thousand years would not place them on that high ground on which our common people are now setting out. Ours could not have been so fairly put into the hands of their own common sense had they not been separated from their parent stock & kept from contamination . . . by the intervention of so wide an ocean.[18]

John Adams, who had been active in foreign affairs since the beginning of the Revolution, repeatedly warned his countrymen to avoid the devious schemes of European diplomacy.[19] And Alexander Hamilton pointedly reëmphasized the most venerable concept of all with his argument that Europe and America belonged to essentially different spheres. "The world may politically, as well as geographically, be divided into four parts," he wrote in 1788,

> each having a distinct set of interests. Unhappily for the other three, Europe, by her arms and by her negotiations, by force and by fraud, has, in different degrees, extended her dominion over them all. . . . Let the thirteen States . . . concur in erecting one great American system, superior to the control of all transatlantic force or influence, and able to dictate the terms of the connection between the old and the new world![20]

All the personages just mentioned, except Franklin, belonged to President Washington's official family and were thus able to advise him directly regarding the conduct of foreign affairs. Generally speaking, moreover, their counsel was not ignored. But Washington had convictions, too; and even though his decisions were influenced by his associates, by the precedent which emerged from the Treaty Plan of 1776, and by the moral obligation of the French alliance, the foreign policy he evolved was essentially his own and neatly fitted to the situation with which he had to deal. Far from taking alarm at the theoretical dangers of foreign trade, he regarded a properly conducted international commerce as wholly beneficial. Commenting on the likelihood of a European war in 1790, he declared that the United States should hold fast to the "situation in which nature has placed us, . . . observe a strict neutrality, and . . . furnish others with those good things of subsistence which they want and which our fertile soil abun-

[18] Jefferson to Wythe, Aug. 13, 1786, *ibid.,* V, 153.

[19] *The Works of John Adams,* II, 505; Adams to Livingston, Nov. 11, 1782, and Adams to Lee, Apr. 12, 1783, *ibid.,* VIII, 9, 518.

[20] "The Federalist," No. 11, in John Spencer Bassett, ed., *Selections from "The Federalist"* (New York: Charles Scribner's Sons, 1921), pp. 46–47.

dantly produces . . . ."[21] Nor did he concern himself greatly with the domestic institutions and the specific policies of European kingdoms. For the most part, he confined his remarks to the general divergence of European and American interests and the unfortunate prevalence of strife in the old world. These were the considerations which prompted the advice in his Farewell Address "to steer clear of permanent alliances with any portion of the foreign world, so far . . . as we are now at liberty to do it."[22]

Washington demonstrated the application of his views in the situation created by the outbreak of war between France and England in 1793. Whatever its ideological background, he regarded this struggle, like the other wars of the French Revolution, as an exclusively European matter. Nevertheless, it directly involved his country's standing political connection with France, for even though France did not choose to invoke the alliance of 1778 by requesting American coöperation in the defense of its West Indian territories, the French government raised an equally grave problem when it undertook to exploit the nation's sense of gratitude by using American soil as a base for its own war operations. Acceptance of these designs by the American government would have led to British reprisals and might easily have drawn the United States into war in spite of itself. Therefore Washington called a halt and took immediate steps to safeguard the country's neutrality by means of executive orders and appropriate legislation. Here the questions growing out of the special ties between France and the United States were permitted to rest for the time being. Meanwhile, the American decision for neutrality had focused attention upon a second large problem, that of neutral rights.

The heavy restrictions which the two belligerents imposed upon neutral trade at the outset made it clear that the United States, for the war's duration, could enjoy its transatlantic commerce only at risk of perilous arguments with both sides. Again the President had to act carefully. But instead of looking for safety in a long-term embargo which would have taken American ships off the high seas, he reverted

[21] Washington to Lafayette, Aug. 11, 1790, George Washington, *The Writings of George Washington*, ed. John C. Fitzpatrick (Washington, D. C.: U. S. Govt. Printing Office, 1931–1944), XXXI, 87.

[22] Farewell Address, Sept. 17, 1796, United States, Congress, *A Compilation of the Messages and Papers of the Presidents, 1789–1902*, ed. James D. Richardson (New York: Bureau of National Literature and Art, 1903), I, 223.

to the principles of the Treaty Plan of 1776 and took the position that neutrality had rights as well as duties. It is true that lack of naval power kept him from venturing a really strong assertion of neutral rights at any time, and he gained no important concession from either of the warring governments. He even abandoned, temporarily, an essential part of his argument when he accepted Jay's Treaty of 1794, with its provision that the British, while the war lasted, might continue their troublesome practice of removing enemy property found on neutral ships.[23] But even this agreement conceded nothing in principle; the United States was still free to develop the concept of neutral rights as opportunity might offer. Moreover, Jay's Treaty accomplished its primary objective by enabling the country to remain at peace without giving up any substantial portion of a foreign trade it could scarcely afford to lose. Thus the net result of Washington's actions was to confirm the policy laid down by the Continental Congress and set the course of American foreign policy within limits that called for political isolation but that did not include its economic counterpart, even during a major European war.

So far as it gave the United States an independent economic and political program without violating any definite treaty obligation, this constituted an excellent beginning. But France was still seeking to corrupt American neutrality when Washington retired from office. Ignoring all dictates of international propriety, it tried through an abrupt severance of diplomatic relations in November 1796 to induce the presidential electors to cast their votes for Thomas Jefferson, who, because of his manifest sympathy for the philosophical implications of the revolutionary movement, was widely regarded as the friend of France. Of course, that plan failed. John Adams was chosen as Washington's successor; considering Jefferson's basically isolationist views, French hopes would probably have been disappointed in any event. But the mere fact that such an effort was made indicated that France still presumed upon the existence of the alliance to seek ends never contemplated by that agreement. Now completely at odds with the United States, the French government further tightened its restrictions on neutral trade and confronted the American merchant fleet with what amounted to undeclared war. Finally, under the additional spur of snubs adminis-

[23] Samuel Flagg Bemis, *Jay's Treaty* (New York: Macmillan Co., 1923), pp. 266–267.

tered to American representatives in the XYZ Affair, Congress reacted against such behavior by abrogating all treaties and suspending all trade with France in 1798. A new commercial treaty was signed two years later. The alliance, however, remained dead, and numerous memories which attended its passing were not of a type to encourage like experiments in the future.[24]

Though American foreign policy no longer suffered from this special embarrassment, its other problems did not dwindle. Instead they grew larger as the economic struggle between Great Britain and the Napoleonic Empire was fully joined. The irritating question of impressment assumed a greater role in disputes with the British, and both sides continued to do much as they pleased with neutral trade. Nothing could disguise the fact that the United States was still a military weakling caught in a battle of giants. Nevertheless, Jefferson, as President, followed Washington in upholding the cause of neutral rights as vigorously as circumstances permitted, and Madison finally surpassed them both.

It is true that Jefferson's embargo withdrew American commerce from the high seas during one brief period; but this, like various other measures which Congress enacted between 1806 and 1810 to restrict trade with the belligerents, was an attempt at economic coercion rather than a move to let neutral rights go by default. Presidential resolve to defend the nation's commercial liberty had become so strong, in fact, that it eventually emerged as a prime cause of the War of 1812. The actual declaration of hostilities was carried through Congress by western and southern expansionists who hoped to take Canada from Great Britain and Florida from Spain, Britain's ally. Nevertheless, Madison's request for such a declaration seems to have been founded primarily upon London's failure, until it was too late, to yield anything to the doctrine of neutral rights.[25] Although the war brought no international agreement on this complicated issue, it did reveal that the United States would sometimes fight to uphold its position. The meaning of recent events, in terms of American policy, was obvious. Through neutrality the United States would seek to maintain its isolation from foreign strife; any abandonment of neutrality during a war fought outside the Americas would probably arise from a defense of neutral rights.

[24] See Richard W. Van Alstyne, *American Diplomacy in Action: A Series of Case Studies* (Stanford University, Calif.: Stanford Univ. Press, 1944), pp. 430–432.

[25] See Warren H. Goodman, "The Origins of the War of 1812: A Survey of Changing Interpretations," *Mississippi Valley Historical Review*, XXVIII (Sept. 1941), 171–172.

IV

The obvious corollary to this declared aloofness from European affairs was the exclusion of Europe, so far as was possible, from the affairs of America. Such a policy was implicit in Hamilton's discussion of separate geographical and political areas, and this concept appears to have been shared in greater or less degree by nearly all his prominent contemporaries. In a sense, the Revolution itself was the first step in the accomplishment of this large task. The Treaty of Paris of 1783 left the Republic so narrowly confined by the territory of potentially hostile European states, however, that it tended to restore that feeling of military vulnerability which had limited the growth of American isolationism before the Seven Years' War. No longer the mother country, Great Britain still held Canada, while Spain had title to Florida, West Florida, and Louisiana, not to mention Mexico and vast possessions in Latin America. Furthermore, neither the Canada boundary nor the Florida boundary was undisputed, and the British manifested great reluctance to fulfill their treaty engagements by withdrawing from their posts on American soil in the Great Lakes region. How to loosen this cordon, therefore, constituted a problem in American security.

Boundary adjustments offered a logical beginning, but these alone were not enough. National frontiers would remain vulnerable until the United States spread far beyond its original limits. American territory would cease to be regarded as bargaining material in the larger transactions of European states only when they abandoned the custom of transferring their American colonies to one another at will. Until they stopped seeking new possessions in America, or the enlargement of established holdings, the Western Hemisphere would be prey to recurring foreign ambitions. Without these changes, American isolation would be more a theory than a fact. Nothing but expansion could give the isolationist gospel its territorial fulfillment; only the no-transfer and no-extension principles could free the United States from the dangerous pressure of schemes originating in Europe. Although these various types of action were not consolidated into a tightly knit program until somewhat later, all left their mark on United States foreign policy within two decades of the founding of the national government.

Washington attacked the frontier question at his first opportunity.

By Jay's Treaty, concluded in 1794, he obtained British agreement to evacuate the Northwest Territory, and made a start at settling the Canadian boundary. The next year he reached an understanding with Spain on the Florida boundary, as well as a temporary agreement respecting navigation of the Mississippi. Spain's cession of Louisiana to France in 1800 eventually aroused grave fears on Thomas Jefferson's part and helped stimulate him to launch American expansion through the purchase of that vast area in 1803. However, much greater stress was laid on the no-transfer principle in 1811, when it looked as though Spain might cede Florida to Great Britain. For Congress then, at President Madison's request, not only passed a resolution declaring its opposition to this project, but also gave the President leave to seize the area by force if that were necessary to prevent its transfer.[26]

During the calm which followed the War of 1812, this campaign to delimit the American interests of European powers and to broaden its own territory became a major preoccupation of the United States government. By agreeing, in 1817, to the drastic restriction of naval forces on the Great Lakes, it laid the foundation of a new and growing security along the northern frontier. Another treaty with Britain, concluded the next year, settled the American-Canadian boundary from the Lake of the Woods to the Rocky Mountains, provided for joint occupation of the Oregon Territory, and carried with it the abandonment of Great Britain's standing claim to free navigation of the Mississippi. The area of possible conflict with Spain was notably reduced in 1819 by the Adams-Onís Treaty, which ceded to the United States all Spanish territory east of the Mississippi (East and West Florida) and established a mutually acceptable dividing line between American and Spanish claims from the Sabine River to the Pacific Ocean. Throughout this period, the United States followed the successful rebellion of Spain's Latin American colonies with open, if unofficial, approval and led the world in recognizing the new governments in 1822 and 1823. In 1824, after some negotiation, Russia was barred from further colonial ventures in the Western Hemisphere by an agreement defining the southern boundary of Alaska. These large accomplishments, added to the fortunate circumstance that its own trading interests had led Great Britain to oppose any attempt by Continental powers to help Spain recover its lost possessions, gave the old concept of distinct European

---

[26] Professor Van Alstyne calls this a "focal point of American diplomacy" (*American Diplomacy in Action*, p. 42).

and American spheres the most substantial basis in reality it had yet enjoyed and opened the way for a clear enunciation of that concept as related to United States policy. "In the wars of the European powers in matters relating to themselves," stated President James Monroe in his message to Congress on December 2, 1823,

> we have never taken any part, nor does it comport with our policy so to do. It is only when our rights are invaded or seriously menaced that we resent injuries, or make preparations for our defense. With the movements in this hemisphere we are of necessity more immediately connected . . . . We owe it, therefore, to candor . . . to declare that we should consider any attempt on their part to extend their system to any portions of this hemisphere as dangerous to our peace and safety. With the existing colonies or dependencies of any European power we have not interfered and shall not interfere. But with the Governments who have declared their independence and maintained it, and whose independence we have . . . acknowledged, we could not view any interposition for the purpose of oppressing them, or controlling in any other manner their destiny, by any European power, in any other light than as the manifestation of an unfriendly disposition towards the United States.[27]

In 1823, and for many years thereafter, the Monroe Doctrine owed its real effectiveness to the implicit support of the British Navy. Nevertheless, it was a purely American definition of the country's vital interests and completed the decisive outlines of American foreign policy. Briefly summarized, the axioms which had emerged from an instinctive national faith and almost fifty years of sovereign experience counseled the Republic, for an indefinite period, (1) to avoid alliances or other advance commitments which would enable foreign powers to determine the policy of the United States, either generally or in any given situation; (2) to observe the duties of neutrality with all reasonable strictness during Europe's inevitable wars, but to champion the doctrine of neutral rights as vigorously as possible for the sake of unbroken commercial activity at all times; (3) to expand across the North American continent; (4) to oppose the transfer of American territory from one non-American power to another; and (5) to discourage the acquisition by European states of new territory in the Western Hemi-

[27] Seventh annual message, Dec. 2, 1823, *Messages and Papers of the Presidents,* II, 218.

sphere, or interference by them in the affairs of established American governments.

V

Every one of these principles helped, in some degree, to isolate the United States from Europe; but even when taken all together, they still failed to achieve anything like complete isolation. While the policy, as defined, adhered closely to the main threads of the isolationist tradition, it held no very certain guarantee that the United States would be able to stay out of all European wars. It coupled with the practice of neutrality the demand for freedom of the seas, and experience had proved that any neutrality which implied a strong defense of neutral rights could easily defeat its own purpose. Nor, in any event, did the isolationist ideal completely dominate the American mind. Two further aspirations were rapidly taking shape in the background of American thought, both potentially capable of challenging the national resolve to stay out of European politics. One was the idealism of the international peace movement, which already had a good deal of organized support in the United States.[28] The other was the idealism of democracy—the belief that that country, as the world's most successful republic and leading exponent of the rights of man, could not ignore the struggle for human liberty wherever it might occur.[29] Though isolationism still enjoyed the ascendancy in both policy and thought, its sway was by no means absolute.

During the remainder of the nineteenth century, however, the isolationist aspects of American thought went almost unchallenged, and American foreign policy, ratified by a long chain of successes, went practically unchanged. Since the War of 1812 had completely failed to settle the question of neutral rights, this area of potential conflict between American and European interests remained as broad as ever. Nevertheless, its real significance declined very quickly. The peace established at Vienna in 1815 was an enduring one. Not for one hundred years did the United States again occupy a neutral position in a far-reaching maritime conflict. The wars of the nineteenth century were, on the whole, land-bound and narrowly restricted; the question

[28] For an account of the origins of this movement see Merle E. Curti, *The American Peace Crusade, 1815–1860* (Durham, N. C.: Duke Univ. Press, 1929), pp. 8–14.

[29] See J. Fred Rippy, *America and the Strife of Europe* (Chicago: Univ. Chicago Press, 1938), chap. ii.

of neutral rights became somewhat academic; assumptions concerning the doctrine's real strength grew more and more optimistic; and the ultimate dangers of neutrality in large-scale wars receded like a half-forgotten nightmare. This same world stability kept the international peace movement from becoming an immediate interest of the American government, and the fact that obvious trends of political growth seemed to augur the coming triumph of democracy everywhere kept the nation from excessive worry about the domestic institutions of foreign states.

Under these circumstances the temptation to view American security as a strictly hemispheric problem remained overwhelming. Thanks to its own growing strength and to Europe's general lack of aggressiveness concerning political objectives in the new world, the United States was able to develop its American program without much hindrance. Annexation of Texas and new territorial gains in the Mexican War, in addition to the almost simultaneous division of Oregon with Great Britain and the final settlement of the long-disputed boundary between Maine and New Brunswick, fulfilled the dream of transcontinental expansion and solved the last major frontier problem by the middle of the century, while the purchase of Alaska in 1867 eliminated Russia's one foothold in the Western Hemisphere. Substantial progress was also made south of the Rio Grande. In 1850 the Clayton-Bulwer Treaty provided an Anglo-American agreement for the neutralization of Central America. A generally successful effort during the next fifty years to expand the Monroe Doctrine through a variety of new pretensions and interpretations—a trend which culminated in the pronouncement of the Roosevelt Corollary in 1904 [30]—along with the ejection of Spain from the West Indies, the assumption of new responsibilities in Cuba, and the annexation of Puerto Rico, greatly tightened the concept of vital interest and gave the United States a more prominent role in Latin American affairs generally. This dominance continued to grow with the digging of the Panama Canal, the purchase of the Virgin Islands, and the acceptance of supervisory functions in Haiti, the Dominican Republic, and Nicaragua.

Otherwise, generally speaking, the United States government until the very end of the century limited its contacts with the governments of Europe and Asia to the maintenance of ordinary diplomatic relations and the advancement of national economic interests. After the

---

[30] The best survey of these develop nts is found in Dexter Perkins, *Hands Off: A History of the Monroe Doctrine* (Boston: Little, Brown, and Co., 1945), chap. v.

Spanish-American War, however, a recognizable effort to guide political developments outside the Western Hemisphere began to take shape. Having won a new stake in the Far East through its acquisition of the Philippine Islands, the United States in 1899, with the tacit encouragement of Great Britain, announced its desire to maintain in eastern Asia the principle of commercial equality, secured at least a qualified acquiescence from all the major powers except Russia, and expanded the Open Door into a defense of China's territorial integrity during the Boxer crisis of 1900.

This quasi-international viewpoint was cultivated even more vigorously by President Theodore Roosevelt and linked even more directly with the peace ideal.[31]   By using the services of the Hague Tribunal, Roosevelt helped strengthen the waning prestige of that body,[32] which had been established in 1899 as a permanent court of arbitration, but two other projects were even better calculated to draw the United States closer to the arena of world politics.   First, Roosevelt's good offices certainly helped shorten the Russo-Japanese War; and although his real influence on the terms of the Treaty of Portsmouth was probably not great, that agreement, taken as a whole, was satisfying to his view of American interests in the Far East.[33]   Second, he went out of his way to take part in Europe's squabbles over Morocco. Notwithstanding the small American stake in the Moroccan question, he engaged in a spirited discussion of that issue during the crisis of 1905, saw to it that the United States was represented at the Conference of Algeciras, suggested the compromise eventually adopted by that body, and, with the somewhat reluctant concurrence of the Senate, made the United States a party to the settlement.   In 1913 and 1914 the Wilson administration betrayed an equivalent, if not exactly similar, concern with the problem of war through the "cooling-off" treaties negotiated by Secretary of State William Jennings Bryan. Since none of these ventures gave the United States a definite commitment outside the Western Hemisphere, they cannot be regarded as evidence of policy change.   But they did show a limited tendency to view the problem of national well-being in a setting larger than that afforded by the two Americas.

---

[31] Cf. Henry F. Pringle, *Theodore Roosevelt: A Biography* (New York: Harcourt, Brace, and Co., 1931), p. 372.

[32] Rippy, *America and the Strife of Europe*, p. 171.

[33] Pringle, *Theodore Roosevelt*, pp. 383, 386–387.

VI

Although it loomed as a potential challenge to the isolationist faith, this quickening in the executive department did no violence to the essential nature of American foreign policy. Isolation, as viewed by the policy maker, had never been an end in itself. The real end was national security, and the problem of security had been solved chiefly in terms of the isolationist tradition because the facts of geography had enabled the United States to shun entanglements in which a young and relatively weak member of the family of nations could not hope to hold a winning hand. But the Western Hemisphere—that is, the Americas and nearby waters—did not constitute the only possible basis of national security. For geographical isolation was a passing condition, national interest an expanding concept, security a changing problem; and when security could no longer be guaranteed within the old frame of reference, that frame would have to be made wider. Not even the Monroe Doctrine had established absolute geographical limits of action "when our rights are invaded, or seriously menaced . . . ." These considerations, together with the circumstance that American isolationism had always been tempered by a number of divergent impulses, foretold that the United States would restrict its political activities to the Western Hemisphere only until its conception of American interest was directly threatened, or its sympathies violently aroused, by what transpired in other parts of the world. Now a great power on a rapidly contracting twentieth-century globe, the United States was merely beginning to review its foreign policy in the light of its traditional and necessary objective.

Every line of reëxamination converged upon the First World War; and as the fighting progressed, the isolationist tradition was first undermined, then abandoned. Like the Napoleonic Wars, this was a great maritime struggle. Once again the dispute over neutral rights supplied the immediate cause of American intervention, but behind this loomed the ultimate threat to the nation's security which was derived from the assumed yearning of the Central Powers for unlimited conquest. Portrayed as a war to "bring peace and safety to all nations and to make the world itself at last free," [34] it also appealed to those who

[34] Address of the President, Apr. 2, 1917, United States, Department of State, *Papers Relating to the Foreign Relations of the United States, 1917 Supplement* (Washington, D. C.: U. S. Govt. Printing Office, 1931), I, 202.

shared the idealism of the international peace movement and struck a responsive chord in all Americans who felt that the United States owed something to the general advancement of human rights. Thus President Wilson seized every strand of American thought that was hostile to isolationism, drew them tight, and joined them all at a single point.

In the beginning, this method of dealing with public opinion was highly successful. Americans responded with a crusading zeal which seemed to indicate that they had accepted a new outlook. But ·their very enthusiasm raised hopes that were not fulfilled by the peace; the soaring good will of 1917 dropped rapidly; and national policy could not escape the reaction. While the larger share of American opinion in 1920–1921 probably wanted the United States to join the League of Nations, at least conditionally,[35] it was not vocal enough to keep Senate and President from reaching a stalemate on the question. For the League, whatever its virtues, was inseparable from the war and the peace; and —perhaps because they had filled a relatively minor role in the total war effort—Americans were already inclined to view all three with a certain detachment.

This, added to such factors as prolonged contemplation of secret treaties made by the Allies during the war, differences at the Peace Conference, later squabbles over war debts, evidence of what appeared to be European ingratitude, and disgust with the growing impotence of the League itself, contributed still further to American discontent with the wartime orientation and hurried the return to a nationalistic view of world affairs. The German threat to the United States, even in 1917, had been rather formless, and, especially when seen in retrospect, appeared to offer no real proof that American security was now directly and immediately related to the political and military situation on the European continent. Hence the American people retreated behind the comforting walls of the isolationist tradition, satisfied that the Western Hemisphere should once more be recognized as the essential framework of national interests and that neutrality, buttressed by historical attitudes regarding the avoidance of political commitments, should be the unchanging rule of American policy toward disputes which might arise outside its boundaries.

[35] Thomas A. Bailey, *Woodrow Wilson and the Great Betrayal* (New York: Macmillan Co., 1945), p. 361; also, Denna F. Fleming, *The United States and the League of Nations, 1918–1920* (New York: G. P. Putnam's Sons, 1932), pp. 218–219.

CHAPTER I

The New Neutrality

I

NOT ALL AMERICANS WERE DISILLUSIONED BY THE COUNTRY'S EXPERIENCE with Europe during and after the First World War. Familiar ideals, especially those associated with the international peace movement, retained their hold on many people; and throughout the next two decades the United States had a well-organized body of internationalist opinion which regarded American membership in the League, or, failing this, decisive activity in close coöperation with other states, as the best, indeed the only, way to prevent the outbreak of another war. Though comparatively small, this group was persistently vocal, and it achieved some success in its efforts to mobilize public opinion as the logic of new events supplemented the logic of precept. But isolationism was unquestionably dominant in the postwar era, spreading wider and deeper through the fabric of American thought than it ever had before in history.

As the isolationist outlook resumed possession of the American mind, it derived both real and fancied support from many quarters. Especially useful to isolationist dialecticians were the labors of historians and publicists. Throughout the nineteen-twenties a growing number of writers joined in an ambitious reconsideration of the steps by which the United States had entered the late war, and as they energetically distilled the lessons of that process from the evidence of European and American diplomacy, this relatively limited problem gained an unfortunate, but more or less permanent, connection with the whole question of war responsibility.

Appearing in 1921, before the Versailles war-guilt thesis was seriously questioned, Charles Seymour's *Woodrow Wilson and the World War* presented the submarine issue as the decisive cause of American intervention and the idealism which Wilson persuaded the country to share as the moving force behind American policy once the United States was committed.[1]   This work was but a rearrangement of the ideas current during the war, but it was not off the press before the larger question of Germany's sole responsibility for starting the conflict was placed under attack by Sidney B. Fay.   His three famous articles in the *American Historical Review* in 1920–1921 [2] launched American revisionism, with a moderate thesis of joint responsibility for the events of July and early August 1914.   This view was later expanded in the same author's two-volume *Origins of the War,* published in 1928.[3] Another revision, less sympathetic toward Germany but still removed from the Versailles pattern, was brought forth in 1930 by Bernadotte E. Schmitt's *Coming of the War*.[4] Neither of these studies was immediately concerned with the problem of American intervention, and neither offered much direct comfort to American isolationism.   It was entirely possible to accept the view of either one without retreating to an isolationist position so far as American policy was concerned.   But any reapportionment of blame lent credence to the idea that the former Allied powers were no better than they should have been, and it was only a step from questioning them to questioning America itself.   A current had been set in motion; and the more one doubted the purity of Russia, France, and Great Britain, the more one was inclined to suspect the motives and wisdom of those who had guided the United States into war at their side.

This current got out of hand with the extreme revisionism developed by Harry Elmer Barnes in the middle nineteen-twenties and the direct application of his exaggerated views to the study of American neutrality before 1917.   Barnes first entered the controversy on war guilt as a reviewer of other people's books.   In January 1922 his spirited condemnation of Edward Raymond Turner's new textbook, *Europe since 1870,* appeared in the *New Republic.*   Turner allowed Germany to retain major responsibility for bringing on the war, and Barnes criticized him severely for not paying more attention to the new research based

[1] Charles Seymour, *Woodrow Wilson and the World War* (New Haven: Yale Univ. Press, 1921), pp. 113, 229, 353.

[2] Sidney B. Fay, "New Light on the Origins of the World War," *American Historical Review,* XXV (July 1920), 616–639; XXVI (Oct. 1920), 37–53; XXVI (Jan. 1921), 225–254.

[3] Sidney B. Fay, *The Origins of the World War* (New York: Macmillan Co., 1928), *passim.*

[4] Bernadotte E. Schmitt, *The Coming of the War* (New York: Charles Scribner's Sons, 1930), *passim.*

66522

upon the postwar revelations of European chancelleries.[5] The real quarrel did not begin until two years later, however, when Barnes published a full-length article in the same journal directing still heavier fire at the latest revision of Charles Downer Hazen's standard college text, *Europe since 1815.* Accusing Hazen of willful blindness and obstinacy in maintaining his stern assessment of German war guilt, Barnes expressed the view that the publishers of this book were morally bound to arrange for its revision before "it misinforms and perverts the historical judgement of thousands of college students and general readers . . . ."[6] For several weeks thereafter the *New Republic* served as arena for an acrimonious exchange of letters between Turner and Hazen on the one hand and Barnes on the other.

As this personal struggle subsided, Barnes broadened his attack with a long article in the May 1924 number of *Current History,* which examined the responsibility of each country in some detail and concluded that Austria was most guilty, followed by Russia, France, Germany, and England, in that order.[7] Albert Bushnell Hart replied with a brief dissent in the same number;[8] but the next month *Current History* offered a symposium by a group of leading historians which indicated that, while Barnes was regarded as too precipitate, the major tenets of revisionism were gaining favor with the profession generally.[9] During the next two years *Current History* continued to publish articles bearing on different aspects of the question; and by 1926, when Barnes rounded out his thesis in a book-length treatment, the whole matter had been quite thoroughly publicized.

In his *Genesis of the War* Barnes announced views that were even more extreme than those he had defended in 1924. Here he made Russia and France bear the major guilt, and then he applied the assumption of Allied culpability to the question of how the United States became involved in so unedifying a struggle. Holding that Allied prop-

---

[5] Harry Elmer Barnes, Review of *Europe since 1870,* by E. R. Turner, *New Republic,* XXIX (Jan. 18, 1922), 228–230.

[6] Harry Elmer Barnes, "Seven Books of History against the Germans," *ibid.,* XXXVIII (Mar. 19, 1924), 15.

[7] Harry Elmer Barnes, "Assessing the Blame for the World War," *Current History,* XX (May 1924), 194.

[8] Albert Bushnell Hart, "A Dissent from the Conclusions of Professor Barnes," *ibid.,* pp. 195–196.

[9] Charles Seymour, Raymond Leslie Buell, Carl Becker, and others, "Assessing the Blame for the World War: A Symposium," *Current History,* XX (June 1924), 452–462.

aganda was highly effective in persuading Americans to accept the view that Germany was solely responsible for provoking the war and that German ambition threatened the security of the entire world, Barnes maintained that the Allied governments' heavy purchases and borrowings in the United States largely completed the task of directing American sympathies toward Great Britain and France.[10] Taking advantage of this situation, he continued, the unneutral Wilson, ably seconded by such warmongering assistants as Colonel House and Secretary Lansing, deliberately worked the nation into a declaration of war by presenting the submarine issue and related matters within a mist of idealism.[11]

Barnes's book was followed in 1929 by C. Hartley Grattan's *Why We Fought*. Here the entire volume was devoted to the problem of American intervention. Although Grattan gave new attention to Allied and German propaganda in the United States and was somewhat more sympathetic toward President Wilson, his conclusions were generally the same: that the submarine controversy was less the reason than the excuse for declaring war; that American participation was made inevitable by a complex of deeper, more sinister, and less readily isolated forces than the wartime explanation implied.[12]

This long dispute and its partisan summation in these two works, taken in conjunction with such studies as Harold Lasswell's *Propaganda Technique in the World War* and such refutations of the familiar atrocity story as Sir Arthur Ponsonby's *Falsehood in War-Time*,[13] gave the isolationists a good deal of ammunition by 1930. A considerable, if not overwhelming, weight of scholarly and semischolarly authority had relegated submarine warfare to a secondary position as a cause of intervention, holding instead that America had been the dupe of propaganda, of the profit motive, of warmongering leaders, of a baseless conviction of moral superiority, and of a trumped-up appeal to its better nature. It was enough to confirm popular feeling in its isolationist predilection and to set the stage for the great debate of the nineteen-

10 Harry Elmer Barnes, *The Genesis of the World War: An Introduction to the Problem of War Guilt* (New York: Alfred A. Knopf, 1926), p. 610.

11 *Ibid.*, pp. 624–627, 594–596.

12 C. Hartley Grattan, *Why We Fought* (New York: Vanguard Press, 1929), *passim.*

13 Harold D. Lasswell, *Propaganda Technique in the World War* (New York: Alfred A. Knopf, 1927); and Sir Arthur Ponsonby, *Falsehood in War-Time* (London: G. Allen and Unwin, 1928).

thirties, when generalizations about the last war would be transformed into specific measures against the danger of involvement in the next.

II

Confronted by this determined advance of isolationist sentiment, the internationalists were able to conduct no more than a rear-guard action. Their position grew more desperate as time went on, but their efforts never relaxed, and their work was not entirely futile. Although it had been twice rejected by the Senate, the League of Nations emerged as a prominent issue in the presidential campaign of 1920. The Democratic platform called for American membership in the League. The Republican position was not so clear. Even though many well-known and well-intentioned citizens believed that a Republican victory would constitute the surest guarantee of American participation in international organization, that party actually straddled the issue, and, once in power, chose to interpret the election results as proof that the American people had no desire for League membership.[14] Under Harding the United States did proclaim its undiminished interest in the Far East by sponsoring, and then signing, the three Washington treaties of 1922.[15] But aside from this, Wilson's uninspiring successor went only far enough to recommend in 1923 that the United States join the World Court.[16] After 1920 general interest in such matters flagged rapidly, and within a short time the establishment of any direct relationship between the United States and the League of Nations was palpably hopeless. But those League advocates who, unlike Wilson, believed that half a loaf was better than no bread at all, strove unremittingly to approach their objective in other ways.

Working unofficially, a number of Americans—including Professor James T. Shotwell and David Hunter Miller—gave freely of their advice and labor in connection with the League's own efforts between 1920 and 1925 to strengthen its security system, especially through agree-

[14] Denna F. Fleming, *The United States and the League of Nations, 1918–1920* (New York: G. P. Putnam's Sons, 1932), pp. 453–464.

[15] The Five-Power Naval Treaty, the Four-Power Treaty, and the Nine-Power Treaty, all of which had a direct and immediate bearing upon Pacific and Far Eastern problems.

[16] Denna F. Fleming, *The United States and World Organization, 1920–1933* (New York: Columbia Univ. Press, 1938), p. 239.

ments calculated to define in more specific terms the obligations of member states.[17]   When this movement culminated in the rejection of the Geneva Protocol, and individual European countries began looking for security in regional pacts of the Locarno type, other branches of the American peace movement were already hard at work on plans of their own.

The central theme of these new inspirations was the idea of a general agreement to outlaw war.   Salmon O. Levinson, a wealthy Chicago lawyer, is usually credited with having originated the project.   As early as 1919, he appears to have convinced himself that war should be divested of its legality, so that states which resorted to it could be treated as criminals before the law of nations.   He originally believed that force might be required to implement the scheme, and he offered no special objection to the principle of sanctions in the League's peace machinery. However, in order to gain the support of isolationist senators like William E. Borah and Philander C. Knox—who were disposed to favor his broad thesis but who regarded sanctions of any kind as snares for American policy—Levinson, seemingly without regret, abandoned this part of his program and fell back on the argument that public opinion must be the only force governing relations between states.[18]

Knox died before anything could be accomplished, but Borah eventually assumed legislative direction of the plan and in 1923 asked the Senate to declare, by resolution, that war should be "outlawed as an institution or means for the settlement of international controversies by making it a public crime under the law of nations."[19]   This move came to nothing, but the opening gun in the campaign which was to bring forth the Kellogg-Briand Pact had been fired.

Had it not been for confusion in the American peace movement, Levinson's scheme might have gone no further; but that movement was distracted by the multiplicity of its own factions.   Speaking gen-

[17] For a brief firsthand survey of these efforts, see James T. Shotwell, "Plans and Protocols to End War: Historical Outline and Guide," *International Conciliation*, No. 208 (Mar. 1925), pp. 93–95.

[18] Drew Pearson and Constantine Brown, *The American Diplomatic Game* (Garden City, N. Y.: Doubleday, Doran, and Co., 1935), pp. 12–13; John E. Stoner, *S. O. Levinson and the Pact of Paris: A Study in the Techniques of Influence* (Chicago: Univ. Chicago Press, 1942), pp. 48–49, 81, 89; and Fleming, *The United States and World Organization*, pp. 291–292.

[19] S. Res. 441, Feb. 13, 1923, United States, Congress, Senate, *Journal of the Senate of the United States of America* (Washington, D. C.: U. S. Govt. Printing Office and others, 1814——) (67th Cong., 3rd and 4th sess.), pp. 12–13.

erally, Americans who thought about peace in any but the most nebulous fashion could be divided into three groups: pacifists, internationalists, and nationalists or isolationists. All favored peace, but each looked for it within a particular frame of reference. The pacifists opposed all war as evil, attacking it through such devices as moral argument and refusal to bear arms. The internationalists regarded it as a practical problem to be met through international organization and a planned coöperation among states which did not rule out the possibility of preventive war. Taking a much narrower position than either of the others, the isolationists simply viewed war as an activity from which the United States should abstain except for immediate self-defense, and believed that the American government should assume no obligations that might hamper its freedom in this respect.

It was possible, nevertheless, for members of all three groups to cross each other's lines without receding from their basic convictions. During the early nineteen-twenties the pacifists had supported the internationalists in their demand that the United States become a member of the League. About 1925, however, they began to worry over the likelihood of preventive war under League auspices and hurriedly withdrew from the internationalist camp.[20] Now it was the internationalists' turn to cross lines. With the League manifestly unable to obtain from its members the powers it required for effectiveness, American coöperation with the League seemed, in their eyes, more essential than ever. For the moment, the scheme to outlaw war appeared to be the half loaf that they had been seeking, a half loaf which patience and judicious tactics might eventually make whole. Thus the Levinson-Borah group received help from an unexpected quarter.

Despite his low opinion of Levinson's program,[21] it was James T. Shotwell who furnished the connecting link. Returning home from Germany in March 1927, Shotwell paused briefly in Paris for some talks with the French Foreign Minister, Aristide Briand, and essayed to suggest a means by which the United States might be able to coöperate with the League of Nations in the interest of peace.[22] The upshot of these conversations was Briand's offhand proposal on April 6 that France and the United States conclude an agreement mutually re-

[20] See John W. Masland, "The 'Peace' Groups Join Battle," *Public Opinion Quarterly,* IV (Dec. 1940), 667.

[21] See Stoner, *Levinson and the Pact of Paris,* p. 215.

[22] James T. Shotwell, *On the Rim of the Abyss* (New York: Macmillan Co., 1936), pp. 133–134.

nouncing war between them.[23] Happy with the opening thus provided, Levinson hurried to Paris, while Borah took up the fight at home.
Thanks to his position as chairman, Borah was finally able to confront
Secretary of State Frank B. Kellogg with the unanimous recommendation of the Senate Committee on Foreign Relations that the French
proposal for a bilateral pact be expanded into a general treaty outlawing
war.[24] This weighty advice stirred the reluctant Kellogg to action; the
American plan eventually gained acceptance; and the Kellogg-Briand
Pact was signed in Paris on August 27, 1928.

However it may be evaluated, the Pact of Paris was mainly the
result of American endeavor, and it offered comfort to almost every
shade of American opinion. It was a resounding denunciation of war
to which no one could take exception. Its innocence of both sanctions
and machinery for consultation endeared it to isolationist and pacifist
alike. At the same time, its generosity of principle opened wide inter-
pretative possibilities. Here the internationalists took their stand.
Some argued that the Pact largely destroyed the old legal basis of
neutrality, as between signatories, and obligated the United States to
renounce that condition in future wars.[25] No one who was so minded
could have much trouble deriving a moral obligation from the rather
vague wording of the treaty, nor could he overlook the circumstance
that most of its signatories were also members of the League of Nations.
Legally, a connection was hard to establish. But could the dichotomy
always be upheld in practice? A number of senators thought not. In
the debate on ratification Bruce, of Maryland, lauded the Pact as a move
toward United States adherence to the League.[26] Isolationist Hiram
Johnson quoted an opinion of internationalist David Hunter Miller
which characterized the agreement as being "in effect, a treaty between
the United States and the League," meaning "that the sanctions of

[23] Briand's statement to the Associated Press, Apr. 6, 1927, United States, Department of State, *Papers Relating to the Foreign Relations of the United States, 1927*
(Washington, D. C.: U. S. Govt. Printing Office, 1942), II, 612.

[24] Fleming, *The United States and World Organization*, pp. 294–295.

[25] Among those who ultimately took such a view was Henry L. Stimson, Secretary
of State in the Hoover administration. For the general argument, see Quincy Wright,
"The Meaning of the Pact of Paris," *American Journal of International Law*, XXVII
(Jan. 1933), 59; also see the concurring opinions of Fenwick, Whitton, Vandenbosch,
Graham, and Eagleton, in American Society of International Law, *Proceedings, 1933*,
pp. 55, 147, 152, 157, 163. Cf. the dissenting opinion of Borchard, *ibid.*, pp. 93–94;
also the views of Garner, *ibid.*, pp. 95–96.

[26] United States, Congress, *Congressional Record* (Washington, D. C.: U. S. Govt.
Printing Office, 1874——), LXX (70th Cong., 2nd sess.), 1284.

Article 16 of the Covenant have behind them the moral acquiescence of the United States."[27]   Bingham, of Connecticut, quoted Professor Edwin M. Borchard, of the Yale Law School, who condemned the League as ardently as Miller supported it, to much the same effect.[28] Moses, of New Hampshire, and Reed, of Missouri, unsuccessfully proposed reservations which betrayed their fear that the United States was in danger of being drawn into League activities.[29]

Moreover, the drive for special embargo legislation, the most obvious means by which the United States could dignify the Peace Pact and bring itself into active support of the League, was already under way. In December 1927, while negotiations leading to the treaty were still in a preliminary stage, Representative Burton, of Ohio, had introduced a resolution to prohibit "the export of arms, munitions, and war material to any country engaged in a war of aggression against another, in violation of a treaty, convention, or any other arrangement providing for recourse to peaceful means for the settlement of international differences."[30]   With what appeared to be the identical end in view, moreover, this same gentleman had risen in January 1928 to offer a second resolution, calling for an impartial arms embargo against all belligerent states, aggressors and victims alike.[31]   Now, as anyone might see, an attempt to have the United States discourage foreign wars by halting the sale of war materials to aggressors and treaty breakers was one thing. But an impartial embargo was something quite different.

So the wheel came full circle, and the final alternatives were presented nearly a year before the Peace Pact was ratified.   One choice involved substantial coöperation with the peace machinery of the League; the other might lead to a withdrawal into commercial isolation such as the United States had never before employed except as a temporary coercive measure.   That the fundamental difference between Burton's first and second proposals apparently escaped clear recognition at the time may be ascribed in part to the fact that the country had not yet reached a stage of practical action and in part to the confusion of the peace forces already mentioned.   The main point is that, instead of resolving this confusion,

[27] *Ibid.*, p. 1532.   [28] *Ibid.*   [29] *Ibid.*, p. 623.

[30] The full text is given in Quincy Wright, "The Future of Neutrality," *International Conciliation*, No. 242 (Sept. 1928), pp. 440–441.

[31] It was referred to committee, but not reported.   See United States, Congress, House of Representatives, *Journal of the House of Representatives of the United States of America* (Washington, D. C.: U. S. Govt. Printing Office and others, 1814——) (70th Cong., 1st sess.), p. 1231.

the Peace Pact aggravated it, for the renunciation of war enlisted the support of all peace groups and obscured their dividing lines a second time. Against this background of multifarious proposal, loosely conceived means, and essentially different ends—all of which were labeled "peace" —it was possible for any specific measure which signified one thing to one school of thought to mean something entirely different to another. Thus the arms-embargo idea, frequently united with assumptions based upon the Peace Pact and other treaties, was suggestive to everyone. Using it as a basis, both the isolationists and the internationalists undertook to work out their own schemes of salvation, while the pacifists trailed somewhat aimlessly in their wake. This confusion of intention was to persist until 1933. In the meanwhile, both sides had reason to hope.

III

The opening of extensive Japanese aggression in China in 1931 called attention again to the Peace Pact and inaugurated a new drive to render it more effective. The first important move in this direction was undertaken by Secretary of State Henry L. Stimson, who pronounced his doctrine of nonrecognition on January 7, 1932. In identical notes to China and Japan Stimson announced that the United States did not "intend to recognize any treaty or agreement . . . which may impair the treaty rights of the United States or its citizens in China . . . [or] . . . any situation, treaty, or agreement which may be brought about by means contrary to the covenants and obligations of the Pact of Paris . . . ." [32]

As invoked here, the doctrine of nonrecognition was not without precedent in American foreign policy. In general conception and tenor this note closely resembled the communication handed Japan on May 11, 1915, by Secretary of State William Jennings Bryan, at a moment when conditions in the Far East were not unlike those of 1932.[33] Stimson regarded the doctrine as a kind of sanction—the only one available to him

---

[32] Note to the Chinese and Japanese governments, Jan. 7, 1932, United States, Department of State, *Department of State Press Releases* (Washington, D. C.: U. S. Govt. Printing Office, 1929–1939), No. 119 (Jan. 9, 1932), pp. 41–42.

[33] For a comparison of these notes, see Robert Langer, *Seizure of Territory: The Stimson Doctrine and Related Principles in Legal Theory and Diplomatic Practice* (Princeton, N. J.: Princeton Univ. Press, 1947), pp. 58–59.

at the time. By his own account, it was intended not only to fulfill American treaty obligations to China but also to uphold the "system of coöperative action for the preservation of peace" which had been set up since the World War, and of which he considered the United States a part.[34]

This explicit linking of nonrecognition with the Pact of Paris represented a laudable attempt to uphold the spirit of international coöperation at a moment when more drastic action was not feasible, and in theory there was much to recommend it. The general purpose of nonrecognition, as explained by a leading student of the subject, is "to prevent the validation of a legal nullity."[35] In this sense, a declaration like Stimson's exhibits a certain moral force and leaves the nonrecognizing state free, if necessary, to nullify at a later date the change involved. Beyond this, its effects on small changes of international significance are not altogether clear. But as applied to changes of sovereignty, new governments, and new states, it has certain political and juridical consequences which may greatly hamper the unrecognized state in the conduct of its relations with the outside world, especially if nonrecognition is widely invoked and long continued. Thus Stimson's announcement had potential value as a sanction. Measured in terms of early practical results, however, its utility depended upon the willingness of other powers to join the United States in a rigorous enforcement of the disabilities arising from nonrecognition.[36]

Fully aware of this, Stimson had made a bid for British support before dispatching his notes. But he encountered grievous disappointment as London, on January 11, declined to take any formal action

[34] Henry L. Stimson, *The Far Eastern Crisis; Recollections and Observations* (New York: Harper and Bros., for the Council on Foreign Relations, 1936), p. 233. The obligations here referred to were mainly those of the Nine-Power Treaty.

[35] Hersh Lauterpacht, *Recognition in International Law* (Cambridge, Eng.: Cambridge Univ. Press, 1947), p. 413.

[36] So far as relations between the United States and Japan were concerned, the principal application of the Stimson doctrine lay in the American refusal to recognize the new state of Manchukuo, constituted in 1934. Weighing the accomplishments and shortcomings of nonrecognition when used as a sanction, Langer concludes that it° positive values—political, juridical, and ethical—notably overshadow its weaknesses. See Langer, *Seizure of Territory*, pp. 287–288. For other estimates, largely favorable, see Lauterpacht, *Recognition in International Law*, pp. 415–420; Quincy Wright, "The Stimson Note of Jan. 7, 1932," *American Journal of International Law*, XXVI (Apr. 1932), 346; and James W. Garner, "Non-Recognition of Illegal Territorial Annexations and Claims to Sovereignty," *ibid.*, XXX (Oct. 1936), 686. A less enthusiastic view may be found in Arnold D. McNair, "The Stimson Doctrine of Non-Recognition," *British Yearbook of International Law*, XIV (1933), 73.

regarding the American program.[37]   This show of lethargy in White-hall certainly hindered the expected growth of Stimson's idea, and en-dorsement of his stand by the League of Nations on March 11 [38] was therefore not so helpful as it might otherwise have been.

Nevertheless, Stimson continued doing what he could to buttress the Pact of Paris. Speaking before the Council on Foreign Relations, in August, he asserted that war had been so closely shorn of its legality that it could no longer be considered the "source and subject of rights" and that violators of the Peace Pact had now to be regarded as law-breakers. Striking directly at traditional neutrality, he added: "We no longer draw a circle about them and treat them with the punctilios of the duelist's code." [39]   He went on to emphasize public opinion as the real sanction behind the Pact, pointed out that nonrecognition was one means of bringing it to bear upon specific problems, and concluded that, since "any effective invocation of the power of world opinion postulates discussion and consultation," the Pact of Paris necessarily carried with it the "implication of consultation." [40]

A few days later, President Hoover publicly described the nonrecog-nition doctrine as one of the significant achievements of his administra-tion.[41]   And in a message to Congress on January 10, 1933, he aligned himself even more solidly with his Secretary of State. On the latter's recommendation he urged legislation "conferring upon the President authority in his discretion to limit or forbid shipment of arms for mili-tary purposes in cases where special undertakings of coöperation can be secured with the principal arms manufacturing nations." Such a meas-ure would "at least enable the executive in special cases to place the United States in line with other nations willing to make such sacrifices in the prevention of military conflict." [42]   Clearly enough, the execu-

[37] Stimson, *The Far Eastern Crisis*, pp. 98–99.

[38] Resolution of the Assembly of the League of Nations, Mar. 11, 1932, *Department of State Press Releases*, No. 128 (Mar. 12, 1932), pp. 256–257.

[39] Address by Stimson, Aug. 8, 1932, United States, Department of State, *Papers Relating to the Foreign Relations of the United States, 1932* (Washington, D. C.: U. S. Govt. Printing Office, 1948), I, 577–578.

[40] *Foreign Relations, 1932*, I, 583–584. Cf. discussion in Charles G. Fenwick, "The 'Implication of Consultation' in the Pact of Paris," *American Journal of International Law*, XXVI (Oct. 1932), 787.

[41] See excerpt from speech by President Hoover, Aug. 12, 1932, in Chesney Hill, "Recent Policies of Non-Recognition," *International Conciliation*, No. 293 (Oct. 1933), p. 420.

[42] See Stimson's letter to the President, Jan. 6, 1933, in United States, Congress, House of Representatives, Committee on Foreign Affairs, *House Report No. 2040* (72nd

tive branch of the government was veering away from the worst excesses of isolationism, while the Peace Pact, aided by Stimson's vigorous interpretation, was beginning to assume theoretical lineaments which had long been envisioned by the internationalists.

Although it failed of adoption, the discretionary embargo measure requested by the President found a sponsor in no less a person than Senator Borah.[43] The old man went down fighting stubbornly; but his defense of his resolution made it clear that, far from having been converted to internationalism, he regarded the proposal chiefly as a blow at the munitions makers.[44] The supposed lessons of 1914–1917 were beginning to take a direct bearing on the embargo question. This fact was even more evident in the treatment accorded an identical resolution brought forward in March, at the request of the newly-inaugurated President Roosevelt, by Sam D. McReynolds, Democratic chairman of the House Committee on Foreign Affairs.[45] It was apparent that the isolationists in Congress had grown too strong and, on the whole, too sure of their own objectives to permit the enactment of any discretionary embargo law authorizing the executive to distinguish between aggressor and victim; such a law would involve taking sides and render neutrality impossible! Yet, even though they failed, these two measures furnished a solid bridge of policy between the Hoover and Roosevelt administrations.

While his next move bore no direct relation to the Peace Pact, Roosevelt erected still another bridge when he espoused Stimson's views on consultation at the Geneva Disarmament Conference in May 1933. Faced by what amounted to stalemate among the conferees, and by strident French demands that some measure of security precede disarmament, he allowed Norman Davis, the American representative, to assure that body that the United States was willing to consult with other nations in the event of any threat to the peace. If the nations, in

---

Cong., 2nd sess.) (Washington, D. C.: U. S. Govt. Printing Office, 1933), pp. 3 ff; and the President's message to Congress, Jan. 10, 1933, *Cong. Record,* LXXVI (72nd Cong., 2nd sess.), 1448.

[43] For the text of this resolution, see *Cong. Record,* LXXVI (72nd Cong., 2nd sess.), 2096.

[44] *Ibid.,* p. 3591.

[45] After being passed by the House in April, this measure was held in the Senate for nearly a year. It was eventually approved on February 28, 1934, with an amendment (drafted by Senator Hiram Johnson) which provided that any embargo proclaimed should apply equally to all belligerents. Thus altered, the resolution was returned to the House. Nothing further was done about it.

conference, designated an aggressor in any given situation and decided to take action, the United States, providing it shared the collective judgment, would do nothing which tended to render such measures ineffective.[46] To implement this policy Roosevelt even thought of appointing an ambassador to the League, but desisted out of reluctance to provoke isolationist sentiment in the country.[47] A third bridge was completed in December 1933, when the United States joined other American republics in an agreement not to recognize territorial or other advantages which any state might gain by the use of force.[48]

The Davis pronouncement foreshadowed an attitude which was to serve the Roosevelt administration as a kind of guide in foreign affairs until almost the time of Munich, when such a stopgap policy was no longer even remotely equal to the international situation. Unable to secure anything better, the President from time to time requested the enactment of impartial embargo laws, accepted others which were offered him, and applied them all to this essentially negative support of collective action. But, however they might be used, their impartiality was the keynote so far as Congress was concerned; it was always clear that such acts were adopted only because they appealed to that body's dominant and involvement-conscious, isolationist viewpoint. First in the series was a highly limited statute drawn at the President's request in May 1934 to enable the United States to coöperate with League sanctions in the Chaco war.[49]

Unfortunately, however, the economic policy of the New Deal,

[46] For the complete text of the Davis statement, see *Department of State Press Releases,* No. 191 (May 27, 1933), p. 390. The immediate background of this move is discussed in Cordell Hull, *The Memoirs of Cordell Hull* (New York: Macmillan Co., 1948), I, 224–226. It has been asserted that Roosevelt, before his inauguration, undertook to follow the major foreign policies of the Hoover administration. According to Raymond Moley, the president-elect made such a pledge to Stimson during an extended interview which took place at Hyde Park on January 9, 1933. See Raymond Moley, *After Seven Years* (New York: Harper and Bros., 1939), p. 94; also Stimson, *The Far Eastern Crisis,* p. 226. It is certain, however, that Roosevelt declined to accept his predecessor's somewhat vague recommendations concerning liberal treatment of the war-debt problem.

[47] Hull. *Memoirs,* I, 387.

[48] Article XI, Convention on the Rights and Duties of States, Dec. 22, 1933, United States, Department of State, *Peace and War: United States Foreign Policy, 1931–1941* (Washington, D. C.: U. S. Govt. Printing Office, 1943), p. 201.

[49] See Hull's letter to McReynolds, May 22, 1934, in United States, Congress, House of Representatives, Committee on Foreign Affairs, *House Report No. 1727* (73rd Cong., 2nd sess.) (Washington, D. C.: U. S. Govt. Printing Office, 1934), pp. 1–2; and *Journal of the Senate* (73rd Cong., 2nd sess.), p. 458.

especially during its first year or two, was not designed to complement Roosevelt's foreign political program. Domestic recovery was its first concern, and the premises upon which the recovery effort was originally based demanded a considerable degree of economic nationalism. It is true that Roosevelt's choice of a Secretary of State lent support to the opposite view. Cordell Hull's opinions on the tariff were sufficiently well known to presage the adoption of a much freer trade policy than the nation had enjoyed for some time, but Hull himself was to complain about the President's delay in pressing for the Reciprocal Trade Act, which did not become law until June 1934.[50] And when the results of his early policy are taken into account, it is difficult to avoid the conclusion that in 1933 Roosevelt's foreign and domestic objectives were at serious odds. This variance was especially notable in his refusal to countenance any move approaching cancellation of the war debts, or to follow Hoover in recognizing an essential connection between the war debts and the state of world trade.[51]

Accordingly, Hull attended the London Economic Conference in the early summer of 1933 equipped to deal—and then only partially—with just one of the three economic questions to which the larger states were most attentive. War debts could not be discussed at all. Currency stabilization could be treated only by Treasury experts and within narrow limits. The third issue, that of tariffs and other trade barriers, proved elusive because, lacking the fulcrum of the Reciprocal Trade Act, Hull could only negotiate with individual countries on the somewhat barren assurance that any treaties so concluded would be presented to the Senate for ratification.[52] As a result, Hull achieved nothing; only one of these questions was given even the pretense of serious consideration. This point was gained when Assistant Secretary of State Raymond Moley, then one of Roosevelt's most intimate advisers, suddenly appeared in London as presidential liaison agent and undertook to secure a tentative agreement on currency stabilization. Although Moley claimed that the terms he got fell completely within his written instructions, and had the approval of the Secretary of the Treasury for

---

[50] Hull, *Memoirs*, I, 251, 353–354.

[51] Moley, *After Seven Years*, p. 196. For a similar estimate by a more friendly critic, see Allan Nevins, *America in World Affairs* (New York: Oxford Univ. Press, 1942), p. 97; also Hull, *Memoirs*, I, 248. Roosevelt's view of the war-debt question is explained by Moley in *After Seven Years*, pp. 78–79. Some interesting personal side lights are given in Grace Tully, *F. D. R., My Boss* (New York: Charles Scribner's Sons, 1949), pp. 60–63. [52] Hull, *Memoirs*, I, 250.

good measure, Roosevelt declined to approve the understanding on the ground that the Conference should not allow details to supplant broad objectives. This summary move brought the parley to an end with no accomplishment whatever.[53] Again domestic policy had bulked large in an international question. For whether or not the President gave his true reason for brushing stabilization aside, it was certainly the opinion of Washington experts that such an agreement would have toppled the rising domestic prices which were so basic to the New Deal's recovery program. As one historian has aptly written, the London Economic Conference was a "tragedy of timing." [54]

Thus internationalism achieved a partial victory in the executive branch of the government during 1932 and 1933. As isolationism deepened its entrenchments throughout the country, and as isolationists in Congress took control of the embargo movement which had beckoned to the internationalists with such fair promise ever since 1928, Stimson and Hoover, followed by Roosevelt and Hull, embraced a policy which, however tentative, betrayed a growing concern over the fate of world-peace machinery and a desire to undertake certain limited repairs. But their program was altogether moral and political, touching economic questions most ineffectively just as economic pressures were greatest and at the moment when vigorous action in this domain might have done substantial good. Official internationalism had reached the highest point it was to achieve between the two world wars, but even here it was less than complete. For if President Roosevelt did not repudiate the internationalists, neither did he altogether accept their gospel.

IV

Between 1934 and 1937 American public opinion finished absorbing the lessons of the World War as set forth by scholars and publicists, and by many who were neither. With more information at their disposal, and aware that they were dealing with what had become a vital public

---

[53] Moley places the greatest blame for this failure upon Roosevelt's vacillations; see *After Seven Years*, pp. 247, 250, 256. Hull regards Moley as an officious busybody who caused trouble by working over the heads of the entire delegation; see *Memoirs*, I, 259–262. Cf. Moley's reply to this accusation in his letter to the *New York Times*, Feb. 2, 1948, p. 18, col. 6.

[54] Basil Rauch, *Roosevelt: From Munich to Pearl Harbor* (New York: Creative Age Press, 1950), p. 17.

question, the best of such writers adopted a tone somewhat more temperate than that employed by Barnes and Grattan a few years earlier. They were, on the whole, less concerned with the general problems of war guilt and much more concerned with the specific problems of neutrality.

Neutrality had been subjected to attack in the late nineteen-twenties and early nineteen-thirties with a view to proving that it was incompatible with the League, the Kellogg-Briand Pact, and other evidences of international solidarity. Now the emphasis was changed, and neutrality was painstakingly reëxamined in the light of its avowed objective: Could it be depended upon to keep the nation out of foreign wars? Writers had no difficulty finding lessons in point; and while their arguments in no way undermined the basic American desire for neutrality, they rapidly stripped that condition, so far as it involved the assertion and defense of broad neutral rights, of the little validity that it still retained in the American mind.

One of the opening gambits was furnished by Charles Warren, former Assistant Attorney General of the United States, whose widely read article "The Troubles of a Neutral" appeared in the journal *Foreign Affairs* in 1934 and later obtained broad distribution in pamphlet form. Although he personally favored more vigorous action against disturbers of the peace than had yet been taken, Warren argued cogently that, if the United States wished to stay out of foreign wars in all circumstances, it "must be prepared to impose upon the action of its citizens far greater restrictions than international law requires." [55] Any serious study of the World War, he asserted, permitted no other conclusion. Between 1914 and 1917 this country had secured no final recognition of neutral rights from any of the belligerents; every condition faced by the United States in that period was still "present or possible." [56] Observance of neutral rights by warring nations depended upon expediency rather than law; a belligerent government would continue to observe those rights only so long as it was convinced that the advantage which it might gain from interference with neutral activity was outweighed by the disadvantage of accepting the injured neutral as a possible enemy. It was evident "that the citizens of a neutral nation do not now possess any rights on the high seas which can

---

[55] Charles Warren, "The Troubles of a Neutral," *Foreign Affairs*, XII (Apr. 1934), 377–378.

[56] *Ibid.*, p. 379.

be successfully asserted against a belligerent without danger of such assertion leading to war." [57]

The remedy, of course, was implicit in the argument. Traditional American neutrality, with its strong defense of neutral rights, presented a clear danger of war in circumstances anything like those which had existed during 1914–1917; to avoid that danger the United States would have to abandon its traditional practice. Rounding out his thesis, Warren suggested a number of measures which, if adopted before a conflict started, would enable the country to carry out the necessary self-denial. Among these expedients was that of a law imposing an automatic and impartial arms embargo against all belligerents as soon as a foreign war began, precisely the device which was already suggesting itself to Congress. [58]

Thus Warren cut the dilemma into its component parts, showing that for a power like the United States there was no realistic middle ground between international coöperation and thoroughgoing isolation. Many other writers used a similar approach and achieved similar results. [59] Even the orthodox historical treatments lent comfort to such reasoning. In two books published during the mid-thirties Charles Seymour studied the last war as a historical problem rather than an object lesson, and convincingly explained American intervention in terms of the submarine issue. [60] Arguing that Wilson alone had determined foreign policy, and that no influence could become politically effective unless espoused by him, Seymour refused to attach much importance to the activities of bankers, munitions makers, or industrialists in general; Wilson's total lack of sympathy with their views was almost proverbial. [61] Seymour went on to isolate submarine warfare as the one effective cause of the intervention. [62] His case was impressive, and by undermining parts of the Barnes-Grattan thesis it struck hard at the

[57] Warren, *Foreign Affairs*, XII (Apr. 1934), 388.   [58] *Ibid.*, pp. 380–381.

[59] It would be impractical to give even a partial list here. Perhaps the best guide to this phase of the neutrality debate is Allen W. Dulles and Hamilton Fish Armstrong, *Can We Be Neutral?* (New York: Harper and Bros., for the Council on Foreign Relations, 1936). The authors admit that neutrality could be successfully implemented only with the aid of self-imposed restrictions, although they argue that such a withdrawal from world political and economic activities might have results even more unfavorable than those of war itself. See especially chap. i.

[60] Charles Seymour, *American Neutrality during the World War* (Baltimore: Johns Hopkins Press, 1934); and *American Neutrality, 1914–1917* (New Haven: Yale Univ. Press, 1935).

[61] Seymour, *American Neutrality*, p. 29.

[62] *Ibid.*, p. 171.

isolationist position. At the same time, however, it indirectly confirmed Warren's analysis that any strong defense of neutral rights entailed the risk of war, for it offered no reason to suppose that the submarine issue or some equivalent defiance of American pretensions
would not again arise if the United States clung to established practice.

Professor Edwin M. Borchard used a still different approach. He
was certainly no internationalist, but neither was he an isolationist in the
extreme sense of the word; he found salvation in traditional neutrality
and strict observance of the international law of the nineteenth century,
rather than in novel and complicated trade restrictions whereby the
United States would practically withdraw from the seas. Borchard's
effort, then, was to rehabilitate the tradition. In his book *Neutrality
for the United States,* published in 1937, he sought to do this by arguing
that America had not been really neutral during the First World
War; [63] its treatment of Great Britain and France had differed materially
from its treatment of the Central Powers. If, on the other hand, the
United States had made a genuine effort to fulfill its neutral obligations
in deed as well as in word, insisting at the same time that its rights be
scrupulously observed by all parties, the policy would have succeeded.
Notwithstanding Borchard's considerable powers of exposition, however, his compromise between self-denial and war seemed undependable.
His was a counsel of perfection for everyone in a field of international
behavior where perfection had seldom, if ever, been achieved. The
question of what nations actually did, as opposed to what international
law expected them to do, was almost completely ignored.

A number of other studies, some narrower in scope, some more in-
clusive, appeared side by side with those mentioned above. Among
them was Walter Millis' immensely popular *The Road to War.*[64]
Brilliantly written on a sustained note of artful scepticism, this book
offered a fascinating panorama of the social appeals, cultural ties, economic entanglements, propaganda campaigns, and other forces that
had worked against American neutrality up to 1917. Singling out one
aspect of this titillating thesis, Professor James D. Squires of Colby
Junior College wrote a short but closely reasoned monograph which
exposed the operation of the wartime British propaganda machine both

[63] Edwin M. Borchard and William P. Lage, *Neutrality for the United States* (New
Haven: Yale Univ. Press, 1937). See especially the authors' definition of neutrality,
p. vi.

[64] Walter Millis, *The Road to War; America, 1914–1917* (Boston: Houghton Mifflin
Co., 1935).

at home and in the United States.[65]   Also released at this time were
the memoirs of Robert Lansing, President Wilson's Secretary of State
from mid-1915. Lansing's frank admission that he had never approached the problems of neutrality in a truly neutral spirit simply
added more fuel to the spreading flames.[66]

No consideration of American foreign policy in the middle nineteen-thirties could escape the mental climate engendered by the famous
Nye Committee, for in keeping the neutrality question constantly before the public eye, and in the endless reiteration of a narrowly isolationist viewpoint, the influence of this body was second to none. Established by the Senate in 1934, the Committee opened its hearings in
September of that year. Its original purpose, approved by the Roosevelt
administration, was to investigate the manufacture and sale of arms
and munitions, particularly at the international level. But contrary
to the expectations of the President and Secretary of State, it was
placed under the chairmanship of Gerald P. Nye, one of the Senate's
leading isolationists, and its energies were channeled into an effort to
prove that the true causes of America's recent intervention were to be
found in the policies which bankers and industrialists had selfishly
foisted upon the government during the long months of neutrality.[67]

Provided with a large staff and generous appropriations, the Committee surveyed a good deal of ground in the next two years. Through
lavish use of its authority to summon witnesses and examine records it
uncovered much evidence which not only appeared to support the
arguments of Barnes, Grattan, and Millis, but also helped confirm such
sensational exposés of the international arms traffic as "Arms and the
Men"—an article which appeared in *Fortune* during the spring of 1934,
describing the ability of the armaments makers to "supply everything
you need for a war from cannons to the *casus belli*"—[68] and Helmuth
C. Engelbrecht's *Merchants of Death.*[69]   More than adequately cov-

[65] James D. Squires, *British Propaganda at Home and in the United States from
1914 to 1917* (Cambridge, Mass.: Harvard Univ. Press, 1935).

[66] Robert Lansing, *War Memoirs of Robert Lansing* (Indianapolis: Bobbs-Merrill
Co., 1935), pp. 18–19.

[67] Hull explains that the Roosevelt administration's initial approval of the munitions
investigation was based upon the expectation that a Democrat rather than an isolationist Republican would be made chairman. Nye's appointment, he adds, was a tactical
error on the part of Senator Key Pittman, chairman of the Senate Committee on Foreign
Relations (*Memoirs*, I, 398).

[68] "Arms and the Men," *Fortune*, IX (Mar. 1934), 53.

[69] Helmuth C. Engelbrecht and F. C. Hanighen, *Merchants of Death: A Study of
the International Armaments Industry* (New York: Dodd, Mead, and Co., 1934).

ered by the press and radio, and further illuminated by copious reports
of hearings and conclusions, the work of the Nye Committee received
widespread attention, and its findings were soon deeply embedded in a
receptive public opinion. Its denunciations of the munitions industry
unquestionably had much to do with the final shaping of the arms embargo feature of the new neutrality acts.[70]

Among historians of repute it was probably Charles A. Beard who
found the conclusions of the Nye Committee most alluring. His
hastily written tract, *The Devil Theory of War,* reached the bookshops
in 1936, while the Committee was finishing its labors. Beginning with
a selective examination of various happenings and documents bearing
upon American intervention in 1917, Beard heartily endorsed an expansion of the mandatory and impartial embargo policy with which
Congress had been experimenting more than a year.[71] His method and
much of his material were borrowed from the Committee, and thus its
influence was perpetuated in ever-widening circles. Thanks to such
stimulation, this flood of writing on the lessons of the World War continued to the end of the decade, when three of the best works in the
field—Charles C. Tansill's *America Goes to War,* Alice M. Morrissey's
The American Defense of Neutral Rights, 1914–1917, and H. C. Peterson's *Propaganda for War*—[72] offered a kind of general summing up.

It cannot be doubted that the findings of historians, the arguments of
publicists, and the activities of the Nye Committee had an important
bearing on the development of public opinion in the middle nineteen-
thirties. And although there was a marked lack of unanimity in detailed conclusions, the net effect of all this research and debate was to
crystallize popular thought about a few closely related beliefs and a
definite program which, taken together, constituted isolationism in its
new and most advanced form. At its base lay a conviction that the
natural advantages of geographical position, size, and strength of the

[70] The Committee's hearings were finally published, in forty parts. The main
results of its findings, as expressed in specific recommendations, are set forth in United
States, Congress, Senate, Special Committee to Investigate the Munitions Industry, *Senate
Report No. 944* (74th Cong., 2nd sess.) (Washington, D. C.: U. S. Govt. Printing
Office, 1936), pt. 5, pp. 3–9.

[71] Charles A. Beard, *The Devil Theory of War* (New York: Vanguard Press, 1936),
see especially pp. 122–123.

[72] Charles C. Tansill, *America Goes to War* (Boston: Little, Brown, and Co., 1938);
Alice M. Morrissey, *The American Defense of Neutral Rights, 1914–1917* (Cambridge,
Mass.: Harvard Univ. Press, 1939); and Horace C. Peterson, *Propaganda for War: The
Campaign against American Neutrality, 1914–1917* (Norman, Okla.: Univ. Oklahoma
Press, 1939).

United States made it substantially immune to the effects of any European war. To maintain neutrality during such a struggle might impose many hardships and annoyances upon the American people, but these were as nothing compared with war itself. Americans might prefer the victory of one side or the other, but the victor could never, in any event, seriously threaten the nation's well-being. American security had not been involved in the World War, and it was inconceivable that American security could depend on the outcome of any future European conflict. It followed that the United States had gone to war in 1917 for reasons that had little to do with its vital interests. Certain ideals had been alleged at the time; but that they escaped realization had long been apparent to everyone, and they were not worth the cost in any event. Viewed from this standpoint, American intervention in the First World War became little more than a mechanical process, a huge blunder which materialized inevitably through a definite set of policies and a definite series of acts totally unrelated to fundamental considerations of national security. But these acts and policies, having been identified and analyzed, could be avoided in future if the necessary prohibitions were established in time.

The isolationist gospel was simple and, if one accepted the premise that the United States could always take care of itself regardless of what happened in the rest of the world, it was almost irresistible. While it contended that the nation had to stay out of foreign wars, it admitted that adherence to ordinary neutrality, the traditional means to the end, was a perilous undertaking. The United States had to improve upon accepted standards by relinquishing most of the neutral claims which produce friction with belligerents. Opinions differed as to just what activities should be abandoned, but most isolationists agreed that it was at least necessary to prohibit the export of arms and munitions and the extension of loans to all belligerent states. This, they held, would not only foil the bankers and industrialists whose machinations had been so roundly exposed. It would also provide a new, an exalted, and—more important still—a really dependable type of neutrality. To guarantee that the policy would not be compromised in its early stages, moreover, the essential laws had to be framed at once. For, if the choice were left to executive discretion, who could know that the President would always be as neutral as the people? Obviously Congress would have to man the breach.

According to public-opinion polls, between 70 and 80 per cent of the American people desired a larger Army, Navy, and Air Force in December 1935. But that they were thinking defensively was indicated by a September 1936 survey, which reported that 71 per cent favored a national referendum on any question of declaring war. In March 1936 no less than 82 per cent wanted to prohibit the manufacture and sale of munitions for private profit. In November, 95 per cent thought that the United States should not take part in another conflict like the World War. And in April 1937 it was the belief of 70 per cent that the nation had erred in 1917.[73] The way was now open for consummation of legislative neutrality.

V

It was not surprising that this lopsided growth of sentiment enabled the isolationists in Congress to assume virtually full, though by no means unopposed, control of the embargo movement after 1933. The Mc-Reynolds resolution of that year stands as the great watershed. After its rejection, lines were sufficiently plain to keep true isolationists from supporting any measure which allowed the President to choose between aggressor and victim in connection with the sale of arms. They now knew that the impartial embargo was what they wanted, and pacifists speedily came to agree with them.[74] If international coöperation were able to derive incidental benefit from some law which did not tamper with American neutrality—as in the Chaco embargo of 1934—neither isolationist nor pacifist had any special objection. Otherwise, the embattled internationalists were forced to rely on themselves alone.

As the domestic economy grew better, Roosevelt abandoned his early hesitancy in questions of foreign trade, and some progress was made through commercial arrangement. Passed in June 1934, the Reciprocal Trade Act inaugurated a shift away from the economic nationalism which had marked the New Deal's first year. This had its political bearing. As Hull complacently observed somewhat later, not one of the nations with which the United States made trade agreements under this act was found on the opposite side when war came, and most of them eventually fought the Axis.[75] It is noteworthy too that a special clause in the act was used to withhold tariff reductions from

[73] *Public Opinion Quarterly*, II (July 1938), 387–388.
[74] Masland, "The 'Peace' Groups Join Battle," *ibid.*, IV (Dec. 1940), 668.
[75] Hull, *Memoirs*, I, 365.

Germany—a policy which made the entire program distasteful to that country, as Hjalmar Schacht told Ambassador William E. Dodd in August 1936.[76] The establishment of the Second Export-Import Bank earlier the same year to help finance exports was another move in this direction, and partly overcame the effects of the Johnson Act, with its ban on private loans to governments in default upon their obligations to the United States.[77]

The first general embargo statute, signed on August 31, was passed under the impetus furnished by approaching hostilities between Italy and Ethiopia in the summer of 1935.[78] At the last minute the administration's wishes were revealed again in a bill drafted by the State Department which would have given the President wide freedom to designate the nation or nations to which the embargo should apply, to prohibit loans to such states, to forbid the use of American waters by their submarines, and to caution American citizens that they traveled on the ships of warring states at their own risk.[79] But the act of August 31 followed the pattern set by the Chaco embargo. Frankly experimental and scheduled to run only until February 29, 1936, the most significant provisions related to the arms embargo and to machinery for implementing it.

While the new law permitted no discrimination between the parties to any conflict, it had some application to immediate needs. Since Ethiopia's geographical position hindered reception of imports from the United States in any event, the arms embargo theoretically operated somewhat to Italy's disadvantage. Actually, it permitted the Roosevelt administration to steal the initiative from the League by stopping the shipment of American arms to Mussolini's government before League sanctions began to operate.[80] To inconvenience the Italians still further,

[76] Benjamin H. Williams, "The Coming of Economic Sanctions into American Practice," *American Journal of International Law,* XXXVII (July 1943), 389; and William E. Dodd, *Ambassador Dodd's Diary,* ed. W. E. Dodd, Jr., and Martha Dodd (New York: Harcourt, Brace, and Co., 1941), pp. 344–345.

[77] Benjamin H. Williams, *Foreign Loan Policy of the United States since 1933* (New York: Council on Foreign Relations, 1939), pp. 24–25.

[78] United States, Department of State, *United States Statutes at Large* (Washington, D. C.: U. S. Govt. Printing Office and others, 1845——), XLIX, 1081–1085.

[79] Hull, *Memoirs,* I, 410–411.

[80] Dulles and Armstrong, *Can We Be Neutral?* p. 62. Cf. Hull's memorandum of conversation with the Italian Ambassador, Nov. 22, 1935, United States, Department of State, *Peace and War: United States Foreign Policy, 1931–1941* (Washington, D. C.: U. S. Govt. Printing Office, 1943), p. 294. Hull also explains that he moved ahead of

the administration tried to discourage the sale of other commodities as well.[81] A moral embargo to supplement the legal embargo on arms and munitions was not without merit, but in directing these efforts against Ethiopia as well as against Italy it was needlessly impartial and unduly cautious regarding American neutrality opinion. This venture, which amounted to an extension of the neutrality act, temporarily caused the Roosevelt administration to appear more isolationist than the isolationists themselves.[82]

When this law expired on February 29, 1936, a new one was enacted. Besides reaffirming the impartial arms embargo it prohibited the loaning of money and the extension of credit to belligerent nations, and forbade the sale of their securities in the United States.[83] Congress was still following internationalist recommendations on specific measures, but adapting them to its own views by removing them from executive discretion as far as seemed practicable.

The next significant foreign upheaval was the Spanish civil war, which began in the summer of 1936. Since the joint resolution of February 29 said nothing about domestic conflicts, it was useless here as an instrument of policy. To avoid undermining the ineffectual and somewhat ridiculous nonintervention committee led by Great Britain, therefore, Roosevelt demanded and obtained, in January 1937, a non-discriminatory embargo applying specifically to the Spanish affair.[84] That this move deprived the recognized Spanish government of its rightful opportunity to purchase arms for resisting domestic insurrection weighed as nothing against Roosevelt's determination to coöperate with a nonintervention project which had become a public farce. Even Senator Nye saw the unhappy effect of this regime on the Spanish Republican government, but his attempt to substitute a measure which would have lifted the embargo for the Loyalists alone drew no support from the administration.[85] Here the term "coöperation" was mislead-

---

the League so that American isolationists could not accuse him of following its policies. See *Memoirs*, I, 429.

[81] Hull, *Memoirs*, I, 430. On at least one occasion the President argued that United States policy toward the Spanish civil war was a wholly independent one (Roosevelt to Norman Thomas, Jan. 25, 1937, MS Roosevelt Papers [Official File, Box 422–C]).

[82] Cf. Dulles and Armstrong, *Can We Be Neutral?* pp. 59, 68–69.

[83] *Statutes at Large*, XLIX, 1152–1153.

[84] *Ibid.*, L, 3. For a statement of the purpose of this measure see *Cong. Record*, LXXXI (75th Cong., 1st sess.), 75.

[85] Hull to Pittman, May 12, 1938, *Peace and War*, pp. 419–420.

ing; and while it was perhaps unimportant in the larger scheme of things, Roosevelt's willful blindness in this regard was another item tending somewhat to weaken his later case against the isolationists.[86]

Behind the agitation over the neutrality acts and their use the State Department maintained a close watch over developments abroad. As early as January 1935, Hull joined the American Ambassador at Tokyo, Joseph C. Grew, in recommending a larger Navy.[87] His growing disquietude was further manifested that summer when he endeavored to lay plans for stock-piling tin, but his efforts came to nothing because of England's refusal to apply the cost of such materials against its war debt.[88] With the practical failure of the London Naval Conference in the spring of 1936 the Secretary of State was convinced that disarmament offered little hope as a basis for peace. In his view, the American government faced the question "of when, in the light of chaotic conditions in many areas of the globe, this nation should abandon the undertaking to preserve peace through disarmament and proceed rapidly to arm sufficiently to be able to resist the plainly visible movements toward military conquest by Germany, Japan, and Italy." [89]

But Congress, with the emphatic support of the country, expressed its concern in a different fashion, bringing the new isolationism and the new neutrality to fulfillment in the joint resolution of May 1, 1937. Reënacting the main provisions of its forerunners and making certain large additions, this law forbade the export of arms, munitions, and implements of war to belligerent states and those engaged in civil strife; ordained that no materials of any kind listed in a presidential proclamation bearing on the subject should be exported to such states, except in foreign vessels and after American citizens had yielded all right, title, and interest; prohibited the loaning of money and the extension of credit to any belligerent government; enjoined American citizens against travel aboard the vessels of warring states; forbade the arming of American merchant ships; and empowered the President to restrict the use of American ports and territorial waters by the submarines and armed merchantmen of belligerent nations.[90] Taken altogether, this act represented the most absolute form of neutrality and the most complete program of isolation to which the country had ever been committed.

President Roosevelt's later complaint that such a legislative policy

---

[86] Hull defends this policy in his *Memoirs*, I, 483–484.
[87] *Ibid.*, p. 456.   [88] *Ibid.*, pp. 457–458.   [89] *Ibid.*, p. 455.
[90] *Statutes at Large*, L, 121–128.

interfered with his conduct of foreign affairs did not lack justification. On the other hand, his own somewhat equivocal internationalism, especially before 1937, raises the question of executive leadership. The early deficiencies of the New Deal's economic program have been mentioned. Many similar contradictions stand out in the political sphere. His opposition to the various neutrality acts never ripened into a veto; his occasional requests for impartial embargo legislation, and his use of such laws as were passed, tended to make it appear that he did not find them altogether without merit.[91] There is also the question of just what he would have done if not hampered by such restrictions. While he had delivered numerous moral appeals and was generous with endorsements of international rectitude, his actual foreign policy statements during these years were vague at best.[92]

Furthermore, he still enjoyed all the ordinary controls over foreign affairs. His power to conduct relations with other governments—to frame questions, to make replies, to appoint and withdraw diplomatic agents and special missions—was still of great importance in determining policy.[93] Important also were his freedom to make executive agreements without Senate ratification [94] and his ability to use a considerable array of crisis powers by determining, on his own responsibility, that an emergency existed.[95] Even within the domain of the neutrality acts his course was not always predetermined. It was he who decided when a given foreign situation amounted to war, for even though Congress retained the authority to judge the same question, this power was never invoked and was of doubtful constitutionality in any event. He also decided when the foreign war was ended and the embargo lifted, and he employed as he saw fit all restrictions having to do with the use of American ports and territorial waters by submarines and armed merchant vessels of belligerent nations.[96] In sum, these powers constituted a formidable reserve of presidential authority over the

[91] Nevins, *America in World Affairs*, p. 97.

[92] Cf. Charles A. Beard, *American Foreign Policy in the Making, 1932–1940: A Study in Responsibilities* (New Haven: Yale Univ. Press, 1946), p. 183.

[93] See Louis W. Koenig, *The Presidency and the Crisis: Powers of the Office from the Invasion of Poland to Pearl Harbor* (New York: King's Crown Press, 1944), pp. 21–23; also Edward S. Corwin, *The President: Office and Powers* (New York: New York Univ. Press, 1941), pp. 229–230.

[94] Corwin, *The President*, pp. 235–238; and Wallace M. McClure, *International Executive Agreements* (New York: Columbia Univ. Press, 1941), p. 248.

[95] Koenig, *The Presidency and the Crisis*, pp. 11–13.

[96] *Ibid.*, pp. 36–40.

management of foreign relations, and Roosevelt was to draw against it lavishly as time went on.

In the spring of 1937, therefore, the isolationist Congress and people of the United States confronted a cautiously dissenting executive and a vigorously dissenting internationalist minority with a far-reaching embargo law which had taken form through a long period of growing conviction, bitter argument, and small experiment. While it was capable of hampering the executive direction of foreign policy in some ways, this aspect of the law was not, by itself, nearly so serious as it might have been. The largest question was that of its probable effectiveness in a general war. It had been tested in principle by a number of foreign conflicts; but since none had tested it enough to prove conclusively that it could be effective (as many suspected) only in cases where it was superfluous, the majority of Americans still believed in its value. However, there were many people of influence in the government and in the country who did not accept its fundamental premises, and they were prepared to make the most of its deficiencies when the great crisis developed.

CHAPTER II

Emergence from Isolation

I

THROUGH THE WEEKS IMMEDIATELY FOLLOWING PASSAGE OF THE NEUTRALITY act in May 1937 Europe remained the principal theme of American worries. Misgivings had been aroused by Far Eastern developments in 1932 and 1933, but these had long since moved to the background of public awareness; any disturbance that Japan might be capable of making was regarded as secondary to prospects inherent in the European situation, where, for years, crisis had followed crisis with just enough variation to preserve them from monotony. Since 1933 disarmament had been no more than a lingering aspiration; a rearmed Germany stood defiantly in the Rhineland; Italy rested in smug possession of a new Ethiopian empire; and despite the efforts of the British-sponsored nonintervention committee to seal off that struggle from the rest of the world, meddling by Germany, Italy, and Russia now gave the Spanish civil war many aspects of a European conflict in miniature. That Germany and Italy, Europe's leading advocates of forcible change, were entering a phase of systematic coöperation could not be doubted. Only the previous October they had formalized their growing intimacy with a statement of common purpose which bound them to collaborate in matters of "parallel" interest, especially in Spain, in the economic penetration of the Danube region, and in the defense of Europe against communism.

But notwithstanding this specific orientation of the Rome-Berlin Axis, the Belgian Minister to Moscow had in February of 1937 confided to the American Ambassador, Joseph E. Davies, his belief that Hitler's denunciations of the Soviet Union were chiefly for German consumption and that an understanding between Hitler and Stalin was not beyond possibility—a view which Davies found to be quite general among diplomats in the Russian capital.[1] That European tensions

[1] Joseph E. Davies, *Mission to Moscow* (New York: Simon and Schuster, 1941), pp. 73, 79.

would develop according to no easy formula was made apparent a few days later, however, when Maxim Litvinov, Russian Foreign Commissar, suggested to Davies that the Soviet government was still anti-German in its regard for international coöperation. Litvinov pointed out the totally negative result of the American arms embargo as applied to Spain, and urged Davies to understand that the United States would only succeed in giving the Axis similar encouragement elsewhere if it maintained its existing embargo policy.[2]

But the new neutrality law did not provide for a complete embargo in any circumstances; belligerent governments could still obtain articles other than battle supplies by paying cash on delivery and providing transportation in their own ships. In contrast with Litvinov, therefore, Winston Churchill took a more cheerful view of American policy in his fortnightly letter on foreign affairs written at the end of May. Admitting that no European statesman might count on American military aid in any circumstances that could be foreseen, he still found that Anglo-American friendship had lately reached unprecedented heights, took comfort in reflecting that the cash-and-carry provision of the embargo act at least had "the merit of rendering to superior sea power its full deserts," and advanced the somewhat wry thesis that America's partial withdrawal from the seas in the event of war would dispel the likelihood of any such contention between the United States and Great Britain as had been engendered in 1914 and 1915.[3]

But these were only portents, and immediate business required some attention. Aside from the highly publicized Spanish civil war and memories of events which had preceded it, the most impressive circumstance in Europe during May was the coronation in London of King George VI, in a ceremony full of medieval pageantry. However, events of much deeper significance were occurring elsewhere. On May 8 the German National Socialist Party won a two-thirds majority in the Danzig *Volkstag,* thus giving notice of at least one problem which Sir Nevile Henderson, the new British Ambassador to Berlin, would eventually have to face. But Henderson was not interested in Danzig at the moment. Having just completed a rapid shift from the British Embassy in Buenos Aires, he was now to announce and foster certain changes in London's attitude toward the Nazi government. Stanley

[2] Davies, *Mission to Moscow,* p. 79.

[3] Winston S. Churchill, *Step by Step, 1936–1939* (New York: G. P. Putnam's Sons, 1939), pp. 111–112.

Baldwin was about to retire from Downing Street, and Neville Chamberlain, Prime Minister designate, had decreed an end to fruitless bickering with the dictatorships. In pursuance of his conviction that Hitler was a reasonable man and capable of responding to friendly treatment, he had instructed Henderson to coöperate with the existing regime in Germany as best he might.[4] Nor was this incipient shift in attitude confined to the government of the United Kingdom. In London for the coronation, the dominion prime ministers on May 14 put festivity conscientiously behind them and opened an Imperial Conference to review the possibility of furthering this new trend in British policy with some kind of economic appeasement.[5] Shortly after his arrival in Berlin, Henderson carefully explained the Chamberlain departure in a speech before the German-English Society.[6] But the withdrawal of both Germany and Italy on May 31 from the nonintervention patrol, which had finally been established a month earlier in an attempt to isolate the Spanish civil war, indicated that appeasement's chief potential beneficiaries did not understand exactly what he was talking about. As the summer passed, nevertheless, Chamberlain refused to admit discouragement. Writing to President Roosevelt at the end of September, he even expressed a cautious optimism regarding the prospects for continued European peace.[7]

Although Tokyo won much less attention than London in that spring of 1937, the Far East was not so quiet as it seemed. As a new act in the European drama opened, portentous changes were taking shape in Japan. The unpopular Hayashi government met defeat in the elections of April 30, and Prince Fumimaro Konoye, having accepted the militarists' demand for a program of "national unity," became head of a strongly nationalistic Cabinet on June 4. First fruits of the new regime appeared almost at once. On July 7 the "China Incident," which was destined to grow until it merged imperceptibly with the Second World

[4] Royal Institute of International Affairs, *Survey of International Affairs, 1937*, by Arnold J. Toynbee and others (London: Oxford Univ. Press, 1938), I, 617; and Sir Nevile Henderson, *Failure of a Mission: Berlin, 1937–1939* (New York: G. P. Putnam's Sons, 1940), p. 7.

[5] Whether they viewed this "appeasement" as an effort to achieve economic coöperation with the dictators, or as an attempt to strengthen democratic nations through the creation of more powerful economic ties generally, was never made clear. See *Survey of International Affairs, 1937*, I, 63.

[6] Henderson, *Failure of a Mission*, p. 10.

[7] Chamberlain to Roosevelt, Sept. 28, 1937, MS Roosevelt Papers (Official File, Box 48).

War, began in a clash between Chinese and Japanese troops at the
Marco Polo Bridge, just west of Peiping.

II

Though details of the early fighting remained uncertain for a time,
the general purport of the Japanese move was clear from the start. By
launching a fresh drive outside the limits of Manchuria, Japan was
opening a new chapter of Far Eastern aggression, threatening the interests of every nation that held treaty rights in China, and undermining the precarious structure of world peace. Secretary Hull grasped
this much in a conversation with the Japanese chargé d'affaires on
July 16,[8] and issued a broad statement of American views the same day.
Asserting that there could be no "serious hostilities anywhere in the
world" which did not in "one way or another affect interests or rights
or obligations of this country," he enumerated various principles which
shaped the foreign policy of the United States. The American government advocated peace and self-restraint, deprecated the use of force, and
opposed interference by any state in the domestic affairs of other nations. It believed in the adjustment of international differences by
negotiation, in the performance of established obligations, in the removal of trade barriers, and in the limitation and reduction of armaments. At the same time, while endorsing coöperative effort, it avoided
entangling alliances and commitments.[9]

Framed in such general terms that only by suggestion did it accuse
Japan of wrongdoing, this prudent utterance harmonized with Hull's
belief that the Japanese government served as a kind of permanent arena
for the struggle between moderates and extremists, and that to meet this
latest resurgence of the militarists with an excessively firm tone would
help unite the Japanese nation behind them, confirm their grip on
power, and hinder the moderates in their effort to regain control.[10]
Whatever strength the pronouncement had lay in its moral force, and

---

[8] Memorandum by Hornbeck, July 16, 1937, United States, Department of State,
Papers Relating to the Foreign Relations of the United States: Japan, 1931–1941 (Washington, D. C.: U. S. Govt. Printing Office, 1943), I, 327–328.

[9] Statement by Hull, July 16, 1937, United States, Department of State, *Department
of State Press Releases* (Washington, D. C.: U. S. Govt. Printing Office, 1929–1939),
XVII (July 17, 1937), 41–42.

[10] Cf. Cordell Hull, *The Memoirs of Cordell Hull* (New York: Macmillan Co.,
1948), I, 538.

the prestige of morality was tarnished. In pure righteousness it outdid the Stimson policy of 1932. But it was also less outspoken, while the proved success of aggression, the state of American neutrality law, and the spreading chaos of European appeasement combined to deprive it of any support it might have gained from attendant circumstances. It bespoke an attitude rather than a policy, and no amount of good will could make it appear strong. As late as 1940, President Roosevelt is reported to have said that the management of relations with Japan involved a kind of appeasement.[11]

If the United States could not move forward, however, it could at least decline to withdraw. On August 17 Hull announced that American forces in China were being augmented by a regiment of Marines, and the main outlines of future procedure became clear on September 2, when he informed Ambassador Joseph C. Grew, in Tokyo, that the United States should avoid taking part in the conflict and endeavor to protect American citizens in the threatened areas, but make no direct effort to solidify relations with either China or Japan.[12] So it was to be. Protests against specific acts in violation of American rights would be emphasized by the opportune reiteration of principle. Beyond this, nothing would be done for many months.[13]

On September 1 Japanese Foreign Minister Hirota revealed the terms which he had offered Chiang Kai-shek as the price of stopping the incipient war. They included *de facto* recognition of Manchukuo by the Chinese government, withdrawal of Chinese troops from North China, and cessation of anti-Japanese activities throughout the Chinese Republic.[14] Unprepared to assume the role of mediator,[15] the State Department received this news passively, and on September 10 it announced, without comment, that Japan had closed the entire Asiatic coast to Chinese shipping, from Chinwangtao southward to Pakhoi; that is, for all practical purposes, from the southern boundary of Manchukuo to the northeastern border of French Indo-China.[16] Wishing to avoid trouble in the blockaded zone, President Roosevelt on September 14

[11] Elliott Roosevelt, *As He Saw It* (New York: Duell, Sloan, and Pearce, 1946), p. 12.

[12] Hull to Grew, Sept. 2, 1937, *Foreign Relations: Japan, 1931–1941*, I, 362–363.

[13] For Hull's defense of this policy see his *Memoirs*, I, 536–537.

[14] Memorandum by Grew, Sept. 1, 1937, *Foreign Relations: Japan, 1931–1941*, I, 360.

[15] As late as April 1938, Hull still shied away from any attempt at mediation. See Department of State to the British Embassy, Apr. 14, 1938, *ibid.*, pp. 463–464.

[16] Press release, Sept. 10, 1937, *ibid.*, p. 371.

directed ships owned by the American government not to carry arms and munitions to either China or Japan, and made it clear that privately owned American vessels would engage in such a trade only at their own risk. The same order announced that the question of applying the neutrality act remained upon a twenty-four-hour basis.[17] So far, the United States had merely taken cognizance of happenings in the Far East.

Nor did its intentions become much more explicit as the League of Nations prepared to consider the Chinese appeal for support against Japan. On September 28 Hull instructed Leland Harrison, the American Minister to Switzerland, to "foster . . . the view that the entire question should be treated from the viewpoint of general world interest and concern and on the broadest possible basis." The United States did not wish to suggest anything to the League, he added, and it was unprepared for any kind of joint action. Parallel action might be considered, however. Only in noting that Japan had thus far been less coöperative than China did Hull's instructions waver from a tone of strict impartiality.[18]

The members of the League, especially Great Britain and France, were as reluctant as the United States to cross swords with Japan. The British Prime Minister informed Roosevelt on September 28 that, for the time being, he doubted whether any action by the Western powers could improve the situation in the Far East;[19] and both London and Paris were certainly in accord with the League Assembly on October 6 when it adopted two committee reports declaring Japan guilty of having violated the Nine-Power Treaty and the Pact of Paris, but merely recommended that the parties to the former agreement hold a conference for study of the issues involved. The American government promptly approved this decision. But when the Japanese Ambassador, Hirosi Saito, asked Hull on October 7 whether he had anything further in mind, the Secretary replied that no action was contemplated for the time being.[20]

Hull's admission, coming when it did, must have struck the Japanese

[17] Statement by the President, Sept. 14, 1937, *Department of State Press Releases,* XVII (Sept. 18, 1937), 227.

[18] Hull to Harrison, Sept. 28, 1937, *Foreign Relations: Japan, 1931–1941,* I, 375–377.

[19] Chamberlain to Roosevelt, Sept. 28, 1937, MS Roosevelt Papers (Official File, Box 48).

[20] Memorandum by Hornbeck, Oct. 7, 1937, *Foreign Relations: Japan, 1931–1941,* I, 398.

Foreign Office as reassuring. The League's delegation of responsibility to a nine-power conference, taken in conjunction with the reverberating "quarantine" speech delivered by the President on October 5, had the effect of drawing the United States into the very center of things; yet the Secretary of State judged it wise to keep open a line of retreat.[21] Nor was he alone in this view, to all appearances, for Roosevelt's comments on the Far East in a "fireside chat" delivered October 12 were so eloquent of compromise that he yielded a good part of the leadership he had seemed to promise in his speech a week earlier.[22] Britain made haste to adopt the same tone,[23] and Japan responded by declining to attend the parley on the ground that most satisfactory adjustments could be made through direct negotiations between itself and China.[24] When the conference finally met at Brussels on November 3, it was clear that little would be accomplished.

As events had predicted, the keynote of the discussions was furnished by the United States. The opening address of the American delegate, Norman Davis, was studiously vague, affirming his country's willingness to share common efforts within the scope of treaty provisions, but stressing its lack of commitments outside those provisions.[25] Ten days later he publicly noted Japan's failure to attend the meetings and expressed a hope that the Japanese government would change its mind.[26] Following these tepid statements, the conference on November 15 issued a declaration setting forth its belief that no equitable solution was likely to emerge from direct talks between the combatants.[27] That Japan was still unsure of itself appeared as late as November 16, when Hirota complained to Grew that the United States was taking the lead at Brussels and went on to express concern over the possibility of economic boycott.[28] But he might have spared himself all misgiving, for the United

[21] Hull, *Memoirs*, I, 551.

[22] Radio address by the President, Oct. 12, 1937, *Foreign Relations: Japan, 1931–1941*, I, 401.

[23] Statement by Lord Plymouth, Oct. 21, 1937, Great Britain, Parliament, House of Lords, *The Parliamentary Debates: Official Report*, 5th series (London: H. M. Stationery Office, 1909——), CVI, 1077.

[24] Reply of the Japanese government to the Belgian government, Oct. 27, 1937, and reply of the Japanese government to the Conference, Nov. 12, 1937, Royal Institute of International Affairs, *Documents on International Affairs, 1937*, ed. J. W. Wheeler-Bennett (London: Oxford Univ. Press, 1938), pp. 704, 741.

[25] Address by Davis, Nov. 3, 1937, *Foreign Relations: Japan, 1931–1941*, I, 408.

[26] Statement by Davis, Nov. 13, 1937, *ibid.*, pp. 409–410.

[27] Declaration of the Nine-Power Conference, Nov. 15, 1937, *ibid.*, p. 412.

[28] Memorandum by Grew, Nov. 16, 1937, *ibid.*, p. 413.

States planned no further action.   Admitting its failure to mediate the Far Eastern dispute, the conference adjourned on November 24.

Meanwhile, the Japanese drove ahead in China and took Shanghai on November 8; the war was obviously moving southward. Japan also made progress on the diplomatic front, emerging from relative isolation into explicit psychological alignment with Germany and Italy. This movement had begun a year earlier, when, in the Anti-Comintern Pact of November 25, 1936, Japan and Germany had mutually pledged co-operation in checking the activities of the Third International. Italy closed the triangle by adhering to this agreement on November 6, 1937, and by following its confederates out of the League on December 11. The bargain was then sealed by a number of recognitions. Italy recog-nized Manchukuo on November 29; Japan recognized the Franco government of Spain on December 1; and Hitler, the following Feb-ruary 20, announced Germany's intention to recognize Manchukuo. Aggression now enjoyed the formal sanction of all the aggressors.

In the latter half of 1937 everyone had declined leadership of the democratic powers, and their confused efforts to do something without leadership merely dramatized their weakness and presented them with a full-grown Axis, which now included Tokyo as well as Rome and Berlin.   Speaking to the House of Commons on December 21, British Foreign Minister Anthony Eden supplied an epitaph for the six months just finished. From the very beginning of this dispute, he said, every nation had realized "perfectly well that the thought of action of any kind in the Far East must depend on the coöperation of other nations besides those who are actually members of the League at this time." [29]

The implication was obvious, if not altogether justified. It was true that American policy had been less than energetic, but isolationism and timidity in the United States had met their equivalents abroad. If the country was less disposed to encourage coöperation in defense of law and order than at any time since 1932, the fact remained that the year 1937 offered the American government no one with whom to coöper-ate.[30]   President Roosevelt was only recognizing facts when he ex-plained in a letter to former Secretary of State Stimson that American

[29] Great Britain, Parliament, House of Commons, *The Parliamentary Debates: Official Report,* 5th series (London: H. M. Stationery Office, 1909——), CCCXXX, 1883.

[30] See Viscount Robert Cecil, *A Great Experiment: An Autobiography* (New York: Oxford Univ. Press, 1941), p. 295. For a severe comparison of American policy in 1937 with that in 1932, see A. Whitney Griswold, *The Far Eastern Policy of the United States* (New York: Harcourt, Brace, and Co., 1938), pp. 461–462.

caution at the Nine-Power Conference was based on the attitude of other powers, an attitude which demanded "such obvious leadership on our part that I am sure neither the people of this country nor Congress would have supported it." [31] Actually, Europe had commenced abdicating its traditional Far Eastern role in 1932, when its chances of obtaining a substantial degree of American support had been much better. Now, after its failure in 1937, Europe's former position in Asia was virtually gone. Henceforth the United States would stand nearly alone in its efforts to curb Far Eastern aggression, and would gradually assume the direction of Western policy in that sector of the world.

III

By December 1, 1937, the United States had gained enough experience to establish a norm for the difficult business of upholding its Far Eastern rights through the medium of diplomatic complaint. The protest of that date against interference with the extraterritorial rights of Americans in Manchuria [32] was typical of several hundred others launched during the next four years. Typical also was the Japanese reply. Knowing that the United States could make no formal approach to the unrecognized government of Manchukuo, the Japanese Foreign Office simply stated that the policy of the government of Manchukuo was a matter with which Japan had no concern.[33] Time and again the United States would attempt to grapple with this diplomatic evasion and emerge with nothing that could be firmly grasped. Trying to cope with an undeclared war which was further complicated by the presence nearby of at least one unrecognized government invited frustration.

On the other hand, there were points of friction in which the issues were perfectly direct and clear. The first important incident of this type was the bombing of the American gunboat *Panay* by Japanese planes on December 12, 1937, as she moved up the Yangtze River with three Standard Oil ships bearing American refugees out of the war zone. By undermining the official guise of impartiality which the United States had thus far maintained, the *Panay* affair opened a new phase of American-Japanese relations.

[31] Roosevelt to Stimson, Nov. 24, 1937, MS Roosevelt Papers (Official File, Box 150).
[32] Grew to Hirota, Dec. 1, 1937, *Foreign Relations: Japan, 1931–1941*, I, 154.
[33] Hirota to Grew, Mar. 1, 1938, *ibid.*, p. 155.

While there is reason to believe that the Japanese authorities on the spot, if not the government itself, deliberately manufactured the incident for the purpose of testing American forbearance, Tokyo was certainly not prepared for a breach of relations and saved the amenities by acting promptly. First news of the bombing, together with sweeping apologies, was conveyed to Ambassador Grew by Foreign Minister Hirota, who hurried in person to the American Embassy as soon as he learned of the attack.[34] Nor did he waste time thereafter. On December 14, some three hours before President Roosevelt's demand for formal apologies, guarantees, and suitable monetary damages could be presented in Tokyo, the Japanese Foreign Office stated its readiness to pay compensation and to furnish assurances against similar attacks in the future.[35] After a brief exchange of views Washington chose to accept the Japanese offer, and the crisis was officially terminated on Christmas Day. Nevertheless, the American note of December 25 made it clear that the State Department rejected Japan's explanation of the bombing as an unfortunate accident.[36]

A most delicate situation was thus adjusted with surprising speed. But the settlement did not leave things as they had been before. While Japan's promptness in making amends temporarily caused segments of American public opinion to regard that nation with less hostility,[37] it did not relax underlying tensions. The fact that Japan invited such risks of war offered proof that it had large stakes in view, and American readiness to settle the issue without going into the policy behind it must have convinced the Japanese government that the United States was prepared to endure a great deal. The outcome furnished no guarantee that Japan's basic course would be altered. New friction was inevitable as long as the "China Incident" continued, and the prospect of its termination was becoming more remote each week. Neither his relief at having concluded the settlement nor his abiding confidence that Japanese liberals would regain enough voice in the government to moderate official policy enabled Grew to contemplate the future with "any feeling of

[34] Joseph C. Grew, *Ten Years in Japan* (New York: Simon and Schuster, 1944), p. 233.

[35] Grew to Hull, Dec. 14, 1937, *Foreign Relations: Japan, 1931–1941,* I, 525.

[36] Hull to Grew, Dec. 25, 1937, *ibid.,* pp. 551–552; and Grew, *Ten Years,* p. 240. On April 22, 1938, the Japanese government paid the United States an indemnity of $2,214,007.36.

[37] See Quincy Wright and Carl J. Nelson, "American Attitudes toward Japan and China, 1937–1938," *Public Opinion Quarterly,* III (Jan. 1939), 47.

serenity." He did not yet believe that war would come between the United States and Japan through interference with American interests or treaty rights "or the breaking down of principles for which we stand." But he clearly envisioned the possibility of war through direct attacks on the United States or through an accumulation of incidents like the one just ended.[38]

During this period other Japanese activities, not directly related to the *Panay* affair but largely concurrent with it, tended to strengthen these apprehensions. On December 14 a new pro-Japanese government was set up in the ancient Chinese capital of Peiping. On January 16, 1938, Tokyo announced that it would no longer deal with the Chinese Nationalist government but would plan the establishment of a new regime which could be depended upon for coöperation with Japanese designs.[39] The announcement of this ambitious program made it clear that the China affair was more than an incident to the Japanese government. Especially when viewed in conjunction with Japan's new European attachments, it warned that the Far Eastern crisis was likely to be permanent.

A frame of events surrounding the *Panay* crisis also made it clear that the United States government planned no general withdrawal from the position it had assumed. A joint resolution providing for initiation of a constitutional amendment which would require that any declaration of war be submitted to popular referendum—the measure which Representative Louis Ludlow, of Indiana, had kept before the nation since 1934—was on the point of being forced out of committee at the middle of December. Strong letters of disapproval from the President and the Secretary of State were enough, however, to defeat this move by January 10.[40] At the same time, Hull carefully defined America's Far Eastern position in a letter to the Senate, pointing out that the Asiatic interests of the United States could not be measured only by the number of resident American citizens, the size of American investments, and the volume of American trade. A more fundamental interest was "that orderly processes in international relationships be maintained."[41] And as reports of further outrages against American

[38] Grew, *Ten Years*, p. 240.

[39] Statement by the Japanese government, Jan. 16, 1938, *Foreign Relations: Japan, 1931–1941*, I, 437.

[40] Roosevelt to Bankhead, Jan. 6, 1938, and Hull to Bankhead, Jan. 8, 1938, *Department of State Press Releases*, XVIII (Jan. 15, 1938), 99–100.

[41] Hull to Garner, Jan. 8, 1938, *Foreign Relations: Japan, 1931–1941*, I, 433.

citizens during the occupation of Nanking continued to flow in, President Roosevelt on January 28 asked Congress for larger naval grants, suggesting at the same time that it likewise consider measures to equalize burdens and to eliminate profiteering in the event of war.[42]

Although the presidential request indicated that naval expansion beyond treaty limits was being contemplated for the first time, it was only a muted warning. Aside from this, America's immediate reaction to the *Panay* affair and concurrent developments had been more cautious than forbidding. Neither public opinion nor government policy was calculated to make Japan review what it was doing. On the other hand, the bombing of the *Panay* and the sack of Nanking were to live on in memory and pave the way for a much closer examination of Far Eastern problems during the next year.

IV

While the Far East was unquestionably the largest immediate concern of American diplomacy at the end of 1937 and the beginning of 1938, the problems raised by Japan's course in China merely added to the gravity of a situation that was world-wide. If it had ever existed, the moment for treating aggression in its single episodes was long past. Gone also was the basis for treating it in any other way. The collective hesitation of the League had resolved itself into the separate hesitations of states. No nation was disposed to move until it knew the plans of other nations, and no government wished to commit itself very far in one part of the world lest it become so deeply involved as to risk embarrassment in another part. This dilemma confronted the United States as plainly as it confronted every other country. Even without the new isolationism, America would have found it difficult to escape the general paralysis.

Whatever happened in Asia, the vast unrest of Europe could never be forgotten. Even if the country had been willing to support decisive action, any move in the Far East would have had to be undertaken in full knowledge that it might impair the nation's readiness to meet dangers in Europe. To venture much by itself was a risk which the American government was neither able nor willing to take. The

[42] United States, Congress, *Congressional Record* (Washington, D. C.: U. S. Govt. Printing Office, 1874——), LXXXIII (75th Cong., 3rd sess.), 1187–1188.

world-wide threat of aggression, if met at all, would have to be met on a world-wide scale,[43] and any serious effort in this regard demanded that a new basis for coöperation be provided. Amid the events just narrated, therefore, President Roosevelt worked on a scheme by which he hoped to lay just such a basis.

The first public indication of this move was seen in his famed "quarantine" speech, delivered at Chicago on October 5, 1937, as the League of Nations deliberated over the Chinese appeal against Japan. After commenting at some length upon general conditions, the President noted that the "epidemic of world lawlessness" was spreading. Then he continued in the following words:

> When an epidemic of physical disease starts to spread, the community approves and joins in a quarantine of the patients in order to protect the health of the community against the spread of the disease . . . .
> Most important of all, the will for peace on the part of peace-loving nations must express itself to the end that nations that may be tempted to violate their agreements and the rights of others will desist from such a course. There must be positive endeavors to preserve peace . . . .
> Therefore, America actively engages in the search for peace.[44]

The phrasing of this pronouncement seemed to contemplate action; its timing suggested that it was not entirely unrelated to the Far Eastern problem and decisions being made at Geneva. Since July, according to Sumner Welles, the Under Secretary of State, Roosevelt had entertained a design for exerting pressure on Japan by means of an embargo to be enforced by British and American fleet units, acting jointly. But Chamberlain, as already indicated, was not favorably disposed toward new Far Eastern ventures at that time, while Hull and most of the ranking officers in the United States Navy—with the important exception of Admiral William D. Leahy, Chief of Naval Operations—opposed the project as likely to lead to war.[45] That such action would have invested the "quarantine" idea with tangible meaning is certain. The plan was not implemented, however, and any useful results the presidential utterance might have had in other respects were forestalled

---

[43] Cf. Hull's comment that after the middle of 1935 no major international problem could be considered solely on its own merits (*Memoirs*, I, 397).

[44] Address at Chicago, Oct. 5, 1937, Franklin D. Roosevelt, *The Public Papers and Addresses of Franklin D. Roosevelt, 1937*, comp. S. I. Rosenman (New York: Macmillan Co., 1941), pp. 410–411.

[45] Sumner Welles, *Seven Decisions That Shaped History* (New York: Harper and Bros., 1950), pp. 8, 71–72.

by the decidedly cool attitude of the American government at the Brussels Conference a month later.

Some observers were not impressed. Hans Dieckhoff, the German Ambassador in Washington, thought Roosevelt had merely desired to warn Japan, and he advised his government that the United States would abandon its passive role only if Great Britain should become involved in a new world conflict.[46] Jules Henry, the French chargé d'affaires, likewise shrugged off the Chicago speech, explaining that Roosevelt's words sometimes went beyond the settled policy of the American government. He understood that even the Philippines would be abandoned rather than risk complications with Japan.[47] But domestic opinion was more apprehensive. The President's words suggested an alarming change in national policy. Roosevelt understood, doubtless without surprise, that native isolationists were aroused, and declined to amplify his statement in any way. At a press conference held October 6 he defeated the correspondents' best efforts to learn what was in his mind. Parrying questions neatly, he said only that he had a "clue" as to what might be done.[48]

Not many days passed, however, before another project for international action began to take form. During the month of October the President and Sumner Welles, working together, evolved a plan to call an Armistice Day meeting of the Washington diplomatic corps and propose to the assembled representatives that their governments join the United States in a kind of world peace front which would begin its work by trying to reach agreement on such matters as the essential principles of international conduct, the most effective ways of achieving disarmament, methods of promoting economic well-being, and measures to assure respect for the laws of war. There would be no general conference. Instead, the President would set up an executive committee of ten nations, including the United States. This group would formulate tentative agreements and submit them to the other governments for approval. The hope that inspired this rather nebulous plan was

[46] Dieckhoff to the German Foreign Office, Oct. 9, 1937, United States, Department of State, *Documents on German Foreign Policy, 1918–1945,* Series D (Washington, D. C.: U. S. Govt. Printing Office, 1949——), I, 634–635.

[47] Henry to the French Foreign Minister, Nov. 18, 1937, Germany, Foreign Office, *Roosevelts Weg in den Krieg: Geheimdokumente zur Kriegspolitik des Präsidenten der Vereinigten Staaten* (Berlin: Im Deutschen Verlag, 1943), pp. 37–38.

[48] Press conference, Oct. 6, 1937, Roosevelt, *Public Papers and Addresses, 1937,* p. 424.

that it would tend to establish a common ground for all nations opposing the Axis and stimulate public opinion everywhere. It might even help dissolve the moral support which Japan was drawing from Germany and Italy.[49]

The Armistice Day plan, coming so close upon the heels of the "quarantine" speech, aroused severe dissension in the President's official household. The opposition was led by Hull, who had always disapproved of the Japanese embargo scheme and who, since the spring of 1936, had taken the general position that any form of international action not based upon rearmament of the democratic powers was doomed to failure. Nor could the Secretary forget his annoyance with the "quarantine" speech itself. He was constitutionally opposed to any venturesome public utterance, and this episode merely accentuated his native caution.

Hull takes credit for having urged delivery of the Chicago speech in the first place, but he gravely disapproved of what the President actually said. Having envisaged a somewhat more generalized endorsement of international coöperation, and being given no advance notice of the "quarantine" passage, the Secretary had no chance to register his opposition until the words were out. In view of the country's prevailing isolationism, he considered the moment decidedly unripe for so suggestive a declaration; the American public had to be educated more gradually.[50] As for the Armistice Day plan, he thought it "illogical and impossible." Even if it met with initial success, it would have the undesirable result of lulling the democratic nations "into a feeling of tranquillity . . . at the very moment when their utmost efforts should actually be directed toward arming themselves for self-defense." At all events, he thought it would be futile to start such a move without first consulting Great Britain and France.[51]

Welles had won the first round. But Hull and those who shared his views won the second, and the big offensive was postponed while the President sounded out England. Nor did Hull's misgivings prove unfounded. Since the previous May Chamberlain's new policy of "realism" and determined good-fellowship with the Axis had created psychological obstacles to any advance like that contemplated by

[49] Hull, *Memoirs*, I, 546; Sumner Welles, *The Time for Decision*, 9th ed. (New York: Harper and Bros., 1944), pp. 64–66; and memoranda, Welles to Roosevelt, Oct. 6, 9, 1937, MS Roosevelt Papers (Secretary's File, Box 62).

[50] Hull, *Memoirs*, I, 544–545.

[51] *Ibid.*, p. 547; cf. Welles, *The Time for Decision*, p. 66.

Roosevelt, and one could hardly deny that American diplomatic activity in the same period was little calculated to change British views. Although Chamberlain had publicly endorsed the "quarantine" speech two days after its delivery, he still harbored certain mental reservations. There appeared to be "something lacking" in the quarantine analogy. Besides, the United States had not been receptive to his proposal for some kind of joint mediation at the very beginning of the Sino-Japanese dispute.[52]   And on December 21 he told the House of Commons that the League was wholly inadequate to its purposes, that the way to salvation lay through personal contacts and friendly discussions with the troublemakers.[53]   His entire pattern of thought was unfavorable to large schemes of any kind. He did not deny the existence of American good will for Britain, but he thought it likely to produce nothing except words.[54]

Accordingly, Roosevelt's overtures, when they finally reached London on January 12, 1938, evoked scant enthusiasm. Despite the earnest recommendation of the British Ambassador in Washington, Sir Ronald Lindsay, that the American proposal be accepted without delay,[55] Chamberlain replied courteously, but firmly, that he was pressing for the settlement of specific issues with Germany and Italy. At the moment, Great Britain was considering recognition of Italy's sovereignty over Ethiopia in return for a general Mediterranean understanding; such negotiations as Roosevelt now proposed might afford the Italian government an excuse for delay, or even a pretext for a break. Therefore he suggested postponement.[56]

Chamberlain had proceeded this far without consulting Foreign Secretary Anthony Eden, who was then vacationing in southern France. But Eden now returned to London and, on learning what had taken place, expressed his strong disapproval of the Prime Minister's action. He distrusted appeasement anyhow, and he infinitely preferred coöperation with the United States to questionable arrangements with the Axis. So he immediately set about repairing what he considered the Prime Minister's blunder.[57]

[52] See excerpts from Chamberlain's personal letters in Keith G. Feiling, *The Life of Neville Chamberlain* (London: Macmillan and Co., 1946), pp. 322–325.

[53] *Parl. Debates* (Commons), CCCXXX, 1810, 1812.

[54] Feiling, *Chamberlain*, p. 325.

[55] Winston S. Churchill, *The Gathering Storm* (Boston: Houghton Mifflin Co., 1948), pp. 251–252.

[56] Feiling, *Chamberlain*, p. 336; Welles, *The Time for Decision*, pp. 67–68; and Churchill, *The Gathering Storm*, p. 252.

[57] Churchill, *The Gathering Storm*, p. 252.

In the meanwhile, Roosevelt answered Chamberlain's rebuff with a promise to delay activating his plan while Great Britain pursued direct negotiations with Italy. But he expressed a strong fear that British recognition of Italy's position in Ethiopia would alienate public opinion in the United States and encourage Japan to continue its depredations in the Far East. When delivering this message to the British Ambassador, Hull also expressed himself strongly on the proposed recognition.[58]

Faced with this energetic response, Chamberlain, at Eden's insistence, modified his attitude to some extent in two notes dispatched to Washington on January 21. Here he explained that Great Britain did not intend to favor Italy with *de jure* recognition in Ethiopia except as part of a wider settlement and that, while he could accept no responsibility for the outcome of the President's proposal, he would be glad to see the United States take the initiative. But since he also made it clear that his approval of the American suggestion was limited by a desire to avoid disturbing Germany, Italy, and Japan, he did not leave the President much foundation on which to build.[59] According to Churchill, it was this substantial rejection of Roosevelt's plan which furnished the real cause of Eden's resignation a month later.[60] At all events, Viscount Halifax became Foreign Secretary on February 20, and under his less reluctant direction negotiations with Italy continued. British policy toward the Axis was now irrevocably launched upon its new course,[61] and the President had no good opportunity to revive his foundered scheme.

Thus the grand design came to nothing, but some advance was made during January in a more limited field. Since the previous summer there had been much disquiet in Washington naval circles, especially in the office of the Chief of Naval Operations. Admiral James O. Richardson, then Assistant Chief, was among those deeply concerned about war in the Pacific and repeatedly urged his senior, Admiral William D. Leahy, to convince the President that the United States should not risk commitment there without having allies, as he later put it, "so bound to us that they cannot leave us in the lurch." Looking back upon this period, Richardson felt that his verbal exertions had

[58] *Ibid.*, pp. 252–253. [59] *Ibid.*, p. 253. [60] *Ibid.*, p. 265.
[61] See Alan Campbell Johnson, *Viscount Halifax: A Biography* (New York: Ives Washburn, 1941), p. 450. For a detailed account of the evolution and failure of this peace project, see William L. Langer and S. Everett Gleason, *The Challenge to Isolation, 1937–1940* (New York: Harper and Bros., for the Council on Foreign Relations, 1952), pp. 19–31.

something to do with the mission of Captain Royal E. Ingersoll, Director of the War Plans Division, who visited London at the end of the year.[62]

However persuasive Richardson's advice may have been, the Ingersoll mission was directly inspired by Roosevelt himself. Following Italy's adherence to the Anti-Comintern Pact in November 1937, the President was keenly aware of the possibility that the United States might eventually have to fight a war in two oceans simultaneously, and instructed Leahy to draw up plans against that contingency. Since it was taken for granted that Great Britain would also be involved in such a two-ocean conflict, it was judged wise to discuss the problem of cooperation with British authorities.[63]

According to Ingersoll's account, his special assignment was to explore the question of what the British and American navies could do in the event of a common war with Japan. Reaching London near the end of December, he was taken first to Anthony Eden. But it was not intended on either side that the discussions should be held at the political level, so Ingersoll was relegated from Foreign Office to Admiralty and was finally closeted with Captain Tom Phillips of the Royal Navy's War Plans Section. In their subsequent talks the two men dealt with a single possibility and its related questions: Assuming that both Great Britain and the United States were at war with Japan, what would be the distribution of their respective forces, and what types of joint action could be worked out?

The contemplated situation was obviously more or less hypothetical for the time being. This circumstance, combined with the inability of either negotiator to offer political guarantees, hindered the formulation of any very clear program. There was some talk of basing a British force at Singapore while the United States Fleet gathered at Pearl Harbor. There was also a good deal of speculation regarding the attitude of the Dutch, and Britain was plainly fearful of war in Europe as an additional complication. On the whole, Ingersoll found British naval authorities extremely cautious. Nevertheless, his visit seems to have

[62] Richardson to Stark, Jan. 26, 1940, United States, Congress, Joint Committee on Investigation of Pearl Harbor Attack, *Hearings Pursuant to S. Con. Res. 27, Authorizing Investigation of Attack on Pearl Harbor, Dec. 7, 1941, and Events and Circumstances Relating Thereto* (79th Cong., 1st and 2nd sess.) (Washington, D. C.: U. S. Govt. Printing Office, 1946), pt. 14, exhibit 9, p. 924. Cited henceforth as *Pearl Harbor Hearings*.

[63] Samuel Eliot Morison, *The Rising Sun in the Pacific, 1931—April 1942* (Boston: Little, Brown, and Co., 1948), p. 49.

strengthened the belief that a Pacific war would render Anglo-American naval coöperation inevitable, and this apparently affected strategic thinking in a general way until much more comprehensive plans were laid out during the Washington staff conversations in 1941.[64]

As military understanding thus forged ahead of political agreement, the pace of rearmament quickened slightly. In March 1938 a British mission arrived in the United States to buy planes for the Royal Air Force. The French placed their first aircraft contract with American industry about the same time.[65] And new vistas of naval expansion were opened on March 31 when Great Britain and the United States gave formal notice of their intention to escalate under the London Naval Treaty of 1936, basing this action on the ground that Japan had already exceeded the limitations of that agreement.[66]

V

After so gloomy a beginning the months of 1938 held little promise of achievement in the Far East, and American-Japanese relations generally followed their established pattern from February to the year's end. Principles were enunciated liberally, and the growing volume of American protests against specific Japanese acts revealed a few signs of new stiffness. But such developments were always more successful in emphasizing the gravity of the problem than in working toward its solution. For the time being, at least, the utmost objective of America's Far Eastern policy was to slow the Japanese advance.

But even a purely static defense was judged too venturesome by many in the United States; and the State Department, far from excusing itself for inaction, still found it necessary to justify having done so much. Speaking before the National Press Club on March 17, Hull repeated his now-familiar views on foreign policy and upheld the government's determination not to withdraw completely from China. To let the Far Eastern position of the United States go by default, he de-

[64] Ingersoll's testimony, Feb. 12, 1946, *Pearl Harbor Hearings*, pt. 9, pp. 4273–4276; Richardson to Stark, Jan. 26, 1940, *ibid.*, pt. 14, exhibit 9, p. 924; and Morison, *The Rising Sun in the Pacific*, p. 49.

[65] Edward R. Stettinius, Jr., *Lend-Lease: Weapon for Victory* (New York: Macmillan Co., 1944), pp. 12–13.

[66] Notices of intention to escalate, Mar. 31, 1938, World Peace Foundation, *Documents on American Foreign Relations, 1938-1939*, ed. S. Shepard Jones and Denys P. Myers (Boston: World Peace Foundation, 1939), pp. 486–487.

clared, would merely encourage Japanese wrongdoing and "thus contribute to the inevitable spread of anarchy throughout the world." [67] While there was admittedly nothing heroic in pronouncements of this type, it would have taken a much more effective speaker than the Secretary of State to convince the American people that their government should take a stronger position. According to a Gallup survey made in January, 70 per cent of the citizenry favored complete withdrawal from China. In February 64 per cent disapproved of lifting the ban on arms shipments to China in government-owned vessels. The only hint of popular aggressiveness toward Japan appeared the same month, when 70 per cent of those interviewed voiced a hope that the United States would delay its retirement from the Philippine Islands and the completion of Philippine independence until conditions in the Orient got somewhat better. [68]

As time went on, Japan displayed less intention than ever of mending its ways. After especially strong protests in June against the continued occupation of American property and the vicious bombing of Canton, Grew noted what he described as the first positive signs of a wartime economy and psychology in Japan. Certain Cabinet changes, along with the disappearance from the market of such nonessential things as leather goods and rubber golf balls (Grew, an ardent golfer, being naturally sensitive to such a phenomenon), convinced him that Japan now realized it was "in for a long pull." [69]

Despite the rapid extension of hostilities between China and Japan, the American neutrality act still remained unused, the presidential order of September 14, 1937, having removed nothing but government-owned vessels from the arms trade with those countries. Seizing on the fact that neither government had declared war, Roosevelt argued that full prohibition of arms shipments would be a much more serious blow to agrarian China than to industrialized Japan, and, taking advantage of all the latitude afforded by the law, refused to call the embargo into being. To do otherwise, he said, would make the United States less neutral than it was already. [70] However, he did revive the moral em-

[67] Address by Hull, Mar. 17, 1938, United States, Department of State, *Peace and War: United States Foreign Policy, 1931–1941* (Washington, D. C.: U. S. Govt. Printing Office, 1943), p. 410.

[68] *Public Opinion Quarterly*, II (July 1938), 389.

[69] Grew, *Ten Years*, p. 250.

[70] Press conference, Apr. 21, 1938, Franklin D. Roosevelt, *The Public Papers and Addresses of Franklin D. Roosevelt, 1938*, comp. S. I. Rosenman (New York: Mac-

bargo which had been used so fruitlessly in the Italo-Ethiopian war a few years earlier. On July 1, 1938, the State Department, with obvious if unspoken reference to Japan, announced its reluctance to authorize the shipment of airplanes and aeronautical equipment to countries guilty of bombing attacks against civilian populations.[71] Owing to its discriminatory nature, this differed from the impartial moral embargo of 1935 and, in such form, was destined to become an almost-permanent feature of American policy, applying elsewhere at different times.

From July through September the mounting crisis in Europe relegated the Far East to the background of American calculations. After Munich, however, the United States opened a somewhat more vigorous defense. On October 6 Grew lodged a sharp protest with the Japanese Prime Minister regarding violations of the Open Door, demanding measures for the abolition of discriminatory exchange control in China, the discontinuance of special monopolies and preferences which tended to deprive Americans of the right to engage in Chinese trade and industry, and the cessation of interference with American mails, American property rights, and the right to freedom of residence and travel.[72] After its habit, the Foreign Office met this protest with delayed evasions and counsels of patience.[73] During November, however, Grew began to notice a subtle change in the tone of official Japanese utterances. The observations of Foreign Minister Arita were more direct, less sanctimonious. He no longer intimated that Japan looked to a resurrection of the *status quo* as soon as military necessity was a thing of the past. Now he suggested that a new framework was in the making—a new Far Eastern system in which Japan would have certain essential preferences and other powers would have to settle for what was left. The Open Door, in other words, was to be partly closed.[74]

Military success lay behind the new attitude; all year long the Japa-

millan Co., 1941), p. 287. This claim was not altogether without basis. Up to July 1938 American arms shipments to Japan, except for airplanes, were slightly less than corresponding shipments to China. Thus the moral embargo struck directly at that aspect of the arms traffic which was, on a comparative basis, of greatest benefit to Japan, while the failure to invoke the neutrality act left China free to pursue its quantitative advantage with respect to other types of war-material imports. See tables in Francis Deak, "The United States Neutrality Acts: Theory and Practice," *International Conciliation*, No. 358 (Mar. 1940), p. 101 n.; and Hull, *Memoirs*, I, 557.

[71] Department of State to Airplane Manufacturers, etc., July 1, 1938, *Peace and War*, p. 422.

[72] Grew to Konoye, Oct. 6, 1938, *Department of State Press Releases*, XIX (Oct. 28, 1938), 286.

[73] Grew, *Ten Years*, p. 256.   [74] *Ibid.*, pp. 270–271.

nese armies had pressed steadily southward. On November 3, 1938, Tokyo announced the fall of the Wuhan cities, adding that the Chinese Nationalist government was now but a local regime, and repeating that its extinction was the objective of Japanese policy.[75]   On November 18 the Japanese Foreign Office sent its considered reply to the American note of October 6. Referring to the Open Door, this communication stated:

> . . . any attempt to apply to the conditions of today and tomorrow inap-
> plicable ideas and principles of the past neither would contribute toward
> the establishment of a real peace in East Asia nor solve the immediate
> issues . . . . However, as long as these points are understood, Japan
> has not the slightest inclination to oppose the participation of the United
> States and other powers in the great work of reconstructing East Asia
> along all lines of industry and trade . . . .[76]

Japan had at last come into the open, and the United States met this frank avowal by turning directly to China. Except for its use of the moral embargo and its failure to employ the neutrality act, the American government had thus far given the embattled Chinese little but sympathy and diplomatic support. Now, however, the United States Ambassador in China, Nelson T. Johnson, was called home to dis-cuss what might be done. Financial aid seemed the most promising step for the time being, and the upshot was that on December 15 the Export-Import Bank made the Chinese Republic a loan of $25 million. Though the proceeds of this loan could not be used to buy arms and munitions, they were available for other war supplies needed by the Chinese Army. It was arranged that repayment could be made through the shipment of tung oil to the United States.[77] Outwardly, of course, this was a simple commercial agreement designed to facilitate trade. Nevertheless, its political overtones were clear.

Such lending devices were to be applied frequently as a method of doing international good without running afoul of the neutrality act, until the Lend-Lease program rendered them more or less superfluous. Always discriminatory, this policy had been in the making for some

---

[75] Statement by the Japanese government, Nov. 3, 1938, *Foreign Relations: Japan, 1931–1941*, I, 477.

[76] Arita to Grew, Nov. 18, 1938, *Department of State Press Releases*, XIX (Nov. 19, 1938), 252–253.

[77] Press announcement, Dec. 16, 1938, *Documents on American Foreign Relations, 1938–1939*, p. 271.

time. Since 1932 Japan had been unable to borrow from any agency of the United States government, and China, in 1937, had been extended a small credit of $1,500,000. Now the scale of beneficence was enlarged; before the end of 1941 the United States loaned China a total of $171,500,000. Although China remained the chief object of such attentions, other victims of more powerful neighbors eventually received help in the same way.[78]

On December 22, 1938, Prince Konoye, the Japanese Premier, formally announced that a "new order" had come into being: Japan, China, and Manchukuo, he explained, would henceforth be united in economic coöperation and defense against communism.[79] Taken in conjunction with the Japanese note of November 18, this was a manifesto which could not be ignored, and the United States on December 30 confirmed its decision to yield nothing. Referring to Arita's note of November 18, the State Department granted its awareness that conditions in the Far East had changed indeed. But it pointed out that Japan alone was responsible for most of those changes, and insisted that the United States could not admit the right of any power to constitute itself "the agent of destiny." Declining to recognize the existence of a "new order," it reserved "all rights as they exist" pending the negotiation of new treaties.[80]

The country's Far Eastern policy was still defensive, but its language was growing sharper as the conflict of American interests with Japanese ambitions became more irreconcilable. Casting up his accounts at the end of January, Ambassador Grew morosely contemplated the issues which had been drawn in the past two months and wrote: "Seldom in modern history has a year commenced under more inauspicious circumstances than has 1939 . . . . I cannot see that optimism is justified."[81]

VI

Relations with Japan were never the only problem, however, and usually not even the main one. As has already been suggested, appre-

[78] See Benjamin H. Williams, "The Coming of Economic Sanctions into American Practice," *American Journal of International Law*, XXXVII (July 1943), 393–394.

[79] Statement by the Japanese Prime Minister, Dec. 22, 1938, *Foreign Relations: Japan, 1931–1941*, I, 482.

[80] Grew to Arita, Dec. 30, 1938, *Peace and War*, pp. 445–447.

[81] Grew, *Ten Years*, p. 273.

hension regarding the possible effects of European crises tended to impose restraint in the Far East from the beginning. The care with which the American government took soundings in Europe, its habit of outlining foreign policy only in the broadest possible terms, and its evident reluctance to concentrate upon the Japanese problem all bore witness to its belief that the greatest danger of war, and hence the ultimate threat to American security, was to be found in Europe rather than in Asia.

But it took more than stagnation of American policy in Asia to produce real mobility elsewhere. Thanks to a comparatively long tradition of Asiatic involvement, the administration could avoid surrender in that part of the world without unduly affronting isolationist sentiment at home. But in Europe there was no ready-made position to defend. Even though the country observed European affairs with steadily mounting disquietude,[82] it refused to countenance any but the very smallest advance. Accordingly, the role of the United States in European concerns from Roosevelt's effort to build a peace front at the beginning of 1938 to Germany's absorption of Czechoslovakia in March 1939 was largely one of study and comment.

Study, however, led to conclusions of only the most general sort. Europe had lost its power to rise above a series of temporary expedients, and now offered little but confusion and uncertainty. While final alignments seemed reasonably clear, there was room for doubt even on this point, and it was almost impossible to make confident predictions regarding the stand of given countries on particular issues. Far Eastern tensions certainly augmented European difficulties, and American isolationism kept the United States from contributing to their solution. But Europe's chief problem was still Europe itself.

In October 1937, while considering his Armistice Day project, Roosevelt was by no means certain that the United States, Great Britain, France, and Russia were capable of genuine coöperation.[83] In December he gave Germany up as hopeless. Since 1933 it had been his policy to encourage liberal elements in that country in the belief that they might gain enough influence to change the course of the Nazi government. His appointment to the Berlin Embassy of Professor William E. Dodd, a distinguished historian with strong liberal sympathies and

[82] Philip E. Jacob, "Influences of World Events on U. S. 'Neutrality' Opinion," *Public Opinion Quarterly*, IV (Mar. 1940), 65.

[83] William E. Dodd, *Ambassador Dodd's Diary, 1933–1938*, ed. W. E. Dodd, Jr., and Martha Dodd (New York: Harcourt, Brace, and Co., 1941), p. 428.

an old-fashioned German university background, had been made in hope of establishing cultural rapport between the American way of life and what was best in German civilization.[84] But any sympathy thus engendered had totally failed to reach the German government, and Dodd had long since recognized the failure of his mission.[85]

Anticipating Dodd's retirement, Roosevelt had intended to replace him with Joseph E. Davies, a wealthy lawyer prominently identified with the Democratic party since the time of Wilson, and Ambassador to Russia since the first of the year. But he told Davies on December 8 that he had changed his mind. It was clear, explained the President, that Germany could not be altered from within. Consequently, he would replace Dodd with a career diplomat whose appointment would have no political connotations of any kind; such a man could confine his activities to representing the United States in the narrowest and most formal sense.[86] Later the same month Hugh Wilson, a Foreign Service officer of long experience, assumed the position of American Ambassador to Germany.

As custodian of the Russian puzzle from the beginning of 1937 to June 1938, Davies was undoubtedly one of the busiest men in Europe. He toured Russia with great energy, appeared often in trouble spots outside the Soviet Union, and maintained an unusually close contact with the President. In February 1937 he had enlarged on the possibility of an understanding between Hitler and Stalin. Writing from Copenhagen in August after a brief tour of the Baltic countries, Davies repeated this warning; and from Prague, in September, he canvassed still another possibility, reminding Hull that Finland was almost certain to be used as a base of German operations in the event of a Nazi attack on Leningrad.[87]

Pursuing the latter thought, Davies called attention on March 26, 1938, to Litvinov's recent promise that the Soviet Union would aid Czechoslovakia in the event of a German move against Czech borders.[88] By April 1, however, he was alarmed at what seemed to be Russia's growing tendency to take no heed of Central European affairs.[89] As he took permanent leave of Moscow early in June, he summed up his view of Soviet-American relations in the following points: (1) the Soviet

---

[84] *Ibid.*, p. 3. [85] *Ibid.*, p. 426.
[86] Davies, *Mission to Moscow*, pp. 255–256.
[87] Davies to Roosevelt, Aug. 22, 1937, MS Roosevelt Papers (Secretary's File, Box 28); and Davies, *Mission to Moscow*, p. 217.
[88] Davies, *Mission to Moscow*, pp. 292–293. [89] *Ibid.*, pp. 304–305.

Union was more friendly to the United States than to any other power; (2) the American government could not afford to overlook the importance of Russia's position at Japan's rear; (3) everything possible should be done to discourage Russian isolationism; and (4) communism offered no serious threat to the United States.[90]   Although the United States Ambassador in London, Joseph P. Kennedy, thought there was reason to believe that Russia's self-interest would not permit Soviet leaders to abandon the democracies in any foreseeable event,[91] nothing about eastern Europe seemed beyond doubt except that Moscow required dextrous treatment.

The United States met Germany's seizure of Austria in March 1938 with a frigidity so great that it amounted to nonrecognition.   Replying to Berlin's triumphant announcement of the *Anschluss*, Hull admitted that the United States was compelled to accept the German communication as a statement of fact, added that the American legation in Vienna would be replaced by a consulate general, and requested that Germany now assume responsibility for the Austrian debt to the United States.[92] If he did not explicitly refuse *de jure* recognition, neither did he confirm the legality of the change, and the aseptic tone of his remarks was nicely calculated to throw the implication of dubiety over the whole proceeding.[93]   President Roosevelt went a step further on April 6, directing the Treasury Department to suspend the existing commercial treaty between the United States and Austria,[94] thus denying to Greater Germany the lower import duties hitherto assessed against Austrian goods. While the latter move was normal procedure in such cases, it still had the effect of emphasizing Hull's diplomatic reserve.

There was also a quickening in the tempo of official statement.   Hull on March 17 spoke strongly against isolationism, urged the necessity of upholding rights and principles in all parts of the world, and lauded the benefits of international coöperation.[95]   A few weeks later, when asked for his views on Senator Nye's proposal to repeal the arms embargo for the Spanish Loyalists and give the President authority to

---

[90] Davies, *Mission to Moscow*, p. 418.   [91] *Ibid.*, p. 440.

[92] See two notes, Wilson to Ribbentrop, Apr. 6, 1938, *Department of State Press Releases*, XVIII (Apr. 9, 1938), 465–466.

[93] Cf. Hersh Lauterpacht, *Recognition in International Law* (Cambridge, Eng.: Cambridge Univ. Press, 1947), p. 399.

[94] Roosevelt to Morgenthau, Apr. 6, 1938, *Department of State Press Releases*, XVIII (Apr. 9, 1938), 474.

[95] Speech by Hull, Mar. 17, 1938, *Peace and War*, pp. 416–418.

apply it against the rebels at his own discretion, he carefully explained that he could not recommend passage of such a bill owing to the special circumstances under which the United States was then advancing collective policies in concert with the nonintervention committee.[96] Whatever his argument lacked in realism, this plea of coöperation gave at least verbal support to his thesis of March 17. On June 3,[97] and again on August 16,[98] he spoke in much the same vein.

But Roosevelt failed throughout the spring and summer to elaborate the Secretary's statements in any large degree, and the total effect of these exhortations was modest. Indeed, Hull must have spoken with tongue somewhat in cheek, for the cleavage which had appeared between himself and the President a few months earlier in connection with the Armistice Day plan grew more distinct as the year advanced. It was rapidly becoming evident that the term "coöperation" covered many things and that the only existing basis for action in this domain was support of appeasement. Although he could waver on particulars, Hull regarded such a policy with general disfavor. On the other hand, Sumner Welles and certain ranking members of the diplomatic establishment upheld the idea.[99] Reluctantly or otherwise, the President now leaned in the same direction. Despite his somewhat irritated warning to the British Prime Minister in January, he gradually found merit in Chamberlain's belief that appropriate concessions might loosen Italy's ties with the Axis and thus he adopted a hope which he was not to abandon until the late spring of 1940. By April 1938 he was ready to favor the Anglo-Italian *rapprochement* with his moral support and yielded, over Hull's tacit opposition, to Chamberlain's request that he bestow a public blessing upon the agreement finally concluded by Great Britain and Italy on the sixteenth of that month.[100]

By this treaty the British government recognized Italy's Ethiopian position in exchange for Italian confirmation of the territorial *status quo* in the Mediterranean and accession to the all-but-defunct London

[96] Hull to Pittman, May 12, 1938, *ibid.*, pp. 119–120.

[97] See excerpts from address by Hull, June 3, 1938, *Department of State Press Releases*, XVIII (June 4, 1938), 646.

[98] Radio address by Hull, Aug. 16, 1938, *Documents on American Foreign Relations, 1938–1939*, pp. 21–22.

[99] Louis Fischer, *Men and Politics* (New York: Duell, Sloan, and Pearce, 1941), p. 445; and Robert Bendiner, *The Riddle of the State Department* (New York: Farrar and Rinehart, 1942), pp. 8–9.

[100] Hull, *Memoirs*, I, 581. The request for Roosevelt's support was made on April 14.

Naval Treaty of 1936.[101]   As evidence of his softer mood, Roosevelt at
once announced that the United States believed in the peaceful discussion of international differences and recognized the value of economic appeasement.   While the American government would not venture to comment on the political features of the Anglo-Italian accord,
he added, it did view the pact with "sympathetic interest" as "proof of
the value of peaceful negotiation." [102]   Hull lost no time denying the
truth of an article in the *Baltimore Evening Sun* which alleged that he
was dissatisfied with the presidential statement, and he added the next
day that Roosevelt's words heralded no change in American foreign
policy.[103]   They did bespeak a limited change of attitude, however;
and in view of the Secretary's admitted position on the European appeasement issue, his assurances did not ring altogether true.[104]   It
would seem, at all events, that Roosevelt had said enough for Chamberlain's purpose; whatever its qualifications, this endorsement helped
him persuade the House of Commons to accept the treaty.[105]

Lack of confidence in France was another element of the appeasement philosophy which Hull did not then share.   While Chamberlain
prized his government's excellent relations with France, he did not
regard them as a source of great strength.   French politics were peren-
nially unstable; and since France, in his opinion, was able neither to
"keep a secret for more than half an hour, nor a government for more
than nine months," he did not care to depend on that nation in a
crisis.[106]   A similar, though less outspoken, estimate appears to have
taken root in Washington.   As early as August 1937, Davies had called
the President's attention to France's internal weakness and diminished
prestige; and when Secretary of Labor Frances Perkins returned from a
session of the International Labor Conference at Geneva in June 1938,
she gave the Cabinet her impression that France would collapse if the

[101] Great Britain, Foreign Office, *Agreement between the United Kingdom and Italy,
Consisting of a Protocol with Annexes and Exchanges of Notes, April 16, 1938*, Cmd.
5726 (1938) (London: H. M. Stationery Office, 1938), pp. 8, 29, 30.

[102] Statement by the President, Apr. 19, 1938, *Department of State Press Releases*,
XVIII (May 7, 1938), 527.

[103] Statements by Hull, May 11, 12, 1938, *ibid.* (May 14, 1938), pp. 575-576.

[104] For a less severe opinion on this development, see Langer and Gleason, *The
Challenge to Isolation*, pp. 30-32.

[105] See Royal Institute of International Affairs, *Survey of International Affairs, 1938*,
by Arnold J. Toynbee and others (London: Oxford Univ. Press, 1939), I, 599; and
Documents on German Foreign Policy, 1918-1945, Series D, I, 721.

[106] Quoted in Feiling, *Chamberlain*, p. 323.

real pinch ever came. To this the President listened with attention and seeming approval. Hull disagreed strongly, however, maintaining that his own information justified an altogether different view.[107]

This fundamental lack of rapport between the President and the Secretary of State was even clearer in the fall of 1938. As Europe approached the Munich crisis, Hull feared that Roosevelt's enthusiasm for an active policy would align the United States completely with the forces of appeasement. But his counsels of restraint were only partly effective. There appears to be no evidence that the American government attempted to exert pressure on Chamberlain at any time, and the President refrained from offering the participants either detailed advice or his services as arbitrator. Nevertheless, such influence as he did use was not calculated to discourage the settlement that was eventually made.[108]

Apparently worried that the Prime Minister was losing his hold on the British government and stood in need of moral support, Kennedy reported from London on September 24 that the Cabinet seemed to be split between Chamberlain's supporters and those who wanted to stand absolutely firm. Ambassador William C. Bullitt, in Paris, contributed still further to Washington's sense of urgency when he telephoned later the same day advising the President to send personal appeals for peace to the heads of all states involved.[109] This Roosevelt undertook to do in spite of Hull's conviction that such a move would have negligible results. Accordingly, messages were dispatched to Berlin, Prague, London, Paris, Warsaw, and Budapest on September 26. But the fact that they committed the United States to nothing except the hope for peace suited Hull's views, as did Roosevelt's evasion of a French bid to secure American arbitration, and his failure to approve a suggestion from London that Chamberlain broadcast a justification of his policy to the United States on September 27.[110]

Beyond this, however, the Secretary's forebodings were ignored. On September 27 Welles explained to the French Ambassador, St. Quentin, that Roosevelt's messages of the preceding day were intended to affirm the presence of the United States in the European crisis without arousing

[107] Davies to Roosevelt, Aug. 22, 1937, MS Roosevelt Papers (Secretary's File, Box 28); and Frances Perkins, *The Roosevelt I Knew* (New York: Viking Press, 1946), p. 352.

[108] Hull, *Memoirs*, I, 591. Cf. Charles C. Tansill, *Back Door to War: Roosevelt Foreign Policy, 1933–1941* (Chicago: Henry Regnery Co., 1952), p. 428.

[109] Hull, *Memoirs*, I, 590. [110] *Ibid.*, pp. 591–593.

isolationist sentiment at home.[111] In a further effort to use his influence against war Roosevelt induced nineteen other governments to send peace appeals to Hitler and President Beneš of Czechoslovakia.[112] A special message to Hitler on September 27, pleading for peace but declaring that the United States took no responsibility for ensuing negotiations, and a hopeful appeal to Mussolini, asking that he intervene with the German Chancellor to procure an amicable settlement, rounded out his contribution and, in Hull's opinion, were essential factors in the decision to call the Munich Conference.[113] War had been averted once more. But that the Secretary of State found little joy in the outcome was indicated by his rather sour observation on September 30 that the Munich agreement had begotten an almost "universal sense of relief" as to "immediate peace results."[114] Roosevelt's contemporary view of the Munich settlement is not easy to ascertain. Although Professor Rauch concludes that the President never regarded it as anything but the prelude to war,[115] Roosevelt assured Ambassador William Phillips, in Rome, that he was "not one bit upset over the final result."[116] Sumner Welles, by contrast, was completely outspoken. In a radio address delivered October 3 he expressed great satisfaction with the existing state of things and found that the moment of speaking offered perhaps the best opportunity in two decades to establish "a new world order based upon justice . . . and law."[117]

Although the American government dabbled in appeasement through most of 1938, its direct relations with Berlin were little improved by this policy. On January 14 Hull exchanged bristling opinions with Dieckhoff, the German Ambassador, over the latter's protests against certain distinctly uncomplimentary public statements of ex-Ambassador Dodd concerning Hitler.[118] The German government was so bitter on this point, as a matter of fact, that it momentarily

---

[111] St. Quentin to the French Foreign Minister, Sept. 27, 1938, *Roosevelts Weg in den Krieg,* p. 55.

[112] Hull, *Memoirs,* I, 593. [113] *Ibid.,* p. 595.

[114] Statement by Hull, Sept. 30, 1938, *Peace and War,* p. 430.

[115] Basil Rauch, *Roosevelt: From Munich to Pearl Harbor* (New York: Creative Age Press, 1950), pp. 80–81.

[116] Roosevelt to Phillips, Oct. 17, 1938, Franklin D. Roosevelt, *F. D. R.: His Personal Letters, 1928–1945,* ed. Elliott Roosevelt (New York: Duell, Sloan, and Pearce, 1950), II, 818.

[117] Radio address by Welles, Oct. 3, 1938, *Department of State Press Releases,* XIX (Oct. 8, 1938), 240. For a survey of the reactions of the American press, see Tansill, *Back Door to War,* pp. 428–430.

[118] Memorandum of conversation, Jan. 14, 1938, *Peace and War,* p. 403.

considered the possibility of declining to receive Dodd's successor.[119] On July 7 Hull told Dieckhoff that the United States abhorred "many of the practices of the German Government within their own country."[120] And in the course of a talk with Dieckhoff on September 28, at the height of the Munich crisis, he again criticized German policy in outspoken terms.[121] The meaning of this drift was not lost on Hitler's envoy, for he warned his superiors on September 27 that the American government was "doing everything to suppress the existing but decreasing isolationist tendency among the American people, so that, when the moment comes, the whole weight of the United States can be thrown into the scale on the side of Britain. I consider it my duty to emphasize this very strongly."[122]

All this tended to harmonize with the President's decision of the previous December that the United States would no longer seek to accomplish anything in Berlin through direct action. The growing strain was emphasized in November when Ambassador Wilson was called home for report and consultation following Hitler's week-long pogrom against the Jews. As it turned out, Wilson's recall was permanent; diplomatic relations with Germany were henceforth to be conducted through a chargé d'affaires.

Only in the field of inter-American affairs was there any real progress during the latter part of 1938. Speaking at Kingston, Ontario, on August 18, Roosevelt promised that the United States would not "stand idly by" if Canada were threatened by outside domination other than that represented by the British Empire,[123] thus forecasting the defensive agreement made with Canada two years later. On December 24 the Eighth International Conference of American States, meeting in Lima, Peru, adopted a Declaration of the Principles of the Solidarity of America, which stated that any threat to the peace, security, or territorial integrity of the Americas was the common concern of all the American republics, and provided for joint consultation with a view to the coördination of policy on the invitation of any one of them.

[119] Lammers to Neurath, Jan. 21, 1938, *Documents on German Foreign Policy, 1918–1945*, Series D, I, 685.

[120] Memorandum of conversation, July 7, 1938, *Peace and War*, p. 423.

[121] Memorandum of conversation, Sept. 28, 1938, *ibid.*, pp. 429–430.

[122] Dieckhoff to the German Foreign Office, Sept. 27, 1938, *Documents on German Foreign Policy, 1918–1945*, Series D, II, 982.

[123] Address by Roosevelt at Queen's University, Aug. 18, 1938, Roosevelt, *Public Papers and Addresses, 1938*, p. 493.

Other resolutions approved at the same time reaffirmed earlier pledges of solidarity.[124] In such manner a useful basis was laid for inter-American coöperation in time of crisis.

Between the end of 1938 and the resumption of German aggression in March 1939, the United States watched the aftermath of the Munich settlement and found in its rapid disintegration cause to doubt the ultimate security of America and American institutions if appeasement were indefinitely continued.[125] Public opinion polls indicated that, at the outset, approximately 59 per cent of the American people thought well of Munich. By November, however, 92 per cent doubted that Hitler wanted no more European territory. In January 62 per cent believed Germany would be responsible for any European war that broke out, and the next month the same percentage expected Germany and Italy to attack the United States in the event of war, providing they could first defeat England and France. By March 1939, the proportion favoring a war referendum had sunk to 58 per cent—a drop of ten points since October—and no less than 52 per cent wished to supply the British and French with airplanes and war materials if they became involved in hostilities with the dictatorships.[126]

As public opinion moved, the administration moved also. In his message to Congress on January 4 President Roosevelt cautiously suggested repeal of the arms embargo and spoke of methods "short of war" but "stronger than words" to deter aggressors.[127] On January 14, as he was about to return to France after a three-month stay at home, William C. Bullitt reportedly told the Polish Ambassador, Count Jerzy Potocki, that he had been authorized by the President to convey assurances that the United States was renouncing isolationism and was prepared to place all of its material and financial resources at the disposal of Britain and France in the event of war.[128] Later in the month Roosevelt was

---

[124] Declaration of Lima, Dec. 24, 1938, and other resolutions adopted by the Conference, *Documents on American Foreign Relations, 1938–1939,* pp. 45–48.

[125] See Jacob, "Influences of World Events on U. S. 'Neutrality' Opinion," *Public Opinion Quarterly,* IV (Mar. 1940), 65.

[126] *Public Opinion Quarterly,* III (Oct. 1939), 598–600.

[127] Annual message to Congress, Jan. 4, 1939, Franklin D. Roosevelt, *The Public Papers and Addresses of Franklin D. Roosevelt, 1939,* comp. S. I. Rosenman (New York: Macmillan Co., 1941), pp. 2–4.

[128] Potocki to the Polish Foreign Minister, Mar. 7, 1939, *Roosevelts Weg in den Krieg,* pp. 73–75. Since this collection was issued by the German Foreign Office for obvious propaganda purposes, many of the documents it contains have been questioned as possible fabrications. In this instance, however, the alleged report harmonizes so closely with Bullitt's known views and with his general liking for a strong diplomacy that it cannot be dismissed lightly.

reported to have told the Senate Committee on Foreign Relations that the American frontier was on the Rhine.[129]   Although this statement represented a principle upon which much of his subsequent action was based, and which must have stood close to his inmost convictions at the time, the President retreated hastily when confronted with it, categorically denied the report, and embroidered his denial with some reflections on foreign policy that were decidedly isolationist in tone.[130]   Whether he had made such an assertion or not, his method of spiking the rumor certainly vitiated his theme of January 4 and left popular knowledge of his thoughts as confused as ever.   Notwithstanding the growth of his policy, Roosevelt still insisted on balancing one statement against another.

Within this regime of fits and starts, however, certain details were beginning to add up to a trend.   It was plain that the government was now counting upon the likelihood of war.   Its larger-Navy program had been under way for some time; and while the Navy's greatest strength remained concentrated in the Pacific, a significant redeployment began in January 1939 with the formation of the Atlantic squadron.[131]   The President had tentatively urged renewed study of mobilization measures in January 1938.   In June 1938 he had signed a bill authorizing the government to place "educational orders" with American factories—an arrangement intended to help industry gain skill in war production techniques.[132]   Public opinion now leaned strongly toward Great Britain and France, and the President's recent message to Congress warned that a drive to repeal the arms embargo was a definite prospect.

VII

To sum up, American foreign policy between the middle of 1937 and the spring of 1939 was caution mixed with confusion.   Official efforts to unite internationalist theory with isolationist fact often resulted in

[129] The report was substantially corroborated by Senator Logan of Kentucky, an administration stalwart.   See Raymond Moley, *After Seven Years* (New York: Harper and Bros., 1939), p. 381.

[130] Press conference, Feb. 3, 1939, Roosevelt, *Public Papers and Addresses, 1939*, p. 111.

[131] Samuel Eliot Morison, *The Battle of the Atlantic, 1939–1943* (Boston: Little, Brown, and Co., 1947), p. 14.

[132] United States, Department of State, *United States Statutes at Large* (Washington, D. C.: U. S. Govt. Printing Office and others, 1845——), LII, 707.

failure to distinguish between a coöperation in defense of law and a coöperation in support of expediency. If there was no general retreat from principles, some of them were given strange new uses to justify agreements with Hitler and Mussolini; and there was little advance along practical lines except in the realm of national defense, where the advance was small, and in the domain of inter-American solidarity. All three members of the Axis had fallen noticeably from grace, but not all were regarded with equal despair. Relations with Germany, the most dangerous and defiant of the trio, were worst. The official attitude toward Japan, though stiffening, still embraced a hope that Japanese liberals might recover some influence in their government. Italy was viewed as being especially subject to redemption.

Like the rest of the democratic world, America was irresolute. So far as irresolution sprang from internal causes, it reflected the views of a country devoted to isolation, passionately eager to avoid war, but increasingly doubtful whether this was possible if aggression continued unchecked in Europe and Asia. And in certain details it was the result of divided counsels in the government itself—where one group insisted that any form of coöperation with Britain and France was worse than useless until substantial rearmament could be substituted for the more direct varieties of appeasement, and another group was disposed to countenance the existing policies of London and Paris so long as they promised to accomplish anything whatever.

Yet, in spite of this wavering, there was no longer much doubt as to the ultimate position of the United States if war should come. America's basic strategy was implicit in the world situation and in the course of the American government over the past two years. Europe was the center of policy; action in the Far East awaited developments between the Rhine and the Urals. The period of waiting was drawing to a close, moreover, as conditions which favored a stronger attitude regarding both continents came into being. The United States was slowly putting its defenses in order. Committed to a strategy, the administration was now preparing to abandon some of its tactical uncertainties. And as surrender to Germany brought disillusionment in its wake, public opinion was beginning to throw off its isolationism.

CHAPTER III

Repeal of the Arms Embargo

I

IN THE YEARS PRECEDING THE SECOND WORLD WAR SPRINGTIME SEEMED always to hasten the pace of international activity, but this vernal quickening was especially evident in March and April 1939. If recent experience had built up confidence among the Axis powers, it had also whetted the suspicions of the democracies. Hence Germany's implacable extinction of the Czechoslovak Republic on March 15, less than six months after Munich, was accepted by many as nearly final proof that appeasement satisfied no one; and this, in turn, inaugurated a brisk reëxamination of policy on all sides.

On March 17 Neville Chamberlain delivered an important speech at Birmingham. Since much of the speech was given to a defense of his Munich policy, he was hardly deserting his theme when he carefully distinguished between this last German move and Hitler's earlier aggressions. In this distinction, nevertheless, unfamiliar overtones could be plainly heard. The occupation of the Rhineland, of Austria, and of the Sudetenland, the Prime Minister declared, might be excused on the basis of "racial affinity or of just claims too long resisted." But the seizure of Czechoslovakia "seemed to fall into a different category" and to raise the question, "Is this the end of an old adventure, or is it the beginning of a new?" [1] British leadership was manifestly stirring; as Winston Churchill later remarked, this speech brought him "much closer to Mr. Chamberlain." [2] It also gave British diplomacy a new text, a text which was to have solid meaning by fall.

French opinion, generally speaking, moved in the same direction. The French Ambassador in Berlin, Robert Coulondre, wrote the Quai

---

[1] Speech at Birmingham, Mar. 17, 1939, Neville Chamberlain, *In Search of Peace* (New York: G. P. Putnam's Sons, 1939), p. 274.

[2] Winston S. Churchill, *The Gathering Storm* (Boston: Houghton Mifflin Co., 1948), p. 348.

d'Orsay on March 16 that Germany had now thrown off its mask,[3] and he added a few days later that France would have to join in forcible opposition to Germany.[4] A similar view was delivered by Georges Bonnet, the French Foreign Minister, who stated that France and Britain might be accused of "moral complicity" unless they took a firm position.[5] Even Count Ciano was impressed, pausing in his cynical direction of Italy's foreign affairs long enough to observe that Hitler could never be trusted again, since this act had destroyed not the Czechoslovakia of Versailles but the Czechoslovakia of Munich—[6] which was, partially at least, the German leader's own creation.

While Europe digested its tardy realization that Hitler was unable to keep his word, Germany annexed Memel on March 22 and reopened its latent dispute with Poland over the status of Danzig and the Corridor.[7] But awakening had come, and this new threat brought prompt reactions. On March 31 Chamberlain announced that Great Britain and France would assist Poland to the extent of their ability if the Poles went to war to uphold their independence.[8] France was already committed to this position by the defensive alliance concluded with Poland in 1921. The British guarantee was unilateral, however, and remained so until April 6, when it was made fully reciprocal by a joint declaration of the British and Polish governments.[9] Nor was this all; when Italy undertook the military occupation of Albania on April 7, Britain and France hurried to mend their Balkan fences with unilateral guarantees of Rumania and Greece.[10]

In less than a month the Munich settlement had been overturned, the hopes that enshrined it all but forgotten, vistas of new trouble opened

[3] Coulondre to Bonnet, Mar. 16, 1939, France, Foreign Office, *Le Livre jaune français: Documents diplomatiques, 1938–1939* (Paris: Imprimerie Nationale, 1939), p. 94.

[4] Coulondre to Bonnet, Mar. 19, 1939, *ibid.*, p. 111.

[5] Bonnet to Corbin, Mar. 16, 1939, *ibid.*, pp. 91–92.

[6] Count Galeazzo Ciano, *The Ciano Diaries, 1939–1943*, ed. Hugh Gibson (Garden City, N. Y.: Doubleday and Co., 1946), p. 42.

[7] See Lipsky to Beck, Mar. 21, 1939, Poland, Foreign Office, *Official Documents concerning Polish-German and Polish-Soviet Relations, 1933–1939* (London: Hutchinson and Co., 1939), pp. 61–63.

[8] Statement by Chamberlain, Mar. 31, 1939, Great Britain, Parliament, House of Commons, *The Parliamentary Debates: Official Report*, 5th series (London: H. M. Stationery Office, 1909——), CCCXLV, 2415.

[9] See Polish-German communiqué, Apr. 6, 1939, *Official Documents concerning Polish-German and Polish-Soviet Relations, 1933–1939*, p. 74.

[10] Statement by Chamberlain, Apr. 13, 1939, *Parl. Debates* (Commons), CCCXLVI, 13.

up, and a whole set of new policies formally revealed. A breathing space ensued, the last before the war, as Britain and France began a four-month contest with Germany for an understanding with Russia—whose ultimate purposes had been the subject of growing speculation since the early part of 1937. But the Kremlin's dismissal on May 3 of Foreign Commissar Maxim Litvinov, the supposed apostle of Soviet *rapprochement* with the democracies, gave the Western powers no grounds for optimism. Neither did the appointment of his successor, the enigmatic V. M. Molotov, whose objectives were largely unknown but already suspect. Though Franco-British efforts to reach an understanding with the Soviet government continued well into the month of August, a number of things—among them suspicion of Russian designs on the Baltic states and Finland—made this a losing battle.[11]

The official response of the United States to the events of March went somewhat beyond that of a year earlier, on the occasion of the *Anschluss*. The exports of Bohemia, Moravia, and Slovakia were immediately classed as German for tariff purposes,[12] and on March 18 a 25 per cent countervailing duty was imposed against all German goods entering the United States. Existing law authorized the use of such duties whenever foreign governments paid export bounties to their own producers, and the Treasury Department now held that this was the real effect of the German barter system; but its sudden discovery of that interesting fact obviously grew out of the political climate. The new duty, added to the higher tariffs Germany already paid, left that nation at a serious disadvantage, as compared with other countries, in trade with the United States.[13]

[11] Interesting views of this diplomatic struggle are to be found in Grigore Gafencu, *Last Days of Europe: A Diplomatic Journey in 1939*, tr. E. Fletcher-Allen (New Haven: Yale Univ. Press, 1948), pp. 217–221; and in Lewis B. Namier, *Diplomatic Prelude, 1938–1939* (London: Macmillan and Co., 1948), chap. v. Perhaps the most useful and judicious account of the proceeding is that offered by William L. Langer and S. Everett Gleason, *The Challenge to Isolation, 1937–1940* (New York: Harper and Bros., for the Council on Foreign Relations, 1952), pp. 105–121. These authors point out that Chamberlain always opposed the negotiations with Russia and hoped to revive appeasement discussions with Germany. They believe, on the other hand, that Soviet authorities used the talks with Great Britain and France only to extract greater concessions from Germany.

[12] Commissioner of Customs to all Collectors of Customs, Mar. 17, 1939, United States, Department of State, *Department of State Press Releases* (Washington, D. C.: U. S. Govt. Printing Office, 1929–1939), XX (Mar. 18, 1939), 200.

[13] Treasury Department to Collectors of Customs, Mar. 18, 1939, *ibid.*, p. 203. Cf. Margaret Gordon, *Barriers to World Trade: A Study of Recent Commercial Policy* (New York: Macmillan Co., 1941), pp. 228 n., 408 n. Henry Morgenthau, Jr., gives

Nor was the American answer confined to economic retaliation. On March 17 Welles denounced the annexation,[14] and three days later he applied to it the nonrecognition doctrine.[15] Berlin took note of this attitude by refusing an exaquatur to the American consul general in the former Czech capital until the United States should be prepared to recognize the newly acquired territory. Although the consulate general in Prague remained open without formal German approval until October 14, 1940, this episode demonstrated the growth of tension between the two governments.

The Italian problem was likewise given attention. Receiving the new Italian Ambassador, Prince Ascanio Colonna, on March 22, Roosevelt confronted him with an outspoken lecture on aggression. If war should come, he warned, American sympathies would rest with the democracies, and he assured Colonna that the neutrality act would soon be amended. Mussolini's best course, the President advised, was to throw his influence on the side of peace.[16] When the Duce replied by seizing Albania on April 7, the United States government publicly denounced the act,[17] and the President even requested Hull to study the possibility of stopping draft payments to Italy and Germany by immigrant families in the United States.[18]

Roosevelt next turned directly to Berlin. He sent Hitler a telegram on April 14 suggesting that the German leader extend nonaggression guarantees to some thirty-one European and Near Eastern states.[19] But the Fuehrer was in no mood for conciliatory diplomacy, and he struck back without delay. In a speech to the *Reichstag* on April 28 he rejected and cast derision on Roosevelt's proposal, and underlined his position by denouncing the Anglo-German naval agreements of 1935 and 1937.

Welles credit for the adoption of countervailing duties at this time. Hull opposed them. See Henry Morgenthau, Jr., "The Morgenthau Diaries," *Collier's Magazine,* CXX (Oct. 18, 1947), 16, 71.

[14] Statement by Welles, Mar. 17, 1939, *Department of State Press Releases,* XX (Mar. 18, 1939), 199–200.

[15] Welles to Thomsen, Mar. 20, 1939, *ibid.* (Mar. 25, 1939), p. 221.

[16] Memorandum by Welles, Mar. 22, 1939, MS Roosevelt Papers (Secretary's File, Box 53).

[17] United States, Department of State, *Digest of International Law,* by Green H. Hackworth (Washington, D. C.: U. S. Govt. Printing Office, 1940–1944), IV, 689–690. Also see statement by Hull, Apr. 8, 1939, *Department of State Press Releases,* XX (Apr. 8, 1939), 261; and press release, June 12, 1939, *ibid.* (June 17, 1939), p. 527.

[18] Abstract of memorandum by the President, Apr. 17, 1939, MS Roosevelt Papers (Official File, Box 233).

[19] Roosevelt to Hitler, Apr. 4, 1939, United States, Department of State, *Peace and War: United States Foreign Policy, 1931–1941* (Washington, D. C.: U. S. Govt. Printing Office, 1943), p. 457.

Those treaties were incompatible, he said, with the encirclement of Germany which could now be discerned on every hand.[20]

Thus another series of gestures was made, and again little was affected but the record. Although United States policy during the spring of 1939 had revealed greater annoyance with Germany and larger misgivings over the whole trend of international affairs than in either March or September 1938, it had proved no more capable of slowing events. Effective American participation in the settlement of European problems still awaited vast changes at home—changes in mind, in mood, and in legislation. The issues had been greatly sharpened, however, and were now clear enough to convince the President that this was a favorable moment to seek repeal of the arms embargo. His drive opened on March 19, just four days after German troops entered Prague and three days before his warning to Colonna.

II

The exact shape of this move represented a compromise between the desirable and the possible. Up to now the administration had hoped to amend, not destroy, the arms-embargo feature of the neutrality act. Except in special cases—such as the Chaco and Spanish conflicts, where the impartial embargo was expressly suited to policy—Roosevelt's sporadic efforts to guide the development of this legislation had been aimed at securing a law which would give him wide freedom to prescribe the manner in which the embargo should be applied. But the President and his advisers were finally convinced that the impartial embargo was worse than no embargo at all. Since they also realized the futility of trying to obtain the flexible statute they needed, they decided to concentrate on getting rid of the inflexible law they had.

The basic decision was apparently made as early as November 1938, following Ambassador Wilson's recall from Berlin. Roosevelt told Postmaster General James A. Farley in December that revision of the neutrality act was one of the answers to the foreign situation,[21] and

---

[20] Extract from speech by Hitler, Apr. 28, 1939, Great Britain, Foreign Office, *Documents concerning German-Polish Relations and the Outbreak of Hostilities between Great Britain and Germany on September 3rd, 1939* (New York: Farrar and Rinehart, 1939), pp. 28–32. See also the extract in Germany, Foreign Office, *Documents on Events Preceding the Outbreak of the War* (New York: German Library of Information, 1940), pp. 314–317.

[21] Raymond Moley, *After Seven Years* (New York: Harper and Bros., 1939), pp. 379–380; and James A. Farley, *Jim Farley's Story: The Roosevelt Years* (New York: Whittlesey House, 1948), p. 163.

his message to Congress at the beginning of the new year called attention to the matter. There is some evidence that the President, having given up his initial objective, was now inclined to favor outright repeal of the existing law.[22] But such a program was no more likely to succeed than his earlier request for a discretionary embargo, and it was decided to offer a compromise based on extension of the cash-and-carry principle.

A two-year limitation had been placed on the cash-and-carry provision of the joint resolution of May 1, 1937; it was to expire on the last day of April 1939. Since the idea of cash-and-carry was favored by many congressional isolationists, Democratic tacticians thought that Congress might be persuaded to drop the embargo itself if *all* exports to belligerents, including arms and munitions, were placed permanently on a cash-and-carry basis.

Although it bore no essential relationship to a plan made so long in advance, the liquidation of Czechoslovakia was timed almost perfectly to support these designs. Public opinion was always sensitive for brief periods to European crises, and the proportion of Americans favoring the sale of war materials to Britain and France in the event of hostilities rose from 52 per cent in March to 66 per cent a month later.[23] If launched at once, therefore, the attack on Capitol Hill could expect some endorsement from public uneasiness.

Senator Pittman, still chairman of the Committee on Foreign Relations, was chosen to lead the assault, and he made known his proposal in a radio speech delivered March 19, 1939. His theme, of course, was neutrality. He criticized the existing law as unjust, if not positively unneutral, in such affairs as the war between China and Japan, and maintained that it surrendered legal rights for which the United States had gone to war in 1917. By subjecting all belligerent purchases to cash-and-carry, he went on, the nation could resume its claim to some of those rights, treat everyone with justice, and place its neutrality program on an even sounder basis than it now enjoyed. He also raised the possibility of "further legislation increasing the emergent powers of the President,"[24] but sensibly refrained from laboring the point. With

[22] Memorandum by Roosevelt, Mar. 28, 1939, Franklin D. Roosevelt, *F. D. R.: His Personal Letters, 1928–1945,* ed. Elliott Roosevelt (New York: Duell, Sloan, and Pearce, 1946), II, 873.

[23] *Public Opinion Quarterly,* III (Oct. 1939), 600.

[24] Radio address by Pittman, Mar. 19, 1939, in United States, Congress, *Congressional Record* (Washington, D. C.: U. S. Govt. Printing Office, 1874——), LXXXIV (76th Cong., 1st sess.), 2925–2926.

the stage thus set, Pittman's resolution was brought to the Senate floor the next day and referred to the Committee on Foreign Relations. Entitled the "Peace Act of 1939," this measure provided for repeal of the arms embargo, placed all sales to belligerents on a cash-and-carry basis, and empowered the President, in the event of war, to designate combat zones which American merchant vessels should be forbidden to enter.[25]

But the Senate did not coöperate as eagerly as the bill's sponsors had hoped. Senatorial isolationists were both numerous and unexpectedly stubborn, and it was decided that the proposal might do better in the House, where administration forces were stronger. So the reins were handed to Representative Sol Bloom, of New York, successor to Sam D. McReynolds as chairman of the Committee on Foreign Affairs.[26] At the same time, Hull brought the attitude of the State Department into the open with letters to both houses of Congress urging them to repeal the arms embargo and adopt the changes contained in the Pittman resolution.[27] On May 29 Bloom offered his colleagues a bill which differed only in wording and detail from the Senate proposal.[28]

Everything went smoothly at first, and the Bloom resolution was reported from committee on June 17. The ensuing debate was more arduous, however. Friends of repeal upheld the measure as the best way of keeping the United States out of war, but expounded their thesis in a number of different contexts. Representative Luther A. Johnson, Democrat, of Texas, considered the embargo a threat to peace since, by removing the positive influence of the United States from the world scene, it encouraged other countries to make war.[29] Representative E. V. Izac, Democrat, of California, held that the joint resolution of May 1, 1937, imposed only a partial embargo and declared that no partial embargo could be truly neutral. Specifically, he was worried about continued shipments to Japan.[30] Representative James W. Wadsworth, Republican, of New York, argued that peace for the United States lay in its retention "of the right to do what is best for America when the time comes." Having always counseled freedom of action,

---

[25] S. J. Res. 97, *ibid.,* pp. 2923–2924.

[26] Harold B. Hinton, *Cordell Hull: A Biography* (Garden City, N. Y.: Doubleday, Doran, and Co., 1942), p. 337.

[27] Hull to Bloom and Pittman, May 27, 1939, *Department of State Press Releases,* XX (June 3, 1939), 476–477.

[28] H. J. Res. 306 (76th Cong., 1st sess.), *Cong. Record,* LXXXIV (76th Cong., 1st sess.), 6309.

[29] *Cong. Record,* LXXXIV (76th Cong., 1st sess.), 8324.

[30] *Ibid.*

he opposed the neutrality act just as he had opposed American adherence to the League of Nations after the World War.[31]

Enemies of repeal, on the other hand, denounced the Bloom proposal as a certain move toward war. Representative Paul W. Shafer, Republican, of Michigan, characterized it as a "war-promotion bill clothed in the robes of neutrality . . . [and] just what the international bankers, international war-mongers, and war profiteers desire."[32] Representative J. M. Vorys, Republican, of Ohio, thought it revealed the President's desire "to use the threat of our power to preserve a balance of power in Europe."[33] Representative Martin J. Kennedy, Democrat, of New York, opposed the bill because the people of his district back home were "scared to death" that it would lead to war. "God knows," he added plaintively, "they have enough to worry about without this problem."[34]

Congressional views still had a depressingly familiar ring; and public opinion, whatever its state in April, furnished little help in June. Thanks to this circumstance and to carelessness on the part of Democratic leaders, who neglected to produce some readily available administration votes at the proper time, Representative Vorys managed to insert an amendment restoring the arms embargo. Since Bloom's efforts to delete this provision were unsuccessful, the bill was dropped.[35]

Pittman now undertook to renew the fight in the Senate, but his Committee on Foreign Relations voted on July 11 to postpone further consideration of the matter until the following January.[36] Still unwilling to accept defeat, President Roosevelt entered the struggle in person. On July 14, in a special message, he transmitted to Congress a lengthy argument written by Hull maintaining that repeal of the embargo would be a clear gain for the cause of peace and genuine neutrality. Four days later, on the evening of July 18, he called leading senators of both parties to a meeting at the White House. Here Roosevelt and Hull strove to convince the group that war was imminent. But they achieved nothing. Senatorial attitudes ranged from simple

---

[31] *Cong. Record,* LXXXIV (76th Cong., 1st sess.), 8159.

[32] *Ibid.,* p. 8318.   [33] *Ibid.,* p. 8151.   [34] *Ibid.,* p. 8173.

[35] United States, Congress, House of Representatives, *Journal of the House of Representatives of the United States of America* (Washington, D. C.: U. S. Govt. Printing Office and others, 1814——) (76th Cong., 1st sess.), p. 767; and Hinton, *Cordell Hull,* pp. 338–339.

[36] Cordell Hull, *The Memoirs of Cordell Hull* (New York: Macmillan Co., 1948), I, 648.

pessimism to vehement hostility, and in view of impending congressional adjournment it was decided to postpone further efforts until the next session.[37]

III

While the struggle over neutrality law ran its course in Washington, international tensions continued to grow. Europe moved toward avowed war in a state of mind approaching resignation; Japan plunged still deeper into its work of building a New Order in eastern Asia; and the United States looked on with a kind of impotent nervousness. Franco's capture of Madrid ended the Spanish civil war on March 28, 1939, and the administration's Spanish embargo was lifted April 1. Thus freed of what was perhaps the most embarrassing single aspect of its foreign policy,[38] the American government was finally doing all it reasonably could, within the limits of law and public opinion, to influence events abroad. By this time, however, probably nothing short of direct political commitments to the Western powers could have enabled it to moderate Germany's course. In the absence of so much as a useful embargo policy, the administration's chances of accomplishing anything in Europe were small indeed. In May President Roosevelt warned the Russian Ambassador, Constantine Oumansky, that Stalin would only invite trouble if he made an agreement with Hitler, for Germany would inevitably turn on the Soviet Union as soon as France was defeated.[39] Beyond this, little could be undertaken until new developments stirred the nation again.

As the European contest for Russia's favor continued, England and Turkey, on May 12, pledged themselves to effective coöperation in the event of aggressive moves "leading to war in the Mediterranean area." [40]

[37] Message to Congress, July 14, 1939, Franklin D. Roosevelt, *The Public Papers and Addresses of Franklin D. Roosevelt, 1939,* comp. S. I. Rosenman (New York: Macmillan Co., 1941), pp. 382, 384; and Hull, *Memoirs,* I, 649–650.

[38] As late as January 1939 when Henry T. Hunt, chairman of the Lawyers' Committee on American Relations with Spain, urged the lifting of the Spanish embargo, Welles suggested an answer to the effect that the resolution of January 8, 1937, which was passed unanimously by the Senate and with just one dissenting vote in the House, made it appropriate to let Congress determine whether the embargo should be terminated. See Welles to McIntyre, Jan. 30, 1939, MS Roosevelt Papers (Official File, Box 422-A).

[39] Joseph E. Davies, *Mission to Moscow* (New York: Simon and Schuster, 1941), p. 450.

[40] Statement by Chamberlain, May 12, 1939, *Parl. Debates* (Commons), CCCXLVII, 953.

France and Turkey made a somewhat parallel declaration on June 23.[41] And on May 22 the Rome-Berlin Axis was tightened by a military alliance impressively dubbed the "Pact of Steel." Providing for consultation, economic coördination in time of war, and reciprocal military assistance, this instrument gave the association between Italy and Germany an appearance which was even more monolithic than before.[42]

In the meanwhile, the Far Eastern situation was left pretty much to the United States and Japan. Fully alive to the strength of its position, Japan easily kept the initiative as it moved from one goal to another. But while Hull remained convinced throughout the spring and summer that he should still play a waiting game with Tokyo,[43] Japan's increasing boldness made it appear that even these tactics now required a somewhat harsher tone.

As early as February 10, 1939, the Japanese had seized the large Chinese island of Hainan, thus menacing both the coast of Indo-China and the sea route between Hong Kong and Singapore. This action was followed on March 31 by Japan's annexation of the Spratley Islands, a tiny but strategically important group about four hundred miles west of the southern Philippines. The United States Navy had already surveyed much of this area and considered many of its islands and lagoons valuable for certain types of naval operations. Accordingly, Hull protested the Japanese action and declined to recognize its validity.[44]

Presaging a Japanese drive southward just as Europe was feeling the full effects of the Czechoslovak crisis, these aggressive moves had still other repercussions. In January 1939 a portion of the United States Fleet had been transferred to the Atlantic for the purpose of conducting maneuvers and of paying a ceremonial visit at the New York World's Fair. However, the conjunction of this shift with the events just described aroused serious misgivings in London. On March 22 the British Foreign Office stated that recent developments in Europe made it impossible for Britain to fulfill its intention of transferring a fleet from European waters to Singapore and asked whether the United States would consider returning its ships to the Pacific. Bullitt supplied further enlightenment from Paris about two weeks later, revealing that the British had contemplated reinforcing Singapore with units from the Mediterranean and had desisted only when France warned that, in such

---

[41] *Christian Science Monitor,* June 23, 1939, p. 1, col. 7.
[42] For the text of the treaty see *New York Times,* May 23, 1939, p. 8, cols. 3–6.
[43] Hull, *Memoirs,* I, 638,   [44] *Ibid.,* pp. 628–629,

an event, it would take no further part in joint efforts to construct an anti-Hitler front in eastern Europe. Thus the European and Asiatic situations moved closer together than ever before; and faced by these insistent considerations, Roosevelt ordered the Fleet back into the Pacific on April 15.[45]

Nor was this all. Emboldened by its own successes and Europe's preoccupations, Japan applied still more pressure to foreign interests in China. Between January and July there was some interference with American rights or a bombing of American property on the average of once every three days.[46] Other nationalities fared no better. In June the Japanese blockaded British and French concessions in the Chinese city of Tientsin on the ground that the British were giving asylum to anti-Japanese terrorists.[47] Embarrassed by its new European commitments, Britain opened negotiations on June 15 and accepted a formula on July 24 which for practical purposes granted belligerent rights to Japanese forces in such Chinese areas as were under their control.[48]

Owing to the absence of Ambassador Grew, who had left Japan in May for a five-month vacation in the United States, American representations in Tokyo during this period were even more mechanical than usual. But some advance was made in Washington itself.

Since the beginning of trouble in Asia, the American-Japanese commercial treaty of 1911 had furnished a hindrance to the legal application of economic pressure because of its most-favored-nation stipulation that the United States might not forbid any kind of trade with Japan unless similar prohibitions were established for all other countries.[49] Irritation with the treaty had been growing for some time. On July 18 Senator Arthur H. Vandenberg, of Michigan, still a leading isolationist,

[45] Hull, *Memoirs*, I, 630. At this same time the Naval War Plans Division was informed by British authorities that Great Britain's responsibilities in the Mediterranean would keep the British government from sending a battle force to Singapore in accordance with the general understanding of January 1938. As a result, the Army and Navy drew up a new war plan (Rainbow No. 1) which did not count on the assistance of a British fleet in the Pacific. See Samuel Eliot Morison, *The Rising Sun in the Pacific, 1931—April 1942* (Boston: Little, Brown, and Co., 1948), p. 49.

[46] William C. Johnstone, *The United States and Japan's New Order*, rev. ed. (New York: Oxford Univ. Press, 1941), p. 277.

[47] The *Times* (London), June 17, 1939, p. 12, col. 2.

[48] Statement by Chamberlain, July 24, 1939, *Parl. Debates* (Commons), CCCL, 994.

[49] Article V, Treaty of Commerce and Navigation between the United States and Japan, Feb, 21, 1911, United States, Department of State, *Papers Relating to the Foreign Relations of the United States, 1911* (Washington, D. C.: U. S. Govt. Printing Office, 1918), p. 316.

introduced a Senate resolution calling for the treaty's abrogation.[50] The State Department had been exploring the same idea and, without waiting for the result of this legislative move, on July 26 abruptly gave the six-month notice required to denounce the agreement.[51] This had no effect whatever upon the immediate realities of American-Japanese trade, but it did constitute a warning that American patience was running out and that fairly drastic economic restrictions might be expected later. Meanwhile, Europe raced madly through its last weeks of peace.

Although there was little prospect of current benefit in anything Roosevelt might do to hinder the outbreak of a European war, he continued to explore all possibilities. It was obvious by midsummer that Europe had passed beyond the stage of genuine discussion and that the thinking of its leaders had entered a military phase; each side was so bent on tipping the balance in its own favor that competition for Russian support was now the real focus of diplomacy. Every major government was so deeply concerned with the approaching catastrophe that none could pause to review the whole situation. Only outsiders, those who stood relatively apart from immediate issues, could hope to exercise a moderating influence. The one man in Europe who combined such detachment with the necessary prestige was Pope Pius XII. For the time being, his relationship to the crisis was roughly similar to that of the President, and his record indicated that a working arrangement with the Holy See might be extremely useful to the American government.

The Vatican, which gave considerable weight to the Axis stand against communism, had originally been inclined to think well of Hitlerite Germany. But the more recent development of Nazi foreign policy and the harsh treatment accorded the Catholic Church in Germany succeeded in producing a very different view by the spring of 1939.[52] On March 18 in an interview with the Italian Foreign Minister, Count Ciano, the Pope expressed his concern over Nazi aggression; [53] and at the beginning of May he undertook, through his diplomatic representatives in Berlin, Warsaw, Paris, London, and Rome, to investigate

[50] S. Res. 166 (76th Cong., 1st sess.), *Cong. Record,* LXXXIV (76th Cong., 1st sess.), 9341.

[51] Hull to Horinouchi, July 26, 1939, United States, Department of State, *Papers Relating to the Foreign Relations of the United States: Japan, 1931–1941* (Washington, D. C.: U. S. Govt. Printing Office, 1943), II, 189.

[52] Camille M. Cianfarra, *The Vatican and the War* (New York: E. P. Dutton and Co., 1944), pp. 107–108.   [53] *Ciano Diaries,* pp. 46–47.

the practicality of a new move to avoid war. Although it was made clear to everyone that the Vatican would not participate directly in any discussion among the powers, the American government by late June could feel reasonably certain of the Pope's attitude.[54]

Thus impressed by the Vatican's natural advantages as a potential mediating agency, and even more alive to its possibilities as a source of information—especially on conditions in Germany, Italy, and Spain— not ordinarily available to Washington, Roosevelt considered establishing some kind of relations with the Holy See as early as the beginning of July. Ambassador Phillips, in Rome, favored the idea and advised the appointment of a Protestant with full ambassadorial status to represent the United States at the Vatican. The always-cautious Hull agreed that a Protestant should be chosen for the post, but argued that such an envoy should be accredited not as Ambassador but merely as the President's personal representative.[55] The plan was discussed with Monsignor Ameleto Cicognani, the Apostolic Delegate in Washington, and Cicognani visited Rome in August for conferences with the Pontiff.[56] These soundings were admittedly preliminary and resulted in no definite action for the moment; but in the opinion of James A. Farley, who was granted a papal audience while visiting Europe later that month, the Pope gave evidence of being on extremely intimate terms with the President. As he outlined his peacemaking efforts to the Postmaster General, Pius expressed a firm conviction that Roosevelt would run for a third term in 1940,[57] an opinion identical with one offered Farley a few weeks earlier by the American prelate, Cardinal Mundelein, immediately after the latter had lunched with the President. This was the more remarkable in that it was a view which Farley did not share at that time.[58]

Meanwhile, Germany triumphed over Britain and France in their long struggle for Russian support. On August 23, 1939, a German-Soviet treaty was signed in Moscow providing that neither country would attack, support an attack, or join any grouping of powers directed against the other.[59] There was also a secret additional protocol set-

---

[54] Cianfarra, *The Vatican and the War*, pp. 166–171.
[55] Hull, *Memoirs*, I, 713; and Welles to Roosevelt, Aug. 1, 1939, MS Roosevelt Papers (Secretary's File, Box 54).
[56] Cianfarra, *The Vatican and the War*, p. 178.
[57] *Ibid.*, pp. 181–182; cf. *Jim Farley's Story*, p. 194.
[58] *Jim Farley's Story*, p. 175.
[59] Treaty of Non-Aggression between Germany and the U.S.S.R., Aug. 23, 1939,

ting up spheres of influence in the Baltic states, and in Poland and Rumania.[60] But the treaty itself was enough to convince the world that Germany's hands were now free and that war could not be delayed much longer.

In several quarters there were eleventh-hour attempts to avert hostilities.[61] All efforts failed, of course, but the close parallelism between the activities of President Roosevelt and of Pope Pius XII inspired additional confidence in Vatican policies. On August 24 His Holiness broadcasted to the world an urgent plea for peace. At the same time, Roosevelt sent peace appeals to King Victor Emmanuel of Italy, to Hitler, and to the President of Poland. He suggested, among other things, that an American republic be called in as conciliator. The Pope took up the cue on August 31 by addressing a definite proposal to Germany, Poland, Great Britain, France, and Italy. In it he called for a fifteen-day truce during which the five governments should hold a general conference to study revision of the Versailles Treaty and work out the basis for a pact of nonaggression. Representatives of Belgium, Switzerland, the Netherlands, the United States, and the Vatican might also attend. But even though Great Britain moved at once to support this appeal, it was already too late,[62] and German armies marched into Poland on September 1. As the war started, however, the American government had every reason to continue its study of the advantages to be derived from closer relations with the Holy See.

IV

American fears of a European war had brought the arms embargo into being. Yet, by going to war, Europe paved the way for its withdrawal. The record shows that the American people always became most distrustful of their isolationist convictions precisely at the time when the soundness of those convictions seemed about to undergo a genuine test, and nothing could try the embargo with greater harshness than the very contingency against which the law had been passed. While general support for the idea had declined noticeably in March

United States, Department of State, *Nazi-Soviet Relations, 1939–1941* (Washington, D. C.: U. S. Govt. Printing Office, 1948), pp. 76–77.

[60] Secret additional protocol, Aug. 23, 1939, *ibid.,* p. 78.

[61] See Langer and Gleason, *The Challenge to Isolation,* pp. 193–200.

[62] Cianfarra, *The Vatican and the War,* pp. 183–185. The texts of Roosevelt's messages are given in *Peace and War,* pp. 475–479.

and April, the effects of this change had not extended far enough to repeal the embargo in June and July. How long it might have been retained if peace had continued it is impossible to say. But realization
that Europe had actually gone to war was a sobering, even a frightening,
thought. Although a Gallup poll reported on September 17 that 82
per cent of the American people were confident of an Allied victory,
another survey at the end of the month disclosed that 63 per cent feared
a German attack on the United States if Hitler won in Europe.[63] Long
denied but never forgotten, an old misgiving had once more acquired
the touch of reality. Neutral America was not so serene as it had expected to be, and chance aided design in pointing up the moral.

The war became general with the entrance of Great Britain and
France on September 3, and President Roosevelt spoke to the country
that night. "This nation will remain a neutral nation," he said, "but
I cannot ask that every American remain neutral in thought as well." [64]
By its differences as well as its similarities, this message to the people
recalled Woodrow Wilson's plea of August 18, 1914, which had granted
that the "utmost variety of sympathy and desire . . . with regard to the
issues and circumstances of the conflict" was perfectly natural but ad-
jured the country to "be impartial in thought as well as in action." [65]
In 1914, Wilson had foreseen the difficulties of neutrality almost as
clearly as Roosevelt did in 1939. But the latter's frank admission that
psychological neutrality was now impossible, and his failure to suggest
that sympathy might flow in more than one direction, bespoke a somewhat more vigorous official attitude. Apparently this was no sudden
decision on Roosevelt's part. As early as September 1938 he had expressed a clear resolve to greet a European war in such fashion.[66]

Special radio bulletins later the same evening announced that the
British liner *Athenia*, bound for Montreal with 216 Americans aboard,
had been sunk off the Hebrides. Strictly mindful of the *Lusitania*
precedent, White House secretary Stephen T. Early hastened to assure
the country that the *Athenia* had carried no munitions.[67] On Septem-

[63] *Public Opinion Quarterly*, IV (Mar. 1940), 101–102.
[64] Fireside chat, Sept. 3, 1939, Roosevelt, *Public Papers and Addresses, 1939*, p. 463.
[65] Appeal to the citizens of the Republic, Aug. 18, 1914, Woodrow Wilson, *President Wilson's Foreign Policy: Messages, Addresses, Papers*, ed. James Brown Scott (New York: Oxford Univ. Press, 1918), pp. 67–68.
[66] Roosevelt to Phillips, Sept. 15, 1938, *F. D. R.: His Personal Letters, 1928–1945*, II, 810–811.
[67] *New York Times*, Sept. 4, 1939, p. 1, col. 8.

ber 4 the *New York Times* held Germany responsible for the war, and many other newspapers quickly followed suit.[68]   To one of sufficient age and the least disposition for nostalgia, it must have seemed startlingly reminiscent of events more than twenty years past.

As German armies knifed through Poland during the next three weeks, the American government busily adjusted its relations with a continent at war.   The President issued two proclamations on September 5.   One set forth the country's neutrality under international law, outlining neutral duties as provided by old legislation.[69]   The second gave force to the joint resolution of May 1, 1937, invoking the arms embargo and other provisions—except, of course, the cash-and-carry feature, which had expired at the end of April.[70]   The same day, Roosevelt emphasized his determination to keep belligerent activity at a distance by ordering the formation of a special naval patrol to watch all belligerent craft that might approach the shores of the United States or the West Indies.[71]   On September 6 he announced that the agreement concluded with Britain on June 23, under which American cotton was to be exchanged for Malayan rubber in an effort to create a stockpile of rubber in the United States, had gone into effect.[72]   And on September 8 he readied himself for later developments by proclaiming a "limited national emergency," an act which gave him immediate access to a considerable variety of crisis powers.[73]

At the same time, the belligerents proceeded rapidly with their inevitable maritime arrangements, and meditation over the fate of the *Athenia* had scarcely started before the United States was further reminded of the troubles which beset a trading neutral during a war at

[68] *New York Times,* Sept. 4, 1939, p. 18, cols. 1–2; and Harold Lavine and James Wechsler, *War Propaganda and the United States* (New Haven: Yale Univ. Press, 1940), p. 41.

[69] Proclamation No. 2348, Sept. 5, 1939, United States, National Archives, *Federal Register* (Washington, D. C.: U. S. Govt. Printing Office, 1936——), IV, 3809.

[70] Proclamation No. 2349, Sept. 5, 1939, *ibid.,* p. 3819.

[71] Samuel Eliot Morison, *The Battle of the Atlantic, 1939–1943* (Boston: Little, Brown, and Co., 1947), p. 14.

[72] Press release, Sept. 6, 1939, United States, Department of State, *Department of State Bulletin* (Washington, D. C.: U. S. Govt. Printing Office, 1939——), I (Sept. 9, 1939), 240.   For the text of this agreement, see *Department of State Press Releases,* XX (June 24, 1939), 547–549.

[73] Proclamation No. 2352, Sept. 8, 1939, *Federal Register,* IV, 3851.   For the doctrine of emergency and a list of emergency powers, see Louis W. Koenig, *The Presidency and the Crisis: Powers of the Office from the Invasion of Poland to Pearl Harbor* (New York: King's Crown Press, 1944), pp. 11–13.

sea. France published a contraband list on September 4, as did Germany on September 12 and Britain on September 13.[74] Both sides inaugurated blockade activities almost as soon as the war started, and before a week passed London was flooding the State Department with suggestions regarding the proper attitude toward British contraband-control bases and ways in which American shipping could most effectively coöperate with other blockade measures. Hull scented trouble in all this and, hoping to solve problems as they arose, made arrangements on September 12 for steady consultation with the British government regarding differences arising out of the blockade.[75]

Potential friction with both sides was already building up. An American ship, the S.S. *Wacosta,* was stopped by a German submarine on September 9, searched, and warned that vessels which did not, in the future, obey a U-boat's signals would be fired upon. On September 8 the S.S. *Saccarappa* was seized by the British and released after being disburdened of her cargo. These were quickly followed by many similar incidents.[76] So far as maritime problems were concerned, the Second World War had commenced precisely as did the First.

In part at least, the neutrality act was designed to keep such occurrences to a safe minimum and thus preclude any faltering in the national sense of detachment. If circumstances had been different, this recurrence of maritime troubles might have furnished an argument for strengthening such legislation. But the American sense of detachment was not what it had been a few years earlier. As noted above, the years of successful German aggression had undermined the belief that the United States had no special interest in the results of a European war. Unless fully supported by such a conviction, an impartial embargo could not be effective. As early as September 3, some 50 per cent of the citizenry thought that the arms embargo should be discarded, and the trend remained highly favorable to repeal during the next six weeks. Fifty-seven per cent declared themselves to be of such a mind on September 24, and the proportion rose to 62 per cent ten days later.[77]

---

[74] The texts of the initial French, German, and British announcements regarding maritime policy are given in World Peace Foundation, *Documents on American Foreign Relations, 1939–1940,* ed. S. Shepard Jones and Denys P. Myers (Boston: World Peace Foundation, 1940), pp. 424, 721–722.

[75] Hull, *Memoirs,* I, 680.

[76] For a list of ship detentions by the belligerents, see *Department of State Bulletin,* I (Nov. 4, 1939), 461–462.

[77] *Public Opinion Quarterly,* IV (Mar. 1940), 105–106.

From the administration's point of view it was advisable to strike before the expected inactivity of winter brought a recession of public uneasiness.

Therefore Roosevelt acted promptly and with seeming confidence, for as early as September 11, in a letter to the British Prime Minister, he expressed his belief that the embargo would be repealed within a month.[78] On September 13 he called a special session of Congress for September 21. The next day, Hull indicated what was in his chief's mind by announcing that the United States had yielded none of its rights under international law even though the neutrality act prevented the exercise of some of them at the domestic level. Eight days later Roosevelt went before Congress to ask for repeal of the arms embargo, coupling this proposal with others looking to the reënactment of cash-and-carry and the designation of combat zones. Under this program, he said, the United States would "more probably remain at peace than if the law remains as it stands today . . . because with the repeal of the embargo this Government clearly and definitely will insist that American citizens and American ships keep away from the immediate perils of the actual zones of conflict . . . ."[79]

A familiar compromise, emphasizing the theme of neutrality, was being offered once more!

V

Although conditions now were generally more favorable to repeal of the arms embargo than they had been before the outbreak of war, legislative activity had lost none of its habitual deliberation. In consequence, matters which stood to be directly affected by proposed changes in the neutrality law were held more or less in abeyance during the next six weeks; and American policy in questions of sea-borne commerce was left on a strictly temporary basis, no effort being made to raise sharp issues with any of the belligerents, except in the case of the *City of Flint*, where very special circumstances were involved. For the rest, American shippers were merely advised of the special dangers in European waters growing out of the war.[80]

[78] Roosevelt to Chamberlain, Sept. 11, 1939, *F. D. R.: His Personal Letters, 1928–1945*, II, 919.

[79] Message to Congress, Sept. 21, 1939, Roosevelt, *Public Papers and Addresses, 1939*, p. 518.

[80] Statement by Hull, Oct. 4, 1939, *Department of State Bulletin*, I (Oct. 7, 1939), 343.

Nevertheless, October was filled with alarums and excursions. Discussion of the *Athenia's* sinking continued through the month, with solemn British avowals that she had carried no munitions being ranged against open hints from Berlin that the British themselves had sunk her in order to blacken the reputation of Germany.[81] Intensifying this psychological warfare, Grand Admiral Erich Raeder, Commander-in-Chief of the German Navy, told the United States military attaché in Berlin, on October 5, that the American ship *Iroquois,* then returning from Ireland with a large number of Americans who had been caught in Europe by the war, was to be sunk as she neared the coast of the United States, under circumstances recalling the loss of the *Athenia.* While this tale was heavily discounted in Washington, it aroused enough doubt to prompt the dispatch of a Coast Guard vessel and a number of ships from the neutrality patrol to meet the *Iroquois* and escort her through the last part of her voyage.[82]

The *City of Flint* episode was more complicated. An American ship laden with cargo for the British Isles, the *City of Flint* was captured on October 9 by a German cruiser about twelve hundred miles out of New York. A German crew was put aboard; and the ship entered the neutral port of Tromsö, Norway, on October 21, flying the German flag. After taking on water, she left Tromsö at the order of the Norwegian government and steamed into the Russian harbor of Murmansk two days later. Throughout this odyssey her American crew had remained aboard as prisoners.

As soon as the ship entered Russian waters, the American Ambassador in Moscow, Laurence A. Steinhardt, approached the Russian Foreign Office with inquiries, but was unable to obtain much direct information concerning either the ship or the men aboard her. Finally he tired of such evasion and demanded that the *City of Flint* be turned over to her American crew and allowed to proceed. Pleading the requirements of their own neutrality, the Russians held that the ship would have to leave Murmansk under the same authority which had brought her there in the first place.[83] So far, American representations had proved vain; and still under German auspices, the *City of Flint* was released from Russian waters on October 28. But the vessel was taken

[81] See Lothian to Hull, Oct. 30, 1939, *ibid.* (Nov. 4, 1939), p. 461.

[82] Press release, Oct. 5, 1939, *ibid.* (Oct. 21, 1939), p. 407.

[83] Press release, Oct. 28, 1939, *ibid.* (Oct. 28, 1939), pp. 431–432; also Steinhardt to Hull, Oct. 27, 1939, *ibid.,* pp. 430–431.

into Bergen, Norway, a few days later against the orders of the Norwegian government. This time, the German crew was interned, and the ship was placed in charge of her original master and allowed to proceed.[84] The whole affair had that peculiarly nebulous quality so characteristic of any discussion of neutral rights and duties. It raised some nice legal points and emphasized the frustrations of neutrality,[85] but the chief importance of the episode was the further strain it imposed upon America's none-too-solid ties with Russia.

In spite of all the United States could do, American-Soviet relations deteriorated in almost every way throughout the fall of 1939. Moscow's final intentions seemed vaguer than ever, and immediate policy was summed up in its extension of Soviet influence as far west as was permitted by the secret additional protocol of August 23, which, as it concerned northern Europe, placed Finland, Estonia, Latvia, and that part of Poland which lay east of the Narew and Vistula rivers within the Russian sphere of influence, leaving western Poland and Lithuania to Germany.[86] This work proceeded rapidly in the latter half of September. At the end of the month Nazi Foreign Minister Joachim von Ribbentrop hurried from Berlin to Moscow to conclude another agreement respecting this buffer territory. Under a new protocol signed September 28 Lithuania was transferred to the Russian sphere,[87] and October was not far advanced before Soviet military control of the three Baltic states was as complete, for all practical purposes, as the Soviet hold on eastern Poland.

The United States government watched this process with mixed feelings. Although Russia at the moment looked very much like an enemy to the democracies, it could still be regarded as their potential friend. The likelihood that the Russian understanding with Germany was the product of convenience rather than conviction was not to be ignored, for political convenience, especially in time of war, is often a transitory thing.[88] To maintain as good relations with Russia as possible and to give its rulers no cause for drawing yet closer to Germany was of first importance. This was the thought which animated United States policy in eastern Europe during the fall of 1939. So, notwith-

[84] Press release, Nov. 3, 1939, *Department of State Bulletin*, I (Nov. 4, 1939), 458.

[85] Cf. Charles Cheney Hyde, "The City of Flint," *American Journal of International Law*, XXXIV (Jan. 1940), 92, 94–95.

[86] Secret additional protocol, Aug. 23, 1939, *Nazi-Soviet Relations*, p. 78.

[87] Secret supplementary protocol, Sept. 28, 1939, *ibid.*, p. 107.

[88] Hull, *Memoirs*, I, 702.

standing Poland's formal declaration of war when attacked by Russia in September and his own application of the neutrality act to the concurrent and virtually identical German-Polish conflict, President Roosevelt did not choose to recognize the autumn's hostilities between Poland and the Soviet Union as a war at all. Failure to act was permissible, he argued, because this aspect of the European struggle had little or no relation to the peace of the United States.[89] Thus Russia retained legal access to American war materials, a circumstance from which the Soviet government need not be permitted to draw much profit for the time being but which could prove useful to both countries if alignments suddenly changed. This phase of American policy was already an exercise in higher strategy.

Caution remained the watchword through October and November as the United States sedulously avoided any word or action that could be considered in the least provocative. Even Russian activity in the Baltic states could be justified up to a point. Choosing to view these highhanded incursions as part of an effort by the Soviet government to bolster Russian defenses against Germany, the State Department was inclined to ignore other possible motives. Since neither Estonia, Latvia, nor Lithuania was deprived of nominal independence, as Hull later pointed out, "there was no diplomatic step we felt called upon to take." Yet it was recognized that continued Russian aggression might needlessly enlarge the war to the great detriment of still other small powers.[90] Some limit had to be set, therefore; and by October 11, when he wrote to Soviet President Kalinin expressing a hope that Russia would not make unreasonable demands on Finland,[91] Roosevelt appears to have chosen the Finnish question as the point at which to make a stand.

In similar fashion the President played a waiting game with Italy, adhering to the policy which he had followed in tacit collaboration with Great Britain since the spring of 1938, and with the Vatican since the latter part of August 1939. On September 13, in a long talk with Farley, the President stated his belief that Mussolini was still undecided; he might remain neutral or even join forces with Britain and France. Implying that the nonrecognition policy which he had "inherited" from

[89] Koenig, *The Presidency and the Crisis,* p. 40. For Hull's comments on this development, see his *Memoirs,* I, 685.

[90] Hull, *Memoirs,* I, 701.

[91] Roosevelt to Kalinin, Oct. 11, 1939, *Department of State Bulletin,* I (Oct. 21, 1939), 395.

the Hoover administration had sometimes forced him into attitudes which he would have preferred to avoid, Roosevelt said that Italy's conquest of Ethiopia had been made in "regular fashion" but that he could not extend recognition here without again raising the old problem of Manchukuo. Accordingly, he had tried to enlist Mussolini's patience by having him informed that "time would take care of the situation." [92]

Temporarily, at least, Italy's neutrality was the important thing. This directed new attention to Pope Pius XII. Both Mussolini's failure to declare war at the outset and his suspected misgivings about Russo-German coöperation were in harmony with the views of the Holy See. As a result, relations between the Italian government and the Vatican were better, generally speaking, in the fall of 1939 than they had been for some time in the past.[93] Under these circumstances, the diplomatic coöperation of the Pope in any matter touching Italy was a factor not to be ignored. Roosevelt was toying with other projects too; but he must have had this thought in mind on October 2 when he again raised the question of whether the time was ripe to establish formal relations with the Vatican, pointing out to Hull that such a connection might facilitate dealing with the refugee problem after the war.[94]

Although the President did not then mention His Holiness as a possible ally in bringing the war to an end,[95] there was some talk of a compromise peace during the first week of October. On September 28 Germany and Russia issued a joint declaration calling for an end to hostilities now that the Polish question had been settled by the collapse of the Polish state.[96] Shortly afterward, Washington began receiving hints from such diverse sources as Berlin, Bucharest, Brussels, and Helsinki that a general peace move on the part of the United States would be welcomed. This question was reviewed in a special meeting of State Department experts on October 8, but it was decided that any peace initiative would be ill-advised for the time being in view of Germany's huge successes thus far in the war.[97]

As Washington gingerly probed the European situation, Ambassador Joseph C. Grew, strengthened by a long holiday in the United States and refreshed by many conferences with State Department officials, re-

---

[92] *Jim Farley's Story*, p. 198.
[93] See Cianfarra, *The Vatican and the War*, p. 189.
[94] Hull, *Memoirs*, I, 713.   [95] *Ibid.*, p. 714.
[96] Declaration of the government of the German Reich and the government of the U.S.S.R., Sept. 28, 1939, *Nazi-Soviet Relations*, p. 108.
[97] Hull, *Memoirs*, I, 710–711.

turned to his post in Tokyo. Since his departure five months earlier, Japanese policy had undergone severe strains, the full effects of which could not yet be determined. In May 1939 Baron Hiranuma, Konoye's recent successor as Prime Minister, had suggested a tightening of the Anti-Comintern Pact, subject to the reservation that Japan could not yet promise Germany effective military support of any kind. But Hitler had refused to proceed on this basis, and his August *rapprochement* with Russia, Japan's traditional enemy, had left the Japanese government understandably nonplussed.[98] As a result, Japan had appeared about to slacken its pace when the European war started. The Hiranuma Cabinet fell, and for a time even Hull thought that the Baron's successor, General Nobuyuki Abe, might do something to alter Japan's course.[99] But as Tokyo gave no further indication of revising its Asiatic policy, it was decided that Grew should offer a public warning, in language which could not be misunderstood, that the United States was not to be frightened out of the Far East.

In pursuance of this design Grew spoke before a luncheon meeting of the America-Japan Society on October 19, delivering an address which reached quite unusual heights of diplomatic frankness. The product of deliberate drafting and exhaustive revision,[100] his speech covered both general principles and particular issues, but the development of public opinion at home was Grew's main theme. Asserting that American foreign policy was always closely bound to American public opinion, he assured his listeners that the determination of the United States government not to acquiesce in Japan's Far Eastern program was shared by the whole country. He said: "American public opinion with regard to recent and current developments in the Far East is today very nearly unanimous, and that opinion is based not on mere hearsay or on propaganda but on facts." [101] Since the speech was public and attended by reporters and government officials, this was about as far as the United States could go without resorting to specific threats. But now, unfortunately, threats had to be withheld until the European war took more definite shape.

Only in the field of inter-American relations, where it held a virtual

[98] Joseph W. Ballantine, "Mukden to Pearl Harbor: The Foreign Policies of Japan," *Foreign Affairs,* XXVII (July 1949), 655–656.

[99] Hull, *Memoirs,* I, 717.

[100] Joseph C. Grew, *Ten Years in Japan* (New York: Simon and Schuster, 1944), p. 288.

[101] Address by Grew, Oct. 19, 1939, *Foreign Relations: Japan, 1931–1941,* II, 22.

monopoly of everything that counted, was the United States able to gain a solid advantage during the first two months of the war. Almost immediately after the German invasion of Poland a conference of foreign ministers was summoned to meet at Panama in accordance with procedure laid down the previous December by the Declaration of Lima. The most immediate problem now was that of keeping the war as far as possible from the shores of the Americas, and within this problem the conference found two paramount considerations—the neutrality of waters surrounding the American continents and the future of territory in the Western Hemisphere owned by foreign powers. Under the leadership of Sumner Welles, the United States delegate, decisions were reached on both counts. On October 3, 1939, the conference adopted a resolution opposing the transfer of sovereignty over American territory from one non-American power to another, thus endorsing a time-hallowed corollary of the Monroe Doctrine. The same day, through a statement which became known as the Declaration of Panama, it also established a "safety" zone in the western Atlantic ranging in width from three hundred to one thousand miles. From this zone all belligerent activity was to be excluded.[102]

This measure was especially important, not only because it rounded out President Roosevelt's long efforts to establish an effective kind of hemispheric solidarity, but also because it furnished the main theoretical basis of his Atlantic policy until well into the crucial months of 1941. Strengthening the framework of exclusion even more, the President on October 18 used his authority under the joint resolution of May 1, 1937, to prohibit the use of the territorial waters of the United States by the submarines of all belligerent countries.[103]

VI

Against this background of emergent policy toward ı war in which sides had not yet been fully chosen, the arms embargo died a slow death. Congress got to work briskly enough as it met in special session on September 21, 1939. But no shades of the past had, as yet, been entirely exorcised, and ground with which everyone was familiar had to be covered all over again. The new survey took almost six weeks.

[102] Declaration of Panama, Oct. 3, 1939, *Department of State Bulletin*, I (Oct. 7, 1939), 331–333.
[103] Proclamation No. 2371, Oct. 18, 1939, *Federal Register*, IV, 4295.

Delaying not at all, the Senate started with the Bloom resolution which, fitted with crippling amendments, had passed the House in June. Using the President's new recommendations as a basis, the Committee on Foreign Relations then drew up a substitute bill, which was introduced as an amendment to the House-approved measure on September 29.[104] By early October the debate had settled down in earnest, and it continued without much change or noticeable abatement until late in the month. Practically every senator and congressman who spoke rang variations on the same theme, vehemently insisting that his sole objective in the controversy was peace for the United States. Whatever his attitude toward repeal of the arms embargo, no one proclaimed an enthusiasm for war—even to help the democracies. Differences of opinion related only to method!

Senator Tom Connally, Democrat, of Texas, declared that "our objective, and our only objective, is to keep out of this terrible war," and went on to inform his colleagues that the measure under consideration offered "the greatest possible assurance of any measure that can be devised by any legislative body."[105] Senator E. R. Burke, Democrat, of Nebraska, agreed with him but edged a little closer to the point by explaining that repeal of the arms embargo would lessen America's chances of involvement by shortening the war. He frankly admitted that such a move would favor "the belligerents I want favored, by giving them the chance of coming here with their ships and buying our goods."[106] More oratorically, Senator Robert Wagner, Democrat, of New York, refused to believe that the arms embargo "represented the moral judgment of the American people, our indispensable defense against war, or the symbol of our neutrality."[107]

On the other side, Senator Arthur H. Vandenberg, Republican, of Michigan, appealed to international law and denounced removal of the embargo as a violation of the principle "that the rules of a neutral cannot be prejudicially altered in the midst of a war."[108] Senator W. J.

[104] United States, Congress, Senate, Committee on Foreign Relations, *Senate Report No. 1155* (76th Cong., 2nd sess.) (Washington, D. C.: U. S. Govt. Printing Office, 1939), pp. 10–12.

[105] *Cong. Record*, LXXXV (76th Cong., 2nd sess.), 92.

[106] *Ibid.*, p. 290.   [107] *Ibid.*, p. 241.

[108] *Cong. Record*, LXXXV (76th Cong., 2nd sess.), 95. This argument draws attention to a point which was widely discussed in the fall of 1939. Authoritative opinion disagreed widely; in one poll of international lawyers, Vandenberg's position was both disputed and supported. See *New York Herald-Tribune*, Oct. 25, 1939, p. 28, cols. 5–7. For further observations on the subject, see Lawrence Preuss, "Some

Bulow, Democrat, of South Dakota, thought it would lead inevitably to another attempt by the United States to settle European "boundary disputes." [109] Senator Hiram Johnson, Republican, of California, declaimed that "with embargo repeal we are half in and half out of the war." [110]

Debates in the House added little to the Senate's exposition of the matter. Representative Louis Ludlow, Democrat, of Indiana, called the new resolution "a shining example of the interventionist ideology." [111] Representative J. W. Ditter, Republican, of Pennsylvania liked the law as it stood because it profited "by our past experiences instead of gambling on future experiments." [112]   On the other hand, Representative Luther A. Johnson, Democrat, of Texas, suggested that, if repeal had succeeded in the spring, war might not have broken out.[113]   And Representative Mary Norton, Democrat, of New Jersey, after advising her colleagues to prove their peaceful intentions by first doing away with the arms embargo, incontinently pulled out the stops and hoped that they would then join her in telling "the women of America that this Congress, by its vote, will never consent to send American boys to fight in a European war." [114]

In this manner debate continued through scores of repetitions in both the Senate and the House.   For a time it was by no means clear that congressional views had changed at all over the past few months.   But public opinion had advanced rapidly, continuing in the direction it had assumed with the seizure of Czechoslovakia in March.   And this time public opinion was given a chance to express itself more effectively.

On September 26, five days after Congress met in special session, the Union for Concerted Peace Efforts, an energetic group of prominent internationalists, undertook to form what they called the Non-partisan Committee for Peace through the Revision of the Neutrality Act.   The whole avowed purpose of this organization was expressed in its rather cumbersome title, being restricted to publicizing the weaknesses of the

---

Effects of Governmental Controls on Neutral Duties," American Society of International Law, *Proceedings, 1937*, pp. 110–115; and Clyde Eagleton, "The Duty of Impartiality on the Part of a Neutral," *American Journal of International Law*, XXXIV (Jan. 1940), 99–104.

[109] *Cong. Record*, LXXXV (76th Cong., 2nd sess.), 315.
[110] *Ibid.*, p. 630.   [113] *Ibid.*, p. 338.
[111] *Ibid.*, p. 486.   [114] *Ibid.*, p. 1192.
[112] *Ibid.*, p. 1304.

embargo clause and organizing sentiment on behalf of the cash-and-carry provision. Because their internationalist views were suspect, the organizers of the Non-partisan Committee preferred to keep their own names in the background. So William Allen White—prominent Republican from isolationist Kansas and long famous as editor, author, and confidant of the great—was persuaded to act as chairman.[115] A national headquarters was established in New York City, and its campaign started without delay. Members of the Union for Concerted Peace Efforts and others who were known to sympathize with the Committee's objectives were asked to promote the cash-and-carry idea with their friends, neighbors, and clubs, to organize meetings for discussion of the matter, to circularize local newspapers, and to bombard their senators and congressmen with letters and telegrams.[116] In this manner the Non-partisan Committee conducted an active, though brief, campaign through the month of October, always adhering to the administration's thesis that repeal of the arms embargo was intended solely to bulwark American neutrality and decrease the likelihood of the nation's getting into war.[117]

It is impossible to estimate the influence of the Non-partisan Committee upon the final outcome. The embargo might well have been repealed without its help. But Congress is always sensitive to pressure, especially systematic pressure, and in bringing public opinion to bear directly on those who controlled the decision the Committee did constitute a temporary pressure group. At all events, the new resolution was passed in the Senate on October 27, 1939, by a vote of 63 to 30. And after some disagreement and conference proceedings the House accepted it on November 3, by a vote of 273 to 172.[118] Whatever the explanation, it is certain that Congress was much closer to the prevailing trend of public opinion in adopting repeal at this time than it had been in rejecting such action the previous spring.[119]

The new act went into effect on November 4. It permitted the belligerents to purchase anything they desired in the United States, but

[115] Walter Johnson, *The Battle Against Isolation* (Chicago: Univ. Chicago Press, 1944), pp. 31–32.

[116] *Ibid.,* pp. 42, 46.   [117] *Ibid.,* p. 47.

[118] *Journal of the House* (76th Cong., 2nd and 3rd sess.), p. 43.

[119] Even the evidence transmitted to the White House by that confirmed isolationist General Robert E. Wood tends to support this conclusion. See enclosure to letter from Wood to Stephen Early, Nov. 6, 1939, MS Roosevelt Papers (Official File, Box 1561).

they had to pay cash on delivery and provide their own sea transportation. To make this restriction of American shipping even narrower, vessels of United States registry, no matter what their cargo or destination, would henceforth be totally excluded from large areas of the sea about the coastlines of belligerent countries, as such areas were designated by the President. In its repeal of the arms embargo, however, the joint resolution of November 4, 1939, was much less isolationist than its predecessor. American neutrality, though still generously hedged with self-imposed restrictions, was about to revive part of an old experiment.

VII

Thus war proved stronger than argument, and an effort which had been launched eight months before was finally crowned with success. In the same way, the stimulus of war was manifest in other aspects of American foreign policy. Save for the imposition of countervailing duties against Germany in March, the return of naval units to the Pacific in April, and such hints of stronger economic measures as appeared two months later in the government's notice of intention to abrogate the commercial treaty with Japan, American foreign policy exhibited no definite change from the spring of 1939 to the beginning of the war. Even then caution and delay were still its hallmarks, but the general confusion of the previous four years rapidly gave way to discernible purpose. The central theme of the period from September to November was repeal of the arms embargo. And repeal of the arms embargo, although heralded as a return to neutrality, was obviously calculated to provide Great Britain and France with the access to American war production which they so urgently required.

Otherwise, the American government sought to hedge against a more distant future. Its policy was based on the disturbing realization that the war had not yet assumed a dependable form. So far, it had not spread to the whole of Europe, but unless it could be restricted to existing limits, its final outcome would obviously be decided by states that were yet neutral rather than by the ones already committed. Hoping to control these portentous uncertainties, the United States in the autumn of 1939 adopted certain policies. The Soviet Union would be restrained wherever restraint was practicable, but never at risk of driving it further into the arms of Germany. Italian neutrality would be sedulously cultivated. For this, and for such other purposes as might arise, connections with the Vatican would be broadened. No peace initiative would be undertaken, at least until the Allies' bargaining position improved. And Japan would be put off with new warnings until the United States grew more certain of what it faced in Europe.

CHAPTER IV

The Growth of Partiality

I

By the early part of November 1939 the war in Europe had entered its winter doldrums. The German Army had ceased to move after destroying Poland, and the rest of the conflict was not impressive. Aerial warfare remained lackadaisical. Battle at sea was an unexciting routine of blockade and contraband orders, punctuated by occasional mine explosions and limited submarine forays. Hostilities on the western front did not extend much beyond patrol activity. General inertia, combined with talk of a negotiated peace, made the war a much less fearsome thing than it had been in September. Under these circumstances, Americans regained some of their former assurance about the nation's safety; and as this feeling grew stronger with prolongation of the stalemate, many half-discarded isolationist notions enjoyed renewed popularity.

According to an analysis of public opinion surveys made by Professor Hadley Cantril, of Princeton University, the American fear of the consequences of a possible German victory declined somewhat between September 1939 and April 1940. Since confidence in the ability of France and Great Britain to win a clear-cut victory fell off to about the same extent,[1] it seemed apparent that Germany's quiescence after the battle of Poland had produced a hope that Hitler desired to go no further than absolutely necessary in the larger struggle against Great Britain and France. American public opinion lost none of its overwhelming preference for an Allied victory. But the proportion which favored armed intervention—even to avert a threatened Allied defeat —decreased, according to the American Institute of Public Opinion, from 44 per cent in September 1939 to 23 per cent in February 1940.[2] In

[1] Hadley Cantril, "America Faces the War: A Study in Public Opinion," *Public Opinion Quarterly,* IV (Sept. 1940), chart 1, 396, and chart 3, 398.

[2] *Public Opinion Quarterly,* IV (June 1940), 360.

November about 59 per cent of the people still thought that Congress should not give up the special control over foreign policy which it had assumed by virtue of the neutrality act. That this confidence in the lawmakers had limits was revealed, however, when the proportion of Americans desiring a war-referendum amendment rose from 40 to 60 per cent between early December and the end of January.[3]

While it was undoubtedly real, this abatement of public nervousness as crisis trailed off into relative calm was also deceptive, for the apathy of American sentiment was the direct result of apathy on the part of the belligerents. Fluctuations in popular thought over the last few months indicated pretty certainly that new German successes would make new inroads upon the isolationist belief. America's fundamental distrust of German aims can hardly be overemphasized in this connection. Whether the Nazis had actually laid plans for eventual attack on transatlantic areas could not be known, but in final analysis the answer to this question was unimportant. The German government's reliance on force, its demonstrated faithlessness in international relations, its bitter hostility toward the democratic way of life, and its open threat to the balance of power which had contributed so generously to American security in the past rendered the specter of German victory a fearsome thing even to those who declined to recognize it as a serious possibility.[4] While still deeply reluctant to fight, the American people had admitted, albeit half unconsciously, that they might eventually have to choose between intervention and something worse. But the war had not yet made this choice necessary, and it now seemed that the decision might be comfortably postponed.

In consequence, the external aspect of American policy from November 1939 to the collapse of France in June 1940 was highly reminiscent of the period 1914–1917, being concerned with technical disputes over neutral rights at sea, fruitless efforts to limit or end the war lest its effects become truly disastrous, and attempts to discourage Japanese aggression in the Far East. Behind these resemblances, however, it was different. Despite its powerful isolationism, the country from the beginning sensed a much greater nearness to Europe and its problems than it had during the First World War at any time before 1917. The Roosevelt administration, moreover, had at once slanted its foreign

---

[3] *Ibid.* (Mar. 1940), pp. 103, 109; (June 1940), p. 359.

[4] For a discussion of Hitler's ultimate aims, see Hans L. Trefousse, *Germany and American Neutrality, 1939–1941* (New York: Bookman Associates, 1951), chap. i.

policy toward the nation's decisive preference for an Anglo-French victory and was already working in practical terms to assay the other great neutrals as potential friends or enemies.

II

Using authority conferred upon him by the joint resolution of November 4, 1939, President Roosevelt on that same day proclaimed the existence of a combat zone extending from the southwestern tip of Norway to the northern coast of Spain and westward to the 20th meridian, thus excluding American merchant ships from the waters surrounding the British Isles, from the North Sea, from the entrance to the Baltic, and from most of the Bay of Biscay. On April 10, 1940, as soon as the German occupation of Norway carried the war to the extreme arctic fringe of the Continent, this zone was extended northward to include Norwegian waters and a generous additional sector of the Arctic Ocean, making the Russian ports of Archangel and Murmansk, as well as all Norwegian and Finnish harbors, inaccessible to United States shipping. And on June 11, 1940, during the collapse of France, new combat zones which covered the entire Mediterranean Sea and the southern entrance to the Red Sea were proclaimed.[5] For the time being, however, the Mediterranean was still open, as were Norway and the northern approaches to Finland and Russia. So far as domestic rulings were concerned, American trade could still reach the greater part of neutral Europe.

But beyond the restrictions made in Washington stood the far greater ones imposed by Great Britain and France. Since goods entering neutral areas contiguous to belligerent territory can always be transshipped to new and less innocent destinations, the British and French governments, as in the First World War, placed under searching scrutiny all traffic between continental Europe and the rest of the world. Hence all American ships engaged in trade with the European neutrals were constantly confronted by the rules and restrictions of the Allied

---

[5] Proclamation No. 2374, Nov. 4, 1939, United States, National Archives, *Federal Register* (Washington, D. C.: U. S. Govt. Printing Office, 1936——), IV, 4493; Proclamation No. 2394, Apr. 10, 1940, *ibid.,* V, 1399–1400; and Proclamation No. 2410, June 11, 1940, *ibid.,* pp. 2209–2210. See also Neutrality Act Zone Map, June 13, 1940, World Peace Foundation, *Documents on American Foreign Relations, 1939–1940,* ed. S. Shepard Jones and Denys P. Myers (Boston: World Peace Foundation, 1940), p. 682.

system of maritime control and forced to endure the vexatious physical activities of the Allied blockade.

The inevitability of this situation had, of course, been recognized at the outset. As has been mentioned previously, the British government had launched vigorous efforts early in September 1939 to obtain American coöperation with the Allied blockade policies, and it had agreed in this connection to a plan for regular meetings between British and American experts who would try to settle conflicts of interest as they arose. On the whole, this scheme worked reasonably well, although it was subjected to considerable stress from time to time.

The largest initial problem grew out of Great Britain's request that American merchant vessels bound to Europe call voluntarily at one of the contraband-control bases which the British Navy was setting up to facilitate the examination of cargoes, for some of these bases lay inside the combat zone proclaimed by President Roosevelt on November 4. Obviously, continued insistence that American vessels enter these areas, for whatever purpose, in defiance of American law might soon produce a situation which would fall beyond the competence of the joint board of experts and result in unnecessary tension. Nevertheless, on November 9 London called attention anew to the Allied system of contraband control and reserved all its rights in the matter, thus intimating rather clearly that the program would remain in effect.[6]

A rapid succession of other developments complicated the issue still further. Unprepared for a strong submarine campaign when the war broke out, and somewhat indifferent to its value in any event, Hitler had started with a surprisingly cautious underseas policy, taking special care that neutrals sustained no unnecessary harm. But thanks to the proddings of Grand Admiral Raeder, caution was gradually abandoned, until, by the end of the year, all ships found within the combat zone designated by the United States, except fully lighted ships of neutral nations, were regarded as fair game.[7] This intensification of submarine

[6] Not all the correspondence in this sequence has been published, but its substance is adequately discussed in Hull's note to Lothian, Dec. 14, 1939, United States, Department of State, *Department of State Bulletin* (Washington, D. C.: U. S. Govt. Printing Office, 1939——), II (Jan. 6, 1940), 4.

[7] Reflections of the Commander-in-Chief, Navy, on the outbreak of war, Sept. 3, 1939, United States, Department of the Navy, *Fuehrer Conferences on Matters Dealing with the German Navy, 1939–1941* (Washington, D. C.: Issued in mimeographed form by the Office of Naval Intelligence, 1947), 1939, p. 1. Also conference of the Commander-in-Chief, Navy, with the Fuehrer, Sept. 7, 1939, *ibid.*, pp. 3–4; and report of the Commander-in-Chief, Navy, to the Fuehrer, Dec. 30, 1939, annex 1, *ibid.*, p. 66. Cf.

warfare, combined with the unusual damage wrought in October and November by Germany's lavish use of floating magnetic mines, was bound to provoke retaliation, and on November 27 the Allies formally extended their blockade of German imports to cover exports as well—including German goods exported through neutral countries.[8] This effectively brought all neutral trade in European waters squarely under British surveillance and multiplied the likelihood of dispute.

The United States protested on December 8, holding that "interference with neutral vessels on the high seas by belligerent powers must be justified upon some recognized belligerent right." In view of the generous limits of the combat zone from which American vessels were excluded by domestic law, the note went on, it was difficult to see how any breach of blockade could arise.[9] Hull further pointed out on December 14 that American ships were prohibited by domestic law from entering contraband-control bases within the combat zone, and interpreted the British note of November 9 to mean that Britain intended to divert American vessels to such bases by force if necessary. Under the circumstances, he added, the United States felt that "accommodation and flexibility" were in order for the British government.[10] On December 25 the British Ministry of Economic Defense conceded that in exceptional circumstances, which it refused to define in advance, individual ships might be exempted, on application, from the order of November 27. But it declined to consider any more generalized withdrawal from its position.[11]

Two days later Washington raised another sore point; it objected strongly to the British habit of seizing and censoring United States mails addressed to neutral countries.[12] London replied on January 17 with what amounted to a refusal to alter this practice either.[13] On January 20 the State Department summed up its grievances in a long note which alleged that contraband control at Gibraltar was needlessly

---

Samuel Eliot Morison, *The Battle of the Atlantic, 1939–1943* (Boston: Little, Brown, and Co., 1947), pp. 9–10.

[8] Order-in-Council of the United Kingdom, Nov. 27, 1939, *Documents on American Foreign Relations, 1939–1940*, pp. 705–706.

[9] Kennedy to Halifax, Dec. 8, 1939, *Department of State Bulletin*, I (Dec. 9, 1939), 651.

[10] Hull to Lothian, Dec. 14, 1939, *ibid.*, II (Jan. 6, 1940), 4.

[11] Ministry of Economic Defense, United Kingdom, to U. S. Embassy at London, Dec. 25, 1939, *ibid.*, p. 5.

[12] Kennedy to Halifax, Dec. 27, 1939, *ibid.*, p. 3.

[13] Halifax to Kennedy, Jan. 17, 1940, *ibid.* (Jan. 27, 1940), pp. 91–93.

slow and inefficient, that American vessels had been forced into the belligerent port of Marseilles and made to unload, that British censorship of mails had delayed official letters addressed to United States missions abroad, and that Italian ships were receiving preferential treatment at the hands of the British Navy in the Mediterranean area.[14]

By this time each side had largely completed its case. There was little more to say; and since it was obvious that the dispute would never be allowed to provoke serious ill-feeling in any event, the tempo of the exchanges diminished gradually until renewed activity on the Continent in April and May and Britain's withdrawal of contraband control over American vessels in the Mediterranean on May 24, 1940, directed energies into more important channels. Throughout their course, these dwindling altercations had been so inconclusive and good-natured that they were plainly more for the record than anything else. A London dispatch published in the *New York Times* on February 15, 1940, even suggested the existence of collusion when it asserted that Lord Lothian, the British Ambassador in Washington, regularly discussed the content of his government's notes with the American State Department in advance of their formal presentation.[15]

The true measure of Anglo-American relations during this period is not to be found in the diplomatic struggle over neutral rights but rather in the physical coöperation made possible by repeal of the arms embargo. Immediately after passage of the joint resolution of November 4, Britain and France resumed the arms purchases in the United States which had been interrupted by the outbreak of war in September. Even though new orders placed by Great Britain were not so large as had been anticipated, the American government tended to become more or less directly involved in this program as the weeks passed. For on December 6, 1939, President Roosevelt established a special liaison committee made up of the Secretary of the Treasury and representatives of the War, Navy, and Treasury departments to help secure the latest model weapons, watch over dollar balances, and generally expedite the labors of the British and French purchasing commissions.[16]

During the seven-month period between November 1939 and June 1940 the United States found little occasion for direct dispute with

---

[14] *Aide-mémoire,* Jan. 20, 1940, *ibid.,* p. 93.

[15] *New York Times,* Feb. 15, 1940, p. 3, cols. 5–6.

[16] Edward R. Stettinius, Jr., *Lend-Lease: Weapon for Victory* (New York: Macmillan Co., 1944), pp. 20–21.

Germany on any significant issue. This was owing in considerable measure to deliberate restraint on the part of Germany. Neutral America certainly favored the Allies and might even render them important material assistance, but it could never throw anything like its full weight into the struggle without a declaration of war. Hitler recognized this fact at the outset; however hostile he might be in the ultimate sense, he was determined to cultivate American neutrality for an indefinite period. Nor does he appear to have abandoned this principle of action until almost the day of Pearl Harbor.

But although this objective was kept constantly in view, the Nazi government never wholly confined itself to soft dealing with the United States. It always sought to embarrass the Roosevelt administration by supporting isolationist sentiment in America and, from the summer of 1940, became increasingly occupied with the notion of immobilizing American policy in Europe by encouraging Japan to bring greater pressure in Asia. During the early stages of the war, however, its overwhelming desire was to avoid sharp differences of any kind.

As early as the summer of 1939, even before the war started, there was a notable moderation in the tone of the German press on most subjects pertaining to the United States. A similar change was evident in the public utterances of Nazi officials and in their new avoidance of diplomatic controversy with the American government. It is possible that repeal of the arms embargo in November 1939 for the obvious benefit of Great Britain and France evoked no protest because repeal carried with it the compensatory advantage of excluding American merchant ships from those parts of the Atlantic Ocean where they could be most useful to Germany's enemies. But there is no such explanation for Berlin's neglect to make an issue of those American patrol activities which contributed to the loss of several German vessels within the Atlantic neutrality zone. An outstanding example of Nazi forbearance in this connection was the episode of the German liner *Columbus,* which, in December 1939, was scuttled by her own captain about 450 miles east of Cape May after the United States cruiser *Tuscaloosa* had trailed her all the way from Vera Cruz, giving regular broadcasts of her position throughout the voyage.[17]

Caution also dominated the major aspect of German naval policy; although submarine warfare had gained considerable momentum by the end of the year, this intensification was so nicely adjusted to mari-

[17] See Trefousse, *Germany and American Neutrality,* pp. 26–35, 61.

time developments in the United States that even the U-boat failed to provide a real diplomatic clash.

In view of existing law and proposed changes, the outlook for keeping American merchant vessels fully employed was admittedly not good as the war started. Hence a fairly energetic transfer of American-owned ships to foreign registry by sale or by other means got under way before the end of September. Thanks to Hull's personal intervention, however, this process was slowed to some extent after passage of the new neutrality act in November—especially where a bona fide transfer of ownership could not be shown to accompany change of registry.[18] This limitation of transfer, combined with the relative inactivity of U-boats during the first months of the war, kept the risk of such practices to a minimum. Besides, transferred ships sailed under foreign flags, whatever their real ownership, so their fate was not a matter of which the United States government could take official cognizance in any event. Ships which kept their American registry, on the other hand, were prohibited by domestic law from entering the only real danger areas that existed at this time and were therefore about as safe as ever from German attack. Apart from the difficulties growing out of the Allied blockade, the only serious problem raised in the Atlantic before the summer of 1940 had to do with violations of the huge neutrality zone established by the Declaration of Panama.

The most spectacular invasion of this zone centered about the *Graf Spee* incident. The German pocket battleship *Graf Spee,* which had preyed on Allied commerce in southern waters almost from the beginning of the war, was intercepted by three British cruisers on December 13, 1939, at a point about three hundred miles off Montevideo and well inside the inter-American security belt. The cruisers attacked and kept up a running fight in the direction of the Uruguayan coast, but the battered Nazi vessel was able to hold off her enemies well enough to slip into Montevideo harbor just after midnight. While the British warships lay outside with instructions from London to resume the fight anywhere beyond the three-mile limit if opportunity offered, the German commander landed his dead and wounded and endeavored to ob-

[18] For data on such transfers between October 26, 1939, and April 10, 1940, see United States, Congress, *Congressional Record* (Washington, D. C.: U. S. Govt. Printing Office, 1874———), LXXXVI (76th Cong., 3rd sess.), 2846–2849. Cf. John C. De-Wilde, "The War and American Shipping," *Foreign Policy Reports,* XVI (Apr. 1, 1940), 23; and Cordell Hull, *The Memoirs of Cordell Hull* (New York: Macmillan Co., 1948), I, 699.

tain an extension of the time that he was allowed to remain in port. But the neutral Uruguayan government was adamant, and as the seventy-two-hour period of grace ran out, the *Graf Spee* was forced to leave her refuge. Since her chance of evading her pursuers appeared negligible, she was blown up about seven miles offshore in accordance with orders from Berlin.[19]

Warships of belligerent nations had fought in forbidden waters, and this provided an opportunity for calling new attention to the extended inviolability claimed for the Western Hemisphere. The United States at once joined the twenty other American republics in framing a protest against such invasions of their neutrality belt, the actual note being transmitted to France, Great Britain, and Germany by the President of Panama. But this complaint was founded on weak grounds. Extension of neutrality over so wide an area of the high seas was not greatly unlike a paper blockade unless the zone could be effectively patrolled, and this condition obviously had not been met.[20] As a result, the combined protest was rejected by all three recipients, though Hitler, in consonance with his policy of avoiding trouble with the United States, did give his commanders secret orders against initiating action within the security belt.[21] Immediately afterwards, steps were taken to implement the Declaration of Panama by denying port facilities in the Americas to any ships which failed to observe the rules.[22] This move did not pass beyond the stage of discussion, however. Like most neutral pretensions, the inter-American safety zone was more a theory than a fact.

[19] This is based in large part upon the account by Winston Churchill, who was then First Lord of the Admiralty and in direct contact with the British ships participating in the *Graf Spee* affair. See Winston S. Churchill, *The Gathering Storm* (Boston: Houghton Mifflin Co., 1948), pp. 517–526. The commander of the *Graf Spee* was ordered by Raeder to stay in neutral waters as long as possible, but to take no risk of internment. Owing to the friendlier disposition of the Argentine government, he was to attempt to reach Buenos Aires when forced to leave Uruguayan waters, scuttling his ship if capture seemed unavoidable. See report of the Commander-in-Chief, Navy, to the Fuehrer, Dec. 14, 1939, *Fuehrer Conferences, 1939*, pp. 60–61. See also Uruguay, Foreign Office, *The Uruguayan Blue Book: Outline of Events Prior to the Sinking of the "Admiral Graf Spee" and the Internment of the Merchant Vessel "Tacoma"* (London: Hutchinson and Co., 1940).

[20] Cf. Churchill, *The Gathering Storm*, pp. 513–514.

[21] The texts of the British, French, and German replies are given in *Department of State Bulletin*, II (Feb. 17, 1940), 199–205. See also Trefousse, *Germany and American Neutrality*, p. 41.

[22] Recommendation VII of the Inter-American Neutrality Committee, Apr. 27, 1940, *Documents on American Foreign Relations, 1939–1940*, pp. 137–138.

But as events were to prove, the theory of the neutrality belt was its most useful aspect. The impending collapse of the western front in Europe was about to change the whole nature of the Atlantic war. Adjustments in United States naval policy to meet new conditions would soon make the existing realities of the safety zone largely irrelevant in any event. Beginning in the summer of 1940, the American government would tend more and more to regard the eastern limits of the Western Hemisphere as coinciding roughly with the eastern limits of the inter-American zone and to carry on nonbelligerent, but unneutral, defense activities within this belt. By almost inevitable development, therefore, what was initially conceived as an oversize neutrality area became a vast stretch of defensive waters in the emerging battle of the Atlantic.

III

Another significant phase of American policy at the end of 1939 and the beginning of 1940 centered about the Russo-Finnish war. Lasting from the end of November to the middle of March, this conflict brought to sharp focus a number of long-standing differences between Washington and Moscow. But, as was foreshadowed by its actions in September and October, the attitude of the United States government was determined throughout by its vision of future alignments; it never approached a definite break with the Soviet Union in either political or commercial affairs. Efforts were made to prevent the spread of hostilities to Finland, and the United States even displayed a marked partiality for the Finnish cause when these efforts failed. But action which might encourage Russia to lean more heavily on Germany, or which might otherwise hamper a later *rapprochement* with the democracies, was studiously avoided.

Since it was obvious where American sympathies would lie in the event of a clash between Soviet Russia and Finland, the Finnish government from the outset carried on strenuous efforts to enlist the diplomatic and material support of the United States. With the prospect of Soviet action imminent, the Finnish Minister, Hjalmar Procopé, told Hull on October 5 that Russia was expected to raise the question of bases on Finnish islands in the Gulf of Finland and of securing access to the Åland Islands. He tried to obtain from the Secretary "some kind of express or implied promise to say something" in such an event, but Hull offered no encouragement.[23] Procopé renewed his efforts two days later, announcing that the Finnish Foreign Minister had been invited to Moscow to discuss political questions, and again Hull kept him at a distance. Despite its "genuine friendship" toward Finland, the Secretary stated, the American government could not project itself "into political discussions and controversies between two other countries." [24] This set the tone of American policy for the next two months. The most President Roosevelt felt able to do before hostilities started was to address a message to Soviet President Mikhail Kalinin on October 11 asking the Russians to be moderate in their prospective demands, a plea which was entirely without avail.[25]

On November 29, three days after the frontier clash on the Karelian Isthmus which finally launched the war, Hull took another short step forward with an offer of mediation,[26] and Ambassador Steinhardt talked with Molotov on December 1 in a futile effort to gain acceptance for such a plan.[27] The same day, Roosevelt publicly deplored the fact that the use of force was spreading and that "wanton disregard for law" was "still on the march." [28] At the same time, the possibility of severing diplomatic relations with Russia was given considerable study, and Welles, at least, favored such action. But Roosevelt and Hull preferred to be cautious, and the question was dropped.[29]

Meanwhile, on December 1, the Soviet Union recognized the "Finnish People's Government," a purely artificial creation organized at Moscow's bidding by one Otto Kuusinen, a Finnish Communist who had lived in Russia for twenty years. Holding that it merely supported this regime against the "illegal" regular government of Finland, Russia avoided a formal declaration of war.[30] The American government once more took prompt advantage of this fiction to withhold the appli-

[23] Memorandum by Hull, Oct. 5, 1939, MS Department of State (860D.51/362).

[24] Memorandum by Hull, Oct. 7, 1939, MS Department of State (760D.61/239).

[25] Hull, *Memoirs,* I, 703; and telegram from Steinhardt, Oct. 12, 1939, MS Department of State (760D.61/248).

[26] Statement by Hull, Nov. 29, 1939, *Department of State Bulletin,* I (Dec. 2, 1939), 609.

[27] David J. Dallin, *Soviet Russia's Foreign Policy, 1939–1942,* tr. Leon Denman (New Haven: Yale Univ. Press, 1942), p. 143.

[28] Statement by the President, Dec. 1, 1939, *Department of State Bulletin,* I (Dec. 2, 1939), 609.

[29] William L. Langer and S. Everett Gleason, *The Challenge to Isolation, 1937–1940* (New York: Harper and Bros., for the Council on Foreign Relations, 1952), p. 332.

[30] Dallin, *Soviet Foreign Policy,* p. 133.

cation of its neutrality law from a situation in which Russia was concerned. As a result, neither belligerent was placed under the disabilities of cash-and-carry. In theory, at least, American shipping was still free to enter ports in both countries. This resembled the practice observed toward hostilities in China for the past two and one-half years, but here it was aimed less at helping the victim than at maintaining passable relations with the aggressor. As Hull later noted, ". . . we still wanted to refrain from making Russia a legal belligerent. I could not but feel that the basic antagonisms between Communist Russia and Nazi Germany were so deep and Hitler's ambition so boundless, that eventually Russia would come over to the side of the Allies. We had to be careful not to push her in the other direction." [31]

Within the limits of these hopes, nevertheless, official dissatisfaction with Soviet policy could be revealed by numerous lesser means. Since 1933 the United States had patiently borne the vexatious restrictions imposed on the movement and activity of its consular agents in Russia. Now it began to retaliate in kind. Acting on instructions, Steinhardt refused a *laissez-passer* to a new Russian vice consul assigned to New York. Accordingly, the latter's baggage was subjected to customs inspection as he entered the United States. In Washington, Soviet Ambassador Constantine Oumansky at once protested this denial of customary privilege, arguing that most-favored-nation treatment was proper in such cases. Russia, he said, inflicted no greater disabilities upon American consular officials than upon the like representatives of any other government.[32] But Hull stood firm on the principle of even-handed reciprocity, and Roosevelt backed him up. In a memorandum of December 22, he advised the Secretary of State to match every Russian annoyance with its equivalent and to inform Oumansky that, in view of Russia's current attitude, "the President honestly wonders whether the Soviet Government considers it worthwhile to continue diplomatic relations." [33]

Amid this verbal fencing, Roosevelt called new attention to the moral embargo which he had erected in July 1938 against countries guilty of bombing civilians. Japan had been the target then, but since Russia was widely accused of employing the same freedom in air attacks

[31] Hull, *Memoirs,* I, 707.

[32] Memorandum for the Secretary of State, Dec. 16, 1939, MS Department of State (124.61/144½).

[33] Memorandum by Roosevelt, Dec. 22, 1939, MS Department of State (124.61/144½); and Hull, *Memoirs,* I, 708–709.

on Finnish cities, the new application of his remarks was inescapable. He mentioned the subject generally in a brief statement on December 2,[34] and the State Department on December 15 formally expressed the hope that no one would apply for licenses to export aircraft, aeronautical equipment, aerial bombs, or torpedoes to such countries.[35]   As it applied to Russia, this moral embargo was to last more than a year. The State Department further announced on December 20 that it was halting the "delivery to certain countries of plans, plants, manufacturing rights, or technical information required for the production of high quality aviation gasoline."[36]

While the last move appears to have been directed primarily against Japan, American officials, the President especially, continued to study the means of building up economic pressure against Russia.   On January 27 Roosevelt raised the question of openly curtailing shipments of scrap iron and gasoline to the Soviet Union,[37] and suggested on February 1 that a policy of chartering no ships to Russia might be used instead.[38]   Although this plan was not adopted as an official program, the President did obtain the assurance that no ships would be chartered to the Soviet Union "for good and sufficient domestic reasons."[39]

The Finns, by contrast, received distinctly preferential treatment. According to William C. Bullitt, Russia's expulsion from the League of Nations on December 14 was due at least in part to Roosevelt's influence.[40]   But this, even if true, appears to have been an unacknowledged undertaking; armaments and money were always viewed as the main subjects of possible American-Finnish coöperation.   As a matter of fact, Procopé first began his attempts to obtain an American loan in September 1939.[41]   European requests for money to be used for war purposes

---

[34] Statement by the President, Dec. 2, 1939, Franklin D. Roosevelt, *The Public Papers and Addresses of Franklin D. Roosevelt, 1939,* comp. S. I. Rosenman (New York: Macmillan Co., 1941), p. 589.

[35] Department of State to aircraft manufacturers, etc., Dec. 15, 1939, *Department of State Bulletin,* I (Dec. 16, 1939), 685.

[36] Press release, Dec. 20, 1939, *ibid.* (Dec. 23, 1939), p. 714.

[37] Memorandum by Roosevelt, Jan. 27, 1940, MS Roosevelt Papers (Official File, Box 220).

[38] Abstract of presidential memorandum, Feb. 1, 1940, MS Roosevelt Papers (Official File, Box 434–C).

[39] Memorandum by Berle, Feb. 20, 1940, MS Roosevelt Papers (Secretary's File, Box 62).

[40] William C. Bullitt, "How We Won the War and Lost the Peace," *Life,* XXV (Aug. 30, 1948), 91.

[41] Langer and Gleason, *The Challenge to Isolation,* p. 321.

were still most distasteful to Congress, however, and early in October the Minister was referred to Jesse Jones to discuss a possible credit from the Reconstruction Finance Corporation.[42] Here the matter rested until December 13, when the Export-Import Bank granted Finland a limited credit of $10 million for the purchase of agricultural products in the United States.[43] But Finland, needing money for war materials, had already submitted new requests which on December 28 culminated in a formal application for a loan of $60 million.[44]

The Finns wanted more than the American government was prepared to grant, but they continued to receive favors on a small scale as the question of financial aid underwent further study. During the last half of December the United States Navy undertook to sell Finland forty-four planes,[45] and a scheme was later approved whereby the American grain bought with the credit of December 13 would be sold to Great Britain for dollars which, in turn, could be used for arms purchases in the United States.[46] Turning once more to the loan project, Roosevelt on January 16, 1940, personally urged the Vice President and the Speaker of the House to accept his view that new credits should be extended to Finland,[47] and he continued this offensive with a public statement on February 10 that 98 per cent of the American people sympathized wholeheartedly with the Finnish cause.[48] The truth of this remark was not doubted even in Moscow, for the Russian government had been so disturbed by anti-Soviet feeling in America that it had removed its pavilion from the New York World's Fair shortly after the war started.

Congressional sentiment was also strong, even stronger in some respects than that of the executive departments. On February 7, 1940, a member of the House proposed an amendment to the State Department's supply bill withdrawing all financial support from the American Embassy in Moscow.[49] This move was obviously designed to force a

---

[42] Memorandum by Hull, Oct. 5, 1939, MS Department of State (860D.51/362).

[43] See table of loans granted by the Export-Import Bank in 1939–1940, *Documents on American Foreign Relations, 1939–1940*, p. 554.

[44] Hull to Procopé, Dec. 29, 1939, MS Department of State (860D.51/388).

[45] *New York Times*, Dec. 19, 1939, p. 1, cols. 3–4.

[46] Memorandum by Moffat, Jan. 16, 1940, MS Department of State (860D.51/404).

[47] Roosevelt to Garner and Bankhead, Jan. 16, 1940, *Department of State Bulletin*, II (Jan. 20, 1940), 55.

[48] Speech by the President, Feb. 10, 1940, Franklin D. Roosevelt, *The Public Papers and Addresses of Franklin D. Roosevelt, 1940*, comp. S. I. Rosenman (New York: Macmillan Co., 1941), p. 92.

[49] *Cong. Record*, LXXXVI (76th Cong., 3rd sess.), 1173.

severance of diplomatic relations with Russia, and it so struck legislative fancies that it was defeated by only three votes after the administration brought pressure against its passage.[50]   Meanwhile, Congress responded to the President's fiscal suggestions, and with its assent new credits of $20 million were extended to Finland on March 2.[51]

All these moves bespoke American sympathy for the Finnish cause. But whatever their value as gestures of moral support, they could not enable the Finns to stand indefinitely against the overwhelming numbers of Soviet Russia.   Neither could anything else.   By the beginning of February Russia was using some thirty infantry divisions on the Karelian front, as well as considerable artillery and armor.   It was clear that not even the expeditionary force which Great Britain and France contemplated sending to Finland would be enough to turn the tide.[52]   Besides, this would have merged the northern war with the greater struggle in the south; and war between the Allies and the Soviet Union would have constituted a serious blow to the Russian policy of the United States.   Accordingly, Washington supported new peace efforts at the beginning of March.[53]

Its role was not large at any point.   Arthur Schoenfeld in Helsinki and Steinhardt in Moscow followed the development of these talks as closely as possible,[54] but the American government consciously strove to avoid giving an impression that it was advising the Finns.[55]   United States policy, therefore, contributed little to the success of the negotiations; they succeeded because Finnish resistance was now declining rapidly, because Russia had achieved all immediate objectives, and because neither country desired involvement in the general European war.[56]   For much the same reason—a compelling wish to keep the European conflict from spreading to the Scandinavian Peninsula— Sweden also did what it could to encourage a settlement.[57]   As a

---

[50] Dallin, *Soviet Foreign Policy*, p. 179.

[51] Act to provide for increasing the lending authority of the Export-Import Bank, Mar. 2, 1940, *Documents on American Foreign Relations, 1939–1940*, p. 392.

[52] See John H. Wuorinen, ed., *Finland and World War II, 1939–1944* (New York: Ronald Press Co., 1948), pp. 70–72.

[53] Hull, *Memoirs*, I, 742.

[54] Schoenfeld to Hull, Mar. 4, 1940, and Hull to Steinhardt, Mar. 7, 1940, MS Department of State (760D.61/1201 and 1228B).

[55] Steinhardt to Hull, and Hull to Steinhardt, Mar. 8, 1940, MS Department of State (760D.61/1225).

[56] *Finland and World War II*, pp. 72–73.

[57] Dallin, *Soviet Foreign Policy*, pp. 184–185.   Also see *Finland and World War II*, pp. 74–77.

result, agreement was reached through Finland's acceptance on March 12 of terms which seriously undermined its strategic position and truncated its industrial area but which failed to destroy its independence.

That the war stopped when it did was certainly favorable to the objectives of American policy. Nevertheless, it was growing increasingly difficult to characterize America's relations with the Soviet Union as friendly, and Russia's official attitude during the next few weeks made it perfectly evident that relations could be improved by nothing short of abject submission to the Kremlin's desires in matters of trade. On March 28 Steinhardt was handed a memorandum on Russia's commercial grievances against the United States. In this document the Soviet government complained about the moral embargo, the obstacles encountered by Russian specialists who wished to visit American industrial plants, restrictions on the export from the United States of essential raw materials, and American policy regarding the charter of vessels to the Soviet Union. These protests were immediately taken up in Washington by the tactless and overbearing Oumansky, who developed them orally in two interviews with State Department officials at the beginning of April. But since he obtained no assurance that the United States was prepared to let Moscow dictate its foreign commercial policy, the tension in American-Russian relations did not slacken.[58]

IV

As the small northern war got under way in December 1939, the United States government resumed its search for a means of influencing the greater one at the heart of the Continent. At the same time, it continued its review of Italy's place in the scheme of things and its study of closer relations between White House and Vatican. By the end of 1939 these three questions seemed more intimately connected than ever.

The belief that Italy formed an essential link between Germany and the democracies was strengthened by Mussolini's persistent and ostentatious reserve toward the Russo-German nonaggression pact. In No-

[58] Memorandum prepared for the Secretary of State, Apr. 1, 1940, and memorandum by Hull, Apr. 2, 1940, MS Department of State (711.61/726). Also see memorandum of conversation between Feis, Moffat, and Henderson, on the one hand, and Oumansky and Gromyko, on the other, Apr. 4, 1940, MS Department of State (700.00116—M.E./202).

vember and December Italian newspapers mounted a sustained attack against Bolshevism. In the latter month the Duce even sent Finland a small number of Italian planes.[59] Nor was this mere window dressing, as Mussolini revealed in a personal letter to Hitler written January 4, 1940.[60] It was also believed that the Italian nation foresaw much greater benefits in neutrality, continued for an indefinite time, than in war on any terms. Mussolini did much to encourage such a feeling among the Italian people throughout the autumn,[61] and Ciano gave evidence of official coolness toward both Germany and the war in a speech to the Chamber of Deputies on December 15. Accusing Hitler of trickery, the Foreign Minster complained that Germany, when signing the Pact of Steel in May, had pledged itself not to provoke war before 1943. He also mentioned his annoyance concerning the new friendship between Germany and Russia. While Mussolini had been given advance knowledge of German plans for an understanding with the Soviet Union, Hitler had not kept him informed of the progress of negotiations, and the actual terms of the treaty differed greatly from what he had been led to expect.[62] In addition, the American government continued to hear echoes of the peace talk which had been in the air since October, and it received word from the French Foreign Office on December 14 that Mussolini was about to initiate a move to end the war.[63]

These were only straws. But they did form a kind of pattern, and the design was supplemented by the trend of relations between the Italian government and the Holy See. As has already been noted, Mussolini's neutrality and his unabashed anticommunism had attracted favorable notice from the Vatican ever since the outbreak of the war. The direction of his policy in November and December strengthened him still further in papal esteem. By the end of the year relations between the Vatican and Rome were so cordial that the Pope exchanged visits with the Italian King and Queen in late December.[64] This made it seem plainer than ever that any effort to keep Mussolini from en-

---

[59] Camille M. Cianfarra, *The Vatican and the War* (New York: E. P. Dutton and Co., 1944), pp. 201–202.

[60] Mussolini to Hitler, Jan. 4, 1940, Adolf Hitler and Benito Mussolini, *Les Lettres secrètes échangées par Hitler et Mussolini*, with introd. by André François-Poncet (Paris: Éditions du Pavois, 1946), pp. 55–56.

[61] Cianfarra, *The Vatican and the War*, p. 204.

[62] *Ibid.*, pp. 204–205.   [63] Hull, *Memoirs*, I, 712–713.

[64] Cianfarra, *The Vatican and the War*, p. 206.

tering the war—or, better yet, to ascertain the basis of a compromise peace using the Italian dictator as middleman—stood to profit from the Holy See's coöperation. Thus all three projects drew together as the holiday season passed.

Striking while the iron was hot, Roosevelt first of all made arrangements for systematic communication with the Pope and his Secretary of State. Even if larger hopes should fail to materialize, this would give him regular access to one of the best information centers in the world. The United States had maintained no formal diplomatic relations with the Vatican since 1868, and it was certain that their reëstablishment would cause alarm in the more strongly Protestant sections of the country. So, although the President had considered going back to the earlier relationship by sending the Pope a regularly accredited diplomatic agent, he now decided to stress the informality of his arrangements and took Hull's advice about sending a personal representative who would merely carry the rank of Ambassador. For the new post he selected Myron C. Taylor, an Episcopalian and former chairman of the board of United States Steel, a man who was thoroughly at home in Europe and who had maintained a house in Florence for many years.[65] To disarm criticism still further, his decision was made public in a Christmas letter to the Pope which was released simultaneously with almost identical letters to the president of the Federal Council of Churches of Christ in America and to the president of the Jewish Theological Seminary of America, urging a close association between government and organized religion to deal with the great problems lying ahead. Pope Pius expressed his satisfaction with the presidential design in his Christmas message to the College of Cardinals and on January 7, 1940, sent Roosevelt his formal agreement to receive Taylor.[66]

President Roosevelt's ideas on the question of American participation in a negotiated peace during the winter of 1939-1940 are not altogether clear. It is certain that he gave the problem considerable thought, however, and in late December a special State Department committee was set up under the chairmanship of Sumner Welles to frame proposals for use in the event that a favorable opportunity should arise.[67] Behind this move lay Roosevelt's misgivings concerning a possible Ger-

[65] Myron C. Taylor, ed., *Wartime Correspondence between President Roosevelt and Pope Pius XII* (New York: Macmillan Co., 1947), pp. 3-4.

[66] Cianfarra, *The Vatican and the War*, p. 207; and Pius XII to Roosevelt, Jan. 7, 1940, *Roosevelt and Pius XII*, pp. 21-23.

[67] Langer and Gleason, *The Challenge to Isolation*, pp. 350-352.

man victory, and it seems reasonably evident that he aspired, at least in a general way, to find some basis for ending the conflict before a spring offensive could begin.[68]

Having completed his arrangements with the Holy See, therefore, the President now laid plans for more direct action, hinging them upon a tour of European capitals by the Under Secretary of State. Welles would visit Rome, Berlin, Paris, and London in an effort to learn how the different governments felt about the possibility of an early peace. In specifying the limits of this mission, Roosevelt emphasized that Welles would carry no offers or proposals from the United States and that he, the President, was interested in hearing nothing but genuine peace formulas. Expedients likely to produce only an armed truce did not attract him. The President indicated that Moscow was omitted from Welles's itinerary because he doubted that anything could be accomplished at the Russian capital.[69]

The governments concerned were quickly sounded on their attitudes toward such a mission. All except Germany warmly approved its purpose, and even Berlin agreed to receive the President's emissary, albeit somewhat coldly.[70] On the other hand, the project evoked no great enthusiasm. The reservations of the British government became particularly clear in Chamberlain's expressed misgivings about the wisdom and practicality of the move. The Prime Minister doubted that a stable peace could be negotiated at that time owing to the difficulty of obtaining reliable guarantees against new German aggression; he feared that early peace talks might impair Anglo-French efforts to aid Finland in the war with Russia; and he thought that Welles's activities might bring out divisions among the democracies which could be exploited by the German propaganda machine.[71] Nevertheless, Welles sailed for Europe just before the middle of February 1940, with a schedule that called for talks in Rome, Berlin, Paris, and London, the series to be climaxed by a second visit to the Italian capital. Myron C. Taylor boarded the same liner to take up his duties at the Holy See. Washing-

---

[68] See Langer and Gleason, *The Challenge to Isolation,* pp. 344–345, 362. For further information concerning Roosevelt's views at this time, see Joseph Alsop and Robert Kintner, *American White Paper: The Story of American Diplomacy and the Second World War* (New York: Simon and Schuster, 1940), pp. 85–86.

[69] Sumner Welles, *The Time for Decision,* 9th ed. (New York: Harper and Bros., 1944), pp. 73–74.   [70] *Ibid.,* p. 74.

[71] Chamberlain to Roosevelt (undated), and Chamberlain to Lothian (undated), MS Roosevelt Papers (Secretary's File, Box 62).

ton's reasonably optimistic estimate of Mussolini's position, the immediate order of business, and the fact that the Welles mission coincided exactly with the arrival of an American representative at the Vatican indicated that the major effort was to be focused upon Rome.

The talks proceeded swiftly once Welles reached Europe, but the results were discouraging. The Under Secretary had a pleasant enough conversation with Ciano, but his interview with Mussolini on February 27 led nowhere.[72] He found the going even harder in Berlin. After talking with Ribbentrop, Goering, and Hitler, he left the German capital on March 3 with a distinct impression that the Nazi leaders were thinking in terms of speedy victory and had largely abandoned notions of compromise.[73] While he was received cordially in both Paris and London, British and French leaders were equally barren of practical suggestions for bringing the war to an end. Dominant members of the French government seemed willing to offer concessions to Italy and even thought it possible to negotiate a political and territorial settlement with Germany, although they were not optimistic with regard to obtaining adequate guarantees of French security. British officials appeared somewhat divided as to whether they should seek complete victory and impose a harsh peace or leave the door open to a negotiated peace based upon the acceptance of a de-Nazified Germany as an equal in the family of nations.[74] Thus Welles returned to Rome on March 16 with empty hands.

In the meanwhile, Taylor was received by the Pope, and the two soon reached an informal understanding for concerted action by the United States and the Holy See to preserve Italian neutrality.[75] But events were working against them, for Italy was subjected to new German pressure almost at once. In view of the imminence of Germany's spring offensive, and apparently worried by what Welles might yet

[72] Count Galeazzo Ciano, *The Ciano Diaries, 1939–1943*, ed. Hugh Gibson (Garden City, N. Y.: Doubleday and Co., 1946), p. 212; and Welles, *The Time for Decision*, pp. 78, 87–88.

[73] Welles's Report to the President, MS Department of State (121.840 Welles, Sumner/132½); and Welles, *The Time for Decision*, pp. 119–120. Cf. the Fuehrer's directions for the conference with Welles, Feb. 29, 1940, in United States, Department of State, "German Documents on Sumner Welles Mission, 1940," *Department of State Bulletin*, XIV (Mar. 24, 1946), 459–460; and memorandum of conversation between Goering and Welles at Karin Hall, Mar. 3, 1940, *ibid.*, pp. 460–466.

[74] Welles's Report to the President.

[75] Cianfarra, *The Vatican and the War*, p. 208. Taylor puts the matter less bluntly, but says substantially the same thing (*Roosevelt and Pius XII*, p. 27).

accomplish on his return to Rome, Ribbentrop paid the Italian capital a hurried visit on March 10 and 11. Here he presented his case with urgent plausibility, and before the Nazi's departure Mussolini committed himself to enter the war at Germany's side, stipulating only that he must choose the date of entry to suit his own convenience.[76] As a gesture, Ribbentrop also called on the Pope and the Cardinal Secretary of State, submitting to them a long peace offer which, if generally accepted, would have established Germany as the dominant power on the Continent. But the offer gained no support in Vatican City. Ribbentrop was so far from pressing it, indeed, that the German Foreign Office lost no time issuing a denial that such an offer had been made.[77]

Italy's place in the war, as well as its permanent adherence to the Axis, now appeared to be settled. Within this framework, however, a small margin of doubt remained, if only enough for the slenderest hope. Despite his recent commitment to Ribbentrop, Mussolini was still plagued by nagging indecision; the other was hardly out of Rome before the Duce expressed new misgivings about the spring offensive, indicating to Ciano that he would try to moderate Hitler's intentions on this point at his forthcoming meeting with the German leader, which was scheduled to take place on March 18 in the Brenner Pass.[78]

Welles talked with Mussolini again on March 16. Still dubious of his own brashness, the Italian dictator appeared more conciliatory than in their first interview. Welles spoke of his conversations with Allied leaders and indicated that France and Britain were not unalterably opposed to a compromise if adequate guarantees of security could be offered them.[79] Listening attentively, Mussolini replied that Hitler would have to be convinced of their willingness to negotiate in realistic terms before he could be induced to put off his spring offensive, and asked for permission to convey Welles's assurances to the German leader. But Welles demurred at taking any such initiative on behalf of the Allies and of the United States. As soon as the interview was completed, he informed the President by telephone of Mussolini's request and pointed out that to authorize such a course would encourage the view that Roosevelt "was participating in the determination of such

[76] *Ciano Diaries*, p. 219.
[77] Cianfarra, *The Vatican and the War*, pp. 209–210.
[78] *Ciano Diaries*, p. 200.
[79] *Ibid.*, p. 222; and Welles's Report to the President.

political bases for a negotiated peace as Hitler might be willing to offer."
Since the President concurred, the authorization desired by Mussolini
was not given.[80]   Peace hopes were obviously faltering, and an interview with the Pope further convinced Welles that the most to be
sought was the possibility of keeping Italy out of the war.[81]   As a
result, he started home with no gain except Ciano's agreement to sponsor further communication between Roosevelt and the Duce as circumstances might advise.[82]

An interesting side light on President Roosevelt's labors to encourage peace negotiations in February and March 1940 is supplied by
the fact that he was not willing to let the Welles mission stand alone.
Exactly concurrent with that effort, and nearly identical in purpose, was
the mission of James D. Mooney, an official of General Motors Export
Corporation who had spent considerable time in Germany between the
wars and who had played a small role as intermediary in connection
with the German peace feelers of October 1939.   Acting without publicity, Mooney received independent instructions from the President in
December 1939 and January 1940, and proceeded to Europe at once.
He reached Berlin in February and talked with a number of high German officials—including Hitler, Goering, and Ribbentrop—during the
next three weeks.   He saw Hitler on March 4, just two days after
Welles's conversation with the Fuehrer.   While their talk encompassed
many details, its main point was the question of ending hostilities.
Mooney was at special pains to state that Roosevelt did not wish to act
as arbitrator in any possible peace discussion, but he made it clear that
the President, if asked, would be willing to serve as "moderator"—one
who has no power to decide a question but who merely accepts the duty
of presiding over a conference in accordance with a set of previously defined principles.   This appeared to elicit some momentary interest from
both Hitler and Goering.   But Welles had already found the true
measure of official views in Berlin, and the Mooney mission bore no
more fruit than the efforts of the Under Secretary of State.[83]

So no peace conference materialized in the early spring of 1940, and

[80] Welles, *The Time for Decision*, pp. 139, 140–141.
[81] *Ibid.*, p. 142; and Cianfarra, *The Vatican and the War*, p. 214.
[82] Welles, *The Time for Decision*, pp. 144–145.
[83] Mooney's Report to the President (a series of five letters written in Rome between
March 11 and March 15, 1940, and transmitted to Roosevelt through the facilities of
the Navy Department), MS Department of State.

the die had even been cast against Italian neutrality. It was plain, nevertheless, that Mussolini still hesitated. Efforts to cultivate his misgivings would not cease for another two months.

V

While the United States had always kept many checks upon its Far Eastern policy for the sake of greater freedom to act in Europe, the full measure of this subordination became apparent only with the beginning of the European war. The dubious position of the other great neutrals represented a future military problem. Until the country was prepared materially, as well as psychologically, for effective military action, it was necessary to deal with this problem at the diplomatic level under constant realization that diplomacy can never run too far ahead of military readiness. Diplomacy might eventually have to take action which the country's military position did not justify. But if such risks had to be taken, they would be taken in Europe first.

Public opinion, on the other hand, was following an opposite course. It had reached its height of pusillanimity so far as Japan was concerned during and immediately after the *Panay* crisis. Since then its desire for stronger measures, especially in the economic sphere, had grown rapidly. By August 29, 1939, the American Institute of Public Opinion was able to report that 82 per cent of those consulted wished to prohibit the sale of all war materials to Japan.[84] In other words, the idea of a discriminatory embargo against Japan received overwhelming support at a time when mere repeal of the arms embargo was the most advanced step public opinion would consider in thinking of Europe. Clearly enough, the sentimental lure of neutrality disappeared much faster in one sector than in the other. While the administration's European policy moved just ahead of public opinion, generally speaking, its Asiatic policy lagged somewhere behind; and if Roosevelt was condemned as too venturesome on the one hand, he was criticized as too circumspect on the other.

Japan was more quiet than usual during the first six months of the war, outwardly restricting itself to that infliction of small annoyances which the Japanese government understood so well. Hull attributed this to uncertainty regarding the next moves of Russia and the United

[84] *Public Opinion Quarterly*, IV (Mar. 1940), 115.

States.[85] There was doubtless some truth in this conjecture, but Japan's major ground for hesitation after the beginning of the year was of a different type. In January 1940 the short-lived government of General Abe gave way to a new Cabinet under Admiral Mitsumasa Yonai, who regarded the European war as a priceless opportunity to realize Japan's cherished dream of a new empire embracing southeastern Asia and the Indies. Freedom for this project required a speedy termination of the China Incident by depriving the Chinese Nationalist government of its British and American support. To gain momentum for a strong diplomatic campaign against the United States and Great Britain, therefore, Japan began to seek better relations with Russia and to revive its efforts to obtain a military pact with Germany.[86]

Any thought of *rapprochement* with Russia, of course, bespoke a substantial reorientation of Japanese policy, and as early as November 1939 there was enough evidence of such a turn to arouse misgivings in both London and Paris. This much became clear on November 21 when Lothian offered Welles a combined statement and inquiry, beginning with an observation that the future of Western interests in the Far East was dependent upon the actions of the American government. Since uncertainty regarding the intentions of Mussolini made it impossible for either France or Britain to transfer strength from the Mediterranean, he went on, his government's most advisable course was to seek an agreement with Japan as a means of forestalling attacks on British and French colonial possessions, or on other important interests, in the Orient. Although he feared that such a move would alienate American public opinion, he thought that efforts to further "a direct understanding between China and Japan" based on the realization "that both sides would have to make concessions" offered distinct advantages to the United States as well as to the Allies. The Under Secretary's reply was extremely negative, however. He did not believe that Japan could move against British and French colonial possessions unless it first obtained an agreement with Russia for the partition of China, and he considered that development altogether unlikely. In any event, he concluded, the United States would not exert pressure on China to accept the kind of terms Japan was certain to demand.[87]

[85] Hull, *Memoirs*, I, 730.

[86] Joseph W. Ballantine, "Mukden to Pearl Harbor: The Foreign Policies of Japan," *Foreign Affairs*, XXVII (July 1949), 656–659.

[87] Memorandum by Welles, Nov. 21, 1939, MS Department of State (793.94/15521).

Nor did the American attitude change, even though Grew on November 27 sent the State Department two telegrams calling detailed attention to the new trend in Japanese diplomacy.[88] Instead, a long memorandum which elaborated Welles's statement was prepared by the Division of Far Eastern Affairs and presented to the French and British Ambassadors early in December. This document conceded that Japanese-Soviet agreements concerning fisheries, Sakhalin Island, or the delimitation of frontiers could not be ruled out. A new commercial treaty was also possible, as was a nonaggression pact or some kind of inconclusive political agreement. But none of these possible accords could change the fundamentals of the situation to any extent. Indeed, those very fundamentals made a truly significant understanding between the two nations so unlikely that the United States government saw no reason to "compromise in our principles or surrender any of our material interests in an attempt to dissuade Japan from reaching an accord with the Soviet Union." [89]

But if the American government refused to buy Japan's favor, it also declined for the moment to issue any new threats. Grew's public warning of October 19, 1939, was given no worth-while additions, and the State Department vouchsafed no word of its plans for dealing with American-Japanese trade after the January 1940 expiration of the commercial treaty of 1911.

Hoping to capitalize on the known trend of public opinion, at least one organization made a strenuous effort at the beginning of 1940 to counteract what it regarded as official lethargy. Under the chairmanship of Henry L. Stimson, former Secretary of State and an old hand at Far Eastern problems, the American Committee for Non-Participation in Japanese Aggression entered new and stronger demands for measures to curb Japan. A long letter from Stimson was printed in the *New York Times* on January 11, calling for anti-Japanese embargo legislation.[90] Stimson's argument was reprinted, distributed widely, and given the most generous type of publicity.

But the administration would not allow its hand to be forced. For six months the Senate Committee on Foreign Relations had had in its

[88] Telegrams from Grew, Nov. 27, 1939, MS Department of State (761.94/1159 and 1163).

[89] Memorandum by the Division of Far Eastern Affairs, presented to the French Ambassador on Dec. 2, 1939, and to the British Ambassador on Dec. 6, 1939, MS Department of State (761.94/1176).

[90] *New York Times,* Jan. 11, 1940, p. 4, cols. 2–6.

possession two bills of the type Stimson desired. One of them, introduced by Senator Louis B. Schwellenbach, Democrat, of Washington, lay in the common tradition of special embargo laws. By making it mandatory for the President to embargo the shipment of any goods which would enable the importing country to infringe the sovereignty, the independence, or the territorial or administrative integrity of any nation whose sovereignty the United States was bound by treaty to respect,[91] this bill exactly covered the relationship of the United States to the Japanese campaign in China. That the measure gained no support from the administration is not surprising, since its mandatory character would have forced the American government to adopt a complete change of policy.

The other bill was different, however. It had been framed by Key Pittman, still the administration's leading foreign-policy spokesman in the Senate, and would have accorded the President discretionary authority to impose an embargo against any nation which, having signed the Nine-Power Treaty, had neglected its obligations under that instrument or in any way threatened the lives or property of American citizens in China.[92] Considering the identity of its sponsor, this resolution probably enjoyed the approval of the President and the Secretary of State; since it could be invoked or not, as the executive chose, it might have been useful as a club to brandish over Japanese heads. But as no apparent effort was made to take the bill out of committee, it seemed evident that the administration contemplated no further threats for the time being.

Setting the Stimson group at defiance, the government did nothing as the American-Japanese commercial treaty expired on January 26. Adolph Berle, the Assistant Secretary of State, merely notified the Japanese Ambassador that trade relations between their respective countries would continue on a day-to-day basis, explaining that future commercial understandings would depend upon future developments.[93] Recent extensions of the moral embargo applied to Japan as well as to Russia, however, and the United States in March granted China another loan of $20 million—a move denounced by Tokyo as having the effect of

[91] S. J. Res. 143 (76th Cong., 1st sess.), *Cong. Record*, LXXXIV (76th Cong., 1st sess.), 6473.

[92] S. J. Res. 123 (76th Cong., 1st sess.), *ibid.*, p. 4821.

[93] Hull to Grew, Jan. 23, 1940, United States, Department of State, *Papers Relating to the Foreign Relations of the United States: Japan, 1931–1941* (Washington, D. C.: U. S. Govt. Printing Office, 1943), II, 196–197.

a moral embargo.[94]   But Japan so far was being treated no more harshly than the Soviet Union, although Japan, unlike Russia, could hardly be viewed as a possible future ally.

As spring began, Japan started moving once more. Having decided upon the complete elimination of the Chiang Kai-shek regime, Tokyo on March 30, 1940, inaugurated what was characterized as a "New Chinese National Government." Nanking was chosen as its capital and the notorious political adventurer, Wang Ching-wei, as its head. At the same time, the northern provinces of Hopei, Shansi, and Shantung were accorded semi-independence under a "political affairs commissioner," and Inner Mongolia was placed under the direct rule of the Japanese Kwantung Army. Hull promptly declined to recognize these changes,[95] but he would go no further than that. Rumors were already current that Japan was planning aggressions far to the south, and, as noted, these rumors had an excellent basis in fact. Taking cognizance of the possibilities, Hull issued a new manifesto strongly opposing any change of the *status quo* in the Dutch East Indies.[96]   At this time, only a purely verbal resistance was possible. But as French and British disasters in Europe later that spring augmented Japan's chances of success in southern Asia, the President ordered a significant redeployment of the United States Fleet.

This took place in May when, without warning, the Fleet's base was shifted from the California coast to Pearl Harbor, near Honolulu, on the island of Oahu. Fleet units based on the continental United States had carried out maneuvers and other operations in the Hawaiian area for years, but now the home port itself was being moved westward a distance of more than two thousand miles. Outwardly at least, the transfer was handled in a most casual fashion. While directing maneuvers in Hawaiian waters, Admiral James O. Richardson, Fleet Commander-in-Chief, was suddenly instructed on May 7 to inform the press that the Fleet would remain in Hawaii for further exercises. Richardson was given no explanation at the time and was apparently allowed to believe that the change was only temporary. His efforts to have the Fleet brought back to the California coast on the ground that better

---

[94] Grew to Hull, Mar. 24, 1940, *Foreign Relations of the United States: Japan, 1931–1941*, II, 59.

[95] Statement by Hull, Mar. 30, 1940, *ibid.*, p. 60.

[96] Statement by Hull, Apr. 17, 1940, *ibid.*, p. 282.

training and provisioning facilities were available there proved abortive, however, and the transfer soon became permanent.[97]   The Admiral's objections were probably sound enough on the technical side, but the real utility of the shift had even greater weight. The Fleet's main strength now lay a good deal closer to any possible Japanese drive against the Indies, and the Japanese flank was correspondingly more vulnerable.

The transfer of the Fleet to Pearl Harbor would finally become an important matter in Japanese calculations.   But its immediate effect on policy was negligible, for Japan's course during the first half of June betrayed no fear whatever of American reactions.   Tokyo's campaign for better relations with Moscow resulted on June 9, 1940, in an agreement covering the disputed frontier of Mongolia.[98]   Taking swift advantage of Great Britain's preoccupation with Hitler's vast spring offensive, Japan also submitted new demands regarding the British concession at Tientsin.   To these the British government yielded on June 19, agreeing that Japanese officials might unite with concession police in checking anti-Japanese activities, and that the practically worthless North China currency, issued under Japanese sponsorship for use in the occupied provinces, might circulate within the concession on an equal basis with Chinese national currency.   As a final humiliation, Britain also turned over to the Japanese a quantity of silver held on deposit from the Chinese Nationalist government.[99]

VI

This act of abasement was prompted by the threatened ruin of the British homeland rather than by any weakness in British character, and the United States partook of British fears to such a degree that the niceties of neutral conduct soon lost most of their importance.   The

---

[97] Richardson's testimony, Nov. 19, 1945, United States, Congress, Joint Committee on Investigation of Pearl Harbor Attack, *Hearings Pursuant to S. Con. Res. 27, Authorizing Investigation of Attack on Pearl Harbor, Dec. 7, 1941, and Events and Circumstances Relating Thereto* (79th Cong., 1st and 2nd sess.) (Washington, D. C.: U. S. Govt. Printing Office, 1946), pt. 1, pp. 260–266.   Cited henceforth as *Pearl Harbor Hearings.*

[98] *Bulletin of International News,* XVII (June 15, 1940), 753.

[99] Statement by the Under Secretary of State for Foreign Affairs, June 19, 1940, Great Britain, Parliament, House of Commons, *The Parliamentary Debates: Official Report,* 5th series (London: H. M. Stationery Office, 1909——), CCCLXII, 141–142.

government led the way in this shift. But the nation as a whole required less guidance than might have been expected, for the currents of popular feeling observed in the spring and again in the fall of 1939 quickened tremendously as the prospect of complete German triumph grew stronger.

To a considerable extent, American neutrality had always been illusory. Even when seeking to deny it, the American people were deeply aware of having more in common with Great Britain and France than with Germany. While they distrusted many Allied policies, occasionally suspected Allied intentions, and sometimes made fun of Allied statesmen, they hated Hitler and feared the ways of dictatorship. At best, this sympathy involved recognition of cultural and strategic unities growing out of a long past. At worst, it involved a choice between two evils, and few were in doubt as to which was the greater. No true dilemma ever existed. This greatly simplified the work of those in charge of public enlightenment.

Thanks to their extended broodings over the First World War, Americans were propaganda-conscious in the highest degree. Yet, owing to the basic likeness between Anglo-French and American viewpoints, the Allies could still employ subtlety with assurance of success, while pro-German instruction required such a fundamental distortion of cherished beliefs that it was clearly recognizable as propaganda if it made its point at all. The British and French had only to lift minor obstacles from a stream that already flowed strongly in their direction; the Germans had to stem the whole current. Moreover, persistence of American neutrality—the Allies' worst fear—was Germany's best hope, and as events were to prove, Hitler's very successes on the battlefield could destroy it. Under these circumstances, the Germans labored to little purpose.[100]

The Allies, on the other hand, did much better. Through the winter of 1939–1940 the British and French alike developed systematic campaigns to sway American opinion. The British, not unnaturally, carried the main burden, and the progressive development of the central themes of their propaganda can be illustrated from the speeches of Lord Lothian, the British Ambassador in Washington.

On October 25, 1939, Lothian addressed The Pilgrims—a society of

[100] For an interesting survey of German propaganda efforts in the United States, see Harold Lavine and James Wechsler, *War Propaganda and the United States* (New Haven: Yale Univ. Press, 1940), chaps. vii, viii.

Americans which, like its English counterpart in London, was dedicated to the promotion of fellow feeling between Great Britain and the United States. Examining the history of the Monroe Doctrine, he pointed out that its success through the nineteenth century had rested squarely upon friendly British sea power. World peace, he continued, now demanded a similar basis of Anglo-American coöperation.[101] The present war was not imperialistic; it was a conflict between dissimilar ways of life. India and the dominions, all familiar with the habits of British imperialism, had recognized this truth at once and had joined the mother country in battle of their own free will.[102] Although he did not say it, his obvious conclusion was that the United States should bear in mind that the British were fighting for something much larger than their own material interests.

Fittingly enough, education was the theme of Lord Lothian's talk on November 14 when he spoke at a dinner celebrating the fiftieth anniversary of the founding of Barnard College. The existing situation, Lothian declared, had grown out of the democratic failure to solve three great problems: unemployment, maldistribution of wealth, and war. During the peace to follow education would have to help solve these problems by doing two things. It would have to teach the individual to understand and enjoy his life, and it would have to offer him a preparation for leadership. To this enlightened future Great Britain had already contributed the example of its own educational system, which made both secondary and university training available to all classes.[103]

This talk of a peaceful, sane, and abundant aftermath did no more than skirt the edges of immediate war issues, but most Americans could understand and sympathize with every word. Without much change or addition Lothian developed such concepts until the middle of May— filling out a picture of common traditions, common ideals, and historic unity of interest, emphasizing the un-American and un-English character of totalitarianism, and underlining the common hope for a better world. Not until the entire western front collapsed did he use any form of insistence. Then, on June 4, 1940, he issued a direct warning that Hitler's main objective was to gain possession of the British Fleet,

[101] Speech to the Pilgrims of the United States, Oct. 25, 1939, Royal Institute of International Affairs, *The American Speeches of Lord Lothian, July 1939 to December 1940* (London: Oxford Univ. Press, 1941), pp. 11–15.

[102] *Ibid.*, pp. 16–17.

[103] Speech at Barnard College, Nov. 14, 1939, *ibid.*, pp. 37–39.

pointing out that, if Hitler succeeded, this great bulwark of the Americas against European aggression would be a thing of the past.[104] But in June many Americans were saying the same thing.

Being almost superfluous, British propaganda was effective because it interfered so little with natural processes. Since there were plenty of Americans who were willing to assume the task of convincing themselves and each other, the British wisely permitted Americans to take the lead. Persuasion from domestic sources was not so likely to be regarded as propaganda as was exhortation from abroad, and thus could take full advantage of the fact that the main difference between propagandist and auditor lay not so much in basic conviction as in foresight and in willingness to come to grips with what was clearly foreseen. Of especially great assistance to the British point of view was President Roosevelt himself.[105]

The tone of Roosevelt's fireside chat on the day Britain entered the war has been mentioned. Its text was followed religiously by the whole administration. Indeed, the content and general tone of numerous official statements on war issues showed clearly that psychological neutrality was not only regarded as impossible; it was viewed as positively undesirable.[106] On the other hand, American sensitivity to any hint of physical involvement was frankly recognized, and official arguments throughout the debate on repeal of the arms embargo stressed a return to traditional concepts of neutrality rather than aid to the Allies. The presidential message to Congress in January 1940, however, outlined a dreary picture of what the future might hold if "the vast and powerful military systems" then at large were not destroyed.[107] On March 16 Roosevelt looked beyond the war again and called for a "moral peace" in an international broadcast made on behalf of the Christian Foreign Service Convocation.[108] London seized this chance to maintain full rapport with America by hastily stating its concurrence with the President's views.[109]

[104] Speech before Columbia University alumni, June 4, 1940, *The American Speeches . . .* , pp. 100–101.

[105] As Lavine and Wechsler rightly point out, ". . . in the American political process the president is inevitably the nation's most active and significant propagandist." See *War Propaganda and the United States,* p. 47.	[106] Cf. *ibid.,* p. 63.

[107] Annual message to Congress, Jan. 3, 1940, Roosevelt, *Public Papers and Addresses, 1940,* p. 4.

[108] Radio address by the President, Mar. 16, 1940, *ibid.,* p. 103.

[109] See statement by Chamberlain, Mar. 19, 1940, *Parl. Debates* (Commons), CCCLVIII, 1843–1844.

Large numbers of individuals and groups with no official connections whatever labored to similar effect. Only a few can be mentioned here. Extremely important in building up sympathy for the Allies were the various relief organizations set up by Americans under such titles as "Bundles for Britain" and "Le Paquet au Front." [110] So were the activities of such old-line internationalists as Dr. Nicholas Murray Butler and James T. Shotwell.[111] A useful part of the general effort was a spirited attack on revisionism and an attempt to show that the Peace of Versailles was not so bad as it had been represented.[112] Following the same pattern, Walter Millis—undoubtedly the most popular of between-war debunkers—took back much of what he had written about Great Britain and France, publicly deprecated the lessons many had drawn from his *Road to War,* and explained that the new conflict involved an entirely different situation.[113]

As Hitler's spring offensive started in April 1940, an important new pressure group was formed by William Allen White and Clark Eichelberger who, like White, had been instrumental in the work of the Nonpartisan Committee for Peace through Revision of the Neutrality Act during the fall of 1939. This new organization was called the Committee to Defend America by Aiding the Allies, and its purpose was to encourage the view that neutrality should be openly discarded in favor of a policy of extending every aid to Great Britain and France that could possibly be given without going to war at their side. By June the new campaign was in full swing.[114]

This continual watering of roots that were already healthy achieved practical results in connection with the events of late spring. The logic of the rapid German advance into Denmark and Norway on April 9, the German invasion of the Low Countries on May 10, and the complete disintegration of the western front in the weeks that followed was inescapable. Nor did the administration encourage any desire to escape it. The time for circumlocution and mellow assurances designed to keep the immediacy of the crisis in the background was past, and the

---

[110] Cf. Lavine and Wechsler, *War Propaganda and the United States,* p. 112.

[111] *Ibid.,* pp. 72, 83.

[112] For example, James T. Shotwell, *What Germany Forgot* (New York: Macmillan Co., 1940); and Ellsworth Barnard, "War and the Verities," *Harper's Magazine,* CLXXX (Jan. 1940), 117.

[113] *New York Herald-Tribune,* Feb. 14, 1940, p. 5, cols. 3–6.

[114] Walter Johnson, *The Battle Against Isolation* (Chicago: Univ. Chicago Press, 1944), pp. 64, 81.

American government made no effort to conceal a swiftly mounting alarm as it met successive Allied reverses with dramatic countermeasures.

President Roosevelt denounced the German seizure of Denmark and Norway in scathing terms.[115] To keep the Nazis from gaining control of new resources in the United States, he froze the American assets of those countries on April 10.[116] Events had given Denmark's Atlantic possessions, Iceland and Greenland, a new strategic importance. Acceding to Iceland's own proposal, the State Department in the middle of April agreed to establish direct relations with the Icelandic government.[117] It went a step further on May 1 and announced the opening of a provisional consulate in Greenland.[118] Shortly afterward, the British placed Iceland under military occupation.[119] The German invasions of Luxembourg, Belgium, and the Netherlands called forth new denunciations and new freezing orders.[120]

From the middle of May attention shifted to the fate of British and French armies trying to stem the German advance. On May 15 German forces crossed the Meuse near Mézières, just inside the French border, and by May 19 the Nazis had opened a broad gap in the northern extension of the Maginot line, reaching St. Quentin and Rethel. General Maxime Weygand succeeded Gamelin as French Commander-in-Chief, but the Germans continued almost unhindered. By the end of the month the British evacuation at Dunkirk was under way. This city fell on June 3, and it was evident not only that France stood on the brink of collapse but that the whole Allied cause was in imminent danger.[121]

Throughout this period of growing crisis Roosevelt maintained his efforts to keep Italy from entering the war. Taylor cabled from Rome on April 20 that the Pope was about to address a neutrality appeal to

[115] Statement by the President, Apr. 13, 1940, *Department of State Bulletin*, II (Apr. 13, 1940), 373.

[116] Executive Order No. 8389, Apr. 10, 1940, *Federal Register*, V, 1400.

[117] Press release, Apr. 16, 1940, *Department of State Bulletin*, II (Apr. 20, 1940), 414.

[118] Press release, May 1, 1940, *ibid.* (May 4, 1940), p. 473.

[119] Samuel Eliot Morison, *The Battle of the Atlantic, 1939–1943* (Boston: Little, Brown, and Co., 1947), p. 57.

[120] Executive Order No. 8405, May 10, 1940, *Federal Register*, V, 1678.

[121] The French government considered the possibility of surrender as early as May 25. See William L. Langer, *Our Vichy Gamble* (New York: Alfred A. Knopf, 1947), p. 16.

Mussolini, adding that Cardinal Maglione, the papal Secretary of State, urged the President to do likewise. Bullitt entered a similar plea from Paris. Roosevelt was hesitant, but Taylor repeated his suggestion on April 26.[122] This time the President acted, sending Mussolini a note on April 29 which asked the Italian dictator to exert his influence for a just and stable peace.[123] Mussolini chose to believe that Roosevelt's message contained an implied threat [124] and gave Ambassador Phillips little reason to hope that Italy would remain neutral much longer.[125] His written answer to the President on May 2, suggesting that Roosevelt confine himself to American affairs, was extremely cold.[126] But apparently Mussolini, for all his bluster, was still hesitating. According to Ciano, he did not set a date for entering the war until after May 10.[127]

Just before the middle of May a papal condemnation of Germany and the Vatican's pledge of its moral support to Belgium, Luxembourg, and the Netherlands produced a serious rift between the Italian government and the Holy See.[128] Despite this evidence that Mussolini was growing more unapproachable, Roosevelt appealed to him a second time on May 14, again without effect.[129] By May 25 Britain and France were prepared to deal with the Italian on his own terms and asked Roosevelt to inform Mussolini that if Italy abstained from the war they would agree to satisfy his territorial grievances at the end of the conflict and admit the Italian government to the peace conference as a full participant. In these circumstances, the President preferred not to assume the role of agent,[130] but on May 26 he offered Mussolini the benefit of his influence to help obtain from the British and French what Italy desired.[131] The Duce, however, was now determined to take part in a war which seemed on the point of ending. His refusal to consider this overture elicited the most threatening note Roosevelt had yet sent, one which

---

[122] Hull, *Memoirs*, I, 777–778; and Langer, *Our Vichy Gamble*, p. 11.

[123] Roosevelt to Mussolini, Apr. 29, 1940, United States, Department of State, *Peace and War: United States Foreign Policy, 1931–1941* (Washington, D. C.: U. S. Govt. Printing Office, 1943), p. 520.

[124] Mussolini to Hitler, May 20, 1940, *Lettres secrètes*, p. 63.

[125] Phillips to Hull, May 1, 1940, *Peace and War*, pp. 520–521.

[126] Mussolini to Roosevelt, May 2, 1940, *ibid.*, p. 522.

[127] *Ciano Diaries*, pp. 247, 249.

[128] Cianfarra, *The Vatican and the War*, p. 225.

[129] *Ciano Diaries*, p. 250. See also Roosevelt to Mussolini, May 14, 1940, *Peace and War*, p. 526.

[130] Hull, *Memoirs*, I, 782.

[131] Roosevelt to Mussolini, May 26, 1940, *Peace and War*, pp. 536–537. Cf. *Ciano Diaries*, p. 255.

called attention in pointed words to American support of the democracies.[132]   But this availed nothing.   Ciano told Phillips on May 31 that the die was cast and that Mussolini wanted no "further pressure." [133] The Foreign Minister's statement ended Roosevelt's labors with the Italian leader and prepared the way for the angry "stab in the back" remarks which the President included in his speech at Charlottesville, Virginia, on June 10.[134]

It was during these same weeks of late May and early June that Anglo-American coöperation began to assume a truly active quality, and this development was unquestionably made easier by the formation on May 11 of a new British Cabinet under Winston Churchill.   Although Roosevelt had finally supported many aspects of Chamberlain's policy, especially its Italian phases, he always remained slightly distrustful of British intentions as long as Chamberlain was at the helm. On the other hand, he saw a kindred spirit in Churchill and took a most favorable view of his long opposition to the appeasement of Germany.[135] Under the code name of POTUS (President of the United States) he had been in regular communication with the pugnacious British statesman (designated in these exchanges as "Naval Person") since the latter's resumption of his former duties as First Lord of the Admiralty in September 1939.[136]   Now that Churchill was Prime Minister, close understanding rapidly gave way to explicit coöperation.

This trend became visible almost at once.   As early as May 15, Churchill sent Roosevelt an agitated cable requesting a proclamation of nonbelligerency and a guarantee of all aid short of war.   More specifically, he wanted the loan of forty or fifty destroyers and several hundred war planes and a promise that new credits would be extended to the British government for the purchase of war materials in the United States when Britain's supply of dollars was exhausted.   He also asked Roosevelt to exert pressure on the recalcitrant government of Eire, in whose territory he wished to establish naval bases, by sending an American squadron for a prolonged visit in Irish ports.   "I am looking to you," he concluded, "to keep the Japanese quiet in the Pacific, using

[132] Hull to Phillips, May 30, 1940, *Peace and War*, p. 539.

[133] Phillips to Hull, June 1, 1940, *ibid.*, p. 544.   Cf. *Ciano Diaries*, p. 258.

[134] Address by the President at Charlottesville, Va., June 10, 1940, Roosevelt, *Public Papers and Addresses, 1940*, p. 263.

[135] James A. Farley, *Jim Farley's Story: The Roosevelt Years* (New York: Whittlesey House, 1948), p. 199.

[136] Churchill, *The Gathering Storm*, pp. 440–441.

Singapore in any way convenient." It was a large order; and whatever his opinion of its ultimate wisdom, the President was manifestly unable to grant such an appeal for the time being. This he explained to Churchill in a message dated May 18.[137] But he did make it clear that the United States government was prepared to assume increasingly heavy obligations with respect to the British Empire when he informed the Prime Minister on May 26 that, if the British Fleet should withdraw to Canada following a successful German invasion of the British Isles, the United States would undertake to defend all British possessions in the Western Hemisphere.[138] At the same time, London and Washington drew together in their efforts to obtain assurance that the French Navy would not fall into German hands.

These endeavors were plagued by infinite complications. The French Fleet was the second-most-important naval force in Europe and constituted one of the few real bargaining items still in France's possession. So the French government was determined to keep its freedom of action in this regard as long as it possibly could. Most French leaders were unwilling to face the thought of turning their Navy over to the Germans. But Germany's bargaining power was great as French resistance entered its last days, while Great Britain and the United States could offer little in return for the guarantees they desired. Since the Royal Air Force, after Dunkirk, was regarded as essential to home defense, Britain had practically nothing to spare, and the United States was not much better off so far as immediate resources were concerned. Neither was capable of stopping the German drive in any event, so there was little disposition in either government to risk the little it had for the sake of empty gestures. But the French Cabinet was faced by a situation which offered no other hope and could appreciate no point of view except its own. Approaching hysteria, it kept insisting that the impossible be done. Pending the fulfillment of its requests, it was inclined to treat representations from Washington and London in a somewhat offhand manner.

On May 18, for example, Bullitt had to explain to Alexis Léger of the French Foreign Office the futility of urging Roosevelt to ask Congress for an immediate declaration of war against Germany.[139] It was felt necessary on May 30 to reject the Ambassador's own suggestion that

---

[137] Winston S. Churchill, *Their Finest Hour* (Boston: Houghton Mifflin Co., 1949), pp. 24–25.

[138] Hull, *Memoirs*, I, 772.   [139] *Ibid.*, pp. 767–768.

part of the Atlantic squadron be sent into the Mediterranean as a counterweight to German gains.[140] At the request of the French Premier, Paul Reynaud, Roosevelt did ask the British government to support France's last struggles by throwing units of the Royal Air Force across the Channel, but he accepted the inevitable refusal without pressing Churchill to change his mind.[141] Despite the certainty that no immediate aid would be forthcoming, Reynaud's pleas continued. So did Roosevelt's promises for an indefinite future.[142]

Nevertheless, the question of the French Navy and the related problem of the disposition of French colonies were so vital that long after there was any hope of staving off military collapse in France proper, Britain and the United States continued their efforts to keep France from pulling out of the war. Reynaud's impulse to retire to North Africa with Cabinet and Fleet and carry on the war from that area was the focal point of these exertions. If skilfully carried out, this design would offer at least a temporary solution of both problems. From June 11 to June 13 Churchill himself visited French leaders at Tours, where the government had momentarily established itself to escape the imminent fall of Paris. But he was unable to secure a definite engagement on this point or any other.[143] Turning to another solution, the British Cabinet three days later offered to release France from its undertaking not to conclude a separate peace, on condition that the French Fleet be moved to British ports in advance of the armistice.[144]

Washington supported these efforts as well as it could. Convinced that Reynaud had no thought of surrender, however, Bullitt did not follow the government into the provinces and was unable to maintain direct contact with the seat of authority. Although Hull opposed this course,[145] Roosevelt approved the Ambassador's desire to stay in Paris and help smooth the details of German occupation. So Anthony J. Drexel Biddle, whose position as Ambassador to Poland had been nearly a sinecure since the autumn of 1939, followed Reynaud to Tours, and thence to Bordeaux, as Bullitt's deputy.[146] Whether Bullitt, even with his greater experience in French affairs, could have prevented surrender

[140] For the text of Hull's rejection note, see Langer, *Our Vichy Gamble*, pp. 15–16.
[141] Hull, *Memoirs*, I, 774.
[142] Roosevelt to Reynaud, June 13, 1940, *Peace and War*, p. 550.
[143] Churchill, *Their Finest Hour*, pp. 180–182.
[144] For the texts of the British telegrams of June 16, see Langer, *Our Vichy Gamble*, pp. 36–37.
[145] Hull, *Memoirs*, I, 790.   [146] Langer, *Our Vichy Gamble*, pp. 21–22.

now appears doubtful. But it is certain that Biddle did not succeed. Reynaud mentioned the definite possibility of an armistice in a message to Roosevelt on June 14.[147] He told Biddle the next morning that only an immediate declaration of war by the United States would enable France to continue hostilities from North Africa.[148] Roosevelt answered on June 15, explaining that he could offer no military commitments, but he urged Reynaud to maintain French resistance with the early prospect of more abundant supplies from the United States.[149] Realizing that an armistice was now inevitable, Biddle again raised the question of the Fleet and was told on June 16 that France would not give it up under any circumstances.[150] Well-known divisions in the French government kept this promise from being wholly reassuring, but it was all that could be obtained at the moment of surrender. Clearly the French problem was only beginning for Britain and the United States alike.

Regardless of this collateral issue, the war had finally established a direct and immediate relationship between the British cause and American interests, creating an urgency which could not be met within the framework of neutral inhibitions. On June 5 the White House announced that surplus Army matériel of the First World War—including some five hundred thousand rifles, eighty thousand machine guns, and considerable quantities of field artillery, bombs, and ammunition—was being sold to Great Britain and France. Since these were government stocks, their sale fell under a different rule of international law than the private transactions with foreign governments hitherto permitted. To sell these articles directly threatened the formal neutrality of the United States in a most serious fashion. But even though the administration paid lip service to this dilemma by arranging for the United States Steel Corporation to handle the transfer,[151] its real meaning was plainly evident. The unneutral proclamation desired by Churchill had not been issued, and the government would continue for several months to worry about numerous forms of legality. Nevertheless, the United States had now openly taken the position that international law offered no refuge from the hazards of war and had begun charting its course through that nebulous zone between neutrality and

---

[147] Reynaud to Roosevelt, June 14, 1940, *Peace and War*, p. 552.
[148] Langer, *Our Vichy Gamble*, p. 29.
[149] Roosevelt to Reynaud, June 15, 1940, *Peace and War*, p. 553.
[150] Langer, *Our Vichy Gamble*, pp. 35–36.
[151] Stettinius, *Lend-Lease*, p. 26.

full participation which, for want of a better term, is called nonbelligerency.[152] Speaking to the graduating class of the University of Virginia on June 10, the President described this change in somewhat different words. But his statement left no doubt that the whole essence of neutrality was gone. "In our American unity," he said, "we will pursue two obvious and simultaneous courses: we will extend to the opponents of force the material resources of this nation, and at the same time we will harness and speed up the use of those resources in order that we ourselves in the Americas may have equipment and training equal to the task of any emergency and every defense."[153]

To all appearances, public opinion was significantly abreast of these developments. According to Professor Hadley Cantril's digest of both regular and special surveys of popular feeling, the proportion of the population which favored greater aid to the Allies than was being rendered under cash-and-carry rose from less than 20 per cent in early March to nearly 80 per cent by the middle of June.[154] In May the Gallup organization reported that 62 per cent of Americans thought the United States would be involved in the European war before it ended. At the middle of June, 19 per cent were sufficiently exercised to state that they would vote for a declaration of war within two weeks if given the opportunity. On the whole, the change in public opinion was even more striking than the change in government policy. Nor did this change lack an explanation: by July 7 only 32 per cent of those interviewed still felt certain of ultimate British victory.[155]

VII

Thus the great divide was crossed in the midst of Allied disaster and two related uncertainties, disposition of the French Fleet and England's ability to survive. Notwithstanding the arguments of its

---

[152] For a brief discussion of this concept, see Lawrence Preuss, "The Concepts of Neutrality and Non-Belligerency," *The Annals of the American Academy of Political and Social Science*, CCXVIII (Nov. 1940), 106.

[153] Address by the President at Charlottesville, Va., June 10, 1940, Roosevelt, *Public Papers and Addresses, 1940*, p. 264.

[154] Cantril, "America Faces the War," *Public Opinion Quarterly*, IV (Sept. 1940), chart 2, 397.

[155] *Public Opinion Quarterly*, V (Sept. 1941), 476; and *ibid.*, IV (Dec. 1940), 711, 714. Regarding this general shift in public opinion, see Jerome S. Bruner, *Mandate from the People* (New York: Duell, Sloan, and Pearce, 1944), pp. 20–26.

supporters, from the President down, repeal of the arms embargo was never aimed at strengthening American neutrality. It was hoped that the additional resources which repeal made available to Great Britain and France might help them prolong the stalemate and obtain a compromise peace—or, less conceivably, to win the war and impose a settlement of their own choosing. That was the only real objective of repeal, and that was the objective it failed to reach.

While the stalemate lasted, the United States continued to practice the forms of neutrality in a generally conscientious, if not overvigorous, fashion. But all the time it was moving toward the Allies in spirit and away from Germany. The logic of the whole situation determined this trend. Propáganda, of which there were many different kinds, simply enhanced it. Apparently hopeful of securing Mussolini's coöperation, President Roosevelt explored the possibilities of a compromise peace in February and March. Working with the Holy See, on the one hand, and with the British and French governments, on the other, he exerted himself in May to win Italian neutrality. But when this failed, he ranged himself strongly on the Allied side, rapidly developed his connections with the British government as France sank down in defeat, and went as far as his immediate resources permitted in attempting to minimize the consequences of the Axis victory. Otherwise, the United States moved with exceeding care. Relations with Russia were subjected to great strain during the war in Finland, but a clear break was avoided. Japan was kept under strict observation, and the commercial treaty was finally permitted to lapse. But the only new threat leveled at Tokyo was the basing of the Fleet at Pearl Harbor.

By the middle of June 1940 the experiment in neutrality was finished. Considering what had happened in Europe, the necessity of keeping any aggressive foreign power from gaining control of either the eastern Atlantic or the western Pacific could now be expounded wholly in terms of national defense, and without resort to the suspect formulas of internationalism. Nonbelligerency was the next step.

CHAPTER V

Tactics of the Nonbelligerent

I

EVEN WHILE FRENCH RESISTANCE CONTINUED, THE UNITED STATES HAD rounded a decisive turn in the closely related areas of policy and public opinion. But the formation of a new French government under Marshal Henri Philippe Pétain, the aged hero of Verdun, on the night of June 16 brought matters into yet sharper focus, and France's decision to request armistice terms without delay precipitated another burst of activity in Washington.

So far, nothing had been done to implement the resolution taken by the American republics at Panama in October 1939, when they had declared their uniform opposition to the transfer of American territory from one non-American power to another. Keenly aware that this statement of principle now required a means of execution, the Secretary of State at once summoned a conference of foreign ministers to assemble in Havana on July 21.[1] During the interim, however, the American government acted vigorously by itself. On June 18, following passage of a congressional resolution to this effect,[2] Hull notified the European belligerents that the United States would neither recognize nor acquiesce in any changes affecting the sovereignty of American territory.[3] Although Germany demurred in lordly fashion,[4] the adherence of the United States to traditional policy on this issue was now as clear as it could well be made pending an actual violation.

As a matter of course, all French assets in the United States were

[1] Cordell Hull, *The Memoirs of Cordell Hull* (New York: Macmillan Co., 1948), I, 791–792, 816.

[2] H. J. Res. 556 (76th Cong., 3rd sess.), United States, Congress, *Congressional Record* (Washington, D. C.: U. S. Govt. Printing Office, 1874——), LXXXVI (76th Cong., 3rd sess.), 8559.

[3] Kirk to Ribbentrop, *et al.,* June 18, 1940, United States, Department of State, *Department of State Bulletin* (Washington, D. C.: U. S. Govt. Printing Office, 1939——), II (June 22, 1940), 681–682.

[4] Statement by Hull, July 5, 1940, *ibid.,* III (July 6, 1940), 3.

frozen on June 17,[5] and arrangements were hastily made for British assumption of all French arms contracts in America.[6] The same day, Admiral Harold R. Stark, Chief of Naval Operations, requested the appropriation of $4 billion to construct a two-ocean navy.[7] This was followed by significant changes in the Cabinet. The excessive caution of Charles Edison, acting Secretary of the Navy, and Harry Woodring, Secretary of War, had in recent weeks strengthened Roosevelt's long-standing conviction that changes were necessary. Both had opposed the sale of Army and Navy planes and certain other materials to the Allies, and neither evinced a firm sympathy toward the President's general policies. As a result, he filled these positions on June 20 with two leading Republicans who had long been at odds with many of their party on questions of foreign affairs—choosing Frank Knox, the Chicago publisher, as Secretary of the Navy, and Henry L. Stimson, former Secretary of State, as head of the War Department.[8] Thus he assured a more vigorous administration of these vitally important offices and, at the same time, introduced an element of bipartisanship at the policy-making level.

The President's most insistent worries still centered upon the French Navy, however. France's retirement from the war ended all hope of that force's further coöperation with the British Fleet, and the immobilization of French sea power was now the highest objective to be sought. This was no small matter; if Germany and Italy could add the French Fleet to their existing naval strength, they could easily destroy Britain's position in the Mediterranean and challenge its control of the eastern Atlantic. Regardless of the promises already given, it was obvious that the future of the French Navy still depended upon the armistice terms which might be arranged between France and the victors.

Accordingly, Hull on June 17 instructed Anthony Biddle to give the new Minister of Marine, Admiral Jean Darlan, the most forthright

[5] Executive Order No. 8446, June 17, 1940, United States, National Archives, *Federal Register* (Washington, D. C.: U. S. Govt. Printing Office, 1936——), V, 2279.

[6] Edward R. Stettinius, Jr., *Lend-Lease: Weapon for Victory* (New York: Macmillan Co., 1944), p. 32.

[7] Samuel Eliot Morison, *The Battle of the Atlantic, 1939–1943* (Boston: Little, Brown, and Co., 1947), p. 27.

[8] For the background of this affair, see James A. Farley, *Jim Farley's Story: The Roosevelt Years* (New York: Whittlesey House, 1948), pp. 212–213, 241; Harold L. Ickes, "My Twelve Years with F. D. R.," *Saturday Evening Post*, CCXX (June 5, 1948), 92; and Henry L. Stimson and McGeorge Bundy, *On Active Service: In Peace and War* (New York: Harper and Bros., 1948), pp. 323–324.

warning of which he was capable, pointing out that neglect to insure the Fleet's safety before the armistice would "fatally impair the preservation of the French Empire and the eventual restoration of French independence and autonomy. Furthermore," he declared, "should the French Government fail to take these steps and permit the French Fleet to be surrendered to Germany, the French Government will permanently lose the friendship and goodwill of the Government of the United States." [9]   This threatening manifesto was delivered the next day, whereupon, after some consideration, Foreign Minister Paul Baudouin guaranteed that France would accept no armistice agreement which included surrender of the Fleet. In the event such a concession were demanded, however, he could not promise that the Fleet would be sent to British ports—". . . it might be sent overseas or sunk." [10]   With this Washington had to be momentarily content.

As the situation developed, Hitler rejected Mussolini's plan for taking over the French Navy. He evidently believed that he did not need additional forces in bringing England to terms. It was likewise apparent that he wanted to arouse no special objections on France's part lest French intransigence produce new troubles which would help delay Great Britain's expected capitulation.[11]   That the French government was sincere in its resolve to keep its Fleet out of German hands seems unquestionable. Although the armistice stipulated that all French warships except those released for duty in the colonies should be laid up in home ports under German and Italian control, strong French objections on this point elicited a verbal intimation that the arrangement might not be strictly enforced; [12]   and a major portion of the Fleet was

[9] Hull to Biddle, June 17, 1940, United States, Department of State, *Peace and War: United States Foreign Policy, 1931–1941* (Washington, D. C.: U. S. Govt. Printing Office, 1943), p. 553.

[10] Biddle to Hull, June 18, 1940, *ibid.*, p. 554.

[11] William L. Langer, *Our Vichy Gamble* (New York: Alfred A. Knopf, 1947), pp. 48–49; and conference of the Commander-in-Chief, Navy, with the Fuehrer, June 20, 1940, United States, Department of the Navy, *Fuehrer Conferences on Matters Dealing with the German Navy, 1939–1941* (Washington, D. C.: Issued in mimeographed form by the Office of Naval Intelligence, 1947), 1940, I, 54.

[12] William L. Langer and S. Everett Gleason, *The Challenge to Isolation, 1937–1940* (New York: Harper and Bros., for the Council on Foreign Relations, 1952), pp. 547, 560; and eighth article of armistice terms, in World Peace Foundation, *Documents on American Foreign Relations, 1939–1940*, ed. S. Shepard Jones and Denys P. Myers (Boston: World Peace Foundation, 1940), p. 429. That there were no secret clauses appears from the evidence offered at Pétain's trial in 1945. See France, High Court of Justice, *Le Procès du Maréchal Pétain* (Paris: Éditions Albin Michel, 1945), I, 28, 85.

in fact allowed to remain at Toulon, which was not occupied by the Germans until November 1942, following the Anglo-American invasions of North Africa.

From the French point of view at least, the surrender terms, though stern enough, were less harsh than might have been expected, so armistice agreements were signed with Germany on June 22 and with Italy on June 24. Since it was impossible to foretell just how these agreements might be implemented, neither Great Britain nor the United States felt wholly reassured concerning the safety of the French Fleet, and both governments protested that nothing but Germany's word stood between the ships and their outright appropriation the moment they entered ports under Axis control. But nothing was gained save a repetition of former promises.[13] Taking action alone, therefore, Britain on July 3 seized all French ships in British harbors, immobilized the French squadron at Alexandria, and after the admiral in command refused to permit the Fleet to be disarmed, largely destroyed or disabled that part of it which lay at Mers-el-Kébir, near Oran. While it brought a prompt severance of diplomatic relations between London and the Pétain government, this proceeding reduced French naval power to less threatening dimensions. The Department of State continued to express doubt of France's ability to keep the rest of its Navy out of German hands, but the United States, like Great Britain, was now inclined to believe that neither blandishments nor force could accomplish anything more and to accept conditions as they now stood.[14]

That the situation was not altogether bad even Churchill later admitted.[15] Neither France, its Fleet, nor its overseas empire was being forced to render Germany direct and immediate aid. Besides, it was known that many Frenchmen who still held responsible positions in the government were unalterably opposed to any form of willful collaboration with Germany. It was suspected that even Pétain, despite his authoritarian views, had no aversion to playing a double game with Hitler. Among those who held such an opinion was ex-Ambassador Bullitt, whose information seemed to be as good as anyone's. If judiciously exploited, these footholds might be widened in many ways.

---

[13] Langer, *Our Vichy Gamble,* pp. 56–57.

[14] Memorandum by Hull, Sept. 11, 1940, MS Roosevelt Papers (Secretary's File, Box 69); Langer, *Our Vichy Gamble,* pp. 58–59; and Winston S. Churchill, *Their Finest Hour* (Boston: Houghton Mifflin Co., 1949), pp. 232–237.

[15] Langer, *Our Vichy Gamble,* pp. 76–77. See also Churchill, *Their Finest Hour,* pp. 238–239.

Quickly swallowing its disappointment, therefore, the United States chose to continue ordinary diplomatic relations with the new government in the hope of strengthening all favorable trends in its policy.[16]

II

Nevertheless, the situation was still most critical. The debacle in western Europe had repercussions everywhere, and its effects in Asia went far beyond those Japanese successes with the British at Tientsin which have already been noted. As early as June 17, 1940, Japan made demands on France concerning Indo-China. Three days later the Pétain government was compelled to accept a formula recognizing Japan's "special needs" in China, together with a system of inspection which gave the Japanese substantial control of all traffic through Indo-China.[17] But Tokyo was far from satisfied. On June 25 the Japanese War Minister, Shunroku Hata, issued a formal statement calling attention to the favorable development of international affairs. With visible exultation he added: "We should not miss the present opportunity or we shall be blamed by posterity." [18] At the same time, Japan turned again upon Great Britain, demanding on June 24 that all movements of supplies to Chiang Kai-shek through Burma and Hong Kong be stopped.[19]

London applied to Washington for support. On June 27 Lothian told Hull that Britain was no longer in a position to follow its accustomed policy of yielding to Japan in small matters like that of the Tientsin concession while opposing Tokyo's demands for recognition of the New Order in China. His government believed, Lothian continued, that it would have to seek a general agreement with Japan on Pacific questions unless the United States exerted new pressure in the Far East, either by prohibiting American-Japanese trade or by sending a portion of its Fleet to Singapore. To this diplomatic feeler Hull offered little. He stated that the United States was increasing economic

---

[16] Langer, *Our Vichy Gamble*, p. 65; and Hull, *Memoirs*, I, 805.

[17] Announcement of the Japanese Foreign Office, June 20, 1940, *Documents on American Foreign Relations, 1939–1940*, pp. 270–271.

[18] *Contemporary Japan*, IX (Aug. 1940), 1067. Cf. Tojo's statements before the International Military Tribunal in Tokyo, in *New York Times*, Jan. 6, 1948, p. 28, col. 4.

[19] Statement by Churchill, July 18, 1940, Great Britain, Parliament, House of Commons, *The Parliamentary Debates: Official Report*, 5th series (London: H. M. Stationery Office, 1909——), CCCLXIII, 399.

pressure as fast as it deemed advisible and that the situation in the Atlantic forbade the diversion of American naval power to the Far East. With regard to Lothian's alternative, he added somewhat vaguely that the United States had no objection to a settlement between London and Tokyo provided that the interests of China and the East Indies were not sacrificed.[20] On July 12 Lothian made more specific reference to his government's plan for a three-month closure of the Burma Road, giving Hull to understand that the time thus gained would be employed in trying to arrange a general settlement of the China Incident. Again, however, the Secretary was not helpful. Although he expressed his disappointment regarding the probable sacrifice of Chinese interests, he suggested no other action.[21]

So Great Britain had little choice but to surrender once more, and on July 17 it agreed to halt for a period of three months all shipments to China through Burma and Hong Kong of arms, munitions, gasoline, trucks, and railway equipment. In making this formidable concession Churchill expressed hope that some method of settling the Sino-Japanese conflict would be discovered before the agreement lapsed. The Prime Minister also stated Britain's willingness "to negotiate with the Chinese Government after the conclusion of peace" for the discontinuance of its special privileges in China.[22] This was a brave effort to minimize a damaging confession of weakness. But nothing could disguise Britain's predicament, and its distress was given new emphasis on August 9 when London announced that all of the few British troops still left in China, including about 1,650 men stationed at Shanghai, would be withdrawn for service elsewhere.[23]

Meanwhile, there were important changes in the Japanese government. Admiral Yonai's prolonged failure to discover a basis for a closer understanding with Germany finally cost him his office as Prime Minister, and Prince Konoye formed another Cabinet on July 16, this time composed of ministers who favored totalitarian principles. Especially indicative of future plans was his choice of Yosuke Matsuoka as Foreign Minister. An energetic talker who was not well schooled in

[20] Memorandum by Hull, June 27, 1940, MS Department of State (711.94/1580); and Hull, *Memoirs*, I, 896–898.

[21] Memorandum by Hull, July 12, 1940, MS Department of State (893.24/849).

[22] Statement by Churchill, July 18, 1940, *Parl. Debates* (Commons), CCCLXIII, 399–400.

[23] William C. Johnstone, *The United States and Japan's New Order*, rev. ed. (New York: Oxford Univ. Press, 1941), p. 90.

keeping his thoughts to himself, Matsuoka was known as a leader of Japanese fascists, a confirmed devotee of expansion, and an advocate of the closest possible relations with the European Axis. That he would be the strong man of the Konoye government was taken for granted, and on August 1 he dispelled any lingering doubts as to the scope of his policy by announcing that henceforth Japan would bend its efforts to perfecting the "chain of co-prosperity of Greater East Asia." As the official gloss explained, the term "Greater East Asia" embraced French Indo-China and the Dutch East Indies in addition to Manchukuo, China, and Japan herself.[24] This revealed clearly what the Japanese government had had in mind almost since the beginning of the European war. The geography of the New Order had been formally altered, enabling Konoye and his associates, now at the head of a single-party state, to seize their opportunities without hesitation.

Throughout the spring and early summer of 1940 the United States had continued its fruitless protests against Japanese violations of American rights in China. Grew observed on July 2 that his conversations with Foreign Minister Arita had done little more than keep the door open for still more conversations, adding gloomily: "The vicious circle is complete, and how to break it is a puzzle which taxes imagination." [25] Nor was he greatly reassured when Matsuoka asked him on July 26 to inform Roosevelt that Japan's interest in world peace had not diminished, especially as the Foreign Minister added that the basis of peace must be "adaptation to the development and change" which was so characteristic of the contemporary world.[26] Here the demand for acquiescence in Japanese policy was not even half concealed, and Grew remarked on August 1 that German successes had "gone to the Japanese head like strong wine." [27]

Although it was certainly perturbed, Washington remained as bland as Tokyo during July and the early part of August. Behind this façade, however, an important change in American policy was taking place. On July 2 President Roosevelt signed a new bill ostensibly designed to promote national defense but which contained far-reaching implications for American foreign policy. Vastly enlarging the President's authority over exports, it gave him the undisputed power to ban

---

[24] *Contemporary Japan*, IX (Sept. 1940), 1084.

[25] Joseph C. Grew, *Ten Years in Japan* (New York: Simon and Schuster, 1944), p. 321.

[26] *Ibid*., p. 323.   [27] *Ibid*., p. 325.

completely or to place under licensing control the export of any commodity deemed essential to the defense of the United States.[28] In form, at least, this act was not an amendment to the neutrality law. But its provision for licensing control had the effect of giving the President all the discretionary embargo authority he could have wished.

As recently as June 27, Hull had discouraged British hopes for the application of new economic measures to Japan. But the dangerous trend revealed by the agreement regarding the Burma Road and by changes within the Japanese government speedily convinced Roosevelt that a too extended acquiescence might lose everything. Armed with his new powers, he therefore set about fulfilling the threat implied by denunciation of the commercial treaty of 1911, and announced on July 26 that exports of petroleum, aviation gasoline, tetraethyl lead, and limited categories of scrap iron and steel—all highly essential to Japan's war effort—would be immediately placed under licensing control.[29] This drew a quick protest from the Japanese Ambassador; but using a lesson from Tokyo's own book, the State Department coolly insisted that export controls were being imposed solely in the interests of national defense and were not directed against Japan or any other nation.[30] In the months that followed, as similar controls were extended to a great number of other commodities, economic discrimination against Japan became an extremely significant aspect of United States policy.

Though enough had been done to prove that the American government was not oblivious to Britain's need for assistance in the Far East, the United States still refused to take a firm stand. Speaking of French and British concessions to Japan, Hull remarked on July 16 that such actions as the prospective closing of the Burma Road and the recent submission of traffic through Indo-China to Japanese control raised what the United States viewed as "unwarranted . . . obstacles to world trade."[31] He did not dwell on the strategic implications of these moves, however, and the tone in which he spoke revealed hardly more irritation with Japan for making such demands than with Great Britain and

---

[28] Sec. 6, ch. 508 (76th Cong., 3rd sess.), United States, Department of State, *United States Statutes at Large* (Washington, D. C.: U. S. Govt. Printing Office and others, 1845——), LIV, 714.

[29] Proclamation No. 2417, July 26, 1940, *Federal Register*, V, 2677.

[30] Welles to Horinouchi, Aug. 9, 1940, United States, Department of State, *Papers Relating to the Foreign Relations of the United States, 1931–1941* (Washington, D. C.: U. S. Govt. Printing Office, 1943), II, 219–220.

[31] Press release, July 16, 1940, *ibid.*, p. 101.

France for yielding to them. Similarly, when Japan in August claimed naval and air bases in Indo-China and the right to move troops through that country, Hull merely remarked that any change in the status of Indo-China would have an "unfortunate" effect on American public opinion.[32]

III

The shock produced by France's collapse had not even begun to subside when new changes within that stricken country raised new problems in dealing with its government. On June 24, 1940, Pierre Laval, ex-Foreign Minister and seasoned advocate of collaboration with Germany, entered the government as a Minister of State. From this advantageous position he continued his efforts to give France a wholly authoritarian regime. To this extent, at least, his views were congenial to many prominent Frenchmen, notably Pétain himself and General Maxime Weygand, who had served as Commander-in-Chief during the last stages of resistance to Germany—although both men distrusted Laval in many respects. Laval gained impressive victories as soon as he took office. The French Parliament voted itself out of existence on July 10. Then President Lebrun was removed from office, and Pétain became Chief of State. At the same time, certain aspects of the armistice agreement were clarified. Germany refused to let the French government return to Paris and made it clear that Pétain's authority did not extend beyond the limits of unoccupied France. So the new regime was established provisionally at Vichy, the celebrated watering place, to set about reviving the truncated nation that remained.[33]

By this time it was evident that the postarmistice government of France was going to be neither so liberal nor so independent as might have been hoped. Doubt prevailed regarding its next step, for there were many indications that its policies were being oriented away from Great Britain and the United States. Although Pétain showed no enthusiasm for entering the war against Britain, he was by no means sympathetic to the British cause—especially after the British attack at Mers-el-Kébir—and Laval, whose star was constantly rising, made no secret of his hopes. At the end of July he told Robert D. Murphy,

---

[32] Statement Sept. 4, 1940, *Department of State Bulletin*, III (Sept. 7, 1940), 197.
[33] Langer, *Our Vichy Gamble*, pp. 72–74.

counselor of the American Embassy at Vichy, that he desired Britain's speedy collapse and expected that France would be given an important role in the federation of European states which Hitler meant to establish.[34] With the tide apparently running against those who opposed any collaboration with Germany beyond the terms of the armistice, it was clear that it would be difficult if not impossible to influence the French government.

Spain's attitude rendered the situation even more grim. Though by no means a full partner, General Franco had long been known as an approving connoisseur of Axis enterprises. A German-Spanish pact of friendship, signed March 31, 1939, and ratified on November 29 of the same year, pledged Spain to the most benevolent type of neutrality in conflicts between Germany and its foes, while a variety of secret agreements subjected the Spanish press and police to a considerable degree of German influence.[35] Besides this, Franco could hardly ignore the community of interest established by Axis help in the days of his own rebellion, especially as these ties were now so boldly emphasized by the opportunities and threats inherent in Germany's new grasp on western Europe. Nor did he try to ignore them. His rising pugnacity came to the fore with Italy's declaration of war against France. He declared Spain to be in a state of nonbelligerency on June 12, and on June 14 he had Spanish troops take over the international zone at Tangier, in Morocco. That Franco desired new territory could not be doubted, and his opening moves did not rule out the imminent possibility of Spain's entering the war at the side of the Axis.[36]

A means of attacking the Spanish problem had already been found, however. Spain was a poor country, and its material condition had been especially bad since the civil war. Spain's ability to fight was sadly limited by economics; indeed, its very existence depended upon its ability to import foodstuffs, oil, and other essentials. Particularly since the outbreak of the European war, Germany and Italy had been able to spare very little in the way of raw materials, and the Allies soon began to exploit this advantage. As early as January 1940, France sought to place a checkrein on its southern neighbor in the form of a trade agreement whose operation was understood to be contingent upon

[34] *Ibid.,* p. 83.

[35] Herbert Feis, *The Spanish Story: Franco and the Nations at War* (New York: Alfred A. Knopf, 1948), p. 4.

[36] Sir Samuel Hoare (Viscount Templewood), *Complacent Dictator* (New York: Alfred A. Knopf, 1947), pp. 30, 34.

the maintenance of Spanish neutrality. Great Britain followed this lead on March 18 with a new commercial pact that was similar in purpose if not in form.

The events of May and June altered the situation considerably, however; and hoping to retain some influence at Madrid through a wider application of economic inducements and compulsions, the British government dispatched a new Ambassador to Spain as German armies raced across France. It chose for this exacting mission Sir Samuel Hoare, an ex-Foreign Secretary known in the middle nineteen-thirties for his disposition to compromise with the dictatorships. Though Hoare was an able man and not unacceptable personally, his work did not begin auspiciously. One interview with the Spanish leader convinced him that Franco, anticipating an early British surrender, had no intention of bargaining for a little when he might soon be in position to take a great deal. On July 18 the Caudillo gave Hoare's fear additional cause by laying public claim to Gibraltar. It appeared that German victories now played a larger role in the shaping of Franco's plans than did his own economic needs, and this situation produced almost as much concern in Washington as it did in London.

American policy toward Spain since the war's beginning had been largely an independent one. In August 1939 the Export-Import Bank agreed to finance the shipment of two hundred and fifty thousand bales of cotton to Spain over a ten-month period, but the government made no further effort to guide trade between the United States and Spain. Official inertia, anti-Franco sentiment throughout the country, and uncertainty regarding the fate of American interests in the Spanish telephone system prevented any American action to supplement French and British policy until the spring of 1940. But reports from Alexander Weddell, United States Ambassador at Madrid, called increasing attention to the local situation, and finally, in response to Spanish overtures, the State Department elected to open talks bearing on the provision of a substantial credit to alleviate Spain's dollar shortage.[37]

Since France surrendered before this decision could be conveyed to Madrid, Franco displayed little interest in the prospect of American aid when Weddell finally got a chance to talk with him on June 22. Reviewing all that could be learned, the staff of the American Embassy in

---

[37] Feis, *The Spanish Story*, pp. 23–25; and memorandum of conversation between Weddell and Pétain (then French Ambassador to Spain), Apr. 18, 1940, MS Roosevelt Papers (Secretary's File, Box 72).

Madrid agreed two days later that Spanish intervention on the side of Germany was probable.[38]   Nor did prospects get any better during the next few weeks.   Although Weddell reported on July 3 that he thought Franco was sincerely trying to keep Spain out of the war, he admitted that Germany and Italy were exerting great pressure at Madrid and called new attention to rumors of a possible Spanish or German occupation of Portugal.[39]   A few days later Hoare expressed the opinion that these rumors had no basis in fact, but Weddell continued to find evidence that the possibility of a move against Portugal had to be taken seriously— [40] whereupon Herbert Pell, the American Minister in Lisbon, was directed to see what he could learn at the Portuguese Foreign Office and to stress the interest of the United States in Portugal's South Atlantic islands "as links in the existing aerial communication" between America and Europe.[41]   This was the situation at the middle of July.

The possibility of collaboration with Germany by both France and Spain and the fear that Hitler planned to exploit this opportunity in the near future by launching an attack on Gibraltar raised misgivings to a new high in Washington and in London.   Such a move, of course, would be disastrous to Great Britain's Mediterranean position.   But beyond that was the threat to French territories in Africa's northwestern bulge, an area almost as vital to control of the Atlantic as to dominance over the Mediterranean.

In these circumstances, the thoughts of American officials turned particularly to Dakar, capital of French West Africa.   Although this city was so unimportant in normal times that the United States had not maintained a consulate there for ten years, the existing war situation emphasized the narrowness of the waters which separated West Africa from the eastern hump of Brazil.   At this point the distance between the two southern continents was so small that occupation of the area round Dakar by an unfriendly power would be a distinct menace to the South American coast.   Viewing these potentialities as an essential consideration in any scheme of hemispheric defense, the American government decided on August 6, 1940, to reopen its consulate at

[38] Feis, *The Spanish Story*, pp. 34–35.

[39] Weddell to Welles, July 3, 1940, MS Department of State (852.00/9481).

[40] Telegrams from Weddell, July 8, 1940, MS Department of State (740.0011 European War 1939/4516 and 4528).

[41] Hull to Pell, July 11, 1940, MS Department of State (740.0011 European War 1939/4528).

Dakar. The importance of having an American official on the scene was regarded as so urgent that the Department of State sent one of its most reliable career officers, Thomas C. Wasson, without even pausing to ask Vichy for an exequatur. Governor Pierre Boisson received Wasson cordially enough on his arrival at Dakar, however, and the consular office was functioning again by October 1.[42] It can hardly be argued that the presence of one American consul in French West Africa was in any way decisive through the weeks that followed. Yet the fact remains that Boisson subsequently opposed every German attempt to gain a foothold in France's African possessions, and this experiment helped establish a policy which the United States was to apply in North Africa with conspicuous success during the next two or three years.

IV

The prospect of a German drive to the south, with or without French and Spanish assistance, was only one aspect of the Atlantic situation, however. Equally important was the submarine. Germany's newly won control of France's entire west coast enabled Hitler to base U-boats on French ports and to maintain an intensive submarine campaign much farther into the Atlantic than had been possible from German harbors on the North Sea or in the Baltic.[43] Except for Spain and Portugal, the combat zone now recognized by the United States government embraced the entire coast of Europe as well as the entrance to the Mediterranean. Within the limits of this zone German submarines could operate at will without risk of sinking American ships. Fully alive to this advantage, Germany on August 17, 1940, extended its submarine operations to the utmost boundaries of the American zone in the area surrounding the British Isles.[44] Britain retaliated on August 21 with a blockade covering the full length of Europe's Atlantic coast.[45]

[42] Thomas C. Wasson, "The Mystery of Dakar," *American Foreign Service Journal,* XX (Apr. 1943), 170.

[43] Morison, *The Battle of the Atlantic,* pp. 22–23.

[44] Wagner's testimony, May 13, 1946, International Military Tribunal, *The Trial of German Major War Criminals: Proceedings of the International Military Tribunal Sitting at Nuremberg, Germany* (London: H. M. Stationery Office, 1947–1949), pt. 13, p. 344.

[45] Headnote, in World Peace Foundation, *Documents on American Foreign Relations, 1940–1941,* ed. S. Shepard Jones and Denys P. Myers (Boston: World Peace Foundation, 1941), p. 503.

As maritime warfare was thus intensified, British convoy losses, negligible until after the fall of France, increased sharply.[46]

Obviously the real battle of the Atlantic was now taking shape—with France, Spain, North Africa, West Africa, and the submarine playing heavily in the calculations of both sides. In every sector, moreover, that battle seemed to be running against Britain, threatening the Empire's lifelines at a hundred points. To make matters worse, at the end of the first week in August Hitler opened his campaign to bomb England into submission. The possibility of complete German victory now loomed exceedingly close.

Having thrown off the trammels of conventional neutrality at the beginning of June, the Roosevelt administration formulated its problem in clear terms. The relationship between British survival and American security had been accepted. This acceptance had been confirmed in terms of policy by the practical operation of cash-and-carry and by the recent arms transfer. That Britain would have to receive war materials of all kinds in constantly growing volume if it were to survive at all could not be doubted. But whether the thought of actual military coöperation should be tied in with such day-to-day support of a needed, but still potential, ally was another question.

An answer was soon found, however. On June 11, 1940, and again on June 24, Lord Lothian approached Hull with proposals for joint staff conversations.[47] The wisdom of advance planning was now so patent that it was decided by the end of the month to act on the British suggestions.[48] Henceforward, American support of the British cause assumed a two-fold character in which immediate aid, steadily expanding in volume and variety, was united with the systematic elaboration of strategic and tactical understandings against the day when the American nation might join in actual hostilities at Britain's side. One process rested on the concept of aid short of war; one was based on the realization that such aid might finally prove inadequate. But each complemented the other so handily that the two became almost indistinguishable in practice and could not always be separated even in theory.

One act which partook of both classifications was the controversial destroyer deal: if the acquisition of fifty destroyers strengthened Britain's immediate control of the Atlantic sea lanes, the possession of a string of

---

[46] Morison, *The Battle of the Atlantic*, p. 23.
[47] Hull, *Memoirs*, I, 796–797.
[48] Morison, *The Battle of the Atlantic*, p. 39.

island bases ranging from Newfoundland southward to British Guiana did much to condition later United States naval policy and to make that policy a more effective instrument of the common cause.

Study of this transaction had begun before the fall of France, having originated in Churchill's request of May 15 that forty or fifty American destroyers be made available, on lease, to the British Navy. Although the United States possessed about two hundred destroyers of 1917–1918 vintage from which such a number could conceivably be furnished, Washington's initial reactions were not promising. Under less pressing circumstances in January 1940, President Roosevelt had rejected a suggestion for releasing some of these old vessels to the underequipped Norwegian Navy. He had based this decision on two grounds: first, the ships were needed at home in connection with the expanding activities of the Atlantic neutrality patrol and, second, their sale to Norway would be unlawful.[49] By early summer the United States Navy had recommissioned 172 overage destroyers for its own use, and its need for the others had certainly not been lessened by recent developments in Europe. As Roosevelt informed Sumner Welles on June 1, American naval shortages probably ruled out any destroyer transfer. Such a move would require congressional sanction, which, under the circumstances, "might be very difficult to get." In any event, the ships could not be sold as obsolete, since all were "now in commission and in use" or "in process of being commissioned for . . . use."[50]

Of course it was possible to argue, as many did, that Britain's was the greater need and that any action which helped the British cause would also help the United States. Nevertheless, the whole question was surrounded by legal doubt. On June 28 Congress added still another complication in the form of a law which declared that no property of the American government should be delivered to a foreign country unless the Chief of Staff or the Chief of Naval Operations certified that it was surplus to the needs of the service involved.[51] Considering the tangled situation abroad and the touchiness of public and congressional opinion at home, definition of the circumstances under which an article might be regarded as surplus was no easy task.

[49] Roosevelt to Mrs. J. Borden Harriman, Jan. 9, 1940, Franklin D. Roosevelt, *F. D. R.: His Personal Letters, 1928–1945,* ed. Elliott Roosevelt (New York: Duell, Sloan, and Pearce, 1950), II, 986.

[50] Memorandum by Roosevelt, June 1, 1940, MS Roosevelt Papers (Secretary's File, Box 62).

[51] *Statutes at Large,* LIV, 681.

It is not necessary to review in detail every step leading to the solution of this problem. The passing weeks hardened a conviction that Britain ought to have the destroyers, if at all possible, and that the essential prerequisites to achieving this end were (1) to develop a line of reasoning by which the warships might be declared surplus, and (2) to settle upon a method of by-passing the isolationist opposition which Congress was almost certain to furnish.

As the problem unfolded, it was suggested that the destroyers be turned over to Britain in return for a promise to send the Royal Navy to carry on the war from outlying parts of the Empire if the British Isles themselves were successfully invaded. Churchill refused to offer such a guarantee in exact terms but thought better of a proposal to grant the United States, on lease, a number of areas in British colonies or dominions in the Western Hemisphere for development as naval and air bases.[52] The project was submitted to Attorney General Robert H. Jackson in this form, and his rather involved opinion was delivered on August 27.

Rigidly confining himself to domestic law, Jackson pointed out that an act of March 3, 1883, imposed certain restrictions upon the authority of the Secretary of the Navy to dispose of naval vessels unless the President directed otherwise. Finding that the act of June 28, 1940, represented the only attempt by Congress to limit the President's authority in this regard, and taking cognizance of the bases which the nation stood to gain by way of exchange, he argued that the fifty destroyers might be declared surplus by the Chief of Naval Operations if, in his judgment, "the consummation of the transaction does not impair or weaken the total defense of the United States, and certainly so where the consummation of the arrangement will strengthen the total defensive position of the nation."[53]

Having produced a common-sense formula under which the ships might be declared surplus, Jackson then turned to regular neutrality legislation and found that the act of June 15, 1917, made it unlawful to supply belligerents with "any vessel, built, armed, or equipped as a vessel of war" so long as the United States was a neutral. He read this in connection with the preceding section of the same act, which

[52] Churchill, *Their Finest Hour*, pp. 404–405; and memoranda by Roosevelt, July 22 and Aug. 2, 13, 1940, *F. D. R.: His Personal Letters, 1928–1945*, II, 1048–1052.

[53] Opinion of the Attorney General, Aug. 27, 1940, *Department of State Bulletin*, III (Sept. 7, 1940), 204.

authorized the President to detain any armed vessel until satisfied that it would not engage in hostile operations before reaching another neutral or a belligerent port, and concluded that the statute applied only to vessels specifically built to the order of a belligerent government. Thus it had no bearing whatever upon the fifty old destroyers at issue. Concluding his argument at this point, Jackson advised the President that the transfer was perfectly legal and that it might be handled through an executive agreement.[54]

Negotiations had continued between London and Washington in the meanwhile, and delivery of Jackson's opinion found the understanding virtually complete. Since its reciprocal aspect helped justify the transfer before domestic law and domestic opinion, Roosevelt stubbornly resisted Churchill's wish to treat the exchange of American destroyers for British bases as two separate and unrelated gifts. This threatened to be a stumbling block for a time.[55] But compromise eventually prevailed, the destroyers being rendered in exchange for bases in the Bahamas, Jamaica, Antigua, St. Lucia, Trinidad, and British Guiana, while the United States accepted the Newfoundland and Bermuda concessions as a free gift. This arrangement was formalized by an exchange of notes on September 2.[56] The transfer was announced to Congress the next day, and British crews received the first eight destroyers at Halifax, Nova Scotia, on September 6.[57] On the whole, very little time had been lost.

As was anticipated, this further venture in nonbelligerency aroused no little criticism. Isolationist circles all over the country regarded it as additional proof of Roosevelt's determination to intervene in the European war, while rebukes of a more specialized variety were reserved for the legal arguments used to justify the transaction. Professor Herbert W. Briggs, of Cornell University, seriously questioned the Attorney General's interpretation of domestic law, pointing out that Jackson actually held the act of June 15, 1917, to countenance a violation of international law.[58] Professor Edwin M. Borchard, of the Yale

---

[54] *Department of State Bulletin,* III (Sept. 7, 1940), 206–207.

[55] Hull, *Memoirs,* I, 835–837; Stimson and Bundy, *On Active Service,* p. 358; and Churchill, *Their Finest Hour,* pp. 408–414.

[56] Lothian to Hull, and Hull to Lothian, Sept. 2, 1940, *Department of State Bulletin,* III (Sept. 7, 1940), 199–200.

[57] Morison, *The Battle of the Atlantic,* p. 34.

[58] Herbert W. Briggs, "Neglected Aspects of the Destroyer Deal," *American Journal of International Law,* XXXIV (Oct. 1940), 586–587.

Law School, complained that the opinion was "apparently designed to justify breaches of neutrality or acts of war, perhaps in the hope that they will not result in a state of war," and remarked that it would be interesting to observe the outcome of such a policy.[59] Although he approved the exchange itself and considered Jackson's opinion generally satisfactory with regard to domestic questions, Professor Quincy Wright, of the University of Chicago, returned to his old theme with the statement that the act should have found its international justification in the argument that German and Italian violations of the Pact of Paris left this country free to impose sanctions against them.[60]

Whatever the weaknesses of logic or law in Jackson's argument, the main issue was the value of the exchange in terms of national defense; and considered retrospectively, its wisdom can hardly be doubted. The Attorney General's opinion must therefore be regarded as an adequate, if somewhat imperfect, attempt to carry a necessary policy through a maze of legal hesitations, which had become largely unreal. Although he was not specifically referring to the destroyer transfer, perhaps the clearest summation of the position held by the United States at this time was offered by Professor Charles G. Fenwick, another international lawyer. Agreeing that the United States was no longer neutral in the "normal, technical sense of the term," he added, "It is engaged in defending the fundamental principles of international law upon which the rights and duties of neutrals rest . . . ."[61] Winston Churchill was to put it even more strongly. By "all the standards of history," he wrote later, this act would have "justified the German Government in declaring war" against the United States.[62]

Reactions in Berlin and Rome were unimpressive, however. Although German naval officials were outraged and Hitler himself was deeply annoyed, the Fuehrer declined to abandon his soft American policy. That the destroyer transfer strengthened his determination to make more effective use of Japan as a Pacific counterweight to the United States appears certain,[63] and it is true that Germany on Septem-

---

[59] Edwin M. Borchard, "The Attorney General's Opinion on the Exchange of Destroyers for Naval Bases," *ibid.,* p. 697.

[60] Quincy Wright, "The Transfer of Destroyers to Great Britain," *ibid.,* p. 688.

[61] Charles G. Fenwick, "Neutrality on the Defensive," *ibid.,* p. 699.

[62] Churchill, *Their Finest Hour,* p. 404.

[63] Hans L. Trefousse, *Germany and American Neutrality, 1939–1941* (New York: Bookman Associates, 1951), p. 64; and report of the Commander-in-Chief, Navy, to the Fuehrer, Sept. 7, 1940, *Fuehrer Conferences,* 1940, II, 19–20.

ber 6 again intensified the submarine war against British shipping.[64] But the first expedient was delayed and indirect at best, while the second was aimed primarily at Britain and would doubtless have come anyway to supplement the vast air assault then being delivered against the British Isles. The Italian attitude proved even milder, for Mussolini, according to Ciano, was simply indifferent.[65]

Talks concerning the long-range aspects of British-American co-operation began as the destroyer deal matured. Rear Admiral Robert L. Ghormley, Assistant Chief of Naval Operations, was ordered on July 12 to prepare to visit London as a special observer for "exploratory conversations" with the British Chiefs of Staff. At the same time, Major General George V. Strong, Assistant Chief of Staff, and Major General D. C. Emmons were assigned like missions on behalf of the Army and Army Air Force respectively, while General George C. Marshall, Chief of Staff, opened a series of talks with a British general in Washington.[66] The Ingersoll mission had given the naval problem a kind of introductory survey in January 1938. Now all phases of possible joint action were to be discussed, although naval matters would remain the keynote until after Pearl Harbor.

Ghormley, Strong, and Emmons reached London on August 15. The battle of Britain was not yet beyond its first stage, and the final outcome was still in doubt. Since it would be foolish to frame an ambitious program for filling the United Kingdom with war supplies if the islands seemed about to fall into German hands, a first concern of the mission was to assess Britain's immediate chances of survival. With the aid of various military underlings and civilian observers who conducted related investigations at the same time, the experts soon decided that Britain could hold out—a strong factor in this conclusion being the insistence of Lieutenant Colonel Carl W. Spaatz, who was destined for a meteoric rise to high command, that the Royal Air Force would not lose control of the air over the British Isles.[67]

This judgment was amply confirmed during the weeks that followed,

---

[64] Morison, *The Battle of the Atlantic*, p. 34.

[65] Count Galeazzo Ciano, *The Ciano Diaries, 1939–1943*, ed. Hugh Gibson (Garden City, N. Y.: Doubleday and Co., 1946), p. 294.

[66] Morison, *The Battle of the Atlantic*, p. 40; and Lothian to Roosevelt, July 20, *1940*, MS Roosevelt Papers (Official File, Box 48).

[67] Morison, *The Battle of the Atlantic*, p. 40. For additional details, see John G. Winant, *Letter from Grosvenor Square: An Account of a Stewardship* (Boston: Houghton Mifflin Co., 1947), pp. 48–50.

and by autumn plans were being made for long-range coöperation with Great Britain. Meanwhile, President Roosevelt started to redeem a pledge voiced two years earlier. Meeting Prime Minister W. L. Mackenzie King at Ogdensburg, New York, on August 18, he put his signature to an agreement providing for a joint United States-Canadian defense board.[68] Considering this, the budding destroyer deal, and other projects already begun, Winston Churchill hardly overstated the case two days later when he spoke of the United States and the British Empire as being "somewhat mixed up together . . . for mutual and general advantage." [69]

Other plans for national defense and international coöperation moved on apace. On July 10 Roosevelt asked Congress to provide equipment for two million men. Nine days later the bill elicited by Stark's request for a two-ocean navy became law, authorizing construction of 1,325,000 tons of new fighting ships.[70] On August 21 the United States government created the Joint Aircraft Committee for allocating airplane production in this country, the board being so named because it gave seats to two British representatives.[71] The National Guard was mustered into federal service on August 28, and the Selective Service Act was signed on September 16.

The foreign ministers of the American republics, in conference at Havana, made formal arrangements on July 30 for the provisional administration of European colonies in the Americas. They agreed that a special committee representing the American nations would assume control of any colonial possession threatened by change of sovereignty, and that any one of the American republics might act independently in this regard if faced with an emergency which did not brook delay.[72] The French West Indian island of Martinique constituted the only immediate source of misgiving. Its governor, Admiral Robert, was a Vichy sympathizer; his importance was greatly enhanced by the fact that he had several French warships under his immediate command and custody of some $245 million in gold bullion which was the property of the French government. While the situation was not regarded as urgent enough to warrant invoking the Havana scheme for provisional

[68] Joint statement by Roosevelt and Mackenzie King, Aug. 18, 1940, *Department of State Bulletin*, III (Aug. 24, 1940), 154–155.

[69] *Parl. Debates* (Commons), CCCLXIV, 1171.

[70] *Statutes at Large*, LIV, 779.   [71] Stettinius, *Lend-Lease*, p. 50.

[72] Act of Havana, July 30, 1940, *Department of State Bulletin*, III (Aug. 24, 1940), 138–139.

administration at that time, Washington dispatched Rear Admiral John W. Greenslade to Martinique in August to obtain from Robert effective guarantees concerning the uses to which ships and gold might be put. Greenslade was only partly successful, however, and the problem of Martinique remained for later treatment.[73]

V

As Germany moved from one success to another in western Europe during the spring and summer of 1940, Russia quietly consolidated its gains in the east and north. Having taken what it could from Poland and Finland, and having placed the three Baltic republics under military occupation, Moscow now prepared to extinguish these republics completely by incorporating them into the Soviet Union. Although this move was not helpful to German interests, the German Foreign Office chose to remain friendly, if noncommittal, when Russian troops in Estonia, Latvia, and Lithuania were reinforced in June; and it maintained the same calm when Moscow opened special negotiations with those states to secure the formation of new governments which could be counted upon to acquiesce in Soviet designs.[74] German diplomacy revealed some alarm, however, when Molotov on June 23 told Count Schulenburg, the German Ambassador, that the question of Bessarabia demanded speedy settlement. He added that Russia would have to use force if Rumania declined to hand over that territory peaceably.[75]

The German government was worried, but it still wanted quiet in eastern Europe and prompted Rumania to satisfy Moscow's demands for Bessarabia and northern Bukovina. To stabilize the Balkans even more, Germany and Italy then sponsored a further partition of Rumania, Bulgaria taking southern Dobrudja and Hungary annexing a large part of Transylvania—after which the two Axis powers guaranteed what was left of the despoiled kingdom.[76] These arrangements were completed in August, but they hardly rendered the peace less uneasy. The mutual toleration of Germany and Soviet Russia had begun to wear thin, and

---

[73] Langer, *Our Vichy Gamble*, p. 103.
[74] Weizsaecker to all German missions, June 17, 1940, United States, Department of State, *Nazi-Soviet Relations, 1939–1941* (Washington, D. C.: U. S. Govt. Printing Office, 1948), p. 154.
[75] Schulenburg to Ribbentrop, June 23, 1940, *ibid.*, p. 155.
[76] See Ribbentrop to Schulenburg, Aug. 31, 1940, *ibid.*, pp. 178–180.

the future of eastern Europe's buffer states was again shadowed by the rivalry of the two giants.

Pending the revival of open trouble in the Balkans, however, Russia went calmly ahead with its northern program. The annexation process began with the resignation of the Lithuanian government on June 15. It was completed during the first eight days of August, when Lithuania, Latvia, and Estonia became the fourteenth, fifteenth, and sixteenth "fraternal republics" of the Soviet Union.

Neither Russia's unopposed aggression nor Germany's outward show of acquiescence soothed fears in the United States. For a time, indeed, American officials were extremely pessimistic regarding the likelihood of an eventual break between Germany and the Soviet Union.[77] In June the State Department rejected Soviet protests over the cancellation of Russian orders for American machine tools and other materials. Later the same month, Hull declined to join Great Britain in an attempted *rapprochement* with the Soviet Union. As the Baltic states lost their independence, the American government promptly froze whatever assets they possessed in the United States and refused to accept the annexation as legally valid.[78] President Roosevelt even suggested the possibility of closing certain Russian consulates in the United States by way of reply to the closing of American consular offices in the former Baltic countries.[79]

For its own part, the Soviet government overlooked nothing. On July 27 Oumansky complained again of American commercial restrictions and explained that Welles's public statement respecting Soviet annexation of the Baltic republics was considered "misleading and offensive."[80] Molotov, in a speech delivered August 1, gruffly remarked that he did not intend to dwell upon his government's relations with the United States "if only for the reason that there is nothing good to be said on this matter." While he permitted himself no reference to a definite break, it was evident that the situation could not grow much worse without raising that threat. Nor did the Foreign Commissar's recognition of somewhat improved relations with Japan mitigate his chilling appraisal of that country, especially as he attributed the im-

[77] Cf. Langer and Gleason, *The Challenge to Isolation*, p. 723.

[78] Hull, *Memoirs*, I, 807, 811; and memorandum by Welles, June 18, 1940, MS Department of State (711.61/739).

[79] Memorandum by Roosevelt, Aug. 15, 1940, MS Roosevelt Papers (Official File, Box 220).

[80] Memorandum by Welles, July 27, 1940, MS Department of State (711.61/749).

provement to French weakness in the Far East and to Japan's new orientation southward; in effect, he was applauding the very conditions which were best calculated to increase tension between the United States and Japan.[81] All signs pointed to the conclusion that Soviet-American friendship had reached its lowest ebb since August 1939. As evidence of his belief that no conciliatory gesture would be worth while, Hull in September declined to act on a British request that he aid London's campaign for better relations with Moscow by releasing the impounded funds of the Baltic countries for Russian use.[82]

Still the American government did not relinquish its policy of keeping its door open to Russia. In midsummer Hull authorized Welles to conduct a series of talks with Oumansky to ascertain whether some basis for agreement did not exist, hidden though it might be; [83] and it was to avoid jeopardizing this effort that Welles, who retained some hope of better relations with Russia, advised the President to abandon his idea of closing a few Soviet consulates in this country.[84] In August the State Department opposed attempts to set up Baltic governments-in-exile. In September Ambassador Steinhardt returned to Moscow, having been absent from his post since May. And as Japan moved toward an outright military alliance with the European Axis during the latter part of the month, Soviet-American relations took a distinct turn for the better.

On September 25 Steinhardt relayed a report that Soviet radio and newspaper authorities had been ordered to cease their attacks on the United States.[85] Molotov accorded the Ambassador an unwontedly friendly reception on September 26 and, in Steinhardt's opinion, "gave every indication of a desire to see an improvement in our relations." [86] Hull and his advisers were so impressed by these evidences of cordiality as to formulate a guess that the still-unpleasant Oumansky was working at cross-purposes with his superiors "in an endeavor to strengthen his personal prestige." [87] This new warmth increased so rapidly that,

[81] David J. Dallin, *Soviet Russia's Foreign Policy, 1939–1942*, tr. Leon Denman (New Haven: Yale Univ. Press, 1942), pp. 330–331, 336.

[82] Telegram from Steinhardt, Sept. 22, 1940, and telegram from Hull to Steinhardt, Sept. 25, 1940, MS Department of State (741.61/899); and Hull, *Memoirs*, I, 811.

[83] Hull, *Memoirs*, I, 812.

[84] Welles to Roosevelt, Aug. 19, 1940, MS Roosevelt Papers (Official File, Box 220).

[85] Telegrams from Steinhardt, Sept. 25, 1940, MS Department of State (711.61/753 and 754).

[86] Telegram from Steinhardt, Sept. 27, 1940, MS Department of State (711.61/756).

[87] Telegram, Hull to Steinhardt, Oct. 3, 1940, MS Department of State (711.61/756A).

despite the moral embargo, several American tankers were dispatched to Vladivostok in October with cargoes of aviation gasoline, and a number of licenses were granted for the shipment of machinery previously bought.

In the meanwhile, Japan showed no intention of relaxing its new demands on French Indo-China. Finding no prospect of change, Grew on September 12 reached an important decision and sent the State Department what he called his "green-light" telegram, "perhaps the most significant message sent to Washington in all the eight years of my mission to Japan." Previously he had hoped that the Japanese government would ultimately listen to reason if nothing more than such mild sanctions as the moral embargo and a few carefully chosen export limitations were used against it. But now he recommended that economic measures be greatly intensified.[88]

While this advice was being considered, France yielded to the occupation of northern Indo-China by Japanese troops. Reverting at once to its familiar device of discriminatory loans, the United States on September 25 agreed to buy $30 million worth of tungsten from China and loaned the Chinese government $25 million for currency stabilization. The next day Roosevelt announced an embargo on the export of all scrap iron and steel except to other parts of the Western Hemisphere and to Great Britain.[89] Scheduled to take effect October 16, this appeared to be about what Grew had in mind.

Thus the tentative beginnings of easier relations with the Soviet Union coincided exactly with a stiffening attitude toward Japan, with broadening cracks in Russo-German friendship, and with a *rapprochement* between Berlin and Tokyo. That the diplomatic climate was changing had become quite evident, and the most unmistakable sign of this change was the conclusion in Berlin of the Tripartite Pact on September 27. Stipulating that the three signatory nations—Germany, Italy, and Japan—would assist one another by all political, economic, and military means should any one of them be attacked by a power not then involved in the European war or the Sino-Japanese conflict,[90] this treaty became one of the great pivotal facts in all the diplomatic maneuvers and military calculations of the following year and a quarter.

[88] Grew, *Ten Years*, p. 334; and Grew to Hull, Sept. 12, 1940, *Peace and War*, p. 572.

[89] Press release, Sept. 26, 1940, *Department of State Bulletin*, III (Sept. 28, 1940), 250.

[90] Article III, Three-Power Pact between Germany, Italy, and Japan, Sept. 27, 1940, *Documents on American Foreign Relations, 1940–1941*, pp. 304–305.

A fairly reliable indication that Germany was digging in for a much longer war than Hitler had expected during the summer, the Tripartite Pact threw much light on Nazi policy. Although it did not mention America explicitly, the treaty was obviously directed against the United States. It symbolized Germany's growing appreciation of Japan's value as a Pacific counterweight to American activity in the Atlantic. And by directly relating the course of all three Axis governments to the moves of the United States in either sphere, it clarified for the United States the position of Japan in the Axis, which had been somewhat obscure ever since the conclusion of the Russo-German nonaggression pact in August 1939. Any doubts that might still have existed regarding the strategic unity of the many different questions with which American policy had to deal were dispelled.

The Tripartite Pact also had implications for the Soviet government. Article V provided that the agreement affected "in no way the political status existing at present" between the contracting parties and Russia, but Ribbentrop and Ciano seem to have been privately agreed that it should bring some restraint upon Russian activity in eastern Europe.[91] And even though Moscow's initial distrust of this alliance between Germany and Japan was partly overcome by Ribbentrop's prompt assurance that it was directed exclusively against the United States,[92] and by his subsequent efforts to secure Russia's adherence to the treaty, one effect of this procedure was to place the Soviet government in a position where it either had to join the Axis front or proclaim its decision to follow a relatively independent course.

VI

With the signing of the Tripartite Pact the first phase of America's nonbelligerency came to an end. Launched in haste during the collapse of France, it began more as a series of determined expedients than as a unified policy. But in the three and one-half months which had

[91] In his diary, under date of September 19, 1940, Ciano makes the following statement concerning his own and Ribbentrop's view of the proposed treaty: "He [Ribbentrop] thinks that such a move will have a double advantage: against Russia and against America, which, under the threat of the Japanese fleet, will not dare to move. I express a contrary opinion. The anti-Russian guarantee is very good, but the anti-American sentiment is less appropriate, because Washington will increasingly favor the English." See *Ciano Diaries*, p. 293.

[92] Ribbentrop to Schulenburg, Sept. 25, 1940, *Nazi-Soviet Relations*, p. 195.

elapsed since the French request for an armistice, a number of events had occurred which heartened the Allies. The French Fleet was still not quite in German hands. Both western Africa and Gibraltar were intact. Neither Pétain nor Franco had yet been drawn into outright collaboration with Germany. Invasion of the British Isles had not developed as promised, and it seemed likely that England could hold out at least through the winter. Material aid was being extended to Britain as fast as possible, and long-range staff conversations had already begun in London and Washington. The Tripartite Pact had explicitly drawn Far Eastern happenings into the orbit of European events. Russia's failure to adhere to this treaty would place that country in a semidetached position which might offer some hope that the Soviet Union could be cultivated as an opponent of both Japan in the Far East and Germany in Europe. With the situation thus clarified and the pressure for time somewhat lessened, American policy could henceforth follow a more considered and orderly design.

According to one supposedly informed source, President Roosevelt conferred with Hull and Welles in his bedroom the morning after the Tripartite Pact was signed and decided then and there upon a basic war strategy which would treat the Atlantic and the Pacific as parts of a related whole, but would accord the European theater a definite priority.[93] Thus the drift of American foreign policy over the past three years was authoritatively confirmed, and substance was given to Count Ciano's gloomiest meditations on the three-power alliance. When he heard it proposed for the first time, Ciano had objected that so close an association of Germany and Italy with Japan would merely increase American aid to Britain.[94] Nor did the formalities of signature in Berlin cheer him up. "One thing alone is certain," he told his diary after signing the treaty on Italy's behalf, "one thing alone is certain: that the war will be long."[95]

[93] Forrest Davis and Ernest K. Lindley, *How War Came* (New York: Simon and Schuster, 1942), pp. 154–158.
[94] *Ciano Diaries*, p. 293.   [95] *Ibid.*, p. 296.

CHAPTER VI

The Unfolding of Strategy

I

THE PORTENTOUS DEVELOPMENTS OF THE SUMMER OF 1940 CAUSED THE American government to slough off the major hesitations of public opinion for the first time, and to formulate national policy so as to meet the international crisis. Public opinion was still a significant force, however, and it still held firmly to most of its established beliefs. Its growth since the war's beginning enabled a majority of the American people to countenance as essential to defense most of the activities publicly undertaken by the administration, but there was no sign that it viewed defense as going much beyond conscription, the building of a two-ocean navy, the transfer of destroyers, and the continued sale of war materials to Great Britain on a cash-and-carry basis. Certainly it did not regard intervention as falling within the scope of the defense program, and it was deeply sensitive to any hint that the country's nonbelligerency might lead to full participation in the war. Public opinion was still intractable and had to be guided with the greatest care.

Thus the adjustment of American policy to world events through the summer and fall of 1940 was especially remarkable in that it took place amid the uncertainties of a presidential election, an election made especially complex by the third-term issue. Strong popular feeling on the latter point clearly demanded an urgent reason for the President's attempt to defy tradition, and such a reason could be found only in the crisis abroad. Yet Roosevelt could not use this argument with absolute freedom. To discuss the full implications of the danger confronting America might create an impression that he was leading the country toward war, and it was not hard to believe that such a view would endanger, if not totally undermine, his chances of reëlection. Therefore, although international affairs received much attention during the campaign, the President cautiously avoided a genuine elucidation of the new drift in American activity.

So far as election tactics were concerned, American foreign policy in the autumn of 1940 resembled an iceberg. Enough appeared above the surface to reveal location and direction of progress, but what existed underneath could only be surmised. There was much ground for warnings and guesses, however. Incipient efforts to formulate military and naval strategy in staff conversations with the British were necessarily secret. But the public policy of aid to Britain, especially as revealed in the arms transfer and in the destroyer transfer, had so many obvious corollaries that some private initiatives could be taken for granted. This gave the Republicans their opportunity. Declaring himself heartily in favor of the administration's general policy, Republican candidate Wendell Willkie divided his criticism between the methods employed to carry out that policy and the President's suspected taste for secret understandings with foreign powers, which might draw the United States into war.[1]

Willkie's insinuations were necessarily vague, but they were not implausible enough to be dismissed without a reply. In the waning days of the campaign Roosevelt finally cast off his reserve and delivered a series of nine major speeches to rebut Willkie's imputations concerning his foreign policy. Faced by misgivings of defeat, he made no effort in these talks to appraise the situation realistically. Instead, he dispensed a shower of heartening generalities which in tone, if not in exact word, encouraged his listeners to believe that everything was well in hand. Although too much has been made of these assurances given under stress of a political campaign whose outcome many Democratic leaders considered doubtful, the fact remains that the President's words fell far short of his convictions as formulated in plan and action at that time.[2]

So official utterance left the boundaries of American foreign policy exceedingly vague throughout the autumn, generally allowing public understanding of what was being done to approximate the public view of what ought to be done. This partial concealment had an unfortunate aspect because an old confusion still troubled the American mind. The fatalism and wishful thinking which lay at its root were strikingly revealed by Gallup polls taken in September and October, when just over

[1] For a convenient survey of Willkie's speaking tactics, see Charles A. Beard, *American Foreign Policy in the Making, 1932–1940: A Study in Responsibilities* (New Haven: Yale Univ. Press, 1946), pp. 298–312.

[2] See Robert E. Sherwood, *Roosevelt and Hopkins: An Intimate History* (New York: Harper and Bros., 1948), pp. 189–192. For a less severe view of Roosevelt's equivocations, see Basil Rauch, *Roosevelt: From Munich to Pearl Harbor* (New York: Creative Age Press, 1950), pp. 263–271.

two thirds of the population thought the United States would eventually take part in the European war,[3] but less than one fifth considered it desirable to enter hostilities at once. The irresolution to which this feeling gave birth was reflected in November, when the same cross section that had overwhelmingly favored aid to Britain for months past divided evenly on the question of whether it was more important for the United States to remain out of the war at all costs, or to risk what was necessary in helping England to win it.[4] Of course, this question had already been answered at the policy-making level. But in declining to reveal and explain its answer the administration appeared to suggest that the question itself was out of order. So if public opinion remain confused, the vagaries of the popular mind were not solely responsible for this phenomenon.

The President's reëlection in the face of the third-term issue was certainly a great personal triumph, but that it represented a popular mandate for his conduct of foreign affairs was not so clear. Since he polled less than 54 per cent of the total national vote, the mandate was not overwhelming in any event.[5] And while questions of war and peace furnished the dominant interest of the campaign, the general reluctance to face the ultimate realities of the world situation, as well as Roosevelt's own failure to expound these realities in his speeches as he viewed them in formulating policy, make it impossible to say just how much of the election victory sprang from conscious endorsement of his attitude in foreign affairs and how much of it reflected a simple faith in his ability as a leader.

That the President's campaign statements laid up a considerable store of future embarrassment is plain enough, but it is a moot question whether a less equivocal discussion of policy would have jeopardized the election and destroyed or impaired his ability to carry on the war. There is no doubt that such a course would have entailed considerable risk; for as organized pressure groups multiplied through the summer of 1940, public opinion was subjected to a new stimulation which was increasingly hostile to any suggestion that the United States might eventually have to consider the possibility of fighting in Europe. By fall the agitation was

[3] *Public Opinion Quarterly,* V (Sept. 1941), 476.

[4] *Ibid.* (Mar. 1941), p. 159.

[5] See Edgar E. Robinson, *They Voted for Roosevelt: The Presidential Vote, 1932–1944* (Stanford University, Calif.: Stanford Univ. Press, 1947), p. 22; and Thomas A. Bailey, *The Man in the Street: The Impact of American Public Opinion on Foreign Policy* (New York: Macmillan Co., 1948), p. 97.

in full swing. Leadership of the noninterventionist school had passed from the relatively moderate older groups to such newly founded and virulent organizations as the short-lived No Foreign War Committee and the more notorious Committee to Defend America First.[6] Despite its energetic support of such measures as the arms transfer and the destroyer deal, even the highly reputable Committee to Defend America by Aiding the Allies remained steadfast in its program of aid short of war.[7] Not until the Fight for Freedom Committee was set up in April 1941 did the counsel of intervention receive any organized support.[8] Thus nearly every circumstance indicated the necessity of caution in public statement, at least until after the election.

Owing to these conditions, it was probably inevitable that expediency should be given such a large role in shaping words just as America's non-belligerency was taking definite form. But the essence of policy is rarely verbal, and the misgivings which imposed such restraint on the use of words did not apply in the same measure to deeds. The nation's real preparations for what lay ahead continued, therefore, without much hindrance.

II

Since coöperation at sea was the obvious starting point in the framing of a joint operational strategy, the main burden of the staff conversations in London was assumed at the outset by representatives of the American and British navies. Vice Admiral Ghormley remained in London for the balance of the year, keeping a sharp lookout over British survival power and holding frequent conferences with a special committee of the British Admiralty headed by Sir Sidney Bailey. In October Ghormley reiterated his opinion that England would not succumb to German air attacks and reported substantial agreement concerning the outlines of future naval coöperation between Great Britain and the United States. The question of whether or not a portion of the United States Fleet should be based at Singapore in the event of a Pacific war constituted the main stumbling block.[9] Britain was eager to have American warships

[6] John W. Masland, "Pressure Groups and American Foreign Policy," *Public Opinion Quarterly*, VI (Spring 1942), 116; and Walter Johnson, *The Battle against Isolation* (Chicago: Univ. Chicago Press, 1944), pp. 161–163.

[7] Johnson, *The Battle against Isolation*, pp. 182–183. [8] *Ibid.*, p. 223.

[9] Samuel Eliot Morison, *The Battle of the Atlantic, 1939–1943* (Boston: Little, Brown, and Co., 1947), p. 41.

operating from that great Far Eastern base; the United States was reluctant to send its forces so far afield and uncertain as to what obligations the British might accept in return.[10]   They saw eye to eye on Atlantic questions, however, agreeing that escort duty and antisubmarine warfare should be the initial tasks of the United States Navy in this area.[11]

With these preliminaries disposed of, Admiral Stark turned to the civilian heads of the government for authorization to proceed further. While Roosevelt had apparently settled the war's broad strategic pattern in his own mind as early as the end of September, only formal decisions at the political level could serve as basis for a detailed allocation of forces and a usable plan of operations.   In a memorandum handed to Secretary Knox on November 12 Stark emphasized the importance of formalizing these decisions at once, making it clear that, among various alternatives, he favored the idea of combining a strong hemispheric defense with an offensive strategy in the Atlantic and a defensive strategy in the Pacific. His recommendations were ratified before the end of the month, and Stark lost no time directing Ghormley to arrange for comprehensive staff talks in Washington early in 1941.   Feeling that British notions regarding Singapore would saddle the United States Navy with impossible burdens, he stated that anyone sent by London "should have instructions to discuss concepts based on equality of considerations for both the United States and the British Commonwealth, and to explore realistically the various fields of war coöperation."   Both the invitation and its attached conditions were accepted promptly.[12]

The Navy's preoccupation with escort duty grew steadily in the meanwhile, for this was solidly founded in Britain's need.   As noted earlier, the British shipping problem had remained well in hand during the first months of the war but had grown more serious with the basing of U-boats on French ports in the summer of 1940.   It became particularly urgent in November and December, when the Germans adopted a new submarine tactic—the highly efficient "wolf-pack" method.   Instead of hunting

---

[10] Samuel Eliot Morison, *The Rising Sun in the Pacific, 1931—April 1942* (Boston: Little, Brown, and Co., 1948), pp. 49–50; also, Stark to Hart, Nov. 12, 1940, United States, Congress, Joint Committee on Investigation of Pearl Harbor Attack, *Hearings Pursuant to S. Con. Res. 27, Authorizing Investigation of Attack on Pearl Harbor, Dec. 7, 1941, and Events and Circumstances Relating Thereto* (79th Cong., 1st and 2nd sess.) (Washington, D. C.: U. S. Govt. Printing Office, 1946), pt. 16, exhibit 109, pp. 2448–2449.   Cited henceforth as *Pearl Harbor Hearings*.

[11] Morison, *The Battle of the Atlantic*, p. 41.   [12] *Ibid.*, pp. 42–44.

singly, U-boats now attacked convoys in large groups, systematically dogging their course for days at a time and running up tremendous scores in the process.[13]   A greater number of escort vessels and a more intensive antisubmarine campaign were needed at once.

At Stark's direction the Naval War Plans Division had for some time been working on preliminary plans for American naval activity in the event of war.   A draft providing for the assumption of transoceanic escort duty and the establishment of American bases in the United Kingdom was completed in December.   By January 14, 1941, Rear Admiral Richmond K. Turner, director of the War Plans Division, was able to assure Stark that the Navy could inaugurate an escort service between North America and Scotland as early as the beginning of April if the physical preparations were started without delay.[14]   It was quite obvious that weighty political considerations stood between a plan designed for use in time of war and its effective realization in time of official peace, but it was equally obvious that some form of escort duty could not be indefinitely postponed if the policy of aiding Britain were to have any material significance.   Having accepted the full implications of this policy, the Navy was merely drawing in outline the essential bridge leading from staff talks to belligerent action.

III

Still mindful of his new discouragement with affairs in Tokyo, Ambassador Grew paused long enough on October 1, 1940, to review his estimate of diplomatic trends.   First he agreed heartily with the general concept of a defensive strategy in the Pacific, stating his belief that every available means should be used to keep the Pacific free of hostilities "until the issue of the European war had been decided."   But his second point harked back to his "green-light" telegram of September 12.   "This cannot be done," he wrote, "nor can our interests any longer receive their full and proper protection, merely by expressing our disapproval and carefully placing it on record." [15]

As though it were echoing this new endorsement of action, the State Department on October 8 advised all American citizens to leave China,

---

[13] *Ibid.*, p. 25.   [14] *Ibid.*, pp. 44–45.
[15] Joseph C. Grew, *Ten Years in Japan* (New York: Simon and Schuster, 1944), p. 338.

Japan, Manchukuo, Hong Kong, Korea, Formosa, and French Indo-China.[16] At the same time, the War Department announced that an antiaircraft regiment of the California National Guard was being sent to Hawaii; and the Navy Department let it be known a day later that personnel allotments of the United States Fleet in the Pacific were being increased to full wartime strength.[17] Nor were these veiled threats completely lost on the Japanese government. On October 9 Grew was called away from the semiannual golf tournament of the American Club to find that Matsuoka was somewhat unnerved by the prospective evacuation of Americans from the Far East and by concurrent press rumors that the United States was about to extend its embargo measures. Grew's annoyance at missing his game was more than compensated for. As he observed to his diary that night, he had often suggested that a move to recall Americans from the Orient "would have a powerful effect on Japanese consciousness." [18]

This stiffening of American policy, which had begun at the end of September with the announcement of the embargo on scrap iron and steel, did not rest solely on Grew's advice, however. As early as August 26, Lothian asked for Hull's coöperation with regard to the possible reopening of the Burma Road. Britain, he said, was giving special attention to Japan's oil problem and had urged British oil interests in the East Indies to enter no long-term contracts with Japanese buyers. If Hull could induce reluctant Dutch oil producers to follow the British example and thus increase the pressure upon Japan, Lothian thought that Japanese uncertainty regarding the petroleum supply, plus Britain's improving position in Europe and Russia's decreasingly pro-Axis attitude, would make it possible to open the Burma Road about October 15.

Hull promised to work along the lines suggested.[19] But when Lothian returned to the subject on September 30 with a request for the Secretary's views concerning an immediate announcement that the Road would be opened October 17, Hull was less direct. Convinced that the Ambassador really wanted an assurance of tangible American support,

[16] Radio bulletin, Oct. 8, 1940, United States, Department of State, *Papers Relating to the Foreign Relations of the United States: Japan, 1931–1941* (Washington, D. C.: U. S. Govt. Printing Office, 1943), II, 114.

[17] See William C. Johnstone, *The United States and Japan's New Order*, rev. ed. (New York: Oxford Univ. Press, 1941), pp. 316–317.

[18] Grew, *Ten Years*, pp. 346–347.

[19] Memorandum by Hull, Aug. 26, 1940, MS Department of State (893.24/859).

he referred to the "definite and somewhat progressive line of acts and utterances" by which the United States had already demonstrated its opposition to Japanese aggression, but he declined to say how far the American government would go in following up this policy. He added, however, that the United States wanted Great Britain to win the war and admitted that its "acts and utterances with respect to the Pacific area would be more or less affected as to time and extent" by the question of what would most effectively contribute to British success.[20]

A few days later Churchill applied to Roosevelt directly, telling him that the British government had decided to permit resumption of traffic over the Burma Road when the existing agreement expired on October 17. He suggested that an American naval squadron, "the bigger the better," be sent to pay a "friendly visit" at Singapore to discourage any hostile Japanese reaction.[21] Public announcement of the scheduled reopening was made October 8, the very day chosen by the American government to advise the withdrawal of its nationals from the Far East. Then, on October 16, when the Australian Minister in Washington, Richard G. Casey, inquired about American naval plans for the South Pacific, Hull replied that the United States was on a day-to-day basis, adding that Australia would have to judge the matter for itself "in the light of our policies up to this time, the last of our acts being the calling back of American citizens from the Far East."[22]

Although American guarantees had not been explicit, the Secretary's hints had certainly been broad, and the conjunction of these utterances with the perfectly tangible actions of late September and early October made it reasonably clear to any informed observer that Anglo-American coöperation was spreading from the Atlantic and western Europe into the Orient.

Still more evidence that the United States backed London's display of energy was furnished by Secretary Knox during an October conversation with Admiral Richardson, who had journeyed from Hawaii to Washington for the purpose of learning more about the future movements of the Fleet. According to Knox, President Roosevelt contemplated rather extensive action in the Pacific if Japan based any new aggression on the reopening of the Burma Road. This action included

[20] Memorandum by Hull, Sept. 30, 1940, MS Department of State (762.9411/84½).
[21] Winston S. Churchill, *Their Finest Hour* (Boston: Houghton Mifflin Co., 1949), pp. 497–498.
[22] Memorandum by Hull, Oct. 16, 1940, MS Department of State (740.0011 Pacific War/4).

reinforcement of the Asiatic Fleet, a complete embargo on American trade with Japan, and an effort to stop all commerce between Japan and the entire Western Hemisphere with a kind of blockade extending from Honolulu to the Philippines. Needless to say, this revival of a scheme conceived three years earlier as a means of "quarantining" the Japanese Empire was, in Admiral Richardson's opinion, decidedly impracticable.[23]

But Richardson, a somewhat unimaginative professional, was always a harsh judge of naval policy, and especially so when it revealed the amateur's lack of appreciation for training problems and other technical difficulties. Moreover, he was still smarting from old annoyances; he could not forget the shortcomings of Pearl Harbor as a base for the United States Fleet, and his main objective in Washington was not to discuss the grand strategic inspirations of civilians but rather to have the Fleet brought back to the California coast. His worries received scant sympathy, however. During an interview at the White House he was told by Roosevelt that the Fleet was being kept at Hawaii to exercise a restraining influence on Japan. When Richardson expressed doubt that the Fleet, in its existing state of unreadiness, could have much effect to that end, the President cut him off with an assurance that the maneuver was very worth while. The occasion was not a total loss, on the other hand, for Roosevelt unbent enough to deliver some views on the general Pacific situation. He considered war with Japan inevitable. He thought the United States would not fight if the Japanese invaded Thailand, the Isthmus of Kra, or the Dutch East Indies. He doubted that real hostilities would begin even if the Philippines were attacked. But "sooner or later," he declared, the Japanese "would make a mistake and we would enter the war." [24] Assembling these revelations as he departed from Washington, Richardson was convinced not only that American policy had stiffened but that it was stiffening altogether too fast.[25]

While the Admiral's fears were premature, it was clear that the government's recent moves in the Pacific were part of a definite program. According to Hull, he and Roosevelt decided about the middle of October to continue exerting economic pressure against Japan without going far enough to provoke a demand for war among Japanese militarists,

---

[23] Richardson to Hart, Oct. 16, 1940, *Pearl Harbor Hearings,* pt. 14, exhibit 11, pp. 1006–1007.

[24] Richardson's testimony, Nov. 19, 1945, *ibid.,* pt. 1, pp. 265–266.

[25] Richardson to Stark, Oct. 22, 1940, *ibid.,* pt. 14, exhibit 9, pp. 963–964.

to cultivate Tokyo's awareness of American strength in the Pacific, and to discourage all hope that the United States would not fight if necessary.[26]

Whether or not Japan was intimidated by the visible signs of this attitude it is impossible to say, but the Japanese undertook no more large aggressions during the remainder of the year. Instead, they confined themselves to maintaining the positions already gained and to such minor ill works as encouraging Thailand in its boundary dispute with French Indo-China. But Grew had no illusions that Japan was actually changing course. He sensed danger in Tokyo's connivings with the Siamese,[27] and he outlined the final dilemma in a personal letter to the President on December 14: "It seems to me to be increasingly clear that we are bound to have a showdown someday, and the principal question at issue is whether it is to our advantage to have the showdown sooner or to have it later." [28]

This was a pertinent query, but the answer was already in hand. Following closely upon the alarms of October, the strategic decisions made by the government in November had confirmed Asia's place as second in priority. While the particulars of the diplomatic resistance envisaged by Hull and Roosevelt would necessarily emerge from circumstances, it was clear that the United States had elected to delay its showdown with Japan as long as possible.

IV

As it affected southwestern Europe, Gibraltar, and French North Africa, the diplomatic situation remained in constant flux between the summer of 1940 and the spring of 1941. Neither Vichy nor Madrid plunged into full collaboration with the Axis. There were no overt moves against Gibraltar, North Africa, or the Atlantic islands belonging to Spain and to Portugal. London and Washington continued their program of uniting diplomacy with economics. But the scales were always too evenly weighted for comfort, and hope alternated with fear at dizzying speed.

Somewhat disconcerted by Franco's coolness toward its offer of a

[26] Cordell Hull, *The Memoirs of Cordell Hull* (New York: Macmillan Co., 1948), I, 911–912.   [27] Grew, *Ten Years*, pp. 354–355.
[28] Grew to Roosevelt, Dec. 14, 1940, *Pearl Harbor Hearings*, pt. 20, exhibit 179, p. 4267.

trade agreement at the end of June 1940, and fearful that Spain was about to enter the war, the American government set about limiting Spanish oil supplies. At first there was some disposition to tie this procedure in with the order of July 26 directed against Japan. But subtler methods were eventually preferred, and the objective was reached through the withdrawal of American tankers from trade with Spain, delays engineered by the Treasury Department, and undertakings by oil companies not to exceed customary volumes.[29]   Before these arrangements were completed, however, Franco's suspected ardor for immediate war began to cool visibly. Weddell understood that the Caudillo was trying to convince Germany that the economic shortages of his country would keep Spain from entering hostilities for the time being;[30] and when Madrid on August 6 yielded to standing demands on behalf of American interests in the Spanish telephone system, the Ambassador informed the Spanish government that it might have all the American oil it could transport, providing the British blockade did not interfere.

Hoare offered a partial solution to this problem, suggesting that British and Spanish experts draw up an extended supply program which would keep Spain alive but leave no surplus for possible transfer to the Axis. As this work proceeded, Britain offered to countenance the importation of still more oil if Spain would loosen existing restrictions on its domestic use. But the Spanish government replied that a dollar shortage kept it from taking advantage of this opportunity, and here the matter rested. Although British and American policies were now openly linked, Washington did not echo London's enthusiasm for the joint program and refused to expedite it with dollar credits.[31]   The net result of these developments was a considerable decline in the volume of American oil exports to Spain through the rest of the year.[32]

At this juncture the United States was much less disposed than Britain to rely heavily upon the psychological effect created in Spain by Anglo-American economic help and by the prospect of its withdrawal in the event of poor behavior. The American State Department, Hull especially, wanted advance payment for any favors extended; and this attitude covered more than the oil problem. On September 7 Spain requested a $100 million loan for general purchases in the United States.

---

[29] Herbert Feis, *The Spanish Story: Franco and the Nations at War* (New York: Alfred A. Knopf, 1948), pp. 39, 45.

[30] Telegram from Weddell, Aug. 14, 1940, MS Department of State (740.0011 European War 1939/5131).

[31] Feis, *The Spanish Story*, pp. 49–51.   [32] *Ibid.*, p. 46.

After lengthy discussion the plea was tabled for the nonce, although it was agreed that some aid might be provided out of a $50 million fund recently appropriated by Congress for European relief. Weddell received instructions to say that the United States would consider methods of aid in return for a promise not to enter the war, but Hull rejected the Ambassador's entreaties for a more flexible program.[33] Accordingly, Weddell communicated this message to Colonel Juan Beigbeder, the Spanish Foreign Minister, on September 30. Beigbeder's anti-Axis views were well known, and he told Weddell that Spain would not enter the war unless attacked. But he made it clear that no such announcement could be issued publicly.[34] Somewhat reassured, the United States was just preparing to revive the loan project when Hitler took up his long-awaited diplomatic offensive to force Spain and France into the war.[35]

Since there had never been any illusions regarding the Axis desire to secure a commanding position in the western Mediterranean and in French North Africa, or the readiness of powerful circles in both the French and Spanish governments to lend such designs a hand, it was obvious that Hitler's own procrastination was the main cause for his delay in launching a strenuous effort to realize these ambitions. Now that procrastination seemed about to end. Having concluded that Britain was less vulnerable to direct assault than he had first imagined, Hitler was prepared to deal with the Empire's Mediterranean flank. His initial objective was Gibraltar.[36]

Groundwork for the necessary collaboration had already been laid. Pierre Laval, now Foreign Minister at Vichy, had been in active communication with German authorities for weeks,[37] and Madrid had been discussing terms with Berlin since June.[38] When the pro-British Beigbeder was suddenly ousted from the Spanish Foreign Office on October

[33] *Ibid.*, pp. 56–58.
[34] Feis, *The Spanish Story*, p. 60. For an estimate of Beigbeder, see Sir Samuel Hoare (Viscount Templewood), *Complacent Dictator* (New York: Alfred A. Knopf, 1947), p. 33. [35] Feis, *The Spanish Story*, p. 62.
[36] Record of conversation between Ribbentrop and Mussolini, Sept. 19, 1940, International Military Tribunal, *Nazi Conspiracy and Aggression* (Washington, D. C.: U. S. Govt. Printing Office, 1946–1947), IV, 477. Cf. Count Galeazzo Ciano, *The Ciano Diaries, 1939–1943*, ed. Hugh Gibson (Garden City, N. Y.: Doubleday and Co., 1946), p. 293.
[37] See William L. Langer, *Our Vichy Gamble* (New York: Alfred A. Knopf, 1947), p. 84.
[38] Memorandum by Stoehrer, Aug. 8, 1940, United States, Department of State, *The Spanish Government and the Axis: Official German Documents* (Washington, D. C.: U. S. Govt. Printing Office, 1946), p. 3.

17 to be replaced by Ramón Serrano Suñer, Franco's brother-in-law and one of the most outspoken friends of collaboration with Germany in all Spain, it became evident that connivance was about to enter a new phase.[39]

Once he had decided to act, Hitler personally assumed the burden of negotiations. On October 22 he talked with Laval at Montoire and arranged for a conversation with Pétain two days later.[40]   In the interim he sped onward to Hendaye, near the Spanish border, for a meeting with Franco on October 23.   He was especially intent on beating down the price of Spanish coöperation, for the Caudillo's wants were notably immodest.   Franco had already made it clear that he required large donations of grain, oil, and military supplies before considering any move which brought him closer to war.   He also demanded special troops and weapons for capturing Gibraltar, and he wanted title to such French possessions as Morocco and Oran.[41]

In a series of alternating monologues which lasted several hours, the two dictators met and reviewed the situation.   Franco affirmed his spiritual ties with the Axis, but spoke even more eloquently of Spain's needs.   Owing to his country's material shortages, he pointed out, Great Britain was in a position to make things very difficult; both the United States and Argentina, Spain's chief suppliers, took orders from London as far as their economic policies were concerned.   The Fuehrer clucked sympathetically and launched into a disquisition of his own. German military power was great.   England would have been defeated by now except for bad weather, but the end was nonetheless certain. American military power would grow slowly at best; it could be further discounted because the United States was being held in check by the Tripartite Pact.   The main dangers to be feared were occupation of the Azores, the Canaries, or the Cape Verde Islands by the British or Americans, and loss of France's colonial empire to DeGaulle, Great Britain, or the United States.   The danger to the empire would grow tremendously if any partition of Africa were attempted at the present time.[42]

[39] See Hoare, *Complacent Dictator*, p. 33.   For Serrano Suñer's personal statement of his views, see Ramón Serrano Suñer, *Entre les Pyrénées et Gibraltar* (Geneva: Les Éditions du Cheval Ailé, 1948), p. 145.   [40] Langer, *Our Vichy Gamble*, p. 90.
[41] Memorandum of conversation between Hitler and Ciano, Sept. 28, 1940, *The Spanish Government and the Axis*, p. 17.   Cf. *Ciano Diaries*, p. 296.
[42] Record of conversation between Hitler and Franco, Oct. 23, 1940, *The Spanish Government and the Axis*, pp. 21–25.   For additional details, see Feis, *The Spanish*

There were many more contributions from both parties before the talk ended, but its atmosphere of negation was maintained throughout. Franco stood firmly on his demands; and since his help, in Hitler's view, was not worth the price he asked, no fruitful bargain was struck.

Retracing his steps northward, the somewhat chastened Fuehrer saw Laval and Pétain together at Montoire on October 24. But Pétain proved no more tractable than Franco, and again Hitler failed to pin anything down. Whatever their shortcomings in other respects, both the Frenchman and the Spaniard were more devoted to national than to German interests, and both were given to moving slowly. Although agreements of a sort were formulated at both Montoire and Hendaye, they went little beyond the affirmation of principle. Neither provided any real basis for action.[43]

The fact that Hitler's trip to Montoire and thence to the Spanish border was another false alarm did not become immediately apparent, however, for neither Vichy nor Madrid stopped exchanging views with Berlin. Through November, and into December, Laval continued his efforts to widen the narrow opening already made.[44] On November 11, furthermore, Serrano Suñer put his signature to a revision of the Hendaye protocol[45] which, in Hitler's view, provided such a definite basis for action that he immediately ordered the High Command to prepare for the assault on Gibraltar.[46]

But the Fuehrer's promises were too niggardly to render his hold on Spain secure, and Laval's ascendancy in the French government was less absolute than most people thought. On November 18, at Berchtesgaden, Hitler told Serrano Suñer that Franco should ready himself to enter the war in January or February, but this announcement drew nothing from the Spanish Foreign Minister except a storm of protests and evasions.[47] A week later Franco himself pressed for more time and for less elusive assurances regarding Spain's territorial claims and other demands. The most Hitler could obtain by the end of the month was a statement that Franco would not object to German preparations for

---

Story, pp. 94–95; and Carlton J. H. Hayes, *Wartime Mission in Spain, 1942–1945* (New York: Macmillan Co., 1946), pp. 64–65.

[43] Langer, *Our Vichy Gamble*, p. 96; Feis, *The Spanish Story*, pp. 96–97; and Churchill, *Their Finest Hour*, pp. 524–525.

[44] Langer, *Our Vichy Gamble*, p. 108.

[45] Feis, *The Spanish Story*, pp. 111–112.

[46] Directive No. 108, Nov. 12, 1940, *Nazi Conspiracy and Aggression*, VI, 957–959.

[47] Feis, *The Spanish Story*, pp. 115–116.

attacking Gibraltar so long as no date was set for action.[48] The exasperated Fuehrer wrote to Mussolini on December 5 that Spain would have to be brought into the war without delay. Since he wanted Germany's complete forces in hand by April for a grand assault on the British Isles, the time for this subsidiary action was growing short.[49]

But time seemed to be running against him, and his hope for speedy action was soon blasted. At the beginning of December he sought to apply new pressure in Madrid through a special envoy, Admiral Wilhelm Canaris, Chief of German Naval Intelligence. Canaris saw Franco on December 7 and told him that German troops would be prepared by January 10 to undertake the capture of Gibraltar in concert with Spanish forces. But the Caudillo refused even to consider this schedule. Since nothing had been done to make good his economic deficiencies, Spain was not prepared to invite fresh hazards like British or American occupation of Madeira, the Azores, the Canaries, or the Cape Verde Islands. Although Gibraltar might fall quickly, the war was not likely to be short; and Germany would find Spain, in its weakened condition, more a hindrance than a help. For all these reasons Spain could not enter the war at this time, nor was it yet possible to name a later date. Franco could only suggest that Hitler verify his words by sending a German economist to obtain a first-hand impression of Spain's circumstances.[50]

After this it was plain that nothing could be done in the Iberian Peninsula unless German tactics were thoroughly revamped. And to make matters worse for Hitler's designs, Pétain's dismissal of Laval from the Ministry of Foreign Affairs on December 13 announced France's almost simultaneous withdrawal to a more independent position.[51] Having lost both western props at the same time, the Fuehrer abruptly turned his back on Gibraltar and prepared to deal with his eastern problems.

In view of the Montoire-Hendaye conversations, the American State Department changed its mind about reviving the Spanish loan project and decided to make no offer in this regard until the outcome of the talks was less uncertain.[52] The possibility of limited aid through Red Cross shipments was all that remained for the time being, and Weddell

[48] Feis, *The Spanish Story*, pp. 117–118.

[49] Hitler to Mussolini, Dec. 5, 1940, Adolf Hitler and Benito Mussolini, *Les Lettres secrètes échangées par Hitler et Mussolini*, with introd. by Andre François-Poncet (Paris: Éditions du Pavois, 1946), p. 100.

[50] Stoehrer to Ribbentrop, Dec. 12, 1940, *The Spanish Government and the Axis*, pp. 26–28.

[51] Langer, *Our Vichy Gamble*, p. 109.

[52] Feis, *The Spanish Story*, p. 65.

was instructed on November 6 to explain that even these could not be justified unless Franco, in a public announcement, stated his intention not to help the Axis. But the Spanish government thought it necessary to be as coy with Washington as with Berlin. The most Weddell could extract from Serrano Suñer four days later was a private declaration that Spain would resist any effort by German or Italian troops to cross its borders. On October 19 the Minister of Industry and Commerce, Demetrio Carceller, added a word of explanation: Spain certainly had differences with the Axis, but was in no position to advertise that fact so long as German troops were camped on its very frontier.[53] Carceller's point did not altogether lack force.

Urged by London to reconsider the instructions of November 8,[54] Roosevelt now conceded that a formal private declaration of Spain's neutral intentions might take the place of a public one. Franco made a somewhat equivocal reply to this message on November 29. While the Caudillo's new statement was less than satisfactory, it was not assayed as a total loss. After weighing it with some care, Washington again veered toward the loan project.[55] The State Department could not rid itself of hesitations, however, and by the end of the year resumed its insistence that Franco must commit himself openly before he could expect additional favors from the United States.[56]

If the Montoire-Hendaye episode further slackened the leisurely gait of Roosevelt's Spanish policy, it had a somewhat different effect on American relations with France. While the United States had carefully maintained its diplomatic connections with the Pétain government, it had thus far employed them merely to observe developments in France and to issue warnings based on its observations. But the events of October reëmphasized the strength of collaborationist tendencies at Vichy to such a degree that Washington, during the last two months of the year, began to evolve a definite policy for minimizing this danger. Since the problem here was not unlike the problem in Spain, it was only natural that its key should likewise be sought in economics. Approaches, however, were different. The Spanish government could be reached only through Madrid, where pro-Axis feeling was strongest. But the road to France began in North Africa, where the possibility of independent action was much greater than at Vichy itself.

The idea of driving an economic wedge into this strategically im-

[53] *Ibid.*, pp. 101–102.
[54] Churchill, *Their Finest Hour*, pp. 529–530.
[55] Feis, *The Spanish Story*, pp. 104–106.   [56] *Ibid.*, p. 107.

portant area had been under review since August 1940, and Great Britain had intimated in September that American coöperation in setting up a special trade with Morocco would be welcome. Although it held some tentative conversations with Emmanuel Monick, secretary-general of the French administration in Morocco, the State Department postponed action for the moment.[57]   At the beginning of October, however, General Maxime Weygand received from the Vichy government broad powers to arrange for the defense of North and West Africa.[58]   The establishment of such an authority in France's African possessions clarified the situation a great deal; and when A. G. Reed, who managed the Moroccan operations of the Socony-Vacuum Oil Company, reached Washington on October 25 with Monick's commission to promote serious trade talks, the project entered a more active phase.[59]

Although the State Department was still slow to take action, it was impressed by Reed's belief that Weygand meant to keep Germany from absorbing the territory under his control. New proposals by Monick reached Washington through the American chargé d'affaires at Vichy early in November, and it was decided to open discussions with both Monick and Weygand through United States consuls on the spot. At the same time, Robert D. Murphy, counselor of the American Embassy at Vichy, was sent into North and West Africa on a tour of investigation.[60]

Other aspects of American relations with France grew more stable in the meanwhile. Discussions regarding Martinique continued with some appearance of a more coöperative attitude on Vichy's part; then, in November, Admiral Greenslade paid his second visit to the island, rumbled a few threats, and extracted a promise from Admiral Robert that none of the ships under his command would leave port without a ninety-six-hour notice to the American government. In return, the United States agreed to supply the island with food, taking payment from French assets held in America.[61]   There were also favorable developments at Vichy. Striving to calm fears aroused by the Montoire conversations, Pétain in November renewed his assurances against collaboration [62] and followed through by dismissing Laval, as previously noted. Since the anti-British influence of Admiral Darlan remained unimpaired, this was not regarded as a fundamental change of orientation, but the trend

[57] Langer, *Our Vichy Gamble,* pp. 105–106.
[58] *Ibid.,* p. 104.   [59] *Ibid.,* p. 106.   [60] *Ibid.,* pp. 107–108.
[61] Memorandum by Welles, Oct. 7, 1940, MS Roosevelt Papers (Secretary's File, Box 62); and Feis, *The Spanish Story,* p. 104.
[62] Feis, *The Spanish Story,* pp. 98, 101.

was certainly encouraging. So Roosevelt went ahead with his plans for filling the vacant ambassadorship to France. Discovering that his first choice, the aged General Pershing, was not physically able to serve, he selected for this ticklish assignment Admiral William D. Leahy, a former Chief of Naval Operations who had a well-developed political sense and a fund of service experience which gave him something in common with Pétain.[63]

Although the American government was now inclined to take a somewhat more optimistic view of French attitudes than was Great Britain, its policy toward European France was still acceptable enough to Downing Street. It entered no protest when the British on December 10 declined to countenance relief shipments to unoccupied France;[64] and Leahy's instructions, drafted ten days later, made it clear that Washington had no intention of moderating its stand against any form of connivance between French and German officials, especially in questions bearing on the French Fleet.[65] The status of the North African project was not so clear, however. It became apparent in mid-December that Great Britain was disposed to hold back on this matter. The British had lately resumed trade with Morocco under a special agreement, and in September they had invited the United States to join such a program. But they were not eager to open their blockade to an independent exchange of goods between the United States and North Africa.[66]

Thus the year ended in some confusion regarding France and Spain. Open collaboration had still failed to materialize in either country, but the air was heavy with its menace. Although Great Britain and the United States had embarked on what might be described as a common effort to stabilize the western Mediterranean through the use of economic pressures and inducements, Spain was Britain's chief interest,[67] while the

[63] William D. Leahy, *I Was There* (New York: Whittlesey House, 1950), chap. ii; and Roosevelt to Leahy, Nov. 16, 1940, Franklin D. Roosevelt, *F. D. R.: His Personal Letters, 1928–1945*, ed. Elliott Roosevelt (New York: Duell, Sloan, and Pearce, 1950), II, 1080–1081.

[64] Langer, *Our Vichy Gamble*, p. 127. For the general attitude of the British government regarding commerce with unoccupied France, see Churchill, *Their Finest Hour*, p. 512.

[65] Roosevelt to Leahy, Dec. 20, 1940, United States, Department of State, *Peace and War: United States Foreign Policy, 1931–1941* (Washington, D. C.: U. S. Govt. Printing Office, 1943), pp. 596–599.

[66] Langer, *Our Vichy Gamble*, p. 130. By an accord signed on November 29, 1940, Great Britain had drawn Morocco, Spain, and Portugal into a triangular trade agreement (Hoare, *Complacent Dictator*, p. 81).

[67] See Churchill, *Their Finest Hour*, p. 518.

United States leaned increasingly toward an endeavor to solve the problem of French North Africa. If Britain's Spanish policy was hampered
by American reluctance to supply Franco with dollar credits, British
management of the blockade threatened to slow the functioning of any
trade agreement which the United States might conclude with Vichy
representatives in North Africa. Both governments blew hot and both
blew cold, but they were not doing it in exact unison.

V

Early in January 1941 the Japanese government appointed a new Ambassador to the United States, Admiral Kichisaburo Nomura. On the
surface, his selection for this vital post seemed promising. A naval officer
of moderate political views and considerable diplomatic experience,
Nomura enjoyed the special prestige of having recently held the portfolio
of Foreign Affairs. He was friendly to the United States and acquainted
with numerous Americans, most of whom regarded him as decidedly
"western" in his patterns of thought. Among his American associates of
earlier years was Captain Ellis M. Zacharias, a seasoned veteran of Naval
Intelligence, then stationed in Honolulu. When Nomura paused briefly
in that city en route to the United States, Zacharias paid him a visit and
ascertained that the new Ambassador had lost none of his respect for
American power. Nomura quite positively made known his belief that
war with the United States would mean the end of the Japanese Empire.[68]

Grew also took Nomura's appointment as a favorable omen,[69] although Matsuoka's continued presence in the Foreign Office discouraged
any real optimism. Since Matsuoka made no effort to conceal the fact
that he was not sanguine concerning Japanese-American relations, Grew
lost none of his deeper misgivings.[70] At the very least, however, Nomura's attitude might be utilized to gain time. Grew had already
advised delaying a break with Japan until a European settlement was
achieved, and he now learned from Roosevelt himself that it was not
American policy to be turned aside by the Japanese problem. Replying
on January 21 to Grew's foreboding epistle of December 14, the President
made it clear that his basic strategy was fixed, and revealed, by implica-

[68] Ellis M. Zacharias, *Secret Missions: The Story of an Intelligence Officer* (New
York: G. P. Putnam's Sons, 1946), p. 227.
[69] Grew, *Ten Years*, p. 350.   [70] *Ibid.*, p. 336.

t.on, that Japan had been given second place. "I believe," he wrote, "that the fundamental proposition is that we must recognize that the hostilities in Europe, in Africa, and in Asia are all parts of a single world con- flict. . . . Our strategy of self-defense must be a global strategy which takes account of every front and takes advantage of every opportunity to contribute to our total security." [71]

Except for sponsoring a treaty which, on March 11, gave Thailand nearly twenty-two thousand square miles of Indo-Chinese territory,[72] Japan remained outwardly quiescent during the first three months of 1941. But the calm was deceptive, and rumor ran wild. Postwar inves- tigation has disclosed that certain Japanese naval officers early in the year began thinking seriously of an attack on the United States Fleet at its Pearl Harbor base. It seems apparent that Admiral Isoroku Yamamoto, Commander-in-Chief of the Combined Fleet and original exponent of the plan, conceived the idea as a practical measure during the month of January, and it is certain that a tentative report on the matter was drawn up about the middle of February.

Yamamoto's advocacy of the plan was founded on his belief that Japan could not hope to win any possible war against the United States unless the American Fleet in Hawaii were destroyed or seriously crippled at the very outset of hostilities. Because Japan's real objectives lay far to the south, Yamamoto encountered great opposition from the Naval General Staff, and the proposal was not finally accepted as a part of the larger Japanese war plan until early autumn. Even then it did not represent an absolute intention; like projects being formulated in American staff con- ferences, it was regarded as an expedient to be used only if diplomacy failed and the necessary political decision for war were taken. Hence the status of the Pearl Harbor plan was decidedly nebulous in early 1941, and all discussions, of course, were held in utmost secrecy. At this time, nevertheless, a set of ominous rumors did make an appearance. And even before rumor came into the open, American naval experts achieved a curious meeting of the minds with Yamamoto on the subject of Pearl Harbor.[73]

[71] Roosevelt to Grew, Jan. 21, 1941, *Pearl Harbor Hearings,* pt. 20, exhibit 179, p. 4261.

[72] Joint communiqué by Japan, France, and Thailand, Mar. 11, 1941, World Peace Foundation, *Documents on American Foreign Relations, 1940–1941,* ed. S. Shepard Jones and Denys P. Myers (Boston: World Peace Foundation, 1941), pp. 294–295.

[73] United States, Congress, Joint Committee on Investigation of Pearl Harbor Attack, *Investigation of Pearl Harbor Attack, Report Pursuant to S. Con. Res. 27, to Investigate*

A letter from Knox to Stimson dated January 24, 1941, observed that a war with Japan might easily begin with a surprise attack on the Hawaiian base. A copy of this communication was dispatched to Richardson.[74] The next day a joint estimate of the situation prepared by Richardson and Rear Admiral Husband E. Kimmel—who was about to succeed Richardson as Commander-in-Chief of the Pacific Fleet—echoed the Secretary's fear.[75] On January 27 Grew transmitted a report which had come to him from the Peruvian Minister in Tokyo. Somewhat incredulously, this functionary had told Grew that he had received information from many sources alleging that Japan was actually planning such an attack.[76] A copy of Grew's telegram was relayed to Kimmel on February 1. But Naval Intelligence believed this particular alarm had gone far enough, and attached to Kimmel's copy of the message was the following omniscient reassurance: "The Division of Naval Intelligence places no credence in these rumors. Furthermore, based on known data regarding the present disposition and employment of Japanese Naval and Army forces, no move against Pearl Harbor appears imminent or planned in the foreseeable future." [77] Again, however, on February 18, Kimmel indicated in a letter to Stark that he thought a surprise attack on Pearl Harbor was not outside the bounds of reason.[78]

Notwithstanding the optimism dispensed by Naval Intelligence, a war of nerves had been started. The next incitement to Washington's alarm was furnished by London. On February 7 the British Embassy reported confidential information from the British Foreign Office that the staff of the Japanese Embassy in London was preparing to leave before the middle of the month.[79] Numerous "straws in the wind" which tended to credit such a story were listed in an explanatory *aide-mémoire* submitted later the same day.[80]

Behind this disturbing tale lay a good deal of Japanese military plan-

---

Attack on Pearl Harbor on December 7, 1941, and Events and Circumstances Relating Thereto (79th Cong., 2nd sess.), S. Doc. 244 (Washington, D. C.: U. S. Govt. Printing Office, 1946), p. 53. Cited henceforth as *Pearl Harbor Report*. See also Robert E. Ward, "The Inside Story of the Pearl Harbor Plan," United States Naval Institute, *Proceedings*, LXXVII (Dec. 1951), 1272–1273.

[74] Knox to Stimson, Jan. 24, 1941, *Pearl Harbor Hearings*, pt. 14, exhibit 10, pp. 1000–1002.   [75] *Pearl Harbor Report*, p. 75.

[76] Grew to Hull, Jan. 27, 1941, *Pearl Harbor Hearings*, pt. 14, exhibit 15, p. 1042.

[77] Stark to Kimmel, Feb. 1, 1941, *ibid.*, p. 1044.

[78] Kimmel to Stark, Feb. 18, 1941, *ibid.*, pt. 16, exhibit 106, p. 2228.

[79] Memorandum of conversation, Feb. 7, 1941, *ibid.*, pt. 19, exhibit 158, pp. 3442–3443.

[80] *Aide-mémoire* from the British Embassy to the Department of State, Feb. 7, 1941, *ibid.*, p. 3444.

ning. As far back as the previous October, Japanese military and naval authorities had formed the design of seizing advance bases in Indo-China and Thailand from which to launch their contemplated drive into the more distant south and southeast. In January 1941 German and Japanese experts had laid out further plans, agreeing that the occupation of Saigon and a landing on the Malay Peninsula should be followed by the capture of Singapore. It seems to have been understood at the time that all these steps would await a settlement of the China Incident, a German invasion of Britain, or some other major Axis success; but military thinking went ahead so fast that Matsuoka was able to inform the German Ambassador on February 10 that the Singapore attack had actually been planned.[81] While Japanese action was still not so imminent as the British government appeared to believe, reports from London thus had some basis in fact. Nor was the unrest confined to London and Washington; when Otto Tolischus, the American newspaperman, reached Tokyo on February 11 to begin an assignment, he found that city, too, in the throes of a genuine war scare.[82]

Concluding at the outset that Japan would move southward if it moved at all, Roosevelt hurriedly considered means of using the Pacific Fleet as a deterrent. Presumably it was discharging this function at Hawaii, but its restraining force might be even greater if a part of its strength were moved closer to the expected line of Japanese advance. Apparently the President studied a number of projects involving Australia, Singapore, and the Dutch East Indies, but discarded them as uninviting from the standpoint of domestic politics. By February 10, however, he was thinking of sending three or four cruisers, a carrier, and a squadron of destroyers to visit the Philippines.[83] Stark objected strongly to this plan, explaining that if any doubt were cast on the permanence of the move it could have little value as bluff, while if it were allowed to appear that the warships would remain in the Philippines indefinitely, their eventual withdrawal would look very much like a retreat. If a special force had to enter the southwestern Pacific at all, he preferred sending it directly to the East Indies, where it could rely on the support of Dutch naval units and hold a position which was less vulnerable to attack.[84]

---

[81] Joseph W. Ballantine, "Mukden to Pearl Harbor: The Foreign Policies of Japan," *Foreign Affairs,* XXVII (July 1949), 659–660.

[82] Otto D. Tolischus, *Tokyo Record* (New York: Reynal and Hitchcock, 1943), p. 7.

[83] Stark to Kimmel, Feb. 10, 1941, *Pearl Harbor Hearings,* pt. 16, exhibit 106, p. 2148.

[84] Memorandum by Stark, Feb. 11, 1941, *ibid.,* p. 2150.

Apprehensions continued to mount when Churchill, on February 15, predicted an early attack against Dutch possessions in the Indies, adding that such an eventuality would have serious repercussions on the Atlantic war, since it would compel Britain to shift forces from the Mediterranean and the Near East into the Pacific.[85]   But the Former Naval Person called it all off a few days later.   On February 20 he informed Roosevelt that fear of the United States had apparently dissuaded Japan from any immediate ventures of a new type, and added that Matsuoka was about to liquidate this change of plan by visiting Moscow, Berlin, and Rome.[86] The war scare subsided almost as quickly as it had begun, and speculation regarding Pearl Harbor subsided with it.

Nomura reached Washington in the very middle of the February alarm.   President Roosevelt received him on February 14, but no serious discussion was attempted.   After brief remarks concerning the unhappy state of American-Japanese relations the President merely suggested that the Ambassador might want to talk with Hull.[87]   Nor did anything new materialize on March 8 during Nomura's first extended interview with the Secretary of State.[88]   But there was, from the American viewpoint at least, no reason for haste.   On the contrary, delay in seeking conclusions with Japan had been Washington's admitted policy for years; and although its dealings with Japan had been somewhat less timid in recent months, the State Department had adhered to the principle of postponement more consciously than ever since October 1940.   As will be seen presently, Hull now possessed rather full information on German designs for attacking Russia in the late spring—designs which, if carried out, would alter the whole structure of American-Japanese relations. He was aware, moreover, that new Japanese proposals for a Pacific settlement were being framed and was content to await their presentation.

This last development had started to unfold well in advance of Nomura's arrival.   Near the end of January two American missionaries— Bishop James Edward Walsh, Superior General of the Catholic Foreign Mission Society at Maryknoll, New York, and one Father J. M. Drought —had returned from Japan with the opinion that moderate elements in that country could oust the militarists from control of the government

[85] Churchill to Roosevelt, Feb. 15, 1941, *Pearl Harbor Hearings,* pt. 19, exhibit 158, p. 3452.

[86] Memorandum by Churchill, Feb. 22, 1941, *ibid.,* p. 3454.   Cf. Winston S. Churchill, *The Grand Alliance* (Boston: Houghton Mifflin Co., 1950), pp. 177–179.

[87] Memorandum by Hull, Feb. 14, 1941, *Foreign Relations: Japan, 1931–1941,* II, 388.   [88] See memorandum by Hull, Mar. 8, 1941, *ibid.,* pp. 391–392.

and effect a marked reversal of policy if they were assured that the United States would accept an arrangement of Oriental affairs which guaranteed Japanese security.

Through Postmaster General Frank C. Walker, himself a prominent Catholic, Bishop Walsh and Father Drought obtained an interview with Roosevelt and Hull. The two priests revealed that they were already in contact with individuals on the staff of the Japanese Embassy in Washington and stated their belief that Tokyo might recognize the Open Door in China if Japan could be assured of similar trade equality throughout the Far East. Both President and Secretary of State heard them out with some scepticism but agreed that Bishop Walsh and Father Drought should proceed with their conversations at the Japanese Embassy in an effort to obtain some proposals in writing. It was understood, however, that they should carry on this work as private individuals; the United States government would take no cognizance of the talks until after Nomura's arrival.[89] As it turned out, there was nothing to report before April. In the meanwhile, both sides limited their formal exchanges to generalities.

VI

Even during the period of Hitler's concentration on the affairs of the western Mediterranean, his problems in the east were not ignored. The gradual infiltration of Finland by Nazi troops after the German-Finnish transit agreement of September 22, 1940, was one aspect of Germany's eastern policy, but attention shifted increasingly to the Balkan area where latent differences between Germany and the Soviet Union were now coming to sharp focus. German pressure had helped force Rumania to grant Russian demands for Bessarabia and the Bukovina in July, and Hitler had sponsored a further dismemberment of that country in August for the joint satisfaction of Hungary and Bulgaria. Rumania, however, did not forsake its new orientation toward Berlin. During the September crisis which followed the last partition, King Carol was forced to leave the country, and Rumania fell under an authoritarian regime headed by a pro-Nazi army officer, General Ion Antonescu. With the new ruler's permission, German troops began to occupy Rumanian territory in October.[90] Hitler's principal objective was still that of keeping

[89] Hull, *Memoirs,* II, 984–985.
[90] See Ribbentrop to Tippelskirch, Oct. 9, 1940, United States, Department of State,

the Balkans quiet, for unrest in the area not only lessened its use to Germany as a source of food and raw materials but also gave the British and the Russians an opportunity to fish in troubled waters, each for their own advantage. Hoping, then, to achieve greater stability in general—and to check Russia in particular—Germany continued its eastward deployment of troops and exerted pressure on the nations beyond the frontier to adhere to the Tripartite Pact. Hungary, Rumania, and Slovakia submitted to this program in the latter part of November.

But a new source of trouble opened in the meanwhile. Annoyed by the German occupation of Rumania without Italian participation, Mussolini decided to proceed immediately with his contemplated invasion of Greece.[91] His offensive started October 28 and ran into difficulties almost at once, as the Greeks put up a much stronger resistance than anyone had anticipated. Now it was Hitler's turn to be annoyed; with the greatest irresponsibility his Italian confederate was upsetting his careful arrangements for peace in the Balkans. Writing to Mussolini on November 20, he complained bitterly that he had not been properly informed of Italian designs until it was too late to make his objections effective, and suggested that further operations be deferred to a more favorable time.[92]

But it was evident that Balkan tranquillity was not the whole key to the Russian problem. During the second week of November Molotov finally accepted an invitation to confer with German leaders in Berlin. This visit produced a good deal of conversation on the points at issue between them but no worth-while results.[93] Berlin did not give up at once, however, and proposed a broad agreement between Russia and the members of the Tripartite Pact calling for mutual nonaggression guarantees, recognition of spheres of influence, and economic coöperation.[94] But Russia wanted more than any of the others was prepared to give. On November 26 Molotov refused to consider the German proposal unless Nazi troops were withdrawn from Finland. He also demanded the establishment of a Soviet sphere of influence in Bulgaria, as well as permission to set up a military and a naval base within range of the Bosporus,

Nazi-Soviet Relations, 1939–1941 (Washington, D. C.: U. S. Govt. Printing Office, 1948), p. 206.   [91] *Ciano Diaries,* p. 300.

[92] Hitler to Mussolini, Nov. 20, 1940, *Lettres secrètes,* p. 82.

[93] See memorandum of conversation between Molotov and Ribbentrop, Nov. 13, 1940, *Nazi-Soviet Relations,* p. 254.

[94] See undated draft of agreement between the members of the Three-Power Pact and the Soviet Union, *ibid.,* p. 256.

freedom of action in the zone between Russia's southern boundary and the Persian Gulf, and renunciation of Japanese coal and oil rights in northern Sakhalin.[95] Abandoning his hope of drawing Russia into close collaboration with the Axis, Hitler now commenced to examine the other side of the record.

What he found was by no means uncongenial. His position was admittedly a good deal stronger than it had been in August 1939, and collaboration with his eastern neighbor seemed proportionately less necessary. Why negotiate where he might command? With the failure of his efforts in mid-December to gain French and Spanish aid for a move against Gibraltar and North Africa, therefore, Hitler adopted the solution offered by a Russian war. Tentative plans for invading the Soviet Union had been under consideration for some time, and he straightway ordered the High Command to finish its preparations by the ensuing May 15. This step was taken on December 18, 1940.[96]

German confidence was great, but German progress had slowed notably since the middle of the year. Britain had stood firm, in growing rather than diminishing strength. Neither France nor Spain had succumbed to the Fuehrer's blandishments. And now, just as the invasion of Russia was being ordained, the Italian offensive in Greece failed miserably and the British swiftly ejected Mussolini's armies from the positions they had assumed in western Egypt at the conclusion of Marshal Rodolfo Graziani's successful drive in September.

On the last day of the year Hitler indited another long epistle to his partner in Rome, revealing some—but not all—of his thoughts. Generally speaking, he was still optimistic. Only one final effort, he thought, would be required to crush England. France and Spain, to be sure, had played him false. Laval's dismissal he attributed to Weygand's influence, while Spain's refusal to collaborate betrayed Franco's stupidity. There was not much hope that Franco would change his mind, however.[97] At the other end of Europe the Russian problem was growing daily; Soviet machinations were at the bottom of unrest in the Balkans. Moscow needed watching, but he did not expect any Russian initiative against Italy and Germany as long as Stalin lived. The situation in North Africa was unfortunate, though not fatal. At all events, it could not be retrieved for the time being. Summer would be upon them before

---

[95] Schulenburg to Ribbentrop, Nov. 26, 1940, *ibid.*, pp. 258–259.
[96] Directive No. 21, Dec. 18, 1940, *ibid.*, p. 261.
[97] Hitler to Mussolini, Dec. 31, 1940, *Lettres secrètes*, pp. 104–107.

German help could arrive, and German armor was not yet properly equipped for operations in such temperatures.[98] Hitler said nothing of his plans for attacking Russia, but it was obvious that his western program had been temporarily suspended.

German intentions were no secret to the United States. As luck would have it, the American commercial attaché in Berlin, Sam E. Woods, enjoyed a connection with an anti-Nazi German so situated as to know the inner workings of his government. Through special arrangements, the two met frequently in a Berlin motion picture theater, where the German dropped notes in Woods's pocket. In this way the American government learned that conferences reviewing plans to attack Russia had been under way since August; and news of the decision made in December reached Hull before the end of January. Eventually Woods even learned the main outlines of the German strategic plan. Suspecting that the German government had planted these reports for reasons of its own, Hull sent them to the Federal Bureau of Investigation for analysis. But its experts considered them probably authentic.[99] This offered hope that America's policy of restraint toward the Soviet Union was about to pay large dividends and raised the question of what might be done to hasten such an outcome.

An obvious course was to give Moscow fair warning of what portended and to show a willingness to overlook Russia's habitually bumptious attitude by permitting a more generous flow of American exports to the Soviet Union. As soon as the State Department was convinced of the truth of reports from Berlin, Welles told Oumansky what he knew of German plans. But the effect was slight. While the Ambassador apparently transmitted the report to his government, he betrayed neither surprise nor gratitude and did not even bother to ask for details.[100]

About the same time, January 21, the moral embargo which had prevailed against the Soviet Union since December 1939 was lifted.[101] This further increased the trade which had been carried on under the licensing system since October 1940. It also raised new differences with London, for the British government was now disposed to take a sour view of any commerce helpful to Russia. On February 5 Lord Halifax —who, because of Lord Lothian's recent death, had just been appointed

---

[98] *Lettres secrètes*, pp. 109–110.   [99] Hull, *Memoirs*, II, 967–968.

[100] *Ibid.*, p. 968; and David J. Dallin, *Soviet Russia's Foreign Policy, 1939–1942*, tr. Leon Denman (New Haven: Yale Univ. Press, 1942), p. 332.

[101] Hull, *Memoirs*, II, 969.

British Ambassador to the United States—made known his government's conviction that substantial amounts of goods were passing through Russia to Germany. Hull replied that American exports to the Soviet Union were carefully regulated on a weekly basis and that he did not believe their volume had increased enough to provide cause for alarm. Explaining American policy in more detail, he added that Russia was sensitive in such matters and argued that the stiff bargains which Moscow had driven with Berlin indirectly strengthened the democratic cause. "Our purpose," he concluded, "is to give less occasion for Soviet officials to feel unkindly toward this Government, especially in the event of some pivotal development where the slightest influence might tip the scales at Moscow against us in a most damaging and far-reaching way." [102] Five days later, Hull answered another protest in substantially the same way.[103] Since there was no British blockade of the sea route to Vladivostok, the American government, preoccupied with Russian sensibilities, felt free to ignore London's misgivings without further argument.

Aid to Britain was still the most arresting aspect of United States policy, however. Nor were its possibilities lost upon Berlin as German preparations for the new spring offensive moved forward. In a conference held February 4, 1941, the German High Command agreed that American aid to Britain was fast becoming effective and pointed out that Japan and the Tripartite Pact held the key to the problem. A Japanese drive into Malaya and the Indies would at least divert American war materials from Britain to the Pacific; and if it led the United States to enter hostilities at Britain's side, this result would be more than offset by Japan's consequent declaration of war on America.[104] Encouraged by Matsuoka's recent assurances concerning an attack on Singapore, Ribbentrop proceeded on February 13 to take new soundings from General Hiroshi Oshima, the decidedly pro-Nazi Japanese Ambassador in Berlin.

Starting with an effort to explain away the Russian pact of August 1939 and Germany's failure to bring England to terms in the summer of 1940, the Foreign Minister spent some time reaching the point. But finally it came out, hedged with the customary verbiage. While Hitler

---

[102] *Ibid.*, pp. 970–971.
[103] *Ibid.*, p. 971; and Halifax to Roosevelt, Feb. 11, 1941, MS Roosevelt Papers (Secretary's File, Box 73).
[104] Annex 1, report of the Commander-in-Chief, Navy, to the Fuehrer, Feb. 4, 1941, United States, Department of the Navy, *Fuehrer Conferences on Matters Dealing with the German Navy, 1939–1941* (Washington, D. C.: Issued in mimeographed form by the Office of Naval Intelligence, 1947), 1941, I, 17–18.

manifestly had the situation well in hand, said Ribbentrop, Japanese coöperation would greatly speed the inevitable victory. Above all, Japan should not delay while opportunity knocked. Under existing circumstances, a major drive against Britain in the Far East would have decisive results for the whole conflict. At the same time, Japan would quickly secure the dominant position in Asia which could never be achieved except by war. The surprise of Japanese intervention, coupled with the unpreparedness of the United States, would discourage action by that country. And even if Washington did choose to send its Fleet beyond Hawaii, Japan could dispose of it without trouble. The Tripartite Pact had been important to German success in Europe and equally so to Japanese success in the Far East. Germany and Japan were bound by a tie that could not be ignored, for Japan must know that realization of its imperial idea was contingent upon German victory. Oshima heard him out with becoming humility. But it was obvious that, in spite of his pro-German views, his enthusiasm did not burn so brightly as the speaker's.[105]

While winter thus moved on toward spring, Washington did nothing to advance its Spanish policy. On the other hand, considerable progress was made in negotiations for a trade agreement with North Africa.

Having completed his first-hand investigations, Murphy on January 17 submitted an optimistic report concerning Weygand's position.[106] In the meanwhile, it appeared that Vichy was being subjected to heavy pressure for the reinstatement of Laval, and Washington became impatient to get on with the understanding before something happened.[107] This led to further discussions with the British, but their views on the shipment of American goods to North Africa were substantially unchanged. While they offered no serious objections to trade with Morocco—where, indeed, they were still plying a commerce of their own—Algeria and Tunisia were different. They placed less faith than did the United States in Weygand's dependability and hinted that they did not understand how adequate safeguards against re-export could be established.[108] Striving to gain an immediate benefit of some kind, the British on February 7 offered to sanction the proposed agreement if its

[105] Extract from report of conference between Ribbentrop and Oshima, Feb. 13, 1941, *Pearl Harbor Hearings,* pt. 19, exhibit 165, pp. 3644–3647. For an extended analysis of German policy in this connection, see Hans L. Trefousse, *Germany and American Neutrality, 1939–1941* (New York: Bookman Associates, 1951), pp. 91–101.

[106] Langer, *Our Vichy Gamble,* p. 129.

[107] *Ibid.,* p. 134.   [108] *Ibid.,* p. 132.

operation were made contingent upon the release of British and neutral shipping held in Moroccan ports, but Hull declined this suggestion.[109] A few days later, however, the knot was cut and London was advised that the United States intended to go ahead with the program regardless of British objections. At the same time, Murphy was directed to return to North Africa and begin definite negotiations.[110]

Since the ground had been thoroughly prepared, understanding was achieved quickly. The Murphy-Weygand Agreement was initialed in Algiers on February 26, 1941, and accepted in both Vichy and Washington during the next two weeks.[111] That its terms were favorable to American interests could hardly be denied. It not only promised the Weygand regime numerous civilian commodities which would make its hold on the native population much more secure but also admitted American control officers to the chief North African cities, thus furnishing the United States government an unusual opportunity to maintain a close watch over developments there.

Nevertheless, Britain continued to frown darkly. By the middle of March the British government was suggesting, in effect, that the Murphy-Weygand Agreement either be discarded completely or extended to unoccupied France on a much larger scale in return for sweeping guarantees against collaboration of any kind. But Washington rejected both alternatives. Hull told Halifax on March 15 that he disagreed in principle with the idea of requiring a *quid pro quo* in these dealings with France,[112] and the prospect of continued Anglo-American friction over the North African aid program remained just about as strong as ever.[113]

VII

The disagreements which troubled certain aspects of Anglo-American policy hardly touched its direct application to the war. Building upon foundations laid in the second half of 1940, the relationship of the United States and Great Britain entered an important new phase in the opening months of 1941.

With the election safely behind him, President Roosevelt obviously felt much less hampered in the domain of public statement. Although he still dealt with one thing at a time, he turned generally from denial to

---

[109] Hull, *Memoirs*, II, 950.
[110] Langer, *Our Vichy Gamble*, p. 134.
[111] *Ibid.*, p. 135.
[112] Hull, *Memoirs*, II, 954.
[113] See Langer, *Our Vichy Gamble*, p. 139.

affirmation and stated on November 8 that half of America's future war production would be alloted to Great Britain.[114] Whether this announcement was meant to be statistically accurate is not important. Taken in conjunction with the known fact that American war production was then entering a period of tremendous growth, his words certainly emphasized the vast extent of the British-aid program and helped prepare the ground for consideration of Britain's ability to pay for what it got.

Although the administration had carefully refrained from laboring this point, it had always been obvious that the cash-and-carry program offered no final solution to the problem of supplying Great Britain and other countries with materials needed to carry on the war. Since loans were ruled out by law—and apparently by public sentiment as well—it was clear that even a nation favored by the United States could profit from its access to American factories only so long as it possessed enough dollar exchange to cover its purchases. War expenditures had dissipated Britain's supply of dollars much faster than it could be replenished through exports and services; whatever the inherent wealth of the British Empire, a prospective dollar shortage compelled England by December 1940 to impose serious restrictions on its purchases in the United States.[115] Feeling that the American government had already reached the limit of feasible action through the direct transfer of Army and Navy surpluses, many authorities were convinced that another solution must be found.[116] How far this belief progressed before the election is impossible to decide, but it is certain that British finances gave the State Department serious concern during most of November. Returning to Washington on November 23 from a visit to England, Lord Lothian added to the sense of urgency by pointing out that his government was near the end of its cash resources.[117] The matter was then brought to a head by Winston Churchill's letter of December 8.

At this moment Roosevelt was placidly enjoying a Caribbean voyage aboard the cruiser *Tuscaloosa,* and the Churchill letter was delivered to him by seaplane on December 9. The Prime Minister took advantage of

[114] Press conference, Nov. 8, 1940, Franklin D. Roosevelt, *The Public Papers and Addresses of Franklin D. Roosevelt, 1940,* comp. S. I. Rosenman (New York: Macmillan Co., 1941), p. 563.

[115] See Edward R. Stettinius, Jr., *Lend-Lease: Weapon for Victory* (New York: Macmillan Co., 1944), p. 60.

[116] Henry Morgenthau, Jr., "The Morgenthau Diaries," *Collier's Magazine,* CXX (Oct. 18, 1947), 72.   [117] Hull, *Memoirs,* I, 871–872.

the opportunity to discuss a number of things, including freedom of the seas, escort duty by United States naval and air forces, and the stubborn neutrality of Eire.[118]   But his real message concerned finances.   Despite the most strenuous efforts to raise money, he wrote, Britain would soon run out of cash for American purchases; and he ventured the opinion that it would "be wrong in principle and mutually disadvantageous in effect" for his country, after waging the common fight, to emerge from the war "stripped to the bone." [119]   Roosevelt considered the matter for several days, and before the cruise was finished he expounded the main outlines of Lend-Lease to his traveling companion, Harry L. Hopkins.[120] According to Henry Morgenthau, the idea was the President's own— conceived in one of those "brilliant flashes" which now and again amazed his subordinates—and a much more direct solution than anyone expected.[121]   Without further ado the Treasury Department set to work on details.[122]

Roosevelt gave the Lend-Lease idea its public launching in a press conference held December 17 immediately after his return to Washington.   Sketching in a deep background, he began his discourse with a lecture on the economic lessons of the First World War, observing reflectively that no major war had ever been "lost through lack of money."   He next pointed out that British war contracts were a positive aid to the defense of the United States because they stimulated war production and created new manufacturing facilities.   Coming then to the heart of his talk, he proposed that the United States government take over British orders in this country, turn them into American orders, and lease the materials so obtained—or sell them on mortgage—to countries resisting aggression.   This procedure was justified, he stated, by the argument that such articles "would be more useful to the defense of the United States if they were used in Great Britain than if they were kept in storage here."   He was striving, he explained, "to eliminate the dollar sign." [123]

In the more polished phrases of his annual message the President offered his program to Congress on January 6, 1941.   Emphasizing that he

---

[118] For the complete text of this letter, see Churchill, *Their Finest Hour*, pp. 558–567.
[119] *Ibid.,* p. 566.
[120] Sherwood, *Roosevelt and Hopkins*, p. 224.
[121] "The Morgenthau Diaries," *Collier's Magazine*, CXX (Oct. 18, 1947), 74.
[122] Hull, *Memoirs*, I, 873.
[123] Press conference, Dec. 17, 1940, Roosevelt, *Public Papers and Addresses, 1940*, pp. 605–607.

did not recommend a loan, he stated that he was thinking of arrangements which would enable certain countries to obtain war materials from the United States within the framework of its own defense program. He intimated that payment in kind would be forthcoming at the end of the war and assured his listeners that the United States would not heed the aggressors' complaints even if they chose to regard such conduct as a breach of international law.[124] As drafted by Treasury experts during the first week in January,[125] the Lend-Lease bill was introduced on January 10.

Meanwhile, steps were taken to ensure that neither British penury nor congressional delay might interrupt the aid program. To sustain manufacturing processes, the British were advised on December 18, 1940, to place new orders for about $3 billion worth of war materials.[126] Roosevelt portrayed the United States as the "arsenal of democracy" in a fireside chat delivered December 29, thus placing the country firmly in its new role.[127] And on January 7, 1941, Harry Hopkins departed for London to discuss further plans with members of the British government.[128]

In England Hopkins had a busy time inspecting war damage, receiving estimates of Great Britain's war potential, and carrying on discussions with British leaders. He found them grimly confident but not at all buoyant. Churchill was preoccupied with questions of supply; he did not then believe that the war would ever reach a stage that demanded the employment of great numbers of men in mass combat.[129] Foreign Secretary Anthony Eden expressed greatest concern about Japan and its intentions. This was just before the February war scare already described, and Eden nourished a conviction that Japan was about to attack British possessions in the Far East. He insisted that Britain had to know what the United States planned to do if Japan moved against Singapore or the Dutch East Indies.[130] The strain of the long crisis was evident on every hand. But while Hopkins was unable to offer many of the commitments desired by his hosts, his assurances regarding the Lend-Lease program and the general outlines of United States policy certainly

---

[124] Annual message to Congress, Jan. 6, 1941, *Documents on American Foreign Relations, 1940–1941*, pp. 29–30.

[125] "The Morgenthau Diaries," *Collier's Magazine*, CXX (Oct. 18, 1947), 74.

[126] Forrest Davis and Ernest K. Lindley, *How War Came* (New York: Simon and Schuster, 1942), p. 120.

[127] Fireside chat, Dec. 29, 1940, Roosevelt, *Public Papers and Addresses, 1940*, p. 643.

[128] Sherwood, *Roosevelt and Hopkins*, pp. 230–231.

[129] *Ibid.*, pp. 238–239.

[130] *Ibid.*, p. 259; and Churchill, *The Grand Alliance*, p. 23.

boosted morale, as did his parting promise that he would arrange at once for the repair of damaged British warships in American yards.[131]   In an effort to expedite the adoption of Lend-Lease by making prospective tax increases less distasteful to the American public, Hopkins shortly after his return used his new intimacy with Churchill to suggest an official statement concerning the extent of British financial sacrifices occasioned by the war.[132]

During the interim, preparations for staff talks in Washington were completed. These discussions got under way on January 29. American naval units in the Atlantic were formally organized as the Atlantic Fleet on February 1 and were placed under the command of Admiral Ernest J. King. Throughout that month the Navy's preoccupation with Atlantic sea lanes continued, and a special support force designed for escort duty was constituted on March 1.[133]   As soon as this force was put to its intended use, war and nonbelligerency would commence to overlap.

Such a development lay very close to the center of popular fears. But regardless of its hazards for domestic politics, American participation in convoy work was the inevitable concomitant of Lend-Lease. The whole project would be reduced to absurdity if materials supplied at American expense were permitted to go to the bottom on the way to the British Isles. With the adoption of Lend-Lease it would no longer be a question of whether the United States Navy should be used for convoy duty, but rather a question of when such action might become absolutely necessary. Nor could this time be long in coming.

While airing his views to newspapermen in December, President Roosevelt had shrugged off the problem of delivery as a mere detail, saying, ". . . you don't have to send an American flag and an American crew on an American vessel." [134]   As presented to Congress, moreover, the bill itself made no reference to convoys. But that the administration was thinking of convoys was proved by the organization of the naval support force on March 1, and Stimson put the issue squarely before the President as early as January 22. In a memorandum on the Lend-Lease bill, he said: "In matériel the assistance rendered by this bill during the coming six months will be insignificant. . . . It is my belief that

---

[131] Davis and Lindley, *How War Came,* p. 184.

[132] Hopkins to Churchill, Feb. 17, 1941, MS Roosevelt Papers (Secretary's File, Box 80).

[133] Morison, *The Battle of the Atlantic,* p. 51.

[134] Press conference, Dec. 17, 1940, Roosevelt, *Public Papers and Addresses, 1940,* p. 610.

consideration should be given to measures which will at the same time secure the life line of British supplies across the Atlantic and relieve the convoy duty units of her fleet which are sorely needed elsewhere." [135]

While Roosevelt evidently shared the Secretary's belief, he refrained from any open espousal of convoys. In this he was probably wise, for Congress was so alert to the issue and so opposed to the whole convoy idea that the Lend-Lease Act, as finally passed on March 11, 1941, categorically stated that it did not authorize or permit convoy activities by the United States Navy or the operation of any American ship in a combat zone forbidden to it by the neutrality act of 1939.[136] Even so, the Act was a formidable instrument and represented a great advance in American policy. It disposed of inter-Allied financial problems at a stroke; and as a continuing and ever-expanding program of aid, it formed a much more decisive break with neutrality than any previous measure with a definite beginning and a recognizable end.

By the middle of March 1941, therefore, the United States had assumed almost its full place in the world crisis. Nothing short of an immediate declaration of war could have rendered its alignments more clear. Indeed, as confirmed by strategic understandings at the military level, wide diplomatic coöperation, and the assurance of unprecedented subsidies, these ties were rapidly gaining the strength of a formal alliance. Thanks to the Tripartite Pact and to well-founded expectations of a German attack on the Soviet Union, the United States was now warming toward Russia as fast as conditions permitted. It was also embarked upon a long-term program of limited aid to French North Africa. These two policies, combined with American slowness in Spain, revealed the chief differences between Great Britain and the United States. For in spite of recurring alarms about Japan, the two governments were united in the belief that action in the Pacific should be restricted to maintaining the *status quo* while they pressed for a decision on the other side of the world.

[135] Memorandum by Stimson, Jan. 22, 1941, *Pearl Harbor Hearings,* pt. 20, exhibit 179, p. 4280.

[136] Sec. 3 (d), chap. 11 (77th Cong., 1st sess.), United States, Department of State, *United States Statutes at Large* (Washington, D. C.: U. S. Govt. Printing Office and others, 1845———), LV, 32.

CHAPTER VII

Plans, Expedients, and Battle at Sea

I

THE BRITISH-AMERICAN STAFF CONVERSATIONS WHICH OPENED IN WASHINGton on January 29, 1941, lasted throughout the debate on Lend-Lease and into the final week of March. The preliminary talks held in London during the last half of 1940 had revealed some discord with respect to the Far East and other areas of possible coöperation, and these differences survived to complicate the new discussions. But the delegates reached substantial agreement by March 27. On that date they finished a long report which embodied their main conclusions and recommendations.

This document carefully avoided the question of an Anglo-American alliance. The preamble made it clear that the talks were conducted wholly at strategic and operational levels by ranking military and naval officers without authority, on either side, to discuss binding political commitments. All recommendations, moreover, were subject to later approval by the civilian heads of the two governments.[1] As expressed in the report, the purpose of the conversations was

To determine the best methods by which the armed forces of the United States and British Commonwealth, with its present Allies, could defeat Germany and the powers allied with her, should the United States be compelled to resort to war . . . [and]

To reach agreements concerning the methods and nature of Military Coöperation between the two nations, including the allocation of the principal areas of responsibility, the major lines of the military strategy to be pursued by both nations, the strength of the forces which each may be able to commit, and the determination of satisfactory command arrange-

---

[1] Report of the United States–British staff conversations, Mar. 27, 1941, United States, Congress, Joint Committee on Investigation of Pearl Harbor Attack, *Hearings Pursuant to S. Con. Res. 27, Authorizing Investigation of Attack on Pearl Harbor, Dec. 7, 1941, and Events and Circumstances Relating Thereto* (79th Cong., 1st and 2nd sess.) (Washington, D. C.: U. S. Govt. Printing Office, 1946), pt. 15, exhibit 49, p. 1488. Cited henceforth as *Pearl Harbor Hearings.*

ments both as to supreme Military control, and as to unity of field command in cases of strategic and tactical joint operations.[2]

They achieved harmony on all the main points. It was ordained that military and naval coöperation should be founded upon continuous study of war plans. For the time being, at least, the exchange of intelligence data and technical information should receive special emphasis. To facilitate this trading of knowledge, American military and naval missions should be established in London, and similar British agencies should be set up in Washington.[3] Joint planning should be carried on through these bodies until the United States entered the war, when their functions should be taken over by a more formally constituted joint authority known as the Supreme War Council.[4]

Coöperation beyond this point was to be governed by the joint basic war plan annexed to the staff report. Commonly known as ABC-1, the short title of the entire report, this plan set forth a strategy adapted to a world-wide conflict. Taking account of potential as well as of present belligerents, it assumed that if the United States went to war against Germany and Italy, hostilities with Japan would soon follow. The plan recognized, of course, that such an enlargement of the war would not diminish Great Britain's need for American supplies; the British should continue to receive as much direct material aid as possible.[5] In other respects, however, major roles were assigned on a geographical basis.

For obvious reasons the western Atlantic (north of 25 degrees south latitude and west of 30 degrees west longitude) and the eastern Pacific (east of 140 degrees east longitude, except north of 30 degrees north latitude where this zone reached the Asiatic coast) were designated as areas of American responsibility.[6] British areas included the United Kingdom and home waters, the eastern Atlantic, the Mediterranean, the

[2] *Pearl Harbor Hearings*, pt. 15, exhibit 49, pp. 1487–1488.

[3] *Ibid.*, p. 1494; and Samuel Eliot Morison, *The Battle of the Atlantic, 1939–1943* (Boston: Little, Brown, and Co., 1947), p. 49.

[4] The Supreme War Council became the Combined Chiefs of Staff in January 1942. Although the Council is not mentioned specifically in either the basic report or any of its various annexes as they appear among the exhibits of the Pearl Harbor investigating committee, Professor Morison, who had full and reliable sources of information, states that the Council was provided for in the staff agreement (*The Battle of the Atlantic*, p. 48).

[5] United States–British Commonwealth joint basic war plan, Mar. 27, 1941, *Pearl Harbor Hearings*, pt. 15, exhibit 49, p. 1504. See also the report of the United States–British staff conversations, Mar. 27, 1941, *ibid.*, p. 1489.

[6] Joint basic war plan, *ibid.*, pp. 1504–1505, 1511.

Middle East, and India (as well as the Indian Ocean from 92 degrees east longitude westward to the coast of Africa).[7]   Between the Indian area and the Pacific area lay a third major region subdivided into the Far Eastern area (southeastern Asia, the Netherlands Indies, and the Philippines) and another area embracing Australia and New Zealand. By implication at least, this was made a region of joint responsibility, where each nation with substantial interests (Great Britain, the United States, the Netherlands, Australia, and New Zealand) would deal primarily with the defense of its own territory but would, in addition, coöperate with the others under British strategic control to defend the entire region.[8]

Of course, responsibility was not exclusive in any zone.   It was understood that joint action should be employed whenever it became necessary or feasible.[9]   But to render the major obligation as exact as possible, specific tasks were assigned for each area.   The plan even tried to estimate the forces which would be available to carry out these assignments. Only with regard to the Far Eastern sector was the understanding notably vague.   During his informal conversations in London the previous autumn, Rear Admiral Ghormley had reported certain differences arising out of British insistence that a portion of the American Fleet should be based at Singapore.   The views of the two governments were still far apart on this and on a number of related matters.   Another obstacle to more detailed plans for the defense of this region was uncertainty concerning the views of other Far Eastern powers.   China, of course, was not expected to do anything outside its own borders.   But the Dutch had worth-while naval and air forces in the Indies, and consultation with representatives of their government was an obvious necessity before proceeding further.

When all was said and done, however, the Far East was admittedly secondary.   The plan followed established concepts by treating the Atlantic and Europe as the decisive theaters and assumed that the United States would bring its principal effort to bear in this part of the world.[10] Although its Pacific Fleet was assigned such formidable tasks as that of gaining control over the Caroline and Marshall Islands while diverting Japanese land forces from any move against the Malay Barrier, the main duty of the United States lay on the other side of the American con-

---

[7] *Ibid.*, pp. 1504, 1531.   [8] *Ibid.*, pp. 1515–1520.
[9] Report of the United States–British staff conversations, Mar. 27, 1941, *ibid.*, p. 1493.
[10] *Ibid.*, p. 1491.

tinent. For the war's early stages, at least, its role there was conceived of as primarily naval, involving support of the Anglo-American position in the western Atlantic. Accordingly, its forces were to devote themselves to the kind of jobs for which they were now being prepared. They were to protect the sea communications of the associated powers by escorting, covering, and patrolling, and by destroying the raiding forces of the enemy. They were to break up Axis sea communications by capturing or destroying vessels which traded directly or indirectly with the enemy. They were to defend the territory of the associated governments in the Western Hemisphere and prevent the extension of enemy power into this area. Finally, they were to prepare for the occupation of the Azores and the Cape Verde Islands.[11]

The Washington report was not immediately accepted by either government. But it served as foundation of a new Army-Navy basic war plan which was drawn up in the course of the next month; and along with this plan—known as Rainbow No. 5—it was approved by the Secretary of the Navy on May 28 and by the Secretary of War on June 2.[12] President Roosevelt declined to express any kind of official sanction for the time being on the ground that the master war plan which constituted the heart of the report had not been finally accepted by the British government.[13] Nevertheless, he was obviously satisfied with its arrangements; and even though many of them could not go into effect until the United States entered the war, the exact correspondence of tasks assigned to American naval forces in the Atlantic with the preparations which these forces had been undergoing since the autumn of 1940 made it perfectly clear that the Navy could begin some of its duties in this area without waiting for either the outbreak of hostilities or presidential approval of ABC-1.

Against this background of strategic planning, detailed naval preparations continued without abatement. The special patrol group formed on March 1 immediately began serious training in antisubmarine warfare, and the Navy sent Captain Louis Denfeld to the British Isles in search

[11] Joint basic war plan, *Pearl Harbor Hearings*, pt. 15, exhibit 49, p. 1506.

[12] Report of the United States–British staff conversations, Mar. 27, 1941, *ibid.*, p. 1485; and Kimmel's testimony, Jan. 15, 1946, *ibid.*, pt. 6, p. 2502. For the Navy's section of this plan, see WPL-46, Navy basic war plan—Rainbow No. 5, *ibid.*, pt. 18, exhibit 129, pp. 2880–2941.

[13] Gerow's testimony, Dec. 5, 1945, *ibid.*, pt. 3, p. 995. As late as July, the British government would say only that it was "in general agreement" with the Washington staff report. See Halifax to Welles, July 4, 1941, MS Roosevelt Papers (Secretary's File, Box 74).

of bases for the European end of a transatlantic escort system. As Denfeld hurriedly chose two pairs of sites adapted to the needs of destroyers and naval aircraft—Gare Loch and Loch Ryan in western Scotland, Londonderry and Lough Erne in Northern Ireland—Secretary Knox informed the President on March 20 that the Navy was almost ready to commence escort-of-convoy operations between North America and Great Britain. He added that he contemplated sending twenty-seven destroyers and four squadrons of flying boats to the Irish bases about the middle of September, together with some fifteen thousand troops.[14]

Meanwhile, transport difficulties in the Atlantic grew steadily worse. Between September 1939 and March 1941 Great Britain lost 923 merchant ships with a total capacity of nearly four million tons, while non-British sinkings—many of which had a direct bearing on the amount of cargo space available to Great Britain—accounted for about six hundred more ships and upwards of two million additional tons.[15] A modicum of satisfaction could be derived from the destruction of five German submarines by the Royal Navy in March. But toward the end of the month U-boats started operating much farther west than had been their earlier habit, thus improving the opportunity to strike eastbound convoys during that unprotected interval between the return of their Canadian escorts to North America and the moment when they were joined by British escorts based on the United Kingdom.[16] This move was announced on March 26 by an order of the German government which proclaimed a new operational zone in the North Atlantic extending from the latitude of southern France to a northern limit well beyond the Arctic Circle and westward to the three-mile limit of Greenland. Within these boundaries all vessels faced the threat of destruction.[17] The danger posed by this enlarged zone of operations became evident almost at once, for ten ships of a twenty-two-ship convoy were sunk on the night of April 3 by a German "wolf-pack" in the neighborhood of 28 degrees west.[18]

Such an extension of U-boat warfare was of more than indirect concern to Washington. Following concepts laid down in the Declaration

[14] Morison, *The Battle of the Atlantic*, pp. 53–54.
[15] See the tabulation by the British Admiralty, in World Peace Foundation, *Documents on American Foreign Relations, 1940–1941*, ed. S. Shepard Jones and Denys P. Myers (Boston: World Peace Foundation, 1941), p. 613.
[16] See Morison, *The Battle of the Atlantic*, p. 56.
[17] German notice of a zone of operations, Mar. 26, 1941, *Documents on American Foreign Relations, 1940–1941*, p. 504.
[18] Morison, *The Battle of the Atlantic*, p. 56.

of Panama, the American government now defined the 26th meridian as the dividing line between the Eastern and Western hemispheres.[19]   Since the new German operational zone extended as far west as the 38th meridian in the neighborhood of Greenland, it was clear that Nazi submarines were prowling in waters whose exemption from belligerent activity the United States regarded as essential to its own interests.   A sizable area had been opened to direct conflict between that country and Germany. When this thought was added to growing worry over the magnitude of British shipping losses, Atlantic problems assumed a new urgency.   Reviewing these problems on April 4, Stark wrote to Admiral Kimmel at Pearl Harbor thus: "The situation is obviously critical in the Atlantic. In my opinion, it is hopeless except as we take strong measures to save it." [20]

Such measures had already been started.   On March 30 the United States government took protective custody of sixty-five Axis and Axis-controlled vessels in American ports after finding evidence of sabotage by their crews.[21]   On April 7 Stark ordered the transfer of two destroyer squadrons from the Pacific to the Atlantic Fleet as well as the battleships *Idaho, Mississippi,* and *New Mexico;* the carrier *Yorktown;* and the light cruisers *Philadelphia, Brooklyn, Savannah,* and *Nashville.*[22] Two days later the United States assumed a temporary protectorate over Greenland by virtue of a somewhat informal agreement with the Danish Minister in Washington, and coldly rejected Copenhagen's prompt disavowal of its representative—apparently on the ground that the Danish government, owing to German occupation of the country, was no longer a free agent.[23]

In addition, on April 9 ten Coast Guard cutters equipped for escort

[19] Stark's testimony, Jan. 3, 1946, *Pearl Harbor Hearings,* pt. 5, p. 2292.

[20] Stark to Kimmel, Apr. 4, 1941, *ibid.,* pt. 16, exhibit 106, p. 2150.

[21] Cordell Hull, *The Memoirs of Cordell Hull* (New York: Macmillan Co. 1948), II, 927.   See also Hull to Colonna, Apr. 3, 1941, United States, Department of State, *United States and Italy, 1936–1946: Documentary Record* (Washington, D. C.: U. S. Govt. Printing Office, 1946), pp. 25–26.

[22] Stark to Kimmel, Apr. 7, 1941, *Pearl Harbor Hearings,* pt. 11, p. 5503; and Morison, *The Battle of the Atlantic,* p. 57.

[23] Hull to Roosevelt (undated), MS Roosevelt Papers (Secretary's File, Box 62); Roosevelt to Hull, Apr. 18, 1941, Franklin D. Roosevelt, *F. D. R.: His Personal Letters, 1928–1945,* ed. Elliott Roosevelt (New York: Duell, Sloan, and Pearce, 1950), II, 1142–1143; and Hull, *Memoirs,* II, 935, 938–939.   The text of this agreement is given in United States, Department of State, *Department of State Bulletin* (Washington, D. C.: U. S. Govt. Printing Office, 1939——), IV (Apr. 12, 1941), 445–447.

duty were transferred to the British.[24]   On April 10 President Roosevelt asked Congress for authority to requisition any foreign vessels in American waters whose services were deemed essential to national defense.[25] The same day, he opened the Red Sea to American shipping by proclaiming the abolition of the combat zone at its southern extremity.[26] A new operations plan issued to the Atlantic Fleet by Admiral King on April 18 confirmed the 26th meridian as the eastern boundary of the Western Hemisphere, announcing that the Western Hemisphere included Greenland, the Azores, the Gulf of St. Lawrence, the Bahamas, the Caribbean Sea, and the Gulf of Mexico.   The plan continued as follows: "Entrance into the Western Hemisphere by naval ships or aircraft of the belligerents other than those powers having sovereignty over territory in the Western Hemisphere is to be viewed as possibly actuated by an unfriendly interest toward shipping or territory in the Western Hemisphere." [27]

This last was a partial answer to the German notice of March 26, and Roosevelt filled it out almost immediately by extending and formalizing a practice which was already more or less common to ships of the neutrality patrol.   On April 21 he issued an order directing units of the Atlantic Fleet to "trail" all German and Italian merchant ships, naval vessels, and aircraft encountered within the limits of the Western Hemisphere as defined by Admiral King and to broadcast their movements in plain language every four hours.[28]   Since lurking British ships and planes were the most obvious beneficiaries of such a policy, this represented another step toward belligerent action.   Indeed, the first direct clash between German and American naval units had already taken place.   For on April 10, while cruising off the coast of Iceland, the United States destroyer *Niblack* had noted the approach of a submarine. Although the submarine, presumably German, had withdrawn when the *Niblack* dropped depth charges, this incident revealed the plain shape of things to come.[29]

[24] Forrest Davis and Ernest K. Lindley, *How War Came* (New York: Simon and Schuster, 1942), p. 187; and Morison, *The Battle of the Atlantic*, p. 36.

[25] Message of the President to Congress, Apr. 10, 1941, *Documents on American Foreign Relations, 1940–1941*, p. 630.

[26] Proclamation No. 2474, Apr. 10, 1941, United States, National Archives, *Federal Register* (Washington, D. C.: U. S. Govt. Printing Office, 1936——), VI, 1905–1906.

[27] Quoted in Morison, *The Battle of the Atlantic*, p. 61.

[28] Stark's testimony, Jan. 3, 1946, *Pearl Harbor Hearings*, pt. 5, pp. 2292–2293.

[29] Morison, *The Battle of the Atlantic*, p. 57.

II

The pilgrimage of the Japanese Foreign Minister to Moscow, Berlin, and Rome, which Churchill had predicted as he called off the February war scare, began in March. That Germany wanted Japan at the earliest possible date to activate plans for expansion in the deep south had recently been made clear; and as Matsuoka rolled westward over the seemingly endless distances of the Trans-Siberian Railway, German designs for embroiling Japan in a Far Eastern war to relieve British and American pressure in the Atlantic still bubbled yeastily.

On March 18 Hitler reviewed the situation once more in a conference with Admiral Raeder. The Admiral felt that Japan should be pressed to attack Singapore without delay and made no secret of his concern over reports from Tokyo that such a move could not be undertaken before German troops landed in England—a fairly remote prospect, then, considering Berlin's plans for an eastern campaign. Since Raeder believed fear of Russia also had much to do with Japan's reluctance to project a drive into Malaya and the Indies, he advised the Fuehrer to tell Matsuoka of his plans for attacking the Soviet Union.[30] What Hitler thought of this counsel is not recorded. But Matsuoka's visit did afford an opportunity to renew the arguments used on Oshima a few weeks earlier; and when Matsuoka finally reached Berlin after talking with Stalin in the Russian capital, both Hitler and Ribbentrop were chafing for action.

Discussion began on March 27 with an interview between Matsuoka and Ribbentrop. Although it was no small triumph to outdo his visitor in loquacity, the German Foreign Minister was himself a prolific talker and dominated the conversation. Opening with his customary lecture on German strength and enemy weakness, Ribbentrop recited statistics on the size of the *Wehrmacht,* assured his listener that submarine warfare in the Atlantic would soon be greatly intensified, and stated that German forces now in Tripoli under General Erwin Rommel had turned the tide of Italian defeat in North Africa. Most of the Balkan countries now adhered to the Tripartite Pact, while Spain was very close to it —at least in spirit—and Turkey was being sounded on the possibility

[30] Report of the Commander-in-Chief, Navy, to the Fuehrer, Mar. 18, 1941, United States, Department of the Navy, *Fuehrer Conferences on Matters Dealing with the German Navy, 1939–1941* (Washington, D. C.: Issued in mimeographed form by the Office of Naval Intelligence, 1947), 1941, I, 32–33.

of joining. As he had done with Oshima in February, Ribbentrop next tried to explain away the nonagression pact with Russia, adding in strict confidence that Germany's relations with the Soviet Union, while correct, were no longer very friendly. Russia was doing many things contrary to German interests, especially in the Balkans. If the Russians ever presented a direct threat, declared the Foreign Minister, Hitler would crush them without mercy.[31]

Swinging round again to the British, Ribbentrop expressed the view that Churchill would have yielded long ago had it not been for Roosevelt's encouragement to go on fighting. Germany was uncertain whether the United States really meant to enter the war and knew that American aid to Britain would remain ineffective for some time to come. Nevertheless, it furnished the hope which kept England from pulling out of the war; and the primary goal of the Tripartite Pact was to scare America into a change of course before its aid became dangerous. The capture of Singapore by Japan would doubtless accomplish this end. It would intimidate Roosevelt by undermining the position of Britain in the Far East without giving him a pretext for war that was satisfactory to American public opinion, and it would lead directly to the consummation of Japan's New Order.[32]

This session ended before Matsuoka could offer any comment, but the attack was resumed in the afternoon by the Fuehrer himself. After closely duplicating Ribbentrop's monologue of the morning, Hitler repeated his conclusions. Matsuoka now availed himself of the day's first good opportunity to speak, indicating his general agreement with Hitler's theme but adding that he was not yet complete master of the situation at home. There was much opposition in Japan, especially among the intelligentsia, to the course suggested. Even the Imperial Family wished to avoid a definite break with the United States and Great Britain. He would do his best to propagate his own views and those of the Fuehrer after his return, but he could offer no pledge on behalf of his government for the time being.[33]

Toward the end of the interview Matsuoka alluded to his recent interview with Stalin. He said that he had urged the advantages of Rus-

---

[31] Memorandum of conversation between Matsuoka and Ribbentrop, Mar. 27, 1941, United States, Department of State, *Nazi-Soviet Relations, 1939–1941* (Washington, D. C.: U. S. Govt. Printing Office, 1948), pp. 281–285.

[32] *Ibid.*, pp. 286–288.

[33] Memorandum of conversation between Hitler and Matsuoka, Mar. 27, 1941, *ibid.*, pp. 292–295.

sian participation with Germany and Japan in a common front against the Anglo-Saxon powers and that Stalin had promised him an answer to this proposition on his return journey through Moscow.[34] But his hosts were not enthusiastic. After sleeping on the possibility of a Soviet-Japanese *rapprochement,* Ribbentrop essayed to change Matsuoka's orientation with an assurance that Japan need not hesitate to attack Singapore from fear of leaving its own rear unprotected. If Russia offered any threatening moves against Japan, Germany would strike at once. A nonaggression pact or a neutrality agreement between Japan and the Soviet Union, he ruminated, "probably would not altogether fit the framework of the present situation."[35] On second thought, however, Ribbentrop seems to have considered this advice too strong, for he explained to Matsuoka on March 29 that Germany did not necessarily disapprove of a simple neutrality pact. Such an arrangement, he added pointedly, might even help Japan get about its main task, which was the reduction of Singapore.[36]

There were further conversations in the German capital both before and after Matsuoka's side trip to Rome. But these led nowhere. Notwithstanding Hitler's assurance of German help if aggression in the south led to war with the United States, the other clung to his initial attitude. Even the prospect of receiving the Fuehrer's personal counsel on the best means of taking Singapore did not attract him,[37] and a definite Japanese move was still far from agreed on when Matsuoka left Berlin on April 4. Everything considered, the apostle of change in Asia had not done badly at the shrine of Europe's new order. By almost any reckoning, he had yielded less than he had gained. As payment on a multitude of half promises which committed him to nothing, he had obtained Berlin's reluctant clearance for his proposed understanding with Moscow.

Although his subsequent negotiations in the Russian capital dragged on for more than a week, Matsuoka succeeded by April 13 in concluding a neutrality pact which, outwardly at least, guaranteed Japan's rear against hostile Soviet action.[38] Lacking detailed knowledge of the Berlin talks, Washington could not assess the full bearing of this treaty on German-

[34] *Nazi-Soviet Relations, 1939–1941,* p. 297.

[35] Memorandum of conversation between Matsuoka and Ribbentrop, Mar. 28, 1941, *ibid.,* pp. 299–302.

[36] Memorandum of conversation between Matsuoka and Ribbentrop, Mar. 29, 1941, *ibid.,* p. 309.   [37] *Ibid.*

[38] Neutrality Pact between Japan and the Soviet Union, Apr. 13, 1941, *Documents on American Foreign Relations, 1940–1941,* pp. 291–292.

Japanese relations. But its implications as to relations between Japan and Russia furnished no excuse for complacency.

Meanwhile, the unofficial exchanges which Bishop Walsh and Father Drought had been commissioned to pursue at the Japanese Embassy had resulted in a new set of proposals, which were conveyed to Hull through Postmaster General Walker on April 9, 1941.[39] These were more accommodating, on the whole, than might have been expected. At least, they seemed to contemplate a broad settlement of the many points at issue between the United States and Japan. On the basis of guaranteed independence for China, withdrawal of Japanese troops from that country without indemnities or territorial changes, recognition of Manchukuo, and "coalescence" of Wang Ching-Wei's regime with his own government, the United States would ask Chiang Kai-shek to negotiate a peace with Japan. In return, Japan would guarantee resumption of the Open Door and "no large-scale concentrated immigration of Japanese into Chinese territory." If Chiang declined this settlement, the United States would discontinue aid to China. So far as non-Chinese issues were concerned, Japan would undertake not to execute its commitments under the Tripartite Pact unless one of the parties to that agreement were *aggressively* attacked by a power not then involved in the European war; the United States would promise to abstain from any "aggressive alliance" designed to assist one nation against another; and both governments would guarantee the independence of the Phillippines.[40]

At the moment, this project was as unofficial on the Japanese side as on the American. But Nomura admitted that he had helped frame the proposals and indicated his willingness to seek his government's approval.[41] Although Hull was not completely satisfied, he agreed a week later that the document might constitute a suitable basis for opening discussions if modified by guarantees on the following points: (1) respect for the territorial integrity and sovereignty of all nations, (2) noninterference in the domestic affairs of other countries, (3) support of the principle of equal commercial opportunity for all nations, and (4) preservation of the *status quo* in the Pacific.[42] Nomura accepted Hull's conditions and referred the whole to Tokyo.

The next move was up to Japan, and what it might be was uncertain

[39] Hull, *Memoirs*, II, 991.

[40] Proposals presented to the Department of State on Apr. 9, 1941, United States, Department of State, *Papers Relating to the Foreign Relations of the United States: Japan, 1931–1941* (Washington, D. C.: U. S. Govt. Printing Office, 1943), II, 398–402.

[41] Memorandum by Hull, Apr. 14, 1941, *ibid.*, p. 403.

[42] Memorandum by Hull, Apr. 16, 1941, *ibid.*, p. 407.

at best. Ambassador Steinhardt had seen Matsuoka during Matsuoka's stay in Moscow, but the summary which he cabled to the State Department on April 11 told very little. According to Matsuoka, Japan recognized no obligation to fight the United States unless it declared war on Germany. He did not think Germany would seize the initiative by declaring war on the United States; but if such a contingency did arise, he hoped that the American government would allow Japan to clarify its intentions before taking action in the Pacific.[43] Outwardly, this statement appeared to reflect the conciliatory spirit of Nomura in Washington. Set against Matsuoka's recent conversations in Berlin and Rome, his infant neutrality pact with Russia, and the beginning of a new effort to liquidate the China Incident, however, it scarcely lessened the impression that Japan was getting ready for action in the south. Under these circumstances, the need for reserve was plain, and Hull awaited Tokyo's reaction to Nomura's proposals in no very trusting frame of mind.

His suspicion was well-founded. Hitler told the impatient Raeder on April 20 that he now had assurances from both Matsuoka and Oshima that Japan would be prepared to strike southward in May. He explained that the Russo-Japanese pact had been concluded with his acquiescence and boasted that this agreement had special value from Germany's standpoint because it restrained any aggressive designs which Japan might harbor with respect to Vladivostok, but left his Oriental ally perfectly free to deal with the problem of southern Asia.[44] Nor did it appear that the Fuehrer was completely misinformed as to Japanese intentions; Tokyo was already pushing demands against Vichy for additional concessions in Indo-China. Again France yielded, and on May 6 the Pétain government signed new agreements which permitted Japanese capital to take part in the development of Indo-Chinese agricultural, mining, and hydraulic enterprises, gave Japanese business firms a larger share in the handling of exports and imports, and provided for the establishment of Japanese schools in that country.[45]

This foretold no moderation of Japanese policy. Neither did the official revision of the draft proposals of April 9, finally submitted on May 12. So far as China was concerned, the only major addition to

[43] Hull, *Memoirs*, II, 993.

[44] Report of the Commander-in-Chief, Navy, to the Fuehrer, Apr. 20, 1941, *Fuehrer Conferences*, 1941, I, 53.

[45] For comment on this treaty, see Virginia Thompson, "The Japan-Indochina Trade Pact," *Far Eastern Survey*, X (June 10, 1941), 116–118.

the suggested peace terms was a stipulation for a Sino-Japanese agreement covering joint defense against communism. But other changes were more significant. Tokyo demanded resumption of normal trade relations with the United States, insisted on reaffirming its obligations under the Tripartite Pact, and asked the American government to consider admitting Japanese immigration on a nondiscriminatory basis.[46] Two days later Matsuoka gave further evidence that Japan had not turned over a new leaf when he informed Grew that he and Konoye were determined to use only peaceful methods in carrying out Japan's southward advance "unless circumstances render this impossible." [47]

In Hull's view the official Japanese proposals of May 12 contained some obvious traps. On May 16 he refused any pledge to discontinue aid to China, even if Chiang Kai-shek did reject the suggested terms, and insisted that the clause calling for joint action against communism should be altered to require nothing more than "parallel measures of defense against subversive activities from external sources." [48] He disclaimed as well all thought of limiting American aid to Britain, making it plain that current negotiations would enjoy little progress unless Japan agreed that its obligations to Germany and Italy under the Tripartite Pact involved no duty to restrict American freedom in this matter.[49]

Thus it became clear at the outset that the two governments were about as far from agreement as ever. But the Japanese proposals of May 12 and the American reply of May 16 did succeed in giving discussion a new impetus and at least the appearance of a new framework, providing the basis for a long series of talks which, with just one major interruption, was to last until October. And, through it all, the Tripartite Pact was to figure increasingly as the primary stumbling block—for Japan's reluctance to disavow any obligations under that instrument proved just as strong as Hull's insistence that nothing more could be done until this fundamental point was settled.

Thus another issue was drawn in the spring of 1941. But even though it did little immediate good, the United States from this moment

---

[46] Draft proposal presented by Nomura, May 12, 1941, *Foreign Relations: Japan, 1931–1941*, II, 420–425.

[47] Hull's testimony, Nov. 23, 1945, *Pearl Harbor Hearings*, pt. 2, p. 419.

[48] Draft suggestion presented by Hull, May 16, 1941, *Foreign Relations: Japan, 1931–1941*, II, 433. His refusal to consider stopping American aid to China was implicit in the omission of such a provision from this draft suggestion.

[49] Oral statement by Hull, May 16, 1941, *ibid.*, pp. 429, 432; also Hull's draft suggestion, May 16, 1941, *ibid.*, pp. 432–433.

forward held a peculiar advantage over its Asiatic opponent. Some time earlier, American cryptographers had broken the Japanese diplomatic code (as well as the code used in broadcasting ship movements), and a regular monitoring system was established by the early part of May.[50]   Owing to the care with which the secret was kept, the Japanese government had no cause to take alarm and change either code, and henceforth the State Department enjoyed almost complete access to messages passing between the Japanese Foreign Office and its missions abroad.   With singular fitness the process by which Japanese messages were intercepted, decoded, and distributed to key officials in the American government became known as "Magic."

III

Thanks to Great Britain's sympathetic relations with Turkey and to the manifest ambitions of both Germany and Russia, the Balkan Peninsula had constituted an area of vast strategic significance from the beginning of the war—while the transfers of Rumanian territory to Russia and Hungary in the summer of 1940, the Italian invasion of Greece a few weeks later, and the rapid extension of German influence throughout the Balkans had greatly heightened its original importance. As a result, the United States had taken a much more direct interest in Balkan affairs since the end of the year.

At the direction of the President, Colonel William J. Donovan visited the numerous Balkan capitals during the month of January 1941 to acquire a first-hand knowledge of local conditions.   Long a prominent attorney in Buffalo, New York, famed as an infantry commander in the First World War, and soon to become chief organizer of the Office of Strategic Services, Donovan was an able man, and he pursued his investigations with marked energy.   Since neither Greece, Bulgaria, nor Yugoslavia had fallen completely into the toils of the Tripartite Pact, these three countries were of greatest interest to Washington.   In Athens and Sofia Donovan called attention to the wish of his government to assist all nations opposed to Germany.[51]   But Yugoslavia was the most important of the trio, and he chose Belgrade as the focal point of his efforts.

[50] See Hull, *Memoirs*, II, 998.
[51] Davis and Lindley, *How War Came*, p. 199.

President Roosevelt had already assured the Yugoslav Minister to the United States, Constantin Fotitch, that Yugoslavia would receive help under the pending Lend-Lease bill if the Belgrade government chose to hold out against the Axis, and Fotitch was doing everything he could to direct such a choice from Washington. But Donovan found that German pressure on Yugoslavia to sign the Tripartite Pact was very great. The Regent, Prince Paul, expressed himself as sympathetic to Britain, while both Dragisha Cvetkovich, the Premier, and Alexander Cincar-Markovitch, the Foreign Minister, professed similar feelings. Yet it was obvious that their fear of Germany outweighed their love for the democratic cause and that they could be expected to yield when the pinch came. However, General Dušan Simovich, commander of the Yugoslav Air Force, told Donovan that arrangements had already been made by various officers of the Army and Air Corps to overthrow the Regency if it succumbed to Germany.[52] Not greatly reassured, the State Department continued its efforts to stiffen Paul's resolution through the American Minister in Belgrade, Arthur Bliss Lane.

Lane considered a Yugoslav-Bulgar-Turkish understanding the best hope of keeping Germany from dominating the entire peninsula and suggested on January 25 that Hull urge those governments to adopt a joint defense policy. Hull rejected this advice on January 29, however, and a week later declined Halifax's request that he support British efforts to promote talks between Yugoslavia and Turkey.[53] By this time German troops were moving into Bulgaria. Lane cabled on February 8 that Prince Paul was not disposed to resist German pressure much longer. But Hull was still cautious—and seemingly not very hopeful in any event. In notes to the Bulgarian, Turkish, and Yugoslav governments he merely called attention to the American policy of aiding the democracies and emphasized his belief that Great Britain would win the war.[54] Lane continued to send disturbing reports, and Roosevelt took a hand by authorizing him to tell Paul that American sympathy was greatest for those countries which did not yield to aggression without a struggle. Lane complied on February 22, and after considering this message with its implied threat that American-Yugoslav

[52] *Ibid.*, pp. 200–201.   [53] Hull, *Memoirs*, II, 928.
[54] Hull, *Memoirs*, II, 928–929; and Hull, to Lane, Feb. 9, 1941, United States, Department of State, *Peace and War: United States Foreign Policy, 1931–1941* (Washington, D. C.: U. S. Govt. Printing Office, 1943), p. 619.

friendship might suffer if he gave in too easily, the Regent promised Lane that he would make no agreements with Hitler.[55]

But resistance to Germany was crumbling everywhere north of Greece, and Bulgaria adhered to the Tripartite Pact on March 1. As German forces in that country started moving toward the Greek border to retrieve the situation resulting from the Italian military debacle of the winter just past, Washington learned that Turkey contemplated no military action regardless of what might happen in Greece, while Yugoslav intentions were uncertain at best. Greece alone was prepared to stand firm. London announced that Greece would receive full British aid to oppose a German invasion, and grasping at this last point, Hull assured Halifax on March 3 that the United States would supply the Greeks with war materials to the limit of its ability.[56]

Roosevelt froze Bulgarian credits on March 4, and Hull instructed Lane the next day to continue his efforts with Yugoslav leaders. On March 10 Churchill suggested that British and American diplomats in Moscow, Ankara, and Belgrade join forces in an attempt to work out a scheme for Balkan resistance; he particularly wanted to secure a Russian promise to assist Turkey. But Hull was more pessimistic than ever. A British guarantee of military aid to Yugoslavia and to Turkey was the only further move he considered worth while.[57]

In plain truth, the immediate military situation was hopeless. With vast forces poised to strike, Germany was destined to take control of the Balkans regardless of what any other country (with the possible exception of Russia) said or did. By March 15 Prince Paul's will to resist was petering out. Considering his surrender inevitable, President Roosevelt froze Yugoslav credits on March 24. The Yugoslav government adhered to the Tripartite Pact the next day.[58]

The prediction which General Simovich had made to Donovan in January was speedily fulfilled. The Regency was overthrown on March 27; Simovich formed a new ministry at once; and Yugoslav troops were deployed along the frontiers in anticipation of the Nazi attack. The United States government officially applauded this move, assured King Peter of military supplies, and exerted such influence as

[55] Roosevelt to Hull, Feb. 20, 1941, *F. D. R.: His Personal Letters, 1928–1945*, II, 1126–1127; and Hull, *Memoirs*, II, 930–931.

[56] Hull, *Memoirs*, II, 931.

[57] Churchill to Roosevelt, Mar. 10, 1941, in Winston S. Churchill, *The Grand Alliance* (Boston: Houghton Mifflin Co., 1950), p. 110; and Hull, *Memoirs*, II, 931.

[58] Hull, *Memoirs*, II, 932.

it could to discourage Bulgarian, Rumanian, and Hungarian participation in German designs.[59] But German power, being on the spot, reduced these efforts to futility. The Nazi troops invaded Yugoslavia on April 6 and received that nation's unconditional surrender twelve days later. Meanwhile, German armies likewise moved into Greece. The Anglo-Greek forces proved unable to stand against them, and the entire Balkan Peninsula rested in Hitler's palm by the end of the month.

Under the impetus of these happenings relations between the United States and Russia continued their improvement to the middle of April. Although Moscow was fully as cautious as Washington, its Balkan program achieved general harmony with American views throughout the late winter and early spring. Russian diplomacy was especially active in Yugoslavia; and while the Soviet government avoided giving any direct promise of military aid, it did conclude a treaty of friendship and nonaggression with the regime of General Simovich on April 6, which won Hull's approval.[60] All this was posted to Russia's credit. It seemed to bear out American knowledge of the impending rupture between Germany and the Soviet Union. In consequence, the trickle of American supplies to Russia was maintained. While this trade failed to achieve even the restricted volume of the corresponding period of 1940,[61] it was now highly specialized in such commodities as machine tools and aviation gasoline, and still sufficiently generous to elicit repeated grumblings from London.[62]

But Soviet policy was never an open book, and Moscow still evinced no particular solicitude for American feelings in its direct relations with Washington. When Oumansky told Welles on March 20 that he had been instructed by his government to seek confirmation of the latter's January warning about the Nazi plan to attack Russia,[63] it appeared that

[59] *Ibid.*, p. 933. Cf. Hull to Earle, Apr. 5, 1941, *Peace and War*, p. 638; and Churchill, *The Grand Alliance*, pp. 161–163.

[60] Statement by Hull, Apr. 6, 1941, *Peace and War*, pp. 638–639. For an illuminating estimate of Russian policy in this connection, see Grigore Gafencu, *Prelude to the Russian Campaign: From the Moscow Pact (August 21st 1939) to the Opening of Hostilities in Russia (June 22nd 1941)*, tr. E. Fletcher-Allen (London: Frederick Muller, 1945), pp. 139–150. An ex-Foreign Minister of Rumania, Gafencu was at this time Rumanian Minister in Moscow.

[61] See statistics in David J. Dallin, *Soviet Russia's Foreign Policy, 1939–1942*, tr. Leon Denman (New Haven: Yale Univ. Press, 1942), p. 427.

[62] See statement by the British Minister of Economic Warfare, Mar. 25, 1941, Great Britain, Parliament, House of Commons, *The Parliamentary Debates: Official Report*, 5th series (London: H. M. Stationery Office, 1909——), CCCLXX, 406.

[63] Memorandum by Welles, Mar. 20, 1941, *Peace and War*, p. 638.

Soviet leaders might be on the verge of treating American counsel with more respect than had been their habit. Since Matsuoka was then in the early stages of his European pilgrimage, Welles seized the opportunity to express his belief that the Japanese Foreign Minister's chief objective was a nonaggression pact with Russia and advised Oumansky that the American government felt Russia should decline to enter any type of understanding with Japan, keeping Tokyo rather in a state of prolonged uncertainty.[64] But Russia, like Japan, was interested in protecting its rear, and Welles's counsel was ignored. After the Russo-Japanese neutrality pact was announced, therefore, relations between Washington and Moscow turned perceptibly cooler.

The effect was heightened by Russia's generally exacting attitude in matters of supply and by Oumansky's personal behavior. Notwithstanding the gradual betterment of commercial relations since the fall of 1940, this trade had produced nothing but dissatisfaction in Moscow and annoyance in Washington. The Soviet government persistently demanded scarce materials in much greater quantity than the United States felt it could grant without slighting its commitments to Britain; Soviet policy was not clear enough in any event to encourage special efforts on Washington's part; and Oumansky's roughhewn disdain for tact merely emphasized the querulousness of his superiors. Since the previous summer Welles had handled most of these increasingly unpleasant contacts with the Russian Ambassador. On May 14, however, Oumansky obtained an interview with Hull, displayed vast ill-humor concerning the twenty-two fruitless meetings he had had with the Under Secretary in the last eight or nine months, and accused the American government of hostility toward both his country and himself. Hull could only deny the charge, explaining that the United States, in view of its other obligations, was now unable to maintain full commercial relations with neutral countries.[65]

Since Russia would neither appreciate small favors nor do anything to justify larger ones, Washington thereupon fell into an attitude of reserve which, according to Hull, embraced a determination to offer Moscow nothing, to exact a *quid pro quo* for every concession requested, and to proceed generally on the principle that good relations were no more important to the United States than to the Soviet Union.[66] Since Russian diplomacy, even then, could not operate smoothly under a

[64] Davis and Lindley, *How War Came,* p. 216.
[65] Hull, *Memoirs,* II, 971–972.   [66] *Ibid.,* pp. 972–973.

formula of give-and-take, this coolness was not dissipated until the middle of the year, when Nazi armies stood on Russian soil.

IV

In the campaign to improve economic relations with Spain, Great Britain continued to move well ahead of the United States throughout the spring of 1941, granting the Spanish government a sizable sterling credit, liberalizing its blockade practices with respect to Spanish trade, and working in other ways to satisfy Spanish needs. British officials urged the United States to do likewise,[67] but Washington still distrusted Franco and procrastinated as before. While American authorities subjected the problem to further study, Weddell was instructed to make it clear to the Spanish Foreign Office that the United States meant to continue its policy of aiding Germany's foes regardless of the cost. The Ambassador explained this resolve to Serrano Suñer on April 19, in a wholly unpleasant interview characterized by stinging remarks on both sides.[68]

Weddell favored more constructive action and so informed his superiors. On April 29 he was given permission to approach Franco with word that the United States was prepared to consider arrangements for supplying goods, chiefly agricultural, of which it had a surplus. He was to make no promise regarding scarce articles, however, and was to exact an assurance that Spain would remain out of the war. But this move hinged upon direct contact with Franco at a time when contact with Franco was not to be had. Bearing Weddell a grudge for his sharp comments of April 19—and hoping to drive Spain into fuller collaboration with Germany through pure inertia—Serrano Suñer now kept the American Ambassador from obtaining an interview with his chief. And Franco was apparently content to let the American negotiations rest for the time being, a state of mind which was destined to last through the next six months.[69]

[67] Memorandum by Welles, Mar. 20, 1941, MS Department of State (852.51/546); and Herbert Feis, *The Spanish Story: Franco and the Nations at War* (New York: Alfred A. Knopf, 1948), pp. 130–133.

[68] Telegram from Weddell, Apr. 9, 1941, MS Department of State (740.0011 European War 1939/10142).

[69] Feis, *The Spanish Story*, pp. 133–134. Serrano Suñer disliked Weddell intensely, claiming that he lacked the "diplomatic temperament." See Ramón Serrano Suñer, *Entre les Pyrénées et Gibraltar* (Geneva: Les Éditions du Cheval Ailé, 1948), p. 238.

The tug of war with Great Britain over policy toward Vichy France did not change very rapidly as time went on. Washington had acquiesced readily enough in December 1940 when the British government refused to countenance any plan for regular shipments of food to unoccupied France. But as the budding Murphy-Weygand Agreement carried its North African program into a more active phase, the State Department raised that question once more; and Churchill finally agreed on March 29, 1941, that relief cargoes under Red Cross auspices might be allowed to pass the blockade. The point remained a sore one, however. New difficulties were raised almost at once, and Hull explained to Halifax on April 8 that the whole success of the North African plan depended upon Pétain's situation at Vichy. His idea was that hunger in unoccupied France would tend to undermine the Marshal's authority. Since Britain had come by gradual stages to accept the Murphy-Weygand accord, London again decided that the Red Cross project might be carried out.[70] In consequence, two American food ships loaded with concentrated milk and vitamins reached Marseilles before the end of the month, and small additional shipments followed in May.[71] Nevertheless, the British continued to make it clear that they did not view the North African program as a model for United States policy toward unoccupied France.[72] This being understood, attention commenced to center upon more pressing topics.

By the middle of April reports of new proposals for collaboration between the Vichy government and Germany began to arouse old fears—especially that of German infiltration into North Africa. Discussing this threat with Halifax on April 19, Hull outlined possible countermeasures for British consideration. These included protests by both governments, British or American seizure of Dakar or Casablanca, and an effort to persuade Weygand to request military aid from the outside.[73] Developing this line of thought, the British on April 29 requested that the United States urge Vichy to permit the French Fleet to join their own naval forces in opposing any German effort to send an army across the Mediterranean. At the same time, they wanted American naval units to visit Dakar and Casablanca. But Hull, in spite of what he had told Halifax ten days earlier, now thought London

---

[70] Hull, *Memoirs*, II, 955; and William L. Langer, *Our Vichy Gamble* (New York: Alfred A. Knopf, 1947), pp. 140–141.

[71] Hull, *Memoirs*, II, 957; and Davis and Lindley, *How War Came*, pp. 194–197.

[72] Langer, *Our Vichy Gamble*, p. 140.   [73] *Ibid.*, p. 143.

was moving too fast. If such a request were transmitted to Vichy, he argued, the Germans would undoubtedly hear of it. This might precipitate the very action which was feared. Since the appearance of American warships at Casablanca would be equally provocative, the British suggestion was turned down on both counts.[74]

The immediacy of the crisis could not be denied, however. Thanks in part to the withdrawal of British troops from the Libyan front to resist the Nazi invasion of Greece, Rommel and his Germans during the past two or three weeks had begun to fulfill Ribbentrop's prediction by forcing the British to disgorge their African gains of the previous winter and to retire once more inside the borders of Egypt. Britain's Near Eastern position was deteriorating in other ways as well, and the prospect of a deal between France and its conquerors loomed nearer by the day.

Marshal Pétain and Admiral Leahy were on especially good terms during this period of stress. "He seemed to draw closer to me as his troubles with the Nazis mounted," Leahy has written. "He asked for me often and seemed relieved to have somebody to whom he could unburden himself." [75] But Pétain, for all his value as a symbol, was not the active force in the Vichy regime. Since Laval's expulsion from the government in December 1940 his collaborator's mantle had rested on the shoulders of his personal foe, Admiral Darlan, now Vice Premier as well as Minister of Marine. Thus far Darlan's efforts to negotiate with Germany had achieved little success. But on May 3 he was invited to confer in Paris with Otto Abetz, Hitler's chief representative in occupied France. This time he managed to strike a bargain. Britain's other difficulties had lately been augmented by a revolt in Iraq. To help the Germans exploit this situation, Darlan promised them the use of a Syrian airfield and undertook to provide the rebels with supplies from French military stores in Syria. He also contracted for a number of small adjustments in North Africa. His *quid pro quo* was to be the rearming of six French destroyers and seven torpedo boats, changes in the regulations governing traffic between occupied and unoccupied France, and a reduction in the costs of the German occupation.[76]

This understanding did not provide for an actual German advance

[74] Hull, *Memoirs*, II, 957.
[75] William D. Leahy, *I Was There* (New York: Whittlesey House, 1950), p. 28.
[76] Langer, *Our Vichy Gamble*, pp. 148–149.

into North Africa. But no one regarded the accord as complete in itself. It was clearly just the opening play for much larger stakes than the destruction of British authority in Iraq. Leahy reported that even Pétain understood the seriousness of German designs, though he considered himself powerless to head them off.[77]

The fear that the old soldier's pessimism was well-founded received further confirmation when Darlan journeyed to Berchtesgaden for discussions with Hitler on May 11 and 12. Once more the United States exerted all the verbal pressure of which it was capable. On May 13 Leahy handed Pétain a vigorous protest against any concessions to Germany beyond the terms of the armistice agreement.[78] Two days later Roosevelt went over the Marshal's head with a direct appeal to the French people to uphold the democratic cause.[79] But as tension continued to mount throughout the following week, Leahy decided that verbal efforts were no longer equal to the task at hand and advised Washington to consider the possibility of landing two hundred and fifty thousand troops in North Africa at once to help Weygand resist a potential German invasion. This notion was impracticable on several grounds. Even if public opinion in the United States had been prepared to countenance such a venture, not enough trained men were available. Furthermore, it was not certain that either Pétain or Weygand would support the move.[80] On the other hand, it was possible to bring pressure by calling off the Murphy-Weygand Agreement. As might have been expected, the British government favored this action. But the State Department concluded that nothing could be lost by going ahead with the North African accord, and Welles so informed Halifax on May 23.[81] With this, Washington set itself to await developments.

V

Owing to the special difficulty of making arrangements for a defense of southeastern Asia and the southwestern Pacific, it had been decided as early as the fall of 1940 that any detailed plans for military and naval

[77] Langer, *Our Vichy Gamble*, p. 144. [78] *Ibid.*, pp. 150–151.
[79] Statement by the President, May 15, 1941, *Department of State Bulletin*, IV (May 17, 1941), 584.
[80] See Langer, *Our Vichy Gamble*, p. 153; and Leahy, *I Was There*, pp. 33–34.
[81] Langer, *Our Vichy Gamble*, pp. 154–155.

coöperation in this area would have to be charted on the spot.[82] Admiral Thomas C. Hart, commanding the Asiatic Fleet based at Manila, was therefore authorized to conduct local talks on behalf of the American government. He opened tentative conversations with British officials at Singapore in November 1940, and with Dutch authorities at Batavia in January 1941. Naval officers representing all three powers held another conference at Singapore in February,[83] but it was obvious that not much could be done until the higher-level staff discussions then proceeding in Washington had assigned the Far East a definite place in the larger scheme of things.

As expected, ABC–1 (the Anglo-American joint basic war plan) did little to solve the immediate problems of the Far Eastern commanders. The strategic priority given the Atlantic and European theaters severely limited the forces available for operations in the Asiatic sector; and while this area was covered by a general framework of command arrangements, little was offered in the way of tactical guidance. The task which ultimately confronted Hart and the others, therefore, was essentially that of interpreting the joint basic war plan as it related to the Far East—a design which permitted considerable local freedom within tight general restrictions. To this end formal staff talks were held in Singapore by American, British, and Dutch representatives from April 21 to April 27.

In spite of their nonpolitical character, these discussions largely revolved about the question of how far Japan should be allowed to go before countermeasures were taken by the associated powers—and this, like any attempt to define the *casus belli,* was fundamentally a political matter. After some consideration it was agreed that military and naval countermeasures would become necessary if Japanese forces moved into Portuguese Timor, New Caledonia, the Loyalty Islands, or into any part of Thailand west of 100 degrees east longitude or south of 10 degrees north latitude. Even more important was the view that the three powers ought to take action if a large number of Japanese warships, or a convoy of merchant vessels escorted by warships, were found on a course directed at the Philippine Islands, the east coast of the Isthmus of Kra (southern Thailand), or the east coast of Malaya. Thinking of a possible attack on the Netherlands Indies or Australia, the conferees likewise recommended action if a Japanese force crossed

---

[82] Turner's testimony, Dec. 20, 1945, *Pearl Harbor Hearings,* pt. 4, p. 1929.
[83] *Ibid.,* pp. 1931–1932.

the parallel of 6 degrees north latitude between the Malay Peninsula and the Philippines, a line running from the Gulf of Davao to Weigeo Island, or the Equator east of Weigeo; [84] but it was clear that they viewed the Malay Barrier as the principal line to be maintained. While the British were accorded general strategic control in this sector (as under ABC–1), its actual defense was entrusted almost completely to American and Dutch forces.[85] This last point remained a troubled one, and it would soon become evident that plans for coöperation in the Far East had not yet achieved a form satisfactory to Washington.

This source of discontent lay temporarily in the background, however, as the difficulty of maintaining transportation routes between North America and the British Isles—added to rumors of German plans for invading North Africa, occupying Spain and Portugal, and seizing the Azores and the Canaries—kept the Atlantic in its familiar position as the truly significant area of coöperation throughout the spring of 1941. The situation here was so tense that the United States in late April seriously considered the further transfer to the Atlantic of three battleships, four light cruisers, and two destroyer squadrons— a suggestion which drew applause from the British Chiefs of Staff.[86] It was at this time, moreover, that Churchill—distracted by military defeat in Libya and new rumors of Franco-German collaboration—informed Roosevelt that he regarded the Spanish situation as hopeless, Gibraltar as doomed to be captured or immobilized, and Great Britain as unable to continue the fight beyond August unless the United States entered the war as a full partner.[87]

As it turned out, these fears proved much exaggerated. But Washington was only less pessimistic than London and soon found itself giving effect to numerous provisions of ABC–1 a good deal earlier than that agreement had contemplated. In May the British government started preparations to occupy Grand Canary and the Cape Verde Islands and requested American help in keeping the Germans out of the Azores.[88] Roosevelt directed Stark on May 22 to prepare an expedition

---

[84] Report of American-Dutch-British conversations at Singapore, April 1941, *Pearl Harbor Hearings,* pt. 15, exhibit 50, p. 1564.

[85] *Ibid.,* pp. 1569–1570, 1580–1582.

[86] Turner to Danckwerts, Apr. 25, 1941, *ibid.,* pt. 19, exhibit 158, p. 3457; and Danckwerts to Turner, Apr. 28, 1941, *ibid.,* p. 3458.

[87] Langer, *Our Vichy Gamble,* p. 145; and Churchill to Roosevelt, May 4, 1941, in Churchill, *The Grand Alliance,* p. 235.

[88] Morison, *The Battle of the Atlantic,* p. 66. For the American view of the situa-

of twenty-five thousand men to seize the Azores, allowing him only thirty days to complete the task.[89]   About the same time, plans were made to occupy Martinique if Pétain yielded entirely to German pressure.[90]   Meanwhile, following other plans laid down in the Washington report, the United States Army and Navy observers at London organized large-scale military and naval missions and embarked upon their program of continuous consultation with the British Chiefs of Staff.[91]

In spite of the Navy's preparations for future escort duty, the question of American-escorted convoys was held in abeyance for the time being. Stimson and Knox, the most aggressive members of the Cabinet, had agreed on March 24 that convoying ought to begin very soon. But Roosevelt was still reluctant to act without congressional sanction, and he decided on April 10 that it was not yet practicable to ask for the desired authority.[92]   Stimson, particularly, regarded his caution as excessive. He told the President in round terms that he could expect no spontaneous demand for convoys; he had to seek popular support for the measure by explaining to the country just why it was necessary to take part in such operations. Roosevelt considered gentler methods less dangerous, however, and contented himself with the "trailing" order of April 21.[93]

No amount of reticence at the White House could disguise the fact that the Atlantic war was drawing closer. The brief but spectacular foray of the German battleship *Bismarck* into the North Atlantic in late May aroused much anxiety in the United States. German naval policy assumed an equally menacing aspect in the *Robin Moor* and *ZamZam* incidents. On May 21 Henry S. Waterman, the United States consul at Bordeaux, reported the landing of 140 American survivors of the Egyptian steamship *ZamZam,* which had been captured and sunk by a German warship in the South Atlantic a few days be-

tion in western and southern Europe at this time, see Roosevelt to Churchill, May 4, 1941, *F. D. R.: His Personal Letters, 1928–1945,* II, 1148–1149.

[89] Stark's testimony, Dec. 31, 1945, *Pearl Harbor Hearings,* pt. 5, p. 2113.

[90] Stark's testimony, Jan. 4, 1946, *ibid.,* p. 2310.

[91] Morison, *The Battle of the Atlantic,* p. 55.

[92] Henry L. Stimson and McGeorge Bundy, *On Active Service: In Peace and War* (New York: Harper and Bros., 1948), pp. 367–368. According to the American Institute of Public Opinion, the proportion of Americans favoring the institution of United States convoys to Great Britain rose from 41 per cent in April to 52 per cent at the end of May. See *Public Opinion Quarterly,* V (Winter 1941), 485.

[93] Stimson and Bundy, *On Active Service,* pp. 369–370.

fore.[94]   One day later the American freighter *Robin Moor* was torpedoed, shelled, and sunk by a German submarine while en route from
New York to Capetown.[95]   Neither incident was calculated to sweeten
relations with Germany, and both testified to the growing unrestraint
of naval activity.

VI

Thus May ended with British and American fortunes manifestly on
the downgrade.   Despite the elaboration of a useful joint strategy for
global war, the tide of German success was running high everywhere.
Britain's toehold in the Balkans had entirely ceased to exist; the Imperial lifeline was threatened by a German-sponsored rebellion in Iraq,
the presence of Rommel's victorious forces in Egypt, and prospective
coöperation among France, Spain, and Germany to drive British power
from Gibraltar and to take full control of the western Mediterranean.
Against this danger the United States searched desperately for expedients—throwing its patrol forces deeper into the Atlantic war, planning to seize the Azores and possibly Martinique, and making a grim
bid for retention of influence in North Africa by pushing ahead with
the Murphy-Weygand accord regardless of everything.   Only with
respect to the Navy's assumption of escort duty did the administration
hold back, and preparations were far advanced even here.

Nor did conditions in Asia hold much better promise.   The launching of new talks on a Pacific settlement had been accompanied by no
essential changes in Japanese policy.   Instead, Japan had exacted new
economic concessions from Indo-China, while Matsuoka's neutrality
pact with Russia seemed to give Tokyo additional confidence for an
early military excursion to the south.   The brightest spot on any horizon
was furnished by the prospect of war between Germany and the Soviet
Union.   But pending that development, even America's relations with
Russia—generally on the mend since the fall of 1940—had again taken
a turn for the worse.

[94] Press release, May 21, 1941, *Department of State Bulletin,* IV (May 24, 1941), 636.
[95] See report of the United States Consul at Pernambuco, Brazil, June 12, 1941, *ibid.*
(June 14, 1941), pp. 716–717.

CHAPTER VIII

Unlimited Emergency

I

Up to the spring of 1941 the crisis proclamation issued by president Roosevelt on September 8, 1939, had not been amended, and the United States continued to exist in the presence of what was officially described as a "limited national emergency." Since it involved no abridgement of the President's right to use all the emergency powers belonging to his office, this limitation had no legal meaning whatever.[1] But it constituted the avowed framework of public policy; and, weighed in this scale, it offered an assurance which events had rendered obsolete. While the administration had done much to emphasize the precarious state of national security as the course of the war turned from bad to worse, its statements on foreign affairs had tended to uphold the concept of limited emergency.

However adequate such a concept might have been in the fall of 1939, it no longer portrayed the real gravity of affairs in the spring of 1941. Some authoritative clarification of the world crisis, especially as it related to the battle of the Atlantic, was manifestly in order; and although Roosevelt still refused to demand such downright measures as a grant of authority to institute American convoys between the United States and the British Isles, his speech of May 27 represented a long step forward in the domain of war psychology.

Delivered as a "fireside chat," this address constituted a reasonably detailed lecture on the war situation as a whole. The President surveyed the decay of relations with all three of the Axis powers, charted the development of anxiety and then of anger in the United States, explained the growth of American war production, and reaffirmed the country's determination to see the crisis through in accordance with its

---

[1] See Louis W. Koenig, *The Presidency and the Crisis: Powers of the Office from the Invasion of Poland to Pearl Harbor* (New York: King's Crown Press, 1944), p. 13.

belief in the fundamental rightness of the democratic attitude.[2] Conditions in the Atlantic were the largest single object of his remarks, however, and he dealt in fairly specific terms with the main worries of the American government in this area—namely, the problem of delivering Lend-Lease supplies to Great Britain and the dangers which would accrue as a result of German seizure of the Azores and the Cape Verde Islands.

His words left no room for doubt that the growing effectiveness of German submarine warfare had reduced Britain's control over its transatlantic supply lines to a questionable minimum at best, and he made it plain that he considered the defense of these lines just as vital to American security as to that of the United Kingdom. For reasons discussed in the last chapter, he did not broach the question of American convoys, or the closely related one of American escorts for British convoys, nor did he furnish details regarding the measures already taken in the Atlantic. But he hinted at both in the clearest statement he had yet made concerning the Atlantic war. "Our patrols are helping now," he said, "to insure delivery of the needed supplies to Britain. All additional measures necessary to deliver the goods will be taken. Any and all further methods or combinations of methods, which can or should be utilized, are being devised by our military and naval technicians, who, with me, will work out and put into effect such new and additional safeguards as may be needed." [3]

In a similar manner, and for reasons that were obvious, the President said nothing of American and British plans to occupy the Azores and the Cape Verde Islands. But his discussion of their strategic importance carried an urgency which was nicely calculated to prepare the country for such a move. These islands, he said, "if occupied or controlled by Germany, would directly endanger the freedom of the Atlantic and our own physical safety. Under German domination, they would become bases for submarines, warships, and airplanes raiding the waters which lie immediately off our coasts and attacking the shipping in the South Atlantic. They would provide a springboard for actual attack against the integrity of Brazil and her neighboring republics." [4]

Concluding from his assessment of these and other dangers that the

---

[2] Address by the President, May 27, 1941, United States, Department of State, *Peace and War: United States Foreign Policy, 1931–1941* (Washington, D. C.: U. S. Govt. Printing Office, 1943), pp. 663–664.
[3] *Ibid.*, pp. 669–670.   [4] *Ibid.*, p. 668.

United States faced a crisis of the most serious type, the President brought his remarks to a close by proclaiming the existence of an "unlimited national emergency." [5] This was the real crux of the message. While he again failed to offer the nation a complete statement of American policy in terms of what had already been done and planned, he now said enough to confirm popular apprehension regarding the drift of affairs; and his positive assurance that the country had entered a phase of unlimited emergency could not fail to inaugurate a new epoch in American nonbelligerency at the level of public consciousness.[6] It was obvious that the administration was ready to proceed more openly and to maintain a more consistent effort to carry public opinion along with it.

II

Thanks in part to Weddell's inability to establish direct contact with Franco and in part to the aloofness of the entire Spanish government as the day approached for Germany's invasion of Russia, the Spanish policy of the United States remained at an absolute standstill from April until midsummer of 1941. Considering Madrid's somewhat hostile attitude and what was known of efforts by Hitler and Darlan to produce an agreement which would give Germany virtually undisputed control over North Africa and the western Mediterranean, Franco was suspected of a willingness to collaborate in these moves if the Hitler-Darlan schemes progressed well enough.[7] As far as it could be done subtly, therefore, he was made to feel the weight of American displeasure.

There was no abrupt change in existing commercial relations with

[5] Address by the President, May 27, 1941, *Peace and War*, p. 672; and Proclamation No. 2487, May 27, 1941, United States, National Archives, *Federal Register* (Washington, D. C.: U. S. Govt. Printing Office, 1936——), VI, 2617.

[6] It is perhaps significant that public-opinion surveys taken immediately, or soon, after the "unlimited emergency" speech reflect a generally sharpened appreciation of the dangers confronting the United States. For example, a *Fortune* poll taken in early June shows a substantial increase in the number of people who believed that American armed forces would eventually be sent to Europe. And the American Institute of Public Opinion discovered that the proportion favoring United States escorts for transatlantic convoys rose from 52 per cent to 55 per cent of the population immediately after this address. See *Public Opinion Quarterly*, V (Fall 1941), 485, 487.

[7] See Cordell Hull, *The Memoirs of Cordell Hull* (New York: Macmillan Co., 1948), II, 940–941; and Herbert Feis, *The Spanish Story: Franco and the Nations at War* (New York: Alfred A. Knopf, 1948), pp. 134–136.

Spain. Except for certain vital materials and articles that were scarce even in the United States, Spain had been permitted from the beginning to make any desired purchase in America, the only general restrictions being those imposed by the British blockade and by Spain's own ability to pay. In appearance, at least, this policy was continued. But by the spring of 1941 the needs of the American defense program and the demands of Lend-Lease had subjected to export control a great number of the things Spain wanted, and the Department of State became progressively less eager to clear these, or any other obstacles, out of the way where Spanish orders were concerned. In this fashion a good deal of economic pressure was quietly applied as Washington awaited the outcome of the Hitler-Darlan negotiations and the beginning of Germany's war on Russia.[8]

The period was an anxious one. Up to the end of May there was no clear evidence that American representations at Vichy would succeed in foiling Darlan's plans. In a radio address delivered May 23 the Vice Premier vehemently reasserted his determination to proceed with the agreements which had been outlined in his talks with Abetz and Hitler earlier that month.[9] A few days after this announcement he journeyed once more to Paris, and on May 27 and 28 affixed his signature to three protocols dealing with Syria and Iraq, with North Africa, and with French West and Equatorial Africa.

Bearing out Darlan's earlier understanding with Abetz, the first protocol stipulated that France would release three quarters of its Syrian military stocks to the Iraqi rebels; aid to the limit of its ability in the servicing of German and Italian planes which crossed Syria on their way to Iraq; permit Germany to use Syrian ports, roads, and railways for the movement of troops into Iraq; instruct the rebels how to use the French arms turned over to them; and transmit to the German High Command all the information that could be obtained regarding the strength and disposition of British forces in Iraq.[10] In the protocol regarding North Africa, France agreed to let Germany use the Tunisian port of Bizerte and the railroad from Bizerte to Gabès for the reinforcement and supply of its troops in Libya, to furnish transports and convoy protection for the voyage across the Mediterranean, and to

[8] Feis, *The Spanish Story,* p. 138.

[9] William D. Leahy, *I Was There* (New York: Whittlesey House, 1950), p. 32.

[10] Accord relatif à la Syrie et à Irak, May 27, 1941, in William L. Langer, *Our Vichy Gamble* (New York: Alfred A. Knopf, 1947), appendix 2, p. 402.

sell the Germans a quantity of French trucks and guns.[11] Under the third agreement Dakar was to become a supply base for German submarines, warships, and planes.[12] In return for these large concessions, the Germans promised some vague changes in political and economic arrangements and agreed to a slight strengthening of French military forces in the areas covered by the three protocols.[13]

The Paris accords justified all the fears which had tormented London and Washington through the preceding month. If carried into effect, they would obviously cancel every gain achieved by the United States and Great Britain in France, Spain, and North Africa since June 1940 and, at the same time, would destroy the main safeguards of Britain's Mediterranean position. But in approving these concessions Darlan reckoned without his own government, for the reception given his handiwork at Vichy was less cordial than he expected.

As usual, Pétain held the balance between those who opposed collaboration and those who favored it. That he had at least countenanced the Vice Premier's efforts to deal with Germany may be taken for granted. But when the terms actually obtained became known in Vichy, he listened to warnings that the protocols would mean trouble with both the United States and Great Britain and consented, readily enough, to seek the advice of General Weygand and Pierre Boisson, Governor of West Africa. Accordingly, these dignitaries were summoned to Vichy.[14]

There followed several days of argument. Weygand and Boisson led the opposition to Darlan from the first; and their efforts were seconded by Admiral Leahy who, on being informed of the Paris agreements, threatened Pétain, indirectly at least, with a severance of diplomatic relations. For his part, Weygand expressed fear that acceptance of the accords would provoke uprisings in France and North Africa alike, while both he and Boisson declined to sanction German operations in their respective bailiwicks. This was enough to stem the collaborationist tide, and Darlan's proposals were rejected on June 6.[15]

Since Germany was then preparing to attack Russia in scarcely more than two weeks, Hitler had no immediate opportunity to follow

---

[11] Accord relatif à l'Afrique du Nord, May 27, 1941, *ibid.,* pp. 404–405.

[12] Projet d'accord relatif à l'Afrique Occidentale et Equatoriale, May 28, 1941, *ibid.,* pp. 407–408.

[13] See the agreements listed in notes 10–12, and protocole complémentaire, May 28, 1941, *ibid.,* p. 412.

[14] Langer, *Our Vichy Gamble,* p. 157.   [15] *Ibid.,* pp. 158–159.

up his designs on France and North Africa. As at the time of Laval's dismissal in the previous December, the Fuehrer's eastern problem caused him to turn his back on France at the crucial moment, and Vichy's defiance of his wishes again went unchallenged. Thanks to Darlan's conversations with Abetz at the beginning of May, the Syrian agreement had already been partly carried out. But preoccupation with Russia kept Germany from exploiting even this opportunity to the full. British and Free French forces entered Syria on June 8, and Vichy's rule in that country was ended on July 12.[16]   As a consequence, Britain's hold on the Mediterranean and the Middle East remained as secure as it had been at any time since the fall of France.

But even though another move toward collaboration had failed, the general threat had not been dissipated. Periodic rumors of further German designs on North Africa kept the State Department anxious throughout the summer. It could relax somewhat, however, pending the emergence of a new threat resembling that of the Paris protocols. Meanwhile, the American government went ahead with its established policy toward unoccupied France and the other areas under Vichy control, stubbornly resisting all demands that it transfer its official support to the Free French movement, and putting the Murphy-Weygand accord into effect as rapidly as possible.[17]   By July 1 two tankers had been sent to North African ports, and the American vice consuls who had been stationed in North African cities under the terms of that agreement were beginning to supply Washington with a constant stream of useful information regarding military and political developments in the area.[18]   Considering this, as well as Weygand's successful opposition to Darlan's proposals in June, it was difficult to argue that the Vichy policy of the United States, so far as it concerned North Africa at least, was not yielding dividends.

III

The American people were not the only ones to be concerned at President Roosevelt's "unlimited emergency" speech of May 27. As their owner, Portugal fully understood the role which the Azores and

[16] Langer, *Our Vichy Gamble*, p. 160; and Winston S. Churchill, *The Grand Alliance* (Boston: Houghton Mifflin Co., 1950), pp. 329–331.

[17] Langer, *Our Vichy Gamble*, pp. 182–185; and Hull, *Memoirs*, II, 961.

[18] Langer, *Our Vichy Gamble*, p. 180.

the Cape Verde Islands might play in the battle of the Atlantic. While German designs constituted the fundamental threat to Portuguese sovereignty over the islands, a preventive occupation by Great Britain or the United States was hardly less likely; and the islands could not be defended in either case. Caught in a struggle of the larger powers, the Portuguese government could do nothing but assert its dignity at every opportunity and then await events. Although Portuguese authorities had already discussed the matter with Great Britain and apparently were not averse to a preventive occupation of the islands under proper conditions and guarantees,[19] they were certainly in a mood to question unsolicited remarks hinting at such action, and they quickly took umbrage at Roosevelt's statement of May 27. In a request for clarification submitted three days later, Portugal gingerly explained that the President's direct references to its Atlantic possessions, especially when viewed in the context of his general thesis, did not signify the most honorable intentions on the part of the United States. This being true, it seemed necessary to point out that the American government would hardly be justified in undertaking to violate Portuguese territory.[20]

Considering that preparations to do this very thing had been under way for some time, Hull must have felt temporarily at a loss. But his embarrassment was relieved a few days later by a change in Anglo-American plans. Intelligence reports from Germany and Spain had convinced Churchill that the invasion of Russia was to begin very shortly and that Franco had refused again to permit the occupation of his country by German troops. At the same time, moreover, Darlan's Paris protocols were rejected at Vichy. Thus the Prime Minister's recent despair quickly gave way to optimism. Roosevelt shared his new confidence and agreed that immediate anxiety concerning the Atlantic possessions of Spain and Portugal had been relieved. By the same token, the prospective necessity of getting supplies to Russia enhanced the importance of the northern convoy route, and it was decided that the American troops being groomed for occupation of the Azores should be dispatched to Iceland instead.[21] The Azores plan was not

[19] Churchill, *The Grand Alliance*, pp. 142–143.

[20] Bianchi to Hull, May 30, 1941, World Peace Foundation, *Documents on American Foreign Relations, 1940–1941*, ed. S. Shepard Jones and Denys P. Myers (Boston: World Peace Foundation, 1941), pp. 426–427.

[21] Samuel Eliot Morison, *The Battle of the Atlantic, 1939–1943* (Boston: Little, Brown, and Co., 1947), p. 67.

dropped entirely. But its postponement enabled Hull, with only a minimum of disingenuousness, to inform the Portuguese Minister on June 10 that the islands had been mentioned "solely in terms of their potential value from the point of view of attack against this hemisphere." [22]

Temporarily relieved of their southern project, Washington and London were free once more to concentrate upon the defense of British supply lines, and renewed preoccupation with shipping difficulties in the North Atlantic was soon accompanied by still another change of plans. This one bore directly upon the convoy problem.

As already explained, the United States Navy had been making extensive preparations for transatlantic convoy duty since the beginning of 1941. Indeed, these preparations had advanced so rapidly that bases in Scotland and Northern Ireland were chosen before the end of March, and the service was expected to be in operation by fall. However, the idea of having American escorts accompany their charges all the way to the British Isles had always encountered opposition. Since the beginning of the war the British and Canadians had used a system whereby escort groups based on either side of the Atlantic operated only as far east or west as the vicinity of Iceland and there traded convoys for the return trip. Considerations of economy in the use of men and equipment advised the United States merely to join this system. But President Roosevelt, up to this moment, had carefully distinguished between merchant and troop convoys, declining every suggestion that American warships be permitted to assume responsibility for the troops. Since troopships were moving regularly from Canada to the British Isles, it was clear that American escorts would have to be wastefully selective in their choice of convoy material if they participated in British-Canadian operations. An independent system was the only answer, therefore, and preparations had been made accordingly. But now, about the middle of June, Roosevelt abruptly changed his mind and agreed that American escorts might work with the established service. As a result, plans for transatlantic operations were abandoned; and it was arranged that United States ships, when eventually assigned to escort duty, should confine themselves to that part of the convoy route which lay between North America and Iceland.[23]

[22] Hull to Bianchi, June 10, 1941, *Documents on American Foreign Relations, 1940–1941*, pp. 428–429.
[23] See Morison, *The Battle of the Atlantic*, pp. 54–55.

Though plans were being evolved in anticipation of a German attack against Russia, the time for putting them into effect had not quite arrived. Viewed in retrospect, the month which followed Roosevelt's "unlimited emergency" speech was preëminently a month of waiting— a period of clearly foreseen but still-pending events which threatened to change the whole shape of the war.

If advances in Atlantic planning were confined during most of June 1941 to agreements for future action, it was still possible to emphasize in a number of ways the stiffening attitude of the United States toward the Axis. On May 29 arrangements were made for the training of British fliers in the United States.[24] By an executive order dated June 6 Roosevelt authorized the Maritime Commission to commandeer idle foreign merchant ships in American ports.[25] Five months before, in February, the American consulates in Palermo and Naples had been closed at the request of the Italian government, and the United States had retaliated in March by closing the Italian consulates in Detroit and Newark.[26] In April the State Department had requested the withdrawal of the Italian naval attaché, Admiral Alberto Lais, from Washington on the ground that he had been implicated in the sabotaging of Axis ships in American ports—whereupon Italy had demanded the recall of the United States military attaché in Rome.[27] Now this policy of diplomatic irritation was brought to its logical conclusion. On June 11 the American assets of Germany and Italy were impounded,[28] and the State Department ordered the entire German and Italian consular staffs from the country on June 16 and June 20, respectively.[29]

At the same time, Roosevelt decided to make the *Robin Moor* incident a vital public issue. To give his remarks all the weight he possibly could, he delivered them in the form of a special message to Congress on June 20. He did not mention convoys, nor did he request legislation of any kind. But he strongly reaffirmed the American gov-

[24] *New York Times,* May 30, 1941, p. 5, col. 1.

[25] Executive Order No. 8771, June 6, 1941, *Federal Register,* VI, 2759.

[26] Hull to Colonna, Mar. 5, 1941, United States, Department of State, *United States and Italy, 1936–1946: Documentary Record* (Washington, D. C.: U. S. Govt. Printing Office, 1946), pp. 22–23.

[27] Hull to Colonna, Apr. 2, 1941, *ibid.,* pp. 23–24; and press release, Apr. 9, 1941, *ibid.,* pp. 25–26.

[28] Executive Order No. 8785, June 14, 1941, *Federal Register,* VI, 2898.

[29] Welles to Thomsen, June 16, 1941, United States, Department of State, *Department of State Bulletin* (Washington, D. C.: U. S. Govt. Printing Office, 1939——), IV (June 21, 1941), 743; and Welles to Colonna, June 20, 1941, *ibid.*

ernment's determination not to withdraw from the battle of the Atlantic, denounced the sinking of the *Robin Moor* as an episode in Germany's "declared . . . policy of frightfulness and intimidation," and assured the country that he would demand of the German government "full reparation for the losses and damages suffered by American nationals."[30]   On June 24 the German chargé d'affaires in Washington declined to transmit a copy of this speech to Berlin as requested by the State Department.[31]   Relations with Germany were now taut indeed.

IV

As was indicated in the last chapter, the American government had been much less than satisfied with the Japanese proposals of May 12, 1941.   From the day Nomura presented them Roosevelt and Hull were agreed that they constituted no more than a bare foundation for talks looking to a settlement of differences between the two countries.   That Tokyo's offer required broadening was obvious.[32]   But Hull's counter-proposals of May 16 defined the changes which he regarded as an essential preliminary to serious negotiations, and it was decided to go ahead with exploratory talks in hope that Japan might agree to revise its basic program in accordance with the Secretary's demands.

Supported by two advisers—Colonel Hideo Iwakuro, of the Japanese Army, and one Tadao Wikawa, an official of the Coöperative Bank of Japan—Nomura was received in Hull's apartment the evening of May 20.   At the outset the Ambassador assured his host that the offer of May 12 enjoyed the support of all branches of the Japanese government and declared that its rejection by the United States would damage his prestige in Tokyo.   Stubborn adherence to words, he said, was now their main obstacle.   In view of the principles enunciated by both countries, he felt that agreement could be achieved if they refused to haggle over verbal formulas.   Of course, this optimistic pronouncement totally ignored the objections which Hull had stated on May 16.   When the Secretary alluded to the vagueness of Japanese proposals for liquidating the China venture, Iwakuro entered the conversation to declare that he viewed the Chinese problem as incidental to the main points at issue and went on to make it clear that the Japanese Army contemplated no settlement with China which provided for the withdrawal of all

[30] Message of the President to Congress, June 20, 1941, *Peace and War*, p. 675.
[31] Thomsen to Welles, June 24, 1941, *Department of State Bulletin*, V (Nov. 8, 1941), 363–364.   [32] Hull, *Memoirs*, II, 1001, 1009.

Japanese troops from Chinese territory. Central and southern China might be evacuated over a period of years, but this movement would not extend to Inner Mongolia and adjoining parts of northern China in any event.[33]

Thus the essential falsity of the Japanese peace offer was revealed almost at once. Even Nomura, whose reputation was good and who certainly did not lack the will to do so, could not allay the suspicion which had been created in Hull's mind, for his government had placed him in a straitjacket. A week later, after confessing that he was not privy to the exact views of the Japanese Army, he substantiated Iwakuro's declaration by admitting that some troops would remain permanently in China to coöperate with local authorities in measures of defense against communism. Whether Chiang Kai-shek liked this or not, he added, the Chinese leader would be compelled to agree if the aid that he received from America were suspended in accordance with Tokyo's proposals of May 12.[34]

But Hull was determined not to lose patience and undertook to clarify American views once more. Selecting Japan's adherence to the Tripartite Pact and the withdrawal of Japanese troops from China as the large issues, he gave Nomura a revised draft of his earlier suggestions on May 31, urging that Japan agree to construe its obligations to Germany and Italy in such a way that Japanese-American relations would not be affected if the United States became involved in war "through acts of self-defense." He was prepared to concede that Japan should arrange to evacuate China through direct negotiations with the Chinese government but insisted that troop withdrawals be carried out as rapidly as possible. He also requested further discussion of Tokyo's plan for a joint defense against communism.[35]

Except for details of phraseology, Nomura approved these terms on June 2.[36] But the exceptions were important. Nomura had already expressed his concern regarding verbal difficulties, and after several days of listening to Japanese views on phraseology, State Department

---

[33] Memorandum by Ballantine, May 20, 1941, United States, Department of State, *Papers Relating to the Foreign Relations of the United States: Japan, 1931–1941* (Washington, D. C.: U. S. Govt. Printing Office, 1943), II, 434–435. See also Hull, *Memoirs*, II, 1005.

[34] Memorandum by Ballantine, May 28, 1941, *Foreign Relations: Japan, 1931–1941*, II, 441–443.

[35] American draft proposal, May 31, 1941, *ibid.*, p. 447; and Hull, *Memoirs*, II, 1010.

[36] Memorandum by Hull, June 2, 1941, *Foreign Relations: Japan, 1931–1941*, II, 454–455.

officials could appreciate the force of his observations. While insisting upon the most specific kinds of guarantees from Washington, Tokyo would offer nothing that could not be interpreted in many different ways. The impasse was made complete two weeks later, when Japan reaffirmed its adherence to the Tripartite Pact without qualification.[37]

Hull was sorely tried. But whatever their chance of success, he was resolved to continue the negotiations as long as possible. He issued another statement of the American position on June 21. It contained little that was new. Carefully reviewing what had transpired since May 12, this note again isolated the Tripartite Pact and the China question as the areas of most serious disagreement,[38] specified the items which would have to be settled in connection with the latter problem, and suggested an exchange of letters whereby Japan would interpret the Pact in the sense desired by the United States.[39] As he handed this document to Nomura, Hull once more expressed his belief that agreements on other points would be futile so long as Japan was committed to the active support of Germany.[40]

Having made no progress in five weeks, negotiations between Washington and Tokyo thus finished another cycle. A new one would soon be started, however. For Japan was at least as close to events in eastern Europe as was the United States, and eastern Europe was about to suffer an upheaval which would place international affairs in a new setting.

V

The great change began on June 22, 1941, with Germany's long-awaited invasion of Russia. Judged by the record of the past two years, this was a quarrel between thieves, and the tensions of recent weeks had not improved American opinion of Soviet conduct. Indeed, growing exasperation with Soviet tactics had caused the President on June 14 to freeze all Russian assets in the United States.[41] Great Britain, too, viewed Moscow with notable reserve. Despite the many substantial

[37] Draft document, June 15, 1941, *Foreign Relations: Japan, 1931–1941*, II, 475.

[38] See oral statement by Hull, June 21, 1941, *ibid.*, p. 488.

[39] American draft proposal, June 21, 1941, *ibid.*; and suggested exchange of letters, *ibid.*, p. 490.

[40] Oral statement by Hull, June 21, 1941, *ibid.*, p. 485.

[41] Executive Order No. 8785, June 14, 1941, *Federal Register*, VI, 2898.

indications that Germany planned to attack Russia, Churchill was not convinced until the end of March that such an outcome was inevitable, and this doubt presumably explains his efforts to secure further reductions in trade between the United States and the Soviet Union. On the other hand, neither the United States nor Great Britain could ignore the tremendous opportunity presented by a Russo-German war. It fulfilled that waxing and waning hope which had guided American policy since 1939, and which had periodically influenced British policy as well. Hence Roosevelt and Churchill had agreed in advance to offer Russia their coöperation as soon as Hitler's armies moved.[42]

Churchill led the way on June 22 with a public assurance of British aid and sympathy.[43] The next day Sumner Welles echoed the Prime Minister in a statement which welcomed Russian collaboration in putting an end to the Nazi dictatorship. "In the opinion of this Government," Welles said, "any defense against Hitlerism, any rallying of the forces opposing Hitlerism, from whatever sources these forces may spring, will hasten the eventual downfall of the present German leaders, and will therefore redound to the benefit of our own defense and security." [44] While this argument was more of an attack on the German cause than an endorsement of the Russian, its practical bearing was clear enough. Following Welles's lead, Roosevelt gave Moscow a promise of American support on June 24,[45] made it clear one day later that he did not propose to invoke the neutrality act against Russia,[46] and promptly released Soviet funds.[47] On June 30 Oumansky started negotiations in Washington with a view to obtaining large quantities of war materials for his government. A British military mission was sent to Moscow about the same time, and a Soviet mission headed by General Philip Golikov reached London at the beginning of July.[48] By the end of the month Golikov was explaining his needs in Washington.[49] On his own initiative, the President had in the meanwhile

[42] Churchill, *The Grand Alliance*, pp. 354, 369; and John G. Winant, *Letter from Grosvenor Square: An Account of a Stewardship* (Boston: Houghton Mifflin Co., 1947), p. 203.

[43] Radio speech, June 22, 1941, in Winston S. Churchill, *The Unrelenting Struggle*, comp. Charles Eade (Boston: Little, Brown, and Co., 1942), pp. 172–174.

[44] Statement by Welles, June 23, 1941, *Department of State Bulletin*, IV (June 28, 1941), 755.   [45] *New York Times*, June 25, 1941, p. 1, col. 3.

[46] *Ibid.*, June 26, 1941, p. 1, col. 5.   [47] Hull, *Memoirs*, II, 973.

[48] David J. Dallin, *Soviet Russia's Foreign Policy, 1939–1942*, tr. Leon Denman (New Haven: Yale Univ. Press, 1942), pp. 389–391.

[49] Hull, *Memoirs*, II, 974.

set up a special supply committee to act under the direction of the State Department. This group by the end of July authorized the shipment to Russia of $9 million worth of material.[50]

As far as the European problems of Great Britain and the United States were concerned, Germany's invasion of Russia furnished a great solvent. Almost overnight the main lines of Anglo-American policy toward the Soviet Union became clear and definite. Gone were the alternately cold and warm periods in Russo-American relations. Gone was British discontent with Russo-American trade. And if either Washington or London still cherished misgivings about the state of the Russian mind or the final objectives of Russian policy, these fears could now be swallowed up in the overriding demands of military necessity.

Germany's Russian campaign likewise improved Britain's position in the Mediterranean and in the eastern Atlantic. Ever since the fall of France German machinations at Vichy and Madrid had kept both London and Washington in an almost constant state of nerves. But now—even though the threat to Gibraltar, North Africa, and the Atlantic islands of Spain and Portugal could not be forgotten—it was plain that the danger of a German move to the south or southwest or, indeed, against the British Isles themselves, would be minimal so long as Hitler remained seriously occupied on the Russian front.

Immediate gains in the Pacific were less clear, for the initial effect of the Russo-German war was to place new burdens upon Washington's already complex relations with Japan. On June 10, 1941, a friendly member of the Japanese Diet had informed Grew that Berlin was exerting strong pressure on his government to seize the Dutch East Indies.[51] Added to what was previously known and suspected of Japanese plans, this was ominous news; and Roosevelt had so little confidence in the sincerity of Japanese efforts to work out a worth-while agreement with the United States that Admiral Kimmel was able to persuade him to abandon thought of transferring new battle forces into the Atlantic.[52] Now that Russia's fight for survival gave Tokyo

[50] John R. Deane, The Strange Alliance: The Story of Our Efforts at Wartime Cooperation with Russia (New York: Viking Press, 1947), pp. 87–88.

[51] Joseph C. Grew, Ten Years in Japan (New York: Simon and Schuster, 1944), p. 392.

[52] Kimmel's testimony, Jan. 15, 1946, United States, Congress, Joint Committee on Investigation of Pearl Harbor Attack, Hearings Pursuant to S. Con. Res. 27, Authorizing Investigation of Attack on Pearl Harbor, Dec. 7, 1941, and Events and Circumstances Relating Thereto (79th Cong., 1st and 2nd sess.) (Washington, D. C.: U. S. Govt. Printing Office, 1946), pt. 6, p. 2505. Cited henceforth as Pearl Harbor Hearings.

double assurance against attack from the rear, the American government was rightfully concerned lest Japan choose this moment for opening the conquest of southeastern Asia.

Another prospect, and one which was equally disturbing, arose at the same time. Though Russia was in no position to violate the neutrality agreement of April 13, this same disability did not apply to Japan. In view of the lack of confidence of British and American experts in the Russian power to survive, it appeared likely that the Soviet Union would speedily collapse if a Japanese attack from the east were added to the German attack from the west.

As early as June 22, Hull asked Nomura directly whether Japan were not seeking to close out the China Incident merely to free itself for participation in the European war; and although Nomura promptly denied this, the Secretary was not convinced.[53] Nor were his suspicions unfounded. Throughout the last week of June the Japanese government seriously considered the advisability of attacking Russia at once. Matsuoka, particularly, favored such a course.[54] But an Imperial Conference held on July 2 decided against it for the time being. While the idea was not permanently abandoned, the Conference agreed that an advance in the south should constitute the first order of business. As an initial move, Japan should consolidate its position in Thailand and Indo-China. Meanwhile, the Foreign Office should maintain its efforts to placate the United States and Great Britain. But if diplomacy failed, Japan would not shrink from war.[55]

Thanks to "Magic," the State Department learned the substance of these decisions by July 8.[56] Roosevelt's misgivings would brook no delay, however; and at his direction, Hull invited the Japanese government on July 4 to deny that it planned to go to war with Russia.[57] Tokyo's reply, which came four days later, stated insouciantly that Japan had not yet considered the possibility of attacking the Soviet Union, and then it turned the question by asking whether the United States planned to intervene in the European war.[58] Enclosed was a

[53] Memorandum by Ballantine, June 22, 1941, *Foreign Relations: Japan, 1931–1941,* II, 493.
[54] Konoye memoirs, *Pearl Harbor Hearings,* pt. 20, exhibit 173, p. 3993.
[55] *Ibid.,* p. 4019.
[56] Matsuoka to Nomura, July 2, 1941, *ibid.,* pt. 12, exhibit 1, pp. 1–2.
[57] Hull to Konoye, July 4, 1941 (delivered by Grew on July 6), *Foreign Relations: Japan, 1931–1941,* II, 502–503.
[58] Statement by Matsuoka, July 8, 1941, *ibid.,* p. 503.

copy of a statement given to the Soviet Ambassador in Tokyo on July 2. While Japan hoped to maintain good relations with Russia, it said, this desire was tempered by a resolve to avoid misunderstandings with the other Axis powers. Hence the future policy of the Japanese government would largely depend upon future developments.[59] This was less than reassuring at best, especially as further reports of Japanese plans for eventual action against Russia continued to be received.[60]

To make the situation still more clouded, regular negotiations between Hull and Nomura had been completely sidetracked since June 22. Not even the shape of Anglo-American naval coöperation in the Pacific was clear at this moment, for Marshall and Stark chose July 3 as the date for rejecting plans drawn up in April at the Singapore staff conversations. Arguing that the report contained political decisions which could not be settled in a military agreement, that it accorded the British powers of strategic command which were altogether too broad, that it failed to appreciate the strategic importance of holding the Dutch East Indies, and that it assigned to American and Dutch forces an excessive share of the responsibility for defending British positions in Malaya, they announced to the British Chiefs of Staff that new arrangements would have to be made.[61]

There was little doubt concerning American policy in the Atlantic, however. The opening of hostilities between Germany and Russia convinced Stark that the time for direct action had at last arrived. With the approval of Secretary Knox, he stated his views to the President. As he later expressed it, the Chief of Naval Operations told Roosevelt that he should "seize the psychological opportunity presented by the Russo-German clash" to proclaim the immediate assumption of escort duty by the Navy. Admitting that "such a declaration followed by immediate action on our part" would be likely to involve the country in war, he went on to say that he regarded "every day of delay in our getting into the war as dangerous" and emphasized his belief that "much more delay might be fatal to British survival."[62] Not all of

---

[59] Oral statement by Matsuoka to the Russian Ambassador, July 2, 1941, *Foreign Relations: Japan, 1931–1941*, II, 504.

[60] See Chinese Minister of Communications to Hu Shih, July 8, 1941, *Pearl Harbor Hearings*, pt. 19, exhibit 159, p. 3497; and Chiang Kai-shek to Hu Shih, July 8, 1941, *ibid.*, p. 3496.

[61] Chief of Naval Operations and Chief of Staff to Special Naval Observer and to Special Army Observer in London, July 3, 1941, *ibid.*, pt. 15, exhibit 65, pp. 1677–1679.   [62] Stark to Cooke, July 31, 1941, *ibid.*, pt. 16, exhibit 106, p. 2175.

Stark's advice proved acceptable, but the occupation of Iceland by American troops was about to smooth the way for some of his recommendations.

As early as December 1940, the Icelandic government had suggested the possibility of such an occupation in a direct exchange of views with the United States.[63] But British troops had been stationed in Iceland since May of the same year, and the project actually took shape under British sponsorship. When the occupation of Iceland was substituted for the Azores plan in early June 1941, Churchill offered to make the necessary arrangements with Icelandic officials, undertaking to obtain a formal request for American protection.[64]

In anticipation of this request the First Marine Brigade was moved to Argentia, Newfoundland—the western terminus of the North Atlantic convoy route—on June 22. But the Icelandic Premier, Herman Jónasson, proved unexpectedly reluctant to issue the desired invitation now that the time was ripe, and the Marines sailed from Argentia on July 1 without knowing just how cordial their welcome might be. All difficulties were avoided, however. Jónasson extended a proper request on July 7, and the American convoy entered the harbor of Reykjavik that evening.[65] The occupation was announced in Washington the same day.[66] To save appearances, the exchange of notes which constituted the formal agreement was dated July 1,[67] but the somewhat unorthodox circumstances under which the objective had been gained did not alter its significance. With American forces stationed in an acknowledged zone of operations, the assumption of new duties by the Atlantic Fleet could be expected momentarily.

VI

Events moved slowly during most of June. By the end of the first week in July, however, it was clear that a good deal had transpired during the six weeks just finished. In his "unlimited emergency" speech of May 27 Roosevelt delivered by far the gravest appraisal of the inter-

[63] Hull, *Memoirs*, II, 946.
[64] Morison, *The Battle of the Atlantic*, p. 67.
[65] *Ibid.*, pp. 74–77.
[66] Message of the President to Congress, July 7, 1941, *Department of State Bulletin*, V (July 12, 1941), 15–16.
[67] Jónasson to Roosevelt, and Roosevelt to Jónasson, July 1, 1941, World Peace Foundation, *Documents on American Foreign Relations, 1941–1942*, ed. S. Shepard Jones and Denys P. Myers (Boston: World Peace Foundation, 1942), pp. 454–457.

national situation he had yet made public. He likewise called attention to certain lines of further activity that were under consideration. From the beginning, the Azores expedition had been more or less dependent upon the likelihood of a German drive into Spain, Portugal, or North Africa. Therefore, as soon as this danger was minimized by Vichy's rejection of Darlan's Paris protocols and by the certainty that Hitler was on the verge of attacking Russia, the North Atlantic convoy route once more became the focus of Anglo-American unity; the occupation of Iceland was substituted for the Azores project; and the United States agreed to forego the transatlantic escort service it had planned in order to assume responsibility for the western half of the British-Canadian system.

In the meanwhile, Hull's new series of talks with the Japanese Ambassador made no progress whatever. Although Nomura insisted that he had been commissioned to seek a genuine agreement, Japan's unbending adherence to the Tripartite Pact, its reluctance to work toward an acceptable solution of the Chinese problem, and its new activities in Indo-China led Hull to believe that Japan was preparing new deviltry behind the scenes. He became convinced of this in late June and early July following the outbreak of the Russo-German war. But Tokyo's answer to his question on this point was evasive, and he could do nothing but wait for a reaction to his proposals of June 21.

On the other hand, the break between Germany and Russia was seized upon promptly. The difficulties which both Washington and London had experienced in recent dealings with Moscow were thrown into the background as the United States and Great Britain made a concerted bid for Soviet understanding. And while preparations to furnish the Russians with material aid got under way, the occupation of Iceland by American troops heralded new advances in American naval policy.

CHAPTER IX

Strategic Adjustments

I

The events of late June and early July 1941 produced an important, if subtle, change in the carefully tended relationship between Japan and Germany. To the extent that it confronted the United States with threats of new aggression in the Far East, Japan's determination to forge ahead with the southern program yielded distinct advantages to German policy and bore out Hitler's conception of the Tripartite Pact as a means of using Japan to discourage American action in the Atlantic. Nevertheless, Japan's adoption of this strategy in the circumstances created by the outbreak of the Russo-German war marked that country's withdrawal to a more independent position as far as its European allies were concerned.

Even before Washington learned the results of the Imperial Conference of July 2, Grew caught some overtones of change from his vantage point in the Japanese capital. In an appraisal of the situation written July 6 he noted a growing conviction that the Tripartite Pact exposed Japan to "certain avoidable risks." Taking this as his basic premise, he went on to observe that the Japanese government was somewhat disturbed by Germany's frank expectation that it would be accorded special privileges in China when the New Order was complete, expressed the belief that Japan was no longer sure of its own future in a German-dominated world, and concluded that from now on Tokyo might be expected to act without much regard for German preferences.[1] On July 23, in a telegram to Hull, Grew emphatically reiterated these opinions.[2]

Behind the surface indications which prompted the Ambassador to expound such views lay facts of concrete significance. Although both Hitler and Ribbentrop only three months earlier had used their greatest

---

[1] Joseph C. Grew, *Ten Years in Japan* (New York: Simon and Schuster, 1944), p. 402.
[2] Telegram from Grew, July 23, 1941, MS Department of State (894.00/1074).

eloquence in trying to persuade Matsuoka that his government should immediately launch a heavy assault on British possessions in southeastern Asia, the beginning of Germany's conflict with Russia had temporarily modified their notion of Japan's proper role. They now wanted their Asiatic ally to create a diversion by attacking the Siberian provinces of the Soviet Union.[3]   But Japan considered itself in a good position to reject this plea for assistance. While the general tendency of Matsuoka's diplomacy over the past year had been to emphasize the principle of Axis solidarity, Japan's esteem for the practical manifestations of unity had never been great except where they offered direct promise of advancing Japanese plans; and the outbreak of the Russo-German war gave Tokyo the hope of carrying out those plans without inviting the coöperation of the European Axis, or risking its interference. By dispelling all reasonable threat of interference from Russia, these hostilities considerably reduced Japan's dependence on support from Berlin. It was evident, moreover, that the Reich's greatest energies would be concentrated upon eastern Europe as long as the new conflict lasted, and this appeared to give Japan several months during which it could act to advance and consolidate its program for eastern Asia without fear that Germany might be able to present effective demands for inclusion in the New Order.   Hence Japan's decision to shelve the Russian project in favor of a drive to the south tended to bear out Grew's analysis. Whatever this might mean in other respects, it meant that any benefits which Germany derived from the Japanese connection would be largely incidental to the advancement of Japanese policy.   Japan, in effect, was preparing to work out its own concept of destiny while its friends, as well as its enemies, were busy elsewhere.

Much of this became clear only in retrospect, however, and it could have exerted little influence over American-Japanese relations even if it had been completely known at the time.   While the lack of any move toward Siberia was helpful in itself, Japan was still bent upon a course of aggression which could only intensify friction with the United States.

---

[3] Hans L. Trefousse, *Germany and American Neutrality, 1939–1941* (New York: Bookman Associates, 1951), pp. 123–128. See also memorandum by Amau (Japanese Vice Minister for Foreign Affairs), Aug. 19, 1941, United States, Congress, Joint Committee on Investigation of Pearl Harbor Attack, *Hearings Pursuant to S. Con. Res. 27, Authorizing Investigation of Attack on Pearl Harbor, Dec. 7, 1941, and Events and Circumstances Relating Thereto* (79th Cong., 1st and 2nd sess.) (Washington, D. C.: U. S. Govt. Printing Office, 1946), pt. 18, exhibit 132–A, p. 2948. Cited henceforth as *Pearl Harbor Hearings.*

That Japan had temporarily abandoned one of the major trends indicated by Matsuoka's labors during the past year remained, of course, an issue between Berlin and Tokyo. But if it partly solved one of the problems confronting the American government, it increased the size of another. Being unacquainted with the exact nature of German desires, moreover, Washington could not even be sure that Japan's contemplated movement southward represented an independent decision. Nor did Japan furnish any evidence on this point. Whatever its private differences with Germany, the Japanese government was not prepared to abandon publicly its Axis connections, and in talks with the United States it continued to speak as a faithful member of the Tripartite Pact. So the outbreak of war in eastern Europe served only to interrupt American negotiations with Japan. As the question of an attack on Russia was submerged in the threat offered by Tokyo's perfectly evident designs on southeastern Asia, these negotiations were resumed in circumstances of even greater strain than before.

The interruption was prolonged for another three weeks, however. Since June 21 the American government had been awaiting Tokyo's reaction to Hull's proposals of that date. But no reply was forthcoming even when Matsuoka lost his battle for immediate war with the Soviet Union. As a matter of fact, the intransigent Foreign Minister was finding himself more at odds with his colleagues every day. He promptly opened a new dispute regarding the manner in which the American note should be answered; efforts to reconcile the opposing viewpoints failed; and Konoye reorganized his Cabinet on July 16. While the only important change involved the substitution of Admiral Teijiro Toyoda, whose views were considered moderate, for the troublesome Matsuoka, this event occasioned still more delay in the resumption of talks with the United States. No real answer to Hull's proposals was ever delivered.

Meanwhile, the Secretary of State retired to White Sulphur Springs, West Virginia, for a badly needed rest, and Nomura did what he could to keep the postponement from assuming a look of finality. In an interview with two of Hull's subordinates, on July 15, he adverted once more to the Tripartite Pact, explaining that while Japan was not obligated to fight if the United States "should become involved in the European war through acts of self-defense," it could not give a "blank check" for everything the American government might choose to call "self-defense," but would have to judge events on their merits "in the light of actual circumstances." [4]   Three days later he assured Welles that Matsuoka had received no advance knowledge of German intentions to attack Russia and observed that he had telegraphed the new Foreign Minister to request new instructions concerning his talks with Hull.[5]

But the Japanese Ambassador apparently realized that he was getting nowhere with the State Department. So he changed to another tack and undertook to discuss his problems with Rear Admiral Turner, head of the Navy's War Plans Division. Approaching the latter in the spirit of one naval officer talking to another, Nomura insisted that Japan, like the United States, must be free to take necessary measures for its own defense. He pointed out that American export restrictions were undermining the Japanese economy and advised Turner that Japanese troops would occupy the remainder of Indo-China within the next few days.[6] This admission came as no surprise; a few days earlier the State Department had received a similar warning from Leahy, in France.[7] Relations between Washington and Tokyo were about to enter their most crucial phase.

II

The stationing of American troops on Icelandic soil precipitated no direct countermeasures from Germany. Hitler seemed content to let the battle of the Atlantic go on as it was for the time being. Indeed, he said as much on July 9 when he told Admiral Raeder that he planned no immediate retaliation. The Admiral, considerably aroused by the implications of Roosevelt's latest move, observed that the American occupation of Iceland might be regarded as an act of war and suggested that German naval forces be accorded greater liberty in dealing with United States ships. But Hitler's responsibilities on the eastern front made him cautious; and after explaining at some length that he wanted to avoid further trouble with the United States for another month or two, he directed Raeder to be content with existing instructions.[8]

[4] Memorandum by Ballantine, July 15, 1941, *Pearl Harbor Hearings*, p. 509.

[5] Memorandum by Welles, July 18, 1941, *ibid.*, pp. 515–516.

[6] Turner to Stark, July 21, 1941, *ibid.*, pp. 517–518.

[7] On July 16, at Vichy, Darlan had positively informed Leahy that Japan was about to "occupy bases in Indo-China with the purpose of projecting military operations to the southward." See William L. Langer, *Our Vichy Gamble* (New York: Alfred A. Knopf, 1947), p. 177.

[8] Conference of the Commander-in-Chief, Navy, with the Fuehrer, July 9, 1941,

There was no attempt, however, to deny the validity of the Admiral's worries. Anyone who gave the matter a second thought could understand that the occupation of Iceland involved more than a question of defense. As long as American forces stayed on that island, they would have to be supplied by American ships under the protection of American naval units. And this would extend the responsibilities of the Atlantic Fleet into an area lying somewhat beyond the 26th meridian, which constituted the easternmost limit of American patrol activity as prescribed in the "trailing" order of April 21.

Moreover, considering the extensive and semibelligerent patrol operations in which United States naval forces had been engaged since that time, it was inevitable that public doubts should be raised on the home front concerning the exact functions of the Atlantic Fleet.[9] The popular columnist Joseph W. Alsop reported as early as June 9 that an American destroyer had recently attacked a German U-boat not far off the coast of Greenland. A fortnight later two other columnists—Drew Pearson and Robert S. Allen—asserted that American naval units had already taken part in convoy operations. This was enough to arouse the isolationist wrath of Senator Burton K. Wheeler, who quickly drew up a resolution calling for investigation of the charges. His motion was dropped after preliminary hearings, but not until both Secretary Knox and Admiral Stark were subjected to questioning. Knox admitted the general truth of Alsop's story about the encounter off the coast of Greenland, stating reasonably enough that the destroyer had employed depth charges only in self-defense. Both he and Stark denied that American warships had escorted a single merchant vessel since the beginning of the war except for the *Iroquois* which, laden with homecoming Americans, had been guarded from somewhere off the Grand Banks in the fall of 1939 as a precaution against a rumored plot to destroy her. At the same time, both men categorically refused to discuss what the Navy was actually doing in the Atlantic or to reveal the extent of its coöperation with the ships of other powers.[10]

United States, Department of the Navy, *Fuehrer Conferences on Matters Dealing with the German Navy, 1939–1941* (Washington, D. C.: Issued in mimeographed form by the Office of Naval Intelligence, 1947), 1941, II, 3.

[9] For a detailed summary of this discussion in Congress and the press between March and July 1941, see Charles A. Beard, *President Roosevelt and the Coming of the War, 1941: A Study in Appearances and Realities* (New Haven: Yale Univ. Press, 1948), chap. iii.

[10] United States, Congress, Senate, Committee on Naval Affairs, *Senate Report No. 617* (77th Cong., 1st sess.) (Washington, D. C.: U. S. Govt. Printing Office, 1941).

While their testimony was not conclusive, the Navy's top representatives thus managed to preserve secrecy without resorting to falsehood. But they were interviewed just in time. For on July 11, the very day they appeared before the Senate Committee on Naval Affairs, Roosevelt gave orders that the Atlantic Fleet should be instructed to escort convoys of American and Icelandic ships between the United States and Iceland. Vessels of other nationalities might join such convoys if they desired.[11] That the United States had assumed a broad partnership in the Atlantic war could not be concealed much longer.

The presidential directive was implemented through two orders to the Fleet. Admiral King's Operation Plan No. 5, issued July 15, instructed it to "support the defense of Iceland" and to "capture or destroy vessels engaged in support of sea and air operations directed against Western Hemisphere territory, or United States or Iceland flag shipping." King specified that the occasion for action would arise from the presence of "potentially hostile vessels . . . actually within sight or sound contact of such shipping or of its escort." Operation Plan No. 6, promulgated July 19, decreed the formation of a special task force "to escort convoys of United States and Iceland flag shipping, including shipping of any nationality which may join such United States or Iceland flag convoys, between United States ports or bases, and Iceland." [12] At the same time, a number of Canadian and Free French destroyers and corvettes were assigned to aid the new task force in its duties.[13] Until further arrangements could be made, however, the provision which allowed foreign ships to join Iceland-bound convoys was suspended.[14]

Hitler now thought better of the Spartan restraint he had lately imposed upon Raeder as far as American shipping was concerned, and on July 18 he authorized U-boat commanders to sink United States merchant vessels anywhere inside the original German zone of operations. It was made abundantly clear, however, that this directive did not refer to the current zone of operations (which touched the three-mile limit of Greenland) but only to the earlier one (which corresponded roughly to the American-designated combat zone off the western coast of Europe). Since the order specifically exempted the sea route between the

[11] Stark's testimony, Jan. 3, 1946, Pearl Harbor Hearings, pt. 5, p. 2294.
[12] Quoted in Samuel Eliot Morison, The Battle of the Atlantic, 1939–1943 (Boston: Little, Brown, and Co., 1947), p. 78.   [13] Ibid., pp. 78–79.
[14] Stark's testimony, Jan. 3, 1946, Pearl Harbor Hearings, pt. 5, p. 2295.

United States and Iceland,[15] the freedom thus gained by the German Navy was more a concession in principle than one in fact.

As the United States dipped ever deeper into the Atlantic war, its new friendliness with Russia continued to expand under that brilliant glow of understanding furnished by recognition of a common enemy. Moscow waxed almost genial as its emissaries were received by London and Washington in an atmosphere of solicitous helpfulness, while ex-Foreign Commissar Maxim Litvinov—that enduring and lonely symbol of his government's supposed regard for collective action in the late nineteen-thirties—was hastily dredged up from the limbo to which he had been consigned and put on the radio to return the greetings of Churchill and Roosevelt.[16] The British Ambassador in Moscow, Sir Stafford Cripps, had opened negotiations with Stalin during the interim, and what amounted to a treaty of alliance between Great Britain and the Soviet Union was signed in the Russian capital on July 12. By this accord the two governments undertook to give each other full assistance and support in the "present war against Hitlerite Germany" and promised that neither would consider "an armistice or treaty of peace except by mutual agreement."[17] Meanwhile, presidential adviser Harry Hopkins flew to England in search of new ideas as to how the American government could exploit the situation to the greatest advantage of all three countries.

Hopkins was deep in his second series of conferences with Churchill before the Russo-German war had lasted a month, and it soon appeared that all was not calm beneath the surface of Anglo-Soviet relations despite the many external signs of amity. Russia's position was critical, but already Moscow was talking of peace terms and showing a larger interest in postwar political concessions than in British offers of immediate aid. Nevertheless, Churchill viewed the eastern war with growing confidence and was beginning to hope that the Soviet armies might continue their resistance until winter at least. His most pressing anxiety concerned the valuable battle experience being gained by Hit-

[15] Extract from German Naval File, July 18, 1941, International Military Tribunal, *Nazi Conspiracy and Aggression* (Washington, D. C.: U. S. Govt. Printing Office, 1946–1947), VI, 916.

[16] David J. Dallin, *Soviet Russia's Foreign Policy, 1939–1942,* tr. Leon Denman (New Haven: Yale Univ. Press, 1942), p. 389.

[17] Great Britain, Foreign Office, *Agreement between His Majesty's Government in the United Kingdom and the Government of the Union of Soviet Socialist Republics Providing for Joint Action in the War against Germany (with Protocol), Moscow, July 12, 1941,* Cmd. 6304 (1941) (London: H. M. Stationery Office, 1941).

ler's legions from their endeavors on the Russian front.[18] Whatever the future might hold, the principle objective now was to help the Russians stave off immediate defeat. Until a better knowledge of their needs, desires, and prospects could be obtained, however, it was impossible to discuss the Russian-aid program in detail.

On the other hand, there was much to discuss in connection with the Atlantic war and related aspects of Anglo-American coöperation. Returning to England on June 20 after a flying visit to Washington, Ambassador John G. Winant had carried with him Roosevelt's assurance that the zone covered by United States naval patrols in the Atlantic would soon be extended,[19] and Hopkins was able to show Churchill a penciled line on a map torn from the *National Geographic* which gave the Prime Minister a better notion of what the President had in mind. The United States still defined the 26th meridian as the eastern limit of the Western Hemisphere. But Hopkins' map indicated that Roosevelt proposed to redefine this boundary in such a way that it swung sharply eastward at a point about two hundred miles southwest of Iceland and did not turn north again until it reached a point about two hundred miles southeast of that vital outpost.[20]

Since Hopkins was under orders to discuss no postwar economic or territorial arrangements and to say nothing about the possible entry of the United States into the war, the most troublesome problem on his agenda was to investigate rumors that the British were using articles received under Lend-Lease to build up their export trade in South America and elsewhere.[21] The matter was ultimately left to Winant for solution, and it led him into a disagreeable series of negotiations with Anthony Eden lasting until September 10, when the latter promised on behalf of the British government that Lend-Lease goods would not be used in foreign trade at all, and that items of domestic production similar to those received under Lend-Lease would not be employed for developing new markets or for extending British trade to the detriment of American exporters.[22]

[18] Robert E. Sherwood, *Roosevelt and Hopkins: An Intimate History* (New York: Harper and Bros., 1948), pp. 309, 311.

[19] John G. Winant, *Letter from Grosvenor Square: An Account of a Stewardship* (Boston: Houghton Mifflin Co., 1947), p. 203.

[20] Sherwood, *Roosevelt and Hopkins*, p. 311. A photostatic copy of the map appears on p. 310.   [21] *Ibid.*, pp. 311–313.

[22] Winant, *Letter from Grosvenor Square*, pp. 149–150; also British White Paper, Sept. 10, 1941, in United States, Office of Lend-Lease Administration, *Third Report to*

Otherwise, Hopkins' main conversational themes related to Britain's position in the Middle East and to arrangements for a personal conference between Roosevelt and Churchill. On the first of these points Hopkins stated his government's feeling that the British were spending too much of their substance in a possibly futile effort to maintain their traditional hold on the Middle East. After some thought, Churchill rejected this criticism. Although more than one half of Great Britain's war production over the past eight months had been sent to Egypt and nearby areas, he believed that the strategic importance of this region justified such expenditures of men and matériel.[23] Agreement on the other point was much easier. At least since the beginning of the year both Roosevelt and Churchill had been looking forward to a personal meeting,[24] and a reassessment of Anglo-American strategy at the very highest level seemed particularly desirable now that Russia had entered the war. The question was settled in principle when Hopkins reached London, and he had no difficulty in completing arrangements for a rendezvous at sea off the Newfoundland coast between August 10 and August 15. This led directly to the next stage of Hopkins' odyssey.

Presumably there had been no discussion of a trip to Moscow before Hopkins left Washington,[25] but that the idea should take form during his conversations with Churchill was only natural. Even these preliminary talks in London were frustrated to some extent by ignorance of Russia's attitude, prospects, and needs; and one of the main tasks faced by the President and the Prime Minister in their forthcoming conference was to review the world situation in the light of these very questions. At all events, Hopkins saw that Britain and the United States would operate at a serious disadvantage until they had a more intimate acquaintance with the Russian government than could be obtained through ordinary diplomatic channels, and he decided, as his talks with Churchill drew to a close, that he was the man to establish the necessary rapport with Stalin.[26]

Congress on Lend-Lease Operations (Washington, D. C.: U. S. Govt. Printing Office, 1941), appendix 5, pp. 45–47.

[23] Sherwood, *Roosevelt and Hopkins*, pp. 314–316; and Winston S. Churchill, *The Grand Alliance* (Boston: Houghton Mifflin Co., 1950), pp. 424–425.

[24] See text of Hopkins' undated personal letter to Roosevelt, written from London in January 1941, in Sherwood, *Roosevelt and Hopkins*, p. 243.

[25] Sherwood, *Roosevelt and Hopkins*, p. 318.

[26] According to Sherwood's analysis, the idea was probably Hopkins' own (*ibid.*, p. 317). Winant, however, takes credit for sharing the inspiration (*Letter from Grosvenor Square*, p. 207).

After Churchill approved the idea and volunteered to make arrangements for transportation, Hopkins cabled Roosevelt for the proper authority. This was the evening of July 25.[27]　The President concurred with enthusiasm the next day, and Welles sent Hopkins a message for transmission to the Soviet dictator in Roosevelt's name.[28]　On the night of July 27 Hopkins left Invergordon, Scotland, aboard a Catalina flying boat of the Royal Air Force Coastal Command. While it proved exceedingly uncomfortable to one in his tender health, the trip passed without special incident.

He saw Stalin at the Kremlin the night of July 30. His host appeared both friendly and confident and opened his remarks by denouncing Germany's lack of moral standards in relations with other states. Then, at Hopkins' request, he began to list Russia's immediate and long-range needs. In the first category he mentioned antiaircraft guns, large-caliber machine guns, and rifles for the use of the Soviet Army. His chief requirements for a long war were high-octane gasoline, aluminum for aircraft construction, and the other items which Oumansky and Golikov had requested in Washington. As though to remind him that the United States could act promptly, Hopkins called attention to the two hundred fighting planes, Curtiss P-40's, which had already been promised to Russia, 140 from the British Isles and sixty direct from the United States. He then asked advice on methods of delivery. Owing to the enormous distances involved and to the possibility of Japanese interference, Stalin disliked the route offered by Vladivostok and the Trans-Siberian Railway. Nor could he say much for the route through Iran from the Persian Gulf; its capacity was too limited. On the whole, the route through the North Atlantic, the Arctic Ocean, and the White Sea leading to Murmansk and Archangel was most satisfactory.[29]

Later that evening Hopkins discussed supply with representatives of the Red Army.[30]　The next day he exchanged views with Sir Stafford Cripps in regard to the impending conference between Roosevelt and Churchill. He and Cripps agreed that the two leaders ought to send Stalin a joint message from their place of meeting, and the British Ambassador suggested a draft for such a communication.[31]　That afternoon Hopkins talked with Molotov, explaining the American

[27] Sherwood, *Roosevelt and Hopkins*, pp. 317–318.　　[28] *Ibid.*, pp. 321–322.
[29] For Hopkins' record of this conversation, see *ibid.*, pp. 327–330.
[30] *Ibid.*, p. 330.　　[31] *Ibid.*, p. 331.

government's fear that Japan meant to attack Russia from the east if Russia's war situation grew bad enough. While President Roosevelt did not wish to offer threats that could not be supported, he said, the United States was naturally opposed to any Japanese move against Siberia.[32] Molotov agreed that Japan was not to be trusted and suggested, with some indirection, that an American warning on this score might help keep Tokyo in check.[33]

But only Stalin appeared willing to talk freely; and Hopkins' second interview with the dictator, held the evening of July 31, proved quite fruitful. Stalin began with a detailed analysis of the war situation. While he admitted that Germany had launched its attack with a marked superiority in men, tanks, planes, and various other types of matériel, he believed that the tactics of the Red Army were achieving success. Germany, in his view, lacked enough men to sustain offensive warfare over the whole front and at the same time to guard its extended lines of communication.[34] When he repeated his request for American guns and aluminum, however, Hopkins stated that American aid could not possibly become effective before winter and observed in this connection that his own government planned for a long war. He added that the United States, and possibly Great Britain as well, would be unwilling to send any heavy munitions to Russia until the three powers had an opportunity to discuss the relative strategic importance of each of the several theaters involved. Believing it unwise to hold such a conference until the outcome of current operations on the Russian front was less doubtful, Hopkins suggested delay. Stalin seemed amenable to the conference idea, said that he would be glad to receive British and American representatives in Moscow, and offered to supply American authorities with the designs of Soviet weapons. Since his host had already told him that he thought the Russian front would be stabilized by the beginning of October, Hopkins proposed that the conference meet in the Soviet capital between October 1 and October 15.[35]

During the remainder of the interview Stalin dealt frankly with the possible entry of the United States into the war. Couching his words in the form of a personal message to Roosevelt, he stated that he believed Hitler's greatest weaknesses were to be found in the hatred of

---

[32] Excerpt from Steinhardt's record of this conversation, *ibid.*
[33] Hopkins' record of conversation with Molotov, July 31, 1941, *ibid.*, pp. 331–332.
[34] Hopkins' record of conversation with Stalin, July 31, 1941, *ibid.*, pp. 333–340.
[35] *Ibid.*, pp. 341–342.

his subject populations and in the low morale of the German Army and the German people. He thought a declaration of war by the United States would encourage resistance, on the one hand, and smash Germany's fighting spirit, on the other. In this connection he was prepared to welcome American troops, under their own command, on any part of the Russian front. Replying that he could discuss nothing but matters of supply, Hopkins said that American entry into the war would be decided largely by "Hitler himself and his encroachment upon our fundamental interests." [36]

Hopkins left the meeting greatly impressed by Stalin's personality and by his assurance that the Red Army would keep the Germans at bay through the succeeding winter.[37] Prepared to support a Russian-aid program of the most generous type, he flew back to the British Isles, landing at Scapa Flow on August 2. He was joined by Churchill and his suite aboard the battleship *Prince of Wales,* and the whole party set off for the Atlantic Conference without delay.[38]

III

Throughout July and August 1941 relations between Washington and Madrid continued in the trend they had followed since the first of the year. Neither Franco nor Serrano Suñer evinced the slightest disposition to resume contact with Weddell, and the Caudillo was especially provocative in his annual speech to the Falange on July 17, when he stated that Great Britain had so obviously lost the war that it would be "criminal madness" for the United States to intervene.[39] Under these circumstances, the State Department had no reason to grow more trustful of Spanish policy.

Except that many exports were now subject to licensing control, American trade with Spain was still as free, in theory, as Spain's supply of dollar credits and the operation of the British blockade allowed it to be. But the unofficial delays and impediments mentioned in the last chapter were applied more systematically from the beginning of July, and Welles on August 3 accepted the view long championed by Secretary of the Interior Harold L. Ickes that ships owned or controlled in

[36] Quoted in Sherwood, *Roosevelt and Hopkins,* pp. 342–343.
[37] *Ibid.,* p. 343.   [38] *Ibid.,* pp. 347–348.
[39] Herbert Feis, *The Spanish Story: Franco and the Nations at War* (New York: Alfred A. Knopf, 1948), p. 136.

the United States should not carry oil to Spain or to the Canary Islands.[40] Since Spain's own merchant marine was notably inadequate, this decision created a further hindrance to Spanish-American commerce. In such a manner the economic noose was gradually tightened. The effect was especially evident in the declining volume of Spanish petroleum imports. Beginning in July and continuing for a period of some three months, American shipments of gasoline to Spain were only about one half of normal, while fuel-oil sales amounted to only about two thirds of their accustomed total. Whether Franco admitted it or not, this was a serious matter. Hoping to improve the situation, Minister of Trade Carceller approached Weddell on July 31 with conciliatory advice. Since Spain was still neutral, he told the Ambassador somewhat plaintively, the American government should take Franco's public attitude with a grain of salt. Deeds, after all, were more important than words. But the State Department was not convinced that Carceller spoke with Franco's approval and for another month made no attempt to widen this opening.[41]

Meanwhile, disturbing new rumors accumulated in North Africa and in unoccupied France. From his post in Algiers Murphy, on July 7, sent Washington the details of a report which supposedly had originated in Berlin. According to this story, the Nazi invasion of Russia was nothing more than part of a German scheme to gain absolute control of the Mediterranean. After surrounding the Black Sea, Hitler's armies would turn southward through the Near East and then sweep westward across North Africa, drawing Spain into the war and bringing Dakar and Casablanca firmly under German domination.[42] On July 11 Weygand suddenly left his headquarters for new consultations at Vichy. When he returned to Algiers a few days later, he told Murphy he feared a crisis in September or October. At the same time, Weygand's advisers made it clear that the General's position would be strengthened by definite promises of military aid from the United States. Murphy saw considerable merit in this idea and immediately started a long but fruitless campaign to secure from his government the assurances Weygand was thought to desire.[43]

Washington's coolness toward such a venture grew in part from its tendency to discount Murphy's fears. Viewing the North African situation in much wider perspective, the State Department regarded the

[40] *Ibid.*, p. 138.
[41] *Ibid.*, pp. 139–140.
[42] Langer, *Our Vichy Gamble*, p. 176.
[43] *Ibid.*, pp. 182–183.

immediate future in this part of the world with less pessimism than was evinced by anyone on the spot. Indeed, Murphy's own alarm dwindled notably by the end of the month. After pondering local conditions another two weeks, he even sounded almost optimistic. "It is clear," he admitted in a letter written July 31, "that we have a far greater time margin than we dared hope some months ago." [44]

Nevertheless, the American government maintained its usual diplomatic pressure at Vichy throughout this time of apparent crisis. In mid-July, while Weygand was conferring with Pétain, Roosevelt sent Pétain new warnings against collaboration. But it was Darlan with whom Leahy had to deal, and the Vice Premier would make no promises regarding concessions to Germany. Instead, he told Leahy that the Japanese were about to occupy additional bases in Indo-China. This called forth a new protest against concessions to Japan, but Darlan merely replied that France was helpless. On July 21 he concluded the episode by informing Leahy that Japan had been given control of southern Indo-China.[45] Owing to its very immediacy, this problem at once overshadowed the ebbing worries produced by Murphy's dispatches, and the United States had no choice but to continue its discussion of the matter with Japan.

IV

Though France's new surrender to Japanese demands had not yet been officially proclaimed by either government, Tokyo made no secret of its plans. Nomura finished the revelations he had started in his confidences to Admiral Turner on July 21, 1941, by telling Welles two days later that he "understood" Japan had concluded an agreement with France which permitted the occupation of southern Indo-China by Japanese troops. He did his best, however, to create an impression that the move was only temporary. With the emptiness of phrase which had become such a marked characteristic of Japanese diplomacy, he insisted that no violation of Indo-China's "inherent sovereignty" would occur. The occupation was necessary, he said, for reasons of military security. Free French elements in Indo-China had to be controlled, and Japan

[44] Langer, *Our Vichy Gamble,* p. 183.
[45] William D. Leahy, *I Was There* (New York: Whittlesey House, 1950), pp. 44–45; and Langer, *Our Vichy Gamble,* pp. 176–178.

had to guard its access to food supplies in this region. Expressing hope that the United States would not act hastily, Nomura revealed the main focus of Tokyo's worries by declaring that any further restriction of American oil exports would "inflame" Japanese opinion. He ended his discourse with the news that he now had fresh instructions to seek a general agreement with the United States.[46]

But such outpourings were all too familiar, and Welles's quick reply did not mince words for an instant. In view of what the Ambassador had just told him, he said, all basis for continuing negotiations between their respective governments had disappeared. If Japan occupied the remainder of Indo-China, the United States would have no alternative but to assume that the Japanese government was bent upon a "policy of totalitarian aggression in the South Seas." [47]

The decisive moment in America's relations with Japan had arrived. Diplomatic contact was not broken; several rounds of further negotiation were destined to ensue. Nevertheless, Welles's statement of July 23 marked a genuine turning point in the Far Eastern policy of the United States, a kind of watershed between hope and resignation. Having accepted Japan's latest move as final evidence that Tokyo planned no compromise whatever as basis for a peaceful settlement with the United States, the American government would henceforth place less reliance upon diplomatic persuasion than upon economic pressure. And since it had little expectation that ultimate war could be avoided, its major objective would be to gain time.[48]

After his discouraging exchange of views with the Acting Secretary of State, Nomura tried going directly to the President. He was received at the White House on July 24, but he did no better than at the State Department. Roosevelt grasped the opportunity to deliver a severe lecture on the newest dangers of Japanese policy and bluntly informed his visitor that the United States had so far hesitated to declare an oil embargo only because it did not wish to give Japan an incentive to seize the Dutch East Indies. Whether he planned to impose one now the President did not say, but the drift of his remarks could hardly be mistaken. After this threat of new economic restrictions, he went on to

[46] Memorandum by Welles, July 23, 1941, United States, Department of State, *Papers Relating to the Foreign Relations of the United States: Japan, 1931–1941* (Washington, D. C.: U. S. Govt. Printing Office, 1943), II, 523.

[47] *Ibid.*, p. 525.

[48] See Cordell Hull, *The Memoirs of Cordell Hull* (New York: Macmillan Co., 1948), II, 1015.

suggest a formula which, if accepted, would stabilize conditions in southeastern Asia long enough to permit further study of Japanese-American differences. In brief, he offered to seek an agreement with the British, Dutch, and Chinese providing for the neutralization of Indo-China if Japan would withdraw its troops from that country.[49] The campaign to gain time was already getting under way.

The occupation of southern Indo-China proceeded rapidly in the meanwhile, and Roosevelt's implicit threat materialized long before he received an answer to his proposal. On July 26 he issued an executive order freezing all Japanese assets in the United States.[50] This brought Japanese-American trade to an immediate standstill. As Welles told an anxious Nomura on July 28, all Japanese ships in American ports would be granted clearance by the Treasury Department as soon as it was requested. But he made it plain that such vessels would carry nothing except enough fuel to see them home.[51]

This move had portentous implications. Through the device of placing the export of strategic materials under licensing control the United States had exercised a mounting economic pressure against Japan for more than a year. Since the autumn of 1940 the Japanese had been unable to buy from America such articles as aircraft engines and parts, various minerals and chemicals, aviation lubricating oil, aviation gasoline, and any kind of scrap iron or steel. The advisability of extending these prohibitions had been kept under constant study. In recent weeks the question of stopping all shipments of oil to Japan had been especially vexing. That such action would strike Japan in its weakest spot, militarily speaking, could not be doubted; but, as Roosevelt explained to Nomura on July 24, he did not wish to encourage precipitate Japanese seizure of the Dutch East Indies in an effort to gain a firm hold upon a new source of supply.

Anxiety that the freezing order would, in this way, merely defeat the hope of gaining time was particularly strong in military and naval circles. Commenting upon Japan's newest aggression in a letter written to Admiral Hart on July 24, Stark expressed his belief that Japan would take no further action for a time after seizing the remainder of Indo-

[49] Memorandum by Welles, July 24, 1941, *Foreign Relations: Japan, 1931–1941*, II, 527–529.

[50] Executive Order No. 8832, July 26, 1941, United States, National Archives, *Federal Register* (Washington, D. C.: U. S. Govt. Printing Office, 1936——), VI, 3715.

[51] Memorandum by Welles, July 28, 1941, *Foreign Relations: Japan, 1931–1941*, II, 537–538.

China unless Washington decreed an oil embargo. In such an event, however, he thought that Borneo might be attacked at once. This was the reason why he had always opposed an oil embargo.[52] The same view had already been presented in an official analysis submitted by the Navy's War Plans Division on July 22.[53]

That the civilian heads of the government did not share these misgivings to the full accounted for the freezing order of July 26. Still, the gravity of the action could not be denied. Since the British and Dutch governments impounded Japanese funds in a similar manner,[54] Japan could not rely on the East Indies to make good any of the petroleum deficit thus created unless it seized this area by force. Nor could Tokyo afford much delay in making up its mind. Japanese oil stocks were sufficient for only twelve to eighteen months of wartime consumption. Japan normally imported 80 per cent of its oil from the United States, for domestic wells and synthetic production were capable of filling only about 12 per cent of its needs.[55] The American government held a powerful economic weapon and was now using it freely for the first time. But since it confronted Japan with a choice between surrender and new aggressions, the decision was made at cost of bringing war a good deal closer.

The caution displayed by Stark and others tended to harmonize with the general strategic pattern of the war as viewed in both London and Washington, for this pattern assumed that a diplomacy of restraint would be used to avoid an open break in the Pacific as long as possible. But the order of July 26 was viewed with alarm for still another reason: It undermined specific plans for defense of the American position in the Far East.

Since about 1921 standard military thinking in Washington had taken for granted that the Philippine Islands could not be defended in the early stages of a war between the United States and Japan. As a result, there was to be no attempt to hold even Luzon if such a conflict broke out. Instead, plans called for withdrawal of the Philippine Army

[52] Stark to Hart, July 24, 1941, *Pearl Harbor Hearings,* pt. 16, exhibit 106, p. 2173.

[53] Memorandum by Turner, July 22, 1941, *ibid.,* pt. 5, p. 2384. For further material on the immediate background of the freezing order, see Herbert Feis, *The Road to Pearl Harbor* (Princeton, N. J.: Princeton Univ. Press, 1950), chap. xxxi.

[54] Churchill, *The Grand Alliance,* p. 427.

[55] United States, Strategic Bombing Survey, *The Effects of Bombing on Japan's War Economy* (Washington, D. C.: U. S. Govt. Printing Office, 1946), pp. 79–80, table, p. 134. Cf. Samuel Eliot Morison, *The Rising Sun in the Pacific, 1931—April 1942* (Boston: Little, Brown, and Co., 1948), pp. 63–64.

and the United States Army garrison to the Bataan Peninsula. From this stronghold all efforts would be concentrated upon the retention of Manila Bay until help arrived from across the Pacific.[56] Thus American strategy in the Philippines was envisaged as little more than an attempt to keep a narrow beachhead for the convenience of an eventual rescue expedition.

But a change was in progress by July 1941. The native military establishment seemed to have made great strides under the command of former Chief of Staff Douglas MacArthur, who had resigned from the United States Army in 1937 to accept the rank of Field Marshal under the Philippine government, and MacArthur was now convinced that a Japanese attack might be successfully resisted. His optimism had an appeal to which higher authority was not immune. At the same time, moreover, the Army was gaining an unusual respect for the capabilities of its new bombing plane, the B-17, or Flying Fortress. A number of these craft had been allotted to the British under Lend-Lease, and the Royal Air Force had found them very effective in bombing operations over Germany. It now seemed that they might also be used to bolster the defense of the Philippines. After weighing the whole situation, the General Staff conceded that Luzon and the Visayas might be held, at least for a time, if the strength of MacArthur's army could be increased to two hundred thousand men and if the army could be provided with a sizable force of B-17's to operate against the Japanese invasion fleet and Japanese invasion bases.[57]

On July 26, the day of the freezing order, President Roosevelt nationalized the Philippine Army, making it a part of the United States Army Forces in the Far East.[58] He also recalled MacArthur to active duty, with the rank of Lieutenant General, and placed him at the head of this new command.[59] Far Eastern defense preparations thus achieved a more systematic basis and were oriented to a new plan, but the reinforcements in men and aircraft needed to give the plan a chance of success could not be had for several months. This furnished Marshall and Stark with additional incentives for opposing any move that

[56] Morison, *The Rising Sun in the Pacific*, p. 150; and Jonathan M. Wainwright, *General Wainwright's Story*, ed. Robert Considine (Garden City, N. Y.: Doubleday and Co., 1946), p. 9.

[57] Henry L. Stimson and McGeorge Bundy, *On Active Service: In Peace and War* (New York: Harper and Bros., 1948), p. 388. Cf. Morison, *The Rising Sun in the Pacific*, p. 153.   [58] Military Order, July 26, 1941, *Federal Register*, VI, 3825.

[59] Marshall to MacArthur (undated), *Pearl Harbor Hearings*, pt. 20, exhibit 179, p. 4364; and *General Wainwright's Story*, p. 11.

might provoke sudden action by Japan. That the freezing order did not broaden their time margin is certain. In the days which followed, this much became perfectly evident: Neither Welles's assertion that he could see no basis for continuing the Washington talks nor the freezing order itself seemed to impose the least restraint upon Japanese policy. Foreign Minister Toyoda's first reaction to these developments was a heightened anxiety.[60] But he told Grew on July 27 that, while the offer made by President Roosevelt on July 24 would be carefully examined, it had probably come too late. The freezing order, he went on to say, had had a most adverse effect on Japanese opinion.[61] Nevertheless, Roosevelt was determined to give his hope for a moratorium in southeastern Asia as broad a foundation as possible, and Welles, at his direction, told Nomura on July 31 that the President wished to extend his neutralization offer to embrace Thailand as well.[62]

By the time the Japanese government framed its answer to this proposal, Roosevelt was on his way to the Atlantic Conference, and Hull—having finished his sojourn at White Sulphur Springs—was back at his desk in Washington. The counterproposal which Nomura presented to the Secretary of State on August 6 was not one likely to remove the blight which had fallen upon relations between the two countries, however. Japan offered a promise to station no more troops in the southwestern Pacific area outside of Indo-China, but declined to withdraw its troops from that country until the China Incident was settled. Japan also offered to guarantee the neutrality of the Philippines "at an opportune time" and to lend help in procuring from southeastern Asia such raw materials as were needed by the United States. The American government, on the other hand, should agree to suspend its military preparations in the southwestern Pacific, advise Great Britain and the Netherlands to do the same, help Japan secure raw materials from the Dutch East Indies and elsewhere, restore normal trade relations with Japan, use its good offices to encourage direct negotiations between Chiang Kai-shek and the Japanese government, and recognize the special status of Japan in Indo-China even after the withdrawal of Japanese troops.[63]

This counterproposal emphasized Japan's acute realization of its

[60] Memorandum by Grew, July 26, 1941, *Foreign Relations: Japan, 1931–1941*, II, 533–534.   [61] Memorandum by Grew, July 27, 1941, *ibid.*, p. 535.
[62] Memorandum by Welles, July 31, 1941, *ibid.*, p. 540.
[63] Proposal by the Japanese government, Aug. 6, 1941, *ibid.*, pp. 549–550.

economic plight and underlined a natural reluctance to place the nation's economy altogether at the mercy of the United States and other Western powers by surrendering its newly acquired footholds in southern Asia. Viewed against the background of recent negotiations, however, it had no chance of being accepted in Washington. Hull studied the offer two days and then handed Nomura a statement which characterized it as "lacking in responsiveness to the suggestion made by the President." [64]

Thus ended another brief chapter in a lengthening tale of frustration. But that a further chapter would follow seemed evident from the new offensive which Nomura started before the interview closed. Reviving a project which had been suggested as a kind of afterthought in the Japanese Embassy's unofficial program of April 9,[65] he now expressed a conviction that the best approach to a settlement of differences might be found in a personal meeting between President Roosevelt and Prince Konoye.[66] While Hull gave the Ambassador no encouragement at this time, the offer was not to be dropped abruptly. For it had recently been espoused by Konoye himself,[67] and it was to furnish the only real basis for conversations between the United States and Japan during the next two months.

V

As the *Prince of Wales* steamed westward from Scapa Flow bearing Churchill, Hopkins, and the British delegation toward the Newfoundland coast, Roosevelt and his party made an unobtrusive exodus from Washington. Leaving the capital by train on August 3, they proceeded to New London, Connecticut, where they boarded the presidential yacht *Potomac*. Ostensibly it was a vacation trip, intended to combine fishing with relaxation and a leisurely cruise along the New England coast. This festive atmosphere was carefully preserved. On August 4 Princess Martha of Norway, Prince Karl of Sweden, and a few other members of European royalty then in the United States joined the President on the *Potomac* for a brief round of deep-sea fishing. On the morning of August 5, however, Roosevelt and his party transferred to the cruiser

[64] Document presented by Hull to Nomura, Aug. 8, 1941, *Foreign Relations: Japan, 1931–1941*, II, 553.

[65] Proposal presented to the Department of State, Apr. 9, 1941, *ibid.*, p. 402.

[66] Memorandum by Ballantine, Aug. 8, 1941, *ibid.*, p. 550.

[67] Konoye memoirs, *Pearl Harbor Hearings*, pt. 20, exhibit 173, p. 3999.

Augusta. Already on board were Marshall, King, and Stark. As the *Potomac* continued up the coast, the *Augusta* made direct for her rendezvous, reaching Argentia on August 7.[68] Two days later the *Prince of Wales* arrived.

Roosevelt and Churchill had met once before—in England, during the First World War, when Roosevelt was serving as Assistant Secretary of the Navy.[69] But this was their initial encounter on anything like equal terms, and it would be interesting to know the thoughts of each as they sat at dinner aboard the *Augusta* that evening. Both enjoyed world prestige as leaders of the forces opposing Hitlerism, and certainly they were mainly responsible for the extremely close coöperation which had grown up between the United States and Great Britain over the past year. At the same time, however, each was head of government in his own country, the representative of national hopes, fears, and interests; and each was bound by the constitutional system that gave him office. Besides, one came from a nation which had been at war almost two years, while the other headed a state that was, in most respects, little more than a helpful and partisan bystander.

The practical identity of their larger objectives was clear enough, but that their interests varied in detail was equally patent. Each wished to see how far the other was prepared to go in the several spheres of military and diplomatic action that had to be considered, and the fundamental purpose on both sides was to concert measures for projecting Anglo-American coöperation into the future. There is much evidence that Roosevelt wanted a detailed commitment guaranteeing the purity of British war aims, and it is certain that in recent weeks he had studied the desirability of announcing a generalized peace program.[70] Churchill, on the other hand, apparently hoped for an outright pledge of American intervention.[71] But these were subjects which had to be approached with caution, and their coverage seems to have been partial at best.

[68] Ross T. McIntire (with George Creel), *White House Physician* (New York: G. P. Putnam's Sons, 1946), pp. 130–131.

[69] Sherwood, *Roosevelt and Hopkins*, p. 351.

[70] See Sumner Welles, *Where Are We Heading?* (New York: Harper and Bros., 1946), p. 6. Also memorandum by Berle, June 21, 1941, MS Roosevelt Papers (Secretary's File, Box 78); Roosevelt to Berle, June 26, 1941, in Franklin D. Roosevelt, *F. D. R.: His Personal Letters, 1928–1945,* ed. Elliott Roosevelt (New York: Duell, Sloan, and Pearce, 1950), II, 1175; and Elliott Roosevelt, *As He Saw It* (New York: Duell, Sloan, and Pearce, 1946), pp. 27–31.

[71] See Sherwood, *Roosevelt and Hopkins,* p. 355.

Although no formal agenda had been prepared, it was understood that the following matters would be discussed: (1) a broad declaration regarding the postwar policies of the United States and Great Britain, (2) Anglo-American relations with Russia, (3) the Atlantic war, and (4) Anglo-American relations with Japan.

The first item had practically nothing to do with the immediate conduct of the war, except as it might spur the oppressed peoples of Europe and Asia to new efforts of resistance with its promise of better days. Hence it can be passed over rather briefly. Since Roosevelt apparently feared that the British government might be tempted to enter a web of secret treaties like that which had plagued Wilson after the First World War,[72] he was perhaps even more interested in such a statement than was Churchill. Nevertheless, it was Churchill who took the initiative. On the morning of August 10 he submitted the draft of a joint declaration which was to serve as basis for the Atlantic Charter.

During the next two days this document was given extensive revision, most of the changes being proposed by Roosevelt and Churchill, while the actual task of drafting was entrusted to Sumner Welles and Sir Alexander Cadogan, British Under Secretary of State for Foreign Affairs. Agreement on practically all points was fairly easy, but on two matters they never did reach common ground. Owing to his distrust of isolationist sentiment in the United States and his reluctance to invoke memories of the League of Nations, Roosevelt insisted upon a somewhat less forthright statement regarding the future of international cooperation than Churchill desired, while the Prime Minister proved troublesome on economic questions. He considered himself bound by the system of Imperial preference established in the Ottawa Agreements of 1932 and refused to accept the American statement on policy toward world trade without a hedging qualification which, in Welles's view, destroyed much of its value.[73] But eventually the job was completed. As finally approved on August 12, and as published on August 14, the Atlantic Charter contained its familiar eight points renouncing territorial aggrandizement on behalf of Great Britain and the United States and promising, among other things, the best efforts of the two govern-

[72] Welles, *Where Are We Heading?* p. 6.

[73] The detailed story of the drafting of the Atlantic Charter is given by Welles in *Where Are We Heading?* pp. 6–18. For additional points of interpretation, see memorandum by Welles, Aug. 11, 1941, *Pearl Harbor Hearings,* pt. 14, exhibit 22–C, pp. 1283–1291; Sherwood, *Roosevelt and Hopkins,* pp. 359–360; and Churchill, *The Grand Alliance,* pp. 433–437.

ments to restore self-rule wherever it had been forcibly destroyed, to promote world coöperation in the economic field, and to keep all new aggression in check at the war's end until "a wider and permanent system of security" could be established.[74]

There was considerable discussion of Russia, based largely on Hopkins' findings. Churchill readily accepted the proposed plan for a three-power supply conference in Moscow and undertook to appoint Lord Beaverbrook as his representative "with full power to act for all British departments."[75] They also drew up a joint message for Stalin, which was dispatched as the conference ended. Replete with words of encouragement and guarantees of aid, it closely resembled the draft prepared by Cripps in Moscow.[76]

Though they spent considerable time exchanging views on strategy and operations, the military and naval advisers who accompanied the two leaders made little real progress in either domain. The pattern of American entrance into the Atlantic war was already established; Marshall, Stark, and King had no desire to postulate new commitments elsewhere. They would not yield to British fears regarding the Middle East and the possible extension of Japanese power into the Indian Ocean, nor did they warm to a British proposal for more staff talks at Singapore.[77] But Roosevelt and Churchill, in their own discussions, revived earlier plans for neutralizing the Atlantic islands belonging to Spain and Portugal.

The somewhat uncertain views of the Portuguese government had led Churchill as early as June 18 to suggest special Anglo-American staff conversations to determine possible action if Portugal should not request assistance in the face of an imminent German threat to the Azores.[78] Since that time Roosevelt had undertaken further soundings of official Portuguese intentions. His efforts were not without result and now, on August 11, he read Churchill a letter from the Portuguese dictator, Oliveria Salazar, who, under the stipulated circumstances, appeared to favor a preventive occupation of the islands.

---

[74] Joint declaration, Aug. 14, 1941, United States, Department of State, *Department of State Bulletin* (Washington, D. C.: U. S. Govt. Printing Office, 1939——), V (Aug. 16, 1941), 125–126. [75] Sherwood, *Roosevelt and Hopkins,* p. 359.
[76] Sherwood, *Roosevelt and Hopkins,* p. 331. The text of this message is given in United States, Department of State, *Peace and War: United States Foreign Policy, 1931–1941* (Washington, D. C.: U. S. Govt. Printing Office, 1943), pp. 711–712.
[77] Sherwood, *Roosevelt and Hopkins,* p. 358.
[78] Welles to Roosevelt, June 18, 1941, MS Roosevelt Papers (Secretary's File, Box 76).

Churchill seized this opportunity to emphasize his concern regarding German influence in Spain, and stated that Great Britain planned to occupy the Spanish-owned Canary Islands about the middle of September. Owing to the demands of this operation, he added, Britain would be unable to defend the Azores in fulfillment of a pledge already made to Portugal, so their early occupation by American troops was doubly important. He undertook to negotiate with Salazar and guaranteed that the Royal Navy would forestall any attempt by Germany to prevent such a move when the time for action came. On Roosevelt's complaint that the United States could not at once assume the duty of protecting the Cape Verde Islands too, he promised that British forces would occupy these in addition to the Canaries, turning them over to the United States at a later date.[79] But this was a design for early autumn at best, and, since Hitler did not furnish the expected provocation, one which never matured. Far more significant to the diplomacy of the near future were decisions relating to Japan.

Convinced that the threat to its entire Far Eastern position had become direct and immediate, Great Britain was deeply perturbed over Japanese activity. On August 9, while the Atlantic Conference was just getting under way, Halifax called at the State Department to ask Hull what aid this country would be able to furnish his own government if Japan attacked Singapore or the Dutch East Indies. Always cautious, Hull replied that the answer depended upon the amount of help needed in other theaters when such an attack developed. He added that the matter would be discussed at the proper time.[80] But Churchill, at Argentia, was not to be put off so easily. Thinking of a definite agreement for common opposition to Japan, he did not wish to talk of possible help in a future contingency. He wanted diplomatic action, backed by the threat of military action, which might keep that contingency from arising at all. As he told Welles, ". . . if a war did break out between Great Britain and Japan, Japan immediately would be in a position through the use of her large number of cruisers to seize or destroy all the British merchant shipping in the Indian Ocean and in the Pacific, and to cut the life-lines between the British Domin-

---

[79] Hull, *Memoirs*, II, 941; memorandum by Welles, Aug. 11, 1941, *Pearl Harbor Hearings*, pt. 14, exhibit 22–C, pp. 1275–1278; and Churchill, *The Grand Alliance*, p. 438.

[80] Memorandum by Hull, Aug. 9, 1941, *Peace and War*, pp. 710–711.

ions and the British Isles unless the United States herself entered the war." [81]

He met Roosevelt with plans already formed. To his mind, very strong, parallel declarations by the United States, Great Britain, the British dominions, the Netherlands—and possibly Russia—offered the best hope of checking Japan, at least temporarily.[82] The statement he proposed for delivery from Washington was couched in the following terms:

> Any further encroachment by Japan in the Southwestern Pacific would produce a situation in which the United States Government would be compelled to take counter measures even though these might lead to war between the United States and Japan.
> If any third Power becomes the object of aggression by Japan in consequence of such counter measures or of their support of them, the President would have the intention to seek authority from Congress to give aid to such Power.[83]

What the Prime Minister wanted, in short, was a plain declaration that Japan could make no move against British and Dutch possessions in the Far East without having to fight the United States. Lacking such a declaration, he said, "the blow to the British Government might be almost decisive." [84]

Although he sympathized with Churchill's fears, Roosevelt found the draft much too strong. So threatening a statement would affront Japanese pride and might hasten the very action it was designed to forestall. Moreover, he considered it too limited in scope. The southwestern Pacific was not the only area of possible Japanese action; he wanted to phrase the warning in such a way as to cover an attack on Russia also.[85] The President agreed that Japan should be allowed to go no further but emphasized his belief that every effort should be made to postpone the outbreak of war in the Far East. He therefore undertook to read Nomura a severe lecture on Japanese policy as soon as he returned to Washington and to deliver an even more comprehensive

[81] Memorandum by Welles, Aug. 10, 1941, *Pearl Harbor Hearings*, pt. 14, exhibit 22–B, p. 1273.

[82] *Ibid.*, pp. 1273–1274.   [83] *Ibid.*, p. 1270.

[84] Memorandum by Welles, Aug. 10, 1941, *Pearl Harbor Hearings*, pt. 14, exhibit 22–B, p. 1274. For the Prime Minister's own version of his attitude, which agrees substantially with the American records, see Churchill, *The Grand Alliance*, pp. 438–440.

[85] See Sherwood, *Roosevelt and Hopkins*, p. 356.

warning against new expansion. But this was to be accompanied by a somewhat less definite threat of American counteraction than the Prime Minister had envisaged.[86]

He thought such a course would put off for at least thirty days any Japanese move that might result in war. After some reflection Churchill agreed. Apparently convinced that he had gained a substantial part of what he wanted, he promised to support Roosevelt's statement with one of his own. He even expressed a view that the new joint policy had a "reasonable chance" of preventing war in the Pacific altogether.[87]

With these substantial decisions behind them, the statesmen parted and hurried back to their respective capitals.

VI

The five weeks beginning with the American occupation of Iceland in July 1941 and ending with the Atlantic Conference were, in all likelihood, the most significant period of American nonbelligerency. The country's fundamental position in the world crisis had not been in doubt for more than a year; since the fall of France events had pushed the United States undeviatingly toward a conclusion that was vague only in details. But now the details themselves were beginning to emerge. Germany's attack on Russia had set latent plans in motion, and these bore fruit in just about every sector of United States policy between the end of June and the middle of August.

The assignment of American naval units to escort duty followed hard upon the occupation of Iceland. Thanks to Hopkins' quick journey and to the prompt acceptance of his recommendations, the Anglo-American community of interest with Russia now gave every sign of growing into a useful working partnership. It became clear at the same time that slackening German pressure on the Mediterranean rendered the United States more independent in its dealings with France and Spain. But most important of all was the widening breach with Japan, culminating in Welles's rupture of the Hull-Nomura conversations, Roosevelt's fruitless proposals regarding the neutralization of Indo-China and Thailand, the freezing order of July 26, and the utter

---

[86] Memorandum by Welles, Aug. 11, 1941, *Pearl Harbor Hearings*, pt. 14, exhibit 22–C, pp. 1279–1280.   [87] *Ibid.*, p. 1283.

cessation of American-Japanese trade just as new plans for defense of the Philippines made the prospect of early hostilities with Japan less attractive than ever.

All these threads were gathered up at the Atlantic Conference. Here old designs were confirmed, new ones given shape. Most important of all was the emphasis placed on the Far East. While Europe and the Atlantic lost none of their real priority in strategic planning, relations with Japan were destined to be the central problem of the United States from this moment forward. Though caught between the American embargo and an Anglo-American diplomatic front resolved not to yield another inch, Japan obviously planned no withdrawal. The basic framework of the situation which would bring the United States into the war as a full partner was now complete. Within it neither side could do much except play for time and position.

CHAPTER X

Pacific Negotiations and Atlantic War

I

THE WARNING HE HAD UNDERTAKEN TO GIVE NOMURA FOR TRANSMISSION TO the Japanese government stood first upon Roosevelt's order of business as he parted from Churchill at Argentia. Its exact form still had to be determined, however; in his conversations with the Prime Minister he had outlined the general substance of what he planned to say, but had committed himself to no precise phraseology.[1] Armed with the President's ideas on the subject, Welles flew back to Washington ahead of him to prepare a draft. This was no easy task. Under the circumstances, a statement showing infirmity of purpose could not be counted upon to deter Japan at all. Yet, as Roosevelt had explained to Churchill, anything that resembled an ultimatum might induce that country to act at once. Every word in the proposed declaration had to aim at a delicately balanced emphasis which closed the door on further Japanese expansion but did not lock it against time-consuming talk.

According to Welles's initial draft, completed August 15, 1941, Roosevelt was to state flatly that any new Japanese aggressions of a military nature in any part of the Pacific or the Orient would force the United States government "to take immediately any and all steps of whatsoever character it deems necessary in its own security notwithstanding the possibility that such further steps on its part may result in conflict between the two countries." [2] In its lack of a specific threat that the President would make such a development the occasion for requesting new authority from Congress, this formula was somewhat less vigorous than the one originally suggested by Churchill. But it still

---

[1] Welles's testimony, Nov. 24, 1945, United States, Congress, Joint Committee on Investigation of Pearl Harbor Attack, *Hearings Pursuant to S. Con. Res. 27, Authorizing Investigation of Attack on Pearl Harbor, Dec. 7, 1941, and Events and Circumstances Relating Thereto* (79th Cong., 1st and 2nd sess.) (Washington, D. C.: U. S. Govt. Printing Office, 1946), pt. 2, pp. 539, 541. Cited henceforth as *Pearl Harbor Hearings*.
[2] Draft by Welles, Aug. 15, 1941, *ibid.*, pt. 14, exhibit 22, p. 1261.

raised the prospect of a war for which the United States was not ready, and Hull interposed strenuous objections. Regarding a less bellicose tone as more appropriate to the objectives of American policy, he proposed certain changes. These the President accepted on his return to Washington on the morning of August 17. Meanwhile, on August 16, Nomura had asked Hull whether it would be possible to resume the informal conversations Welles had terminated three weeks earlier, and Roosevelt agreed to include in his remarks an answer to this question.[3]

With Hull in attendance, the President received Nomura at the White House late in the afternoon of August 17, took charge of the conversation with a minimum of preliminaries, and delivered his warning as follows: ". . . the United States will be compelled to take immediately any and all steps which it may deem necessary toward safeguarding the legitimate rights and interests of the United States and American nationals and toward insuring the safety and security of the United States."[4] Nomura, in reply, did not try to argue the merits of Japan's aggressive policy. Instead, he reaffirmed Tokyo's wish to secure a peaceful adjustment of relations with the United States, asked whether his conversations with Hull could be resumed, and stressed his government's eagerness to learn whether the President would consent to meet Prince Konoye for a direct exchange of views.[5] Roosevelt then proceeded to read a second statement which declared, in essence, that the United States was not averse to considering further talks but that the success of any such move depended upon Japan's readiness to submit a much clearer expression of its attitude and desires than had yet been furnished.[6] The rest of the interview was largely devoted to the question of his meeting Konoye. While the President remained somewhat noncommittal, he did allow Nomura to gain an impression that he was not wholly opposed to this idea.[7]

[3] Cordell Hull, *The Memoirs of Cordell Hull* (New York: Macmillan Co., 1948), II, 1018.

[4] Memorandum by Hull, Aug. 17, 1941, United States, Department of State, *Papers Relating to the Foreign Relations of the United States: Japan, 1931–1941* (Washington, D. C.: U. S. Govt. Printing Office, 1943), II, 554–555; and oral statement by the President, Aug. 17, 1941, *ibid.*, pp. 556–557.

[5] Nomura to Toyoda, Aug. 18, 1941, *Pearl Harbor Hearings*, pt. 17, exhibit 124, p. 2751.

[6] Memorandum by Hull, Aug. 17, 1941, *Foreign Relations: Japan, 1931–1941*, II, 555; and oral statement by the President, Aug. 17, 1941, *ibid.*, pp. 557–559.

[7] Nomura to Toyoda, Aug. 18, 1941, *Pearl Harbor Hearings*, pt. 17, exhibit 124, p. 2754.

Three salient facts were now established. In the first place, Roosevelt had made it perfectly clear that any movement of Japanese troops into areas not already under Japanese control would beget serious countermeasures on the part of the United States, for despite the element of moderation introduced by Hull, his warning was a strong one. He had also made it clear that Japan would have to prove its desire for new conversations by giving up its attempts to avoid plain speaking on the real causes of tension in the Pacific. On the other hand, Nomura's absorption in the conference project indicated that Japan was disposed to shelve all consideration of basic issues until Roosevelt signified his willingness to meet Konoye.

Hoping to strike while the iron was hot, Foreign Minister Toyoda approached Grew the very next day with a detailed proposal for such a meeting at Honolulu and urged its desirability with enough conviction to win the Ambassador's enthusiastic support.[8] That Washington did not fully share Grew's enthusiasm could not be doubted in view of its reactions up to this point. But an attitude was in the making, and Hull seems to have taken the lead in determining broad outlines. His experience with Japanese diplomacy had never been happy; its tortuous course in recent months had completed his disillusionment; and he was frankly sceptical of the utility of a leaders' conference now that all else had failed. Outwardly, at least, the Japanese proposal involved nothing more than a change of diplomatic procedure. As soon as it reached a stage of serious discussion, therefore, he took the position that Roosevelt should decline to meet Konoye without a preliminary agreement which indicated a marked change in Japan's attitude on Pacific and Asiatic questions.[9] Since personal diplomacy had a natural fascination for the President, he might have been expected to consider the Japanese offer with fewer misgivings. But he, also, lacked faith in Japan's good intentions and seems to have adopted Hull's view at the outset.

That Konoye was no free agent is now clear. According to his own testimony, the Japanese Premier discussed the conference idea with the War and Navy ministers on August 4, several days before Nomura approached Hull on the topic. The Navy Minister offered no special objection. But the War Minister, General Hideki Tojo, insisted upon an understanding that Japanese policy would not be affected by anything that might happen at the proposed meeting; if Roosevelt declined

<hr>

[8] Memorandum by Grew, Aug. 18, 1941, *Foreign Relations: Japan, 1931–1941*, II, 563–564.   [9] Hull, *Memoirs*, II, 1025.

to settle on proper terms, Japan's war preparations should continue.[10] Although Konoye apparently hoped to overcome his colleagues' opposition, the American suspicion of his offer was certainly not unfounded. Since Konoye was thus estopped from issuing satisfactory preliminary guarantees, the negotiations which followed were doomed from the start. But they promised to consume time; and this, from the American viewpoint, was extremely important, for time to strengthen the nation's Pacific defenses was a primary objective so long as it could be bought without fresh concessions. Having no reason for haste, therefore, the American government let Japan keep the initiative in all matters relating to the leaders' conference. Hull neither accepted nor declined the invitation, and seldom mentioned it except in reply to a direct question. At the same time, he endeavored to keep Britain from introducing new notes of discord. Later that month, for example, when the British chargé d'affaires showed him two drafts of a proposed statement by which Churchill meant to fulfill the pledge he had given at Argentia, Hull's lack of enthusiasm for such a move was so obvious that London dropped the matter without further discussion.[11] Meanwhile, the American talks with Japan continued.

Once more, on August 23, Nomura approached Hull to urge the necessity for a prompt decision. His government feared that agreements detrimental to Japan might be reached at the conference which Great Britain, the United States, and Russia planned to hold soon in Moscow; therefore he wanted to suggest the scheduling of a Roosevelt-Konoye meeting to occur before October 15, preferably during the early part of September. But Hull refused to be hurried, and he gave the Ambassador no satisfaction.[12] Four days later Konoye sent Roosevelt a personal appeal, asking him to set the earliest possible date.[13] Like Hull, the President was evasive; even the selection of a meeting place offered difficulties. Honolulu, he thought, was too far away. Perhaps Juneau, Alaska, would be a more convenient rendezvous.[14] Nomura accepted this location at once and proposed that the meeting be held September 21–25. But Roosevelt still declined to make a firm commitment.[15]

In the meanwhile, American oil shipments to Vladivostok furnished

[10] Konoye memoirs, *Pearl Harbor Hearings,* pt. 20, exhibit 173, p. 4000.
[11] Hull, *Memoirs,* II, 1023.
[12] Memorandum by Hull, Aug. 23, 1941, *Foreign Relations: Japan, 1931–1941,* II, 568.
[13] Konoye to Roosevelt, Aug. 27, 1941, *ibid.,* pp. 572–573.
[14] Memorandum by Hull, Aug. 28, 1941, *ibid.,* p. 571. [15] *Ibid.,* p. 576.

an element of diversion. Acting under instructions which had their origin in German pressure at Tokyo,[16] Nomura complained that the United States was building up Russia's Far Eastern position in a manner threatening to Japan. Hull replied that American supplies were being sent to Russia only for use in the European theater, although he added that a different situation would arise if Japan chose to meddle in the Soviet-German war.[17] Nomura filed another protest a few days later. This time Hull contented himself with a flat statement that such trade was perfectly valid under all the laws of commerce. Any attempt to have it stopped, he said, would be "preposterous."[18]

But the Japanese Foreign Office was not easily rebuffed. It next tried to erect a kind of *modus vivendi* upon the proposed leaders' conference, suggesting to Grew on August 29 that the United States might discontinue oil shipments to Russia and suspend its freezing order relative to Japanese assets until the meeting could be held. Needless to say, Grew could offer no real encouragement,[19] and Roosevelt hastened to make his position absolutely clear. On September 3 he sent Konoye his formal reply to the latter's message of August 27. This note left Tokyo no valid reason to believe that he meant to attend a conference until the two governments reached a preliminary agreement on the main questions at issue.[20] He also explained to Nomura that the terms of any such understanding would have to be taken up with the British, the Chinese, and the Dutch before he could enter a final discussion with Konoye.[21]

II

If there were any changes in United States relations with Spain and France during the months of August and September 1941, they were changes of atmosphere rather than of policy. Neither Vichy nor Madrid supplied the American government with a good reason for doing

---

[16] Memorandum by Amau, Aug. 19, 1941, *Pearl Harbor Hearings*, pt. 18, exhibit 132-A, p. 2948; and Toyoda to Nomura, Aug. 23, 1941, *ibid.*, pt. 17, exhibit 124, p. 2772.

[17] Memorandum by Hull, Aug. 23, 1941, *Foreign Relations: Japan, 1931–1941*, II, 566–567.   [18] Memorandum by Hull, Aug. 27, 1941, *ibid.*, p. 570.

[19] Grew to Hull, Aug. 29, 1941, *ibid.;* and Joseph C. Grew, *Ten Years in Japan* (New York: Simon and Schuster, 1944), pp. 423–424.

[20] Roosevelt to Konoye, Sept. 3, 1941, *Foreign Relations: Japan, 1931–1941*, II, 592.

[21] Memorandum by Hull, Sept. 3, 1941, *ibid.*, p. 588.

either more or less than it had been doing, and there was no departure from the attitude of nervous caution which had virtually immobilized the administration's policy toward Spain since the beginning of the year, and which had prevented any real effort to broaden relationships with France since the activation of the Murphy-Weygand accord. As usual, however, tendencies were observable in both capitals. None could be interpreted with finality, but the Spanish government appeared to show a reviving interest in better relations with the United States, while developments at Vichy took a less favorable turn and created new pessimism regarding the future course of the Pétain regime.

Demetrio Carceller, the Spanish Minister of Trade and Industry, had made overtures at the end of July which were clearly intended to open a new round of economic discussions with the United States. But the State Department, fearing that Carceller spoke solely on his own authority, had declined to carry the matter any further at the time. Although Carceller's ideas were brought up again and studied with more or less care during the next month, the result was the same. His efforts to explain away Franco's public truculence with respect to the democratic cause fell far short of a guarantee that Spain would not eventually enter the war at Germany's side, and Weddell was told on September 18 that Spain would be furnished scarce and essential goods only in return for a definite *quid pro quo*.[22] Spanish good will, by itself, was not enough.

As this decision gradually took shape, the Spanish government made new advances through Juan Cárdenas, its Ambassador in Washington. Restricted petroleum supplies from the United States had accentuated Spain's chronic oil shortage, and oil was a leading consideration when Cárdenas approached Hull early in September with a direct inquiry as to the possibility of a commercial understanding. Still suspicious of Carceller's efforts, Hull gave the Ambassador no encouragement. Cárdenas returned to the subject on September 13, just before leaving on a short visit to Spain, and the Secretary took advantage of this opportunity to assure his caller of American sympathy for the Spanish people. But he also made it clear that this sympathy did not include the Spanish leaders; since their attitude had been "one of aggravated discourtesy and contempt in the very face of our offers to be of aid," the United States could undertake no further approaches. The Ambassador

[22] Herbert Feis, *The Spanish Story: Franco and the Nations at War* (New York: Alfred A. Knopf, 1948), p. 140.

countered with a soft answer, making no effort to defend his government except to suggest that part of the difficulty might be ascribed to a
misunderstanding between Weddell and Serrano Suñer. He said that
he would do his best in his forthcoming consultations with his superiors
to encourage better relations.[23]

Cárdenas was as good as his word. In Madrid, on September 27, he
told Weddell that both Franco and Serrano Suñer would shortly invite
him to call for a general discussion of relations between the two countries. He added that Spain now stood in desperate need of American
help, particularly with respect to gasoline, and asked Weddell to make
allowances for the inexperience of those who directed Spanish foreign
policy. And when the American Ambassador had the promised interview with Serrano Suñer three days later—his first such meeting since
April—the auguries were even more favorable. Especially noteworthy
was the Foreign Minister's apparent state of mind. Until then he had
never shown much interest in economic problems. But now his de-
meanor seemed almost humble as he admitted that Spain was in the
throes of economic strangulation.[24] However one might view the
long-range prospects of American-Spanish relations, it was obvious that
the diplomatic atmosphere of the Spanish capital had warmed again.

If the tone of Washington's conversations with Madrid grew somewhat more friendly in August and September, however, its exchanges
with Vichy sharpened almost by the day. Weygand was again called
before Marshal Pétain on August 8, thus reviving fears that Germany
was making new efforts to gain a territorial foothold in North Africa,
particularly at Bizerte, in Tunisia. Though these apprehensions were
not confirmed by any tangible development, Pétain's next move was no
better designed to inspire confidence in Washington. On August 12 he
proclaimed the suspension of activity by all political parties in France,
and announced the government's assumption of broad new police
powers. These moves, of course, gave the regime an even more totalitarian aspect. When the French Ambassador in Washington, Gaston
Henry-Haye, assured Hull on August 20 that Pétain viewed the change
as little more than an expedient to calm the internal situation, the
Secretary did not try to hide his disbelief. He stated frankly that he
attributed the new measures to the work of pro-German forces behind

[23] Memorandum by Hull, Sept. 13, 1941, MS Department of State (711.52/193);
and Feis, *The Spanish Story*, pp. 140–141.
[24] Weddell to Hull, Sept. 28, 30, 1941, MS Department of State (711.52/198, 199).

the old soldier, and expressed the blunt opinion that the "uppermost purpose of the Laval-Darlan group" was to "deliver France body and soul to Hitler."[25]

Still, Hull made no special threats. Except for its ideological bearing, the decree of August 12, as it now stood, was clearly a domestic issue for which there was no immediate diplomatic remedy. At all events, North Africa was the principal concern; and since American authorities had distinguished no definite move to grant Germany special concessions in that area, the North African situation had to be regarded as fundamentally unchanged. Reports from Murphy and other American representatives on the spot indicated that no serious German infiltration had yet occurred in any part of the territory under Weygand's control.[26] Nor were the Army and Navy disposed to regard North Africa as an immediate military problem. About this same time, the services joined in recommending that Weygand be accorded no guarantee of military aid, at least for the moment.[27] So the new rules of order in unoccupied France failed to alter the main lines of American policy, although they did intensify certain aspects of a closely related problem—the question of the administration's attitude toward General Charles DeGaulle.

Despite its continued relations with Vichy, the American government had already given indirect support to the Free French movement. Since July 1941 Free French authorities had been permitted to buy nonmilitary goods in the United States, and for some time they had been receiving, through the British, Lend-Lease supplies of a military character.[28] This much could be done within the limits of established policy, and the administration had so far been able, without extreme difficulty, to resist the widespread popular demand that it undertake a great deal more on DeGaulle's behalf. But the effect of recent changes in unoccupied France was to enhance popular distrust of the Vichy regime throughout the United States and to make it increasingly difficult for Roosevelt and Hull to avoid altering their course in this respect. The difficulty of their position became especially evident after September 24, when DeGaulle and his adherents were permitted to organize the Free French National Committee in London. Great Britain lost no time according this group a considerable degree of recognition as the *de facto*

[25] William L. Langer, *Our Vichy Gamble* (New York: Alfred A. Knopf, 1947), pp. 184–185; and Hull, *Memoirs,* II, 1039.

[26] Langer, *Our Vichy Gamble,* p. 187.

[27] *Ibid.,* p. 190.   [28] *Ibid.,* p. 175. Cf. Hull, *Memoirs,* II, 1042.

authority in territories under its control, and there was a strong demand in the United States that the American government do likewise, severing its connection with the authoritarian regime of Marshal Pétain once and for all.[29]

But the considerations which had first dictated the Vichy policy of the United States had not yet been overruled. Hull and Roosevelt were still unprepared to vent their annoyance with Pétain by openly transferring the support of the American government to the Free French. So in spite of new tribulations and new suspicions, they resolved to adhere to their existing course until they found more tangible reasons for changing it.

III

From the beginning of the Soviet-German war the United States government afforded Russia all the diplomatic help of which it was capable. American efforts to discourage a Japanese attack on Siberia have been mentioned, and these were duplicated in Europe so far as possible. Hungary, Slovakia, Rumania, and Finland opened hostilities against the Soviet Union almost as soon as Germany. Diplomatic remonstrance with Hungary and Slovakia was obviously useless. But Finland and Rumania seemed to offer greater hope, and although both had received more than adequate provocation for striking at Russia, the United States did its best to secure their withdrawal from the war.

In answer to a question regarding its war objectives, the Rumanian government asserted that it merely planned to have Rumanian troops occupy Bessarabia and the other territory ceded to Russia the year before. Then they would take static defensive positions along the Dniester River.[30] The Rumanian aim, as stated, was certainly not unreasonable in view of all circumstances, and Hull appears to have accepted these assurances without further inquiry at the time.

Finnish policy involved more urgent considerations, however. Owing to its geographical position, Finland was easily capable of threatening the vital northern supply route which led from the Atlantic into the Arctic Ocean and thence to the Soviet ports of Murmansk and Archangel. If the Finnish Army should advance too far eastward, or if German

---

[29] Hull, *Memoirs*, II, 1042; and Langer, *Our Vichy Gamble*, p. 186.
[30] Hull, *Memoirs*, II, 977.

troops were allowed the extensive use of Finnish territory as a base of operations, British and American plans for supplying Russia with badly needed war materials would be seriously jeopardized.

Weighing this possibility well ahead of time, Great Britain as early as June 14 had threatened Finland with economic reprisals if the Finns took part in the expected war against Russia.[31]   Soviet pressure in London and Nazi pressure at Helsinki rapidly increased this tension, and Finland at the end of July initiated an exchange of views which led to a severance of diplomatic relations with the British government.[32]   Not yet totally unsympathetic toward Finland, the United States government remained passive well into August.   But when the Soviet Ambassador in Washington informed the State Department that his government was prepared to grant Finland some territorial concessions in return for its withdrawal from the war,[33] American policy entered a more active phase.

On August 18 Welles communicated the Russian proposal to the Finnish Minister, Hjalmar Procopé, but this action elicited no immediate response from Helsinki.   Following presidential instructions, Hull on September 8 expressed his pleasure at Finland's having recovered so much of the territory lost in 1939–1940, and then suggested to Procopé that his government cease hostilities at once.   When the other returned a vague answer, Hull pointed out that Rumania had undertaken to break off its advance as soon as Odessa fell, clearly implying that here was a suitable example for Finland.[34]   About the same time, he also brought pressure through the American Minister in Helsinki.   This tack seemed to promise better results at first.   Within a few days the Finnish Minister of Industry and Commerce stated that Finnish troops would hold on a defensive line shortly to be reached and would refuse to participate in a German attack on Leningrad.   Hull was so encouraged by this informal pledge that he declined for the time being to consider further action of any kind.   On September 17, indeed, he rejected a British proposal that he start Russo-Finnish peace negotiations by acting as middleman for a definite exchange of views.   When Finland still showed no sign of

[31] John H. Wuorinen, ed., *Finland and World War II, 1939–1944* (New York: Ronald Press Co., 1948), p. 129.   [32] *Ibid.*, pp. 131–132.

[33] David J. Dallin, *Soviet Russia's Foreign Policy, 1939–1942*, tr. Leon Denman (New Haven: Yale Univ. Press, 1942), p. 401.

[34] Hull, *Memoirs*, II, 978–979; and memorandum by Roosevelt, Sept. 6, 1941, Franklin D. Roosevelt, *F. D. R.: His Personal Letters, 1928–1945*, ed. Elliott Roosevelt (New York: Duell, Sloan, and Pearce, 1950), II, 1207–1208.

withdrawing from the war a fortnight later, however, his attitude became crisper; and on October 3 he delivered a number of sharp observations to Procopé which cleared the way for a much stronger offensive at Helsinki during the latter half of the month.[35]

But efforts to restrain Finland were scarcely more than incidental to the larger Russian problem. Here the great question was supply. The stopgap agency created by Roosevelt at the end of June to expedite shipments of war materials to the Soviet Union was supplanted a month later by a new section of the Division of Defense Aid Reports.[36] While it was informal and temporary at best, this authority operated on a somewhat larger scale than its predecessor. Hull saw Oumansky and General Golikov on August 4, about two weeks after the military mission headed by the latter reached the United States, and promised to do his best to see that Russia obtained the needed materials.[37] By September 11 the American government was planning details of a long-range supply program.

On that date Roosevelt, Hull, and Hopkins discussed credits with Oumansky, and the President straightway brought up a point that caused him no little anxiety. It would be very difficult, he explained, to secure Lend-Lease appropriations for Russia. The Soviet Union, unfortunately, was not very popular among certain groups in the United States who enjoyed great influence with Congress. A basic cause of this was Russia's attitude toward religion. The President noted that religious worship was permitted by the Soviet constitution of 1936, and he therefore suggested that the Russian government arrange to give this fact some favorable publicity in the United States before the impending Moscow Conference. Oumansky promised to see what he could do.[38]

Passing to another aspect of the supply question, Roosevelt warned the Soviet Ambassador that Congress would not grant Russia Lend-Lease funds unless the President could furnish official information concerning Russian assets and the extent of the Russian gold supply, together with an estimate of the barter exchange which the Soviet Union could offer. In this connection Roosevelt offered to buy large quantities of manganese, chromium, and other materials produced in Russia, with

---

[35] Hull, *Memoirs*, II, 979–980.

[36] John R. Deane, *The Strange Alliance: The Story of Our Efforts at Wartime Cooperation with Russia* (New York: Viking Press, 1947), pp. 87–88.

[37] Hull, *Memoirs*, II, 974.   [38] *Ibid.*, p. 977.

the understanding that they did not have to be delivered until after the war. Apparently worried by the amount of information requested, Oumansky replied that his government preferred a direct credit to Lend-Lease aid, although Lend-Lease arrangements would be quite acceptable if the other were not forthcoming. But whatever the ultimate form of the supply agreement, it was essential to enlarge the existing program without delay. As a first step, therefore, it was agreed that Russia should be granted an immediate credit of $75 million by the Reconstruction Finance Corporation for purchases in the United States.[39]

Meanwhile, preparations for the Moscow Conference progressed steadily. Because of his recent trip to the Russian capital, as well as his intimate connection with Lend-Lease activities, Hopkins seemed the logical choice to represent the United States in this assignment.[40] Owing to Hopkins' bad health, the President eventually substituted W. Averell Harriman, then serving as Lend-Lease expediter in London; but Hopkins still assumed general charge of the project from Washington. He was able to inform Churchill on September 9 that arrangements were practically complete. A plan showing what the United States could do for both Great Britain and Russia in the field of military supply up to June 30, 1942, would be ready in time for a preliminary Anglo-American conference about September 15. He suggested that the larger discussions in Moscow begin as soon as possible thereafter.[41]

Although he did not waver on the Russian supply program, Roosevelt had not forgotten his concern about its effect on American public opinion. Always sensitive in this regard, he was especially alert where religious feelings were involved. The misgivings with which he confronted Oumansky on September 11 were genuine, and his greatest single worry grew out of the traditional attitude of the Roman Catholic Church toward communism. No effort was made to keep this fact a secret. In a letter written about this same time to Brendan Bracken, the British Minister of Information, Hopkins stressed the anti-Russian sentiment among Catholic groups in the United States.[42] Thus the President's effort to soften Catholic opinion on the Soviet Union constituted another important aspect of his preparations for the Moscow Conference. He elected to work directly with the Vatican.

[39] *Ibid.*
[40] Robert E. Sherwood, *Roosevelt and Hopkins: An Intimate History* (New York: Harper and Bros., 1948), p. 359.
[41] *Ibid.*, p. 385.   [42] *Ibid.*, pp. 372–373.

A basis for such an effort had been prepared almost as soon as Germany launched its attack on the Soviet Union. Roosevelt's personal representative at the Holy See, Myron C. Taylor, had been absent in the United States at that time. But one of Taylor's subordinates, Harold Tittman, had called on both the Pope and the Cardinal Secretary of State during the first week in July to suggest on behalf of the American government that they do nothing which might be interpreted as favoring Germany in its new venture. Apparently they had reassured Tittman to some extent.[43] But Roosevelt was not satisfied, and, hoping to obtain commitments that were more direct or more tangible, he sent Taylor back to Rome early in September armed with a personal message to His Holiness.

This letter argued Russia's case in the most favorable terms possible. Stating that churches were now open in Russia, according to his best information, Roosevelt expressed the belief that there was "a real possibility that Russia may as a result of the present conflict recognize freedom of religion." Having blanketed the religious outlook in a pious hope, he turned without further ado to the hard realities of politics. He started by admitting that Russia was in the grip of a dictatorship "as rigid in its manner of being" as the Nazi government of Germany. But he went on to distinguish one from the other by pointing out that Russia was merely guilty of spreading communism through propaganda, while Germany aimed at world conquest by military aggression. Hence the survival of Russia would be less dangerous than a Nazi victory to both religion and humanity in general. "It is my belief," he concluded, "that the leaders of all churches in the United States should recognize these facts clearly and should not close their eyes to these basic questions and by their present attitude on this question directly assist Germany in her present objectives." [44]

Taylor handed this message to the Pope on September 9.[45] The latter's formal reply, dated September 20, was noncommittal.[46] Nor did his conversation with Taylor bring forth such a statement as Roosevelt probably wished. While the Vatican was not prepared to alter its stand against atheistic communism, said the Holy Father, it viewed the

[43] Camille M. Cianfarra, *The Vatican and the War* (New York: E. P. Dutton and Co., 1944), p. 272.

[44] Roosevelt to Pius XII, Sept. 3, 1941, Myron C. Taylor, ed., *Wartime Correspondence between President Roosevelt and Pope Pius XII* (New York: Macmillan Co., 1947), pp. 61–62.

[45] *Ibid.*, p. 58 n.   [46] See Pius XII to Roosevelt, Sept. 20, 1941, *ibid.*, p. 63.

Russian people, as always, with paternal affection.[47]   A more enthusiastic statement would have better served Roosevelt's immediate purpose, but the Pope, as events proved, had said enough.   Neither then nor later did Catholic authorities in this country express any very serious opposition to the new alignment,[48] and this particular worry gradually receded from the President's mind.

By late September necessary preparations for the Moscow Conference were complete.   Harriman, already in England, traveled to Russia with Lord Beaverbrook and other members of the British mission.   He was joined in the Soviet capital by a group of American experts who had flown directly from the United States, and the crucial three-power talks got under way on September 28, the approximate date suggested by Hopkins in his own conversations with Stalin at the end of July.   The meetings lasted three days and included talks at several different levels.   But the various subcommittees of Russian, British, and American specialists were concerned only with details.   All the real decisions of the parley grew out of the trio of long conversations held by Stalin, Beaverbrook, and Harriman.[49]

In their opening encounter with the Russian leader Harriman and Beaverbrook were given a comprehensive survey of Axis and satellite strength on the Russian front, a generalized list of the Red Army's most urgent needs, and a few comments on possible joint operations.   For the moment at least, Stalin did not seem especially anxious regarding a second front in the west, but he urged the value of having a British expeditionary force in the Ukraine.   When Beaverbrook replied that British forces then accumulating in Iran might be sent into the Caucasus, Stalin became impatient and made it clear that he did not regard such a move as having much pertinence to immediate needs.   Nor did he show a great deal of interest in Beaverbrook's proposal for staff conversations between their two countries.   Instead, he began talking of the eventual peace settlement and German reparations; but the other hurriedly quelled this discussion by pointing out that the war was not yet won.   Harriman brought up the possibility of delivering American bombers to Russia by way of Alaska and Siberia.   He gathered, however, that Stalin did not care to have American pilots flying over this route because he feared complications with Japan.   Harriman also mentioned Roosevelt's concern about the status of religion in the Soviet Union.

[47] *Ibid.,* p. 58 n.
[48] Cf. Sherwood, *Roosevelt and Hopkins,* p. 398.   [49] *Ibid.,* pp. 385–387.

But as his host seemed disinclined to explore this topic, he volunteered to set forth the American attitude in a memorandum.[50]

That swift alteration of mood from cordiality to brusqueness which had already become a staple of Russian diplomatic procedure was observable the next day in their second meeting. Stalin seemed preoccupied and impatient almost to the point of discourtesy. As a result, little was accomplished. But he was genial once more at their final talk on September 30. Beaverbrook opened the session by reading a memorandum which listed the supply commitments that Great Britain and the United States were prepared to make at once. Stalin received the list with enthusiasm, and the meeting continued in an atmosphere of growing warmth.[51] The Russian leader engaged Beaverbrook in a spirited discussion of European politics, suggesting that the Anglo-Russian alliance be extended into the postwar period. In answer to Harriman's request for his views on the Far East, he expressed the belief that Japan could be weaned away from its Axis connection. Finally, he brought the talk to a harmonious close by inviting his guests to dinner.[52]

The results of the conference were embodied in a "confidential protocol" signed by Harriman, Beaverbrook, and Molotov on October 1. It was primarily a supply agreement by which the United States and the United Kingdom undertook to furnish the Soviet Union with a broad selection of armaments and other materials, from destroyers and airplanes to army boots and medical items.[53] The Russian-aid program could now begin in earnest, and Hopkins immediately directed Colonel Philip Faymonville, a Russian-speaking supply expert who had come to Moscow as a member of the Harriman mission, to remain in that city as permanent Lend-Lease supervisor. This choice was dictated by two considerations: Faymonville's thorough knowledge of the Russian language and his belief in the utility of the new supply agreement. Faymonville was one of the few American officers who, at this time, agreed with Hopkins in thinking that the Red Army woulc be able to stop the German advance.[54]

Hoping to obtain a closer view of domestic conditions in Russia, Har-

[50] Sherwood, *Roosevelt and Hopkins*, pp. 387–388.

[51] *Ibid.*, pp. 388–389.   [52] *Ibid.*, pp. 390–391.

[53] Confidential protocol, Oct. 1, 1941, United States, Department of State, *Soviet Supply Protocols* (Washington, D. C.: U. S. Govt. Printing Office, 1948), pp. 3–8, 9–12; and Harriman to Roosevelt (undated, but transmitted Oct. 29, 1941), MS Roosevelt Papers (Secretary's File, Box 71). For Churchill's comments on this agreement, see Winston S. Churchill, *The Grand Alliance* (Boston: Houghton Mifflin Co., 1950), pp. 470–471.   [54] Sherwood, *Roosevelt and Hopkins*, p. 395.

riman did not leave Moscow until several days after the conference ended. Notwithstanding the rebuff he had drawn from Stalin in the course of their first meeting, he used some of this time in striving to impress Soviet officials with the importance of conciliating American religious opinion. But the results of his efforts, on the whole, were not encouraging. Neither Stalin nor Molotov seemed greatly interested in what he had to say; and although Oumansky (who had been superseded in Washington by Maxim Litvinov) assured him that the Kremlin's liberality on this point would be given favorable publicity in the United States, Harriman was never optimistic. According to the best information he could obtain, worshipers were no longer persecuted directly. But the denial of political and economic advancement to believers, close scrutiny by the secret police, and the deliberate educational policy of the Russian government kept religious observance within narrow bounds. Practically no one except women, people over thirty, and persons who were not members of the Communist Party attended church, while youths under sixteen were denied all forms of religious instruction. In Harriman's view, the political philosophy of the Soviet regime was fundamentally incompatible with religious belief. Moscow might give out reassuring statements, he thought, but he doubted that conditions inside Russia would be greatly altered.[55]

To an extent, his fears already had substance. The final communiqué issued by the Moscow Conference on October 1 ended with a statement that the three participating governments were resolved "after annihilation of the Nazi tyranny" to establish a peace which could "enable the world to live in security in its own territory free from fear or need." That this formula omitted two of the Four Freedoms—freedom of speech and freedom of religion—was not lost upon some of those present.[56]

IV

Between mid-August and the end of September American participation in the Atlantic war became virtually complete. The stage had been set in June by Roosevelt's promise to furnish escorts over the western half of the transatlantic convoy route. This undertaking had been partially met in the order of July 11 regarding American convoys to Iceland.

[55] Memorandum by Harriman, *ibid.*, pp. 391–393.

[56] Henry C. Cassidy, *Moscow Dateline, 1941–1943* (Boston: Houghton Mifflin Co., 1943), p. 134.

But the clause which entitled foreign ships to join American and Icelandic vessels in such movements was suspended indefinitely, and Roosevelt took no immediate action on his later pledge to include the whole of Iceland in the patrol area covered by the Atlantic Fleet. Thus the Navy was still committed to many responsibilities not yet assumed when the President returned from Argentia.

After the Atlantic Conference, however, new decisions were made quickly. On August 25, 1941, Roosevelt supplemented Admiral King's Operation Plan No. 5 with an order directing the Fleet to "destroy surface raiders" which attacked or threatened shipping along the route between North America and Iceland. The advance was again prospective, for the operation of this order was suspended until the earlier provision relating to escort for ships that were not of American or Icelandic registry should become effective.[57] But its somewhat elastic terms were clarified on September 3 in another directive which explained that hostile forces should be deemed a menace if they entered the general area of the route to Iceland or if they infringed the neutrality zone established by the Declaration of Panama; and on the same day the patrol area of the Atlantic Fleet—heretofore bounded on the east by the 26th meridian —was given a large bulge at its northern extremity which veered eastward at 53 degrees north latitude, reached a point 10 degrees west at 65 degrees north, and ran on to the Pole along the 10th meridian.[58] This brought Iceland within the patrol area by a safe margin and included another good slice of the German operational zone of March 26. Further specific directions regarding escort techniques were given in Admiral King's Operation Plan No. 7, issued September 1.[59]

Within two weeks of the President's meeting at sea, therefore, his Atlantic program was in effect rounded out. Detailed orders which broadened the scope and deepened the intensity of both convoy and patrol operations were now in hand, awaiting only a date of execution. As soon as this was determined, the United States Navy would become a full partner in the conduct of Atlantic hostilities, though still subject to certain geographical restrictions and unable to claim the belligerent rights which only a declaration of war could bring.

Another project, equally significant of Roosevelt's determination to

[57] Stark's testimony, Jan. 3, 1946, *Pearl Harbor Hearings*, pt. 5, p. 2295.
[58] *Ibid.*
[59] Samuel Eliot Morison, *The Battle of the Atlantic, 1939–1943* (Boston: Little, Brown, and Co., 1947), pp. 84–85.

allow Germany no breathing space, was initiated at the same time. Owing to the vulnerable character of the important supply route leading from the Persian Gulf to the Soviet Union through Iran, Great Britain requested the Iranian government, in August, to expel some three thousand Germans known to be present in that country. When the Shah temporized, Russian and British troops entered his territory, seized the railways, and took control of the more important oil deposits. By the end of the month Churchill was able to give the President an optimistic report on conditions in the Middle East. But stronger British forces in that area were an obvious necessity, and the Prime Minister on September 1 asked American help in moving two divisions—some forty thousand men—from the United Kingdom to the head of the Persian Gulf.[60] This task demanded the employment of United States Army transports. To use its own ships in moving a large consignment of belligerent troops halfway around the world to a recognized theater of operations was a serious step for the American government to contemplate, but Roosevelt was now shedding hesitations with great rapidity. He submitted the proposal to Stark, King, and other naval authorities on September 5 and obtained a favorable reaction immediately. It was decided that transports necessary for the movement of twenty thousand men—half the number mentioned by Churchill—should be made available to the British. It was also decided that these ships should fly the American flag and be manned by their own crews while engaged in this mission.[61]

A few days later the *Greer* incident was revealed to the nation. According to official testimony, the United States destroyer *Greer,* en route to Iceland and well inside the German zone of operations, was informed by a British plane on the morning of September 4 that a German submarine lay some ten miles directly ahead. Following standard orders, the *Greer* proceeded to locate and trail the U-boat by means of her underwater equipment and to broadcast its movements. About an hour later the British plane, having remained in the neighborhood, dropped four depth charges and left. Shortly after noon, when the chase was more than three hours old, the U-boat suddenly altered its course and fired a torpedo at the destroyer. The missile failed to reach its target, and the *Greer* retaliated with a pattern of eight depth charges. A few minutes later, the U-boat launched a second torpedo, which also missed.

[60] Churchill, *The Grand Alliance,* p. 492.
[61] Memorandum by Hopkins, Sept. 6, 1941, in Sherwood, *Roosevelt and Hopkins,* p. 375; and Churchill, *The Grand Alliance,* p. 493.

The *Greer* lost contact with her quarry at this point. But she reëstablished it after a two-hour search, whereupon she tossed out another series of depth charges. Although the search was continued until 6:40 that evening, the *Greer* failed to discover any further trace of her adversary. She then resumed her voyage to Iceland.[62]

As far as immediate damage was concerned, the *Greer* episode was no more serious than the *Niblack's* encounter with a submarine the previous April. But since it became one of those momentous trifles which so often form the visible turning points in international relations, it is important to see the affair in its true light. From the standpoint of immediate circumstances, the *Greer's* conduct was certainly no less aggressive than that of the U-boat. Having been notified of the submarine's presence by a belligerent plane, she deliberately searched until she found the craft and trailed it for more than three hours, broadcasting its movements regularly, before it struck back. During this period, the British plane dropped four depth charges. While it might be argued that the *Greer* refrained from using depth charges until such action was required in her own defense, it must be acknowledged that her own actions contributed directly to the situation which imposed that necessity upon her. Those actions, moreover, were based not on the hurried decisions of her commander but on orders which had applied to the whole Fleet since April.[63] In final analysis, therefore, the *Greer* incident was the logical outcome of mutually hostile German and American naval policies. Together, they rendered such clashes inevitable.

The use which the President made of the episode was likewise the outgrowth of larger policy. According to Hopkins, Roosevelt had been planning, at least since the middle of August, to go before the country some time in September with an explanation of his broadening Atlantic policy. No date was set, but the *Greer* incident furnished such an opportune background for the sort of message the President wished to deliver that he chose to act at once.[64] A brief delay was occasioned by the death of his mother, and he did not give his "shoot-on-sight" speech until September 11. But he was still able to exploit the *Greer's* adventure to the full. Combining indignation with defiance, he castigated

[62] Statement by Stark with regard to the *Greer* incident, World Peace Foundation, *Documents on American Foreign Relations, 1941–1942*, ed. S. Shepard Jones and Denys P. Myers (Boston: World Peace Foundation, 1942), p. 95.

[63] This was emphasized in Stark's report (*ibid.*, p. 96).

[64] Memorandum by Hopkins, Sept. 13, 1941, in Sherwood, *Roosevelt and Hopkins*, p. 370.

Germany's methods of naval warfare at appropriate length and made it clear that American naval forces in the Atlantic would henceforth fight fire with fire, destroying enemy vessels wherever they were encountered.[65] Two days later the Atlantic Fleet received an order, effective September 16, to protect ships of any nationality between North America and Iceland, including convoys in which no American vessels were present.[66] This was the execution clause specified in the various direc-. tives issued over the past two months, and it brought the United States Navy automatically into the war.

Any doubts on this point were resolved by the events of the next fortnight. On September 14 the crew of the Coast Guard cutter *Northland* captured and destroyed a German radio station on the coast of Greenland, after seizing its supply ship. The captured Germans were held as prisoners, the first ones taken by American forces in the Second World War.[67] The term "United Kingdom" was redefined by executive action on September 15 to permit American vessels to carry arms to British overseas colonies and possessions without contravening the neutrality act.[68] The first transatlantic convoy, as distinguished from those bound for Iceland, to be escorted by United States warships left Halifax, Nova Scotia, on September 16.[69] Hull chose September 19 as the date for presenting Germany with a claim for damages of nearly $3 million arising out of the sinking of the *Robin Moor*.[70] He received his answer a week later when the German chargé d'affaires in Washington refused to transmit this demand to Berlin on the ground that it would not beget an appropriate reply from his government.[71]

The same day, September 26, all recent orders affecting United States naval policy in the Atlantic were drawn together in a broad new summary known as Western Hemisphere Defense Plan No. 5. Within the American patrol zone—as extended, of course, by the order of September 3—United States forces were directed to protect all American and foreign ships (except German and Italian) by escorting, covering, and

[65] Address by the President, Sept. 11, 1941, United States, Department of State, *Peace and War: United States Foreign Policy, 1931–1941* (Washington, D. C.: U. S. Govt. Printing Office, 1943), p. 743.

[66] Stark's testimony, Jan. 3, 1946, *Pearl Harbor Hearings*, pt. 5, p. 2295.

[67] Walter Karig (with Earl Burton and Stephen L. Freeland), *Battle Report: The Atlantic War* (New York: Farrar and Rinehart, 1946), pp. 35–37.

[68] Hull, *Memoirs*, II, 1046.   [69] Morison, *The Battle of the Atlantic*, p. 86.

[70] Hull to Thomsen, Sept. 19, 1941, United States, Department of State, *Department of State Bulletin* (Washington, D. C.: U. S. Govt. Printing Office, 1939——), V (Nov. 8, 1941), 364.   [71] Thomsen to Hull, Sept. 26, 1941, *ibid.*

patrolling, and to trail merchant vessels suspected of assisting hostile warships or aircraft. While the order pointed out that the United States was not at war "in the legal sense," [72] the fact that such a reminder was considered necessary spoke eloquently of the new situation.

That the Navy was compelled to operate without benefit of a formal declaration of war did not constitute the only restriction upon United States policy in the Atlantic, however. Lend-Lease had adequately by-passed the antiloan provisions of the joint resolution of November 4, 1939, but other parts of that law were still effective. A few, like the sections providing for government supervision of arms exports and imports and the collection of charitable funds for belligerents, the State Department had always wished to retain.[73] But others—particularly sections 2 and 3, which forbade American merchant ships to enter combat zones, and section 6, which prohibited them from carrying armament—raised genuine obstacles to the most efficient use of the American merchant marine. Specifically, sections 2 and 3 kept American cargo ships from entering ports in the United Kingdom, in European Russia, and in the Mediterranean, while section 6 rendered them incapable of self-defense no matter where they went. Of course, the provisions relating to combat zones had been fathered by the Roosevelt administration. But in persuading congressional isolationists to give up the arms embargo they had long since fulfilled their main purpose. Judged by any standard, moreover, the current situation differed greatly from that of November 1939. Fully aware of this, Hull had advised President Roosevelt as early as June 1941 to begin sounding congressional leaders out on the possibility of revising the neutrality act once more.[74]

Acting on the Secretary's advice, Roosevelt formed the opinion that any major proposal for changing this law would evoke prolonged debate but that there was enough favorable sentiment in both houses of Congress to give revision a fair chance of success. In consequence, a number of amendments involving different degrees of change were drawn up and made ready for use by September 24. But caution prevailed thereafter; for instead of trying to deal with all three offending sections at one time, it was decided by the beginning of October to concentrate first upon section 6, leaving the sections regarding combat zones for subsequent action.[75] Thus preparations were made to abolish

[72] Stark's testimony, Jan. 3, 1946, *Pearl Harbor Hearings*, pt. 5, p. 2296.
[73] Hull, *Memoirs*, II, 1047.
[74] *Ibid.*, p. 1046.   [75] *Ibid.*, pp. 1046–1047.

vexatious restrictions still hedging the use of the American merchant marine.

V

Although War Minister Tojo had reluctantly agreed when Konoye first broached his plan for direct negotiation with Roosevelt, he and other military leaders were pressing for its abandonment by the end of August 1941.[76] That Konoye bore a large share of responsibility for the course of the Japanese government since 1937 cannot be doubted, but he apparently did what he could to avoid war in the fall of 1941. His progress was negligible, however. Another Imperial Conference met on September 6 to lay additional plans for southward expansion, and while it did not rule out further efforts by the Premier to arrange a meeting with Roosevelt, it certainly placed a definite limit upon them. For it approved a schedule of "minimum" demands and "maximum" concessions already drawn up by the Army and Navy, and decided that final war preparations should be made if there was no reasonable prospect of a settlement on these terms by the early part of October. Apparently expecting the United States to influence Great Britain, this program required Washington and London to forswear all aid to China, leaving Japan to settle the China Incident on its own terms. In addition, the United States and Great Britain would have to agree to establish no military bases in the Dutch East Indies, China, or Siberia; to undertake not to increase their existing military forces in the Far East; to restore trade relations with Japan; and to assist Japan in establishing closer economic relations with Thailand and the Indies. Japan was prepared to guarantee the neutrality of the Philippines immediately and to withdraw its troops from Indo-China as soon as a "just peace" was established in the Orient. Until such a peace could be realized, however, Japan would keep its troops in Indo-China, merely promising not to use that country as a base of operations against anyone but the Chinese.[77]

Whether Konoye truly believed that Roosevelt might be persuaded to accept these conditions it is impossible to say, but he did not relax his efforts to meet the President. Inviting Grew to a private dinner the same evening (September 6), he mounted a new offensive and asked that

[76] Konoye memoirs, *Pearl Harbor Hearings*, pt. 20, exhibit 173, p. 4004.
[77] *Ibid*. and pp. 4022–4023.

his statements be transmitted directly to Roosevelt. He allowed Grew to understand that he accepted the four principles laid down by Hull in April as a basis for a Japanese-American settlement: (1) respect for the sovereignty and territorial integrity of all nations, (2) noninterference in the domestic affairs of other countries, (3) respect for the equality of all nations, and (4) nondisturbance of the *status quo* in the Pacific except as it might be altered by peaceful means. Konoye then resorted to still another dubious guarantee, for he assured the Ambassador that his Cabinet was strong enough to adhere to a peaceful program and stated that any commitment given would be observed. Repeatedly stressing the importance of time, he said that he desired as ardently as ever to meet Roosevelt.[78]

His words were fair but poorly scheduled. For September 6 was also the date chosen for Nomura to offer Hull a new memorandum fondly characterized as Japan's response to the American wish for some kind of preliminary agreement. A substantial paraphrase of the demands recently approved by the Imperial Conference, this note completely destroyed any effect that Konoye's supposed acceptance of Hull's four principles might otherwise have had.[79] Speaking to the British chargé d'affaires two days later, Hull was notably pessimistic. In his opinion, there was only about one chance in fifty of reaching an agreement with Japan; the primary objective now was to keep Tokyo as long as possible from initiating further aggression.[80]

Although Hull certainly offered him no encouragement on September 6, Nomura managed to keep up his spirits. On September 17 he cabled Tokyo that Roosevelt was prepared to meet Konoye "if the preliminary arrangements could be made."[81] Taken literally, his words were probably sound enough, but their whole context revealed his inability to appreciate the difference between his government's reading of that phrase and the stipulations envisaged by Hull and Roosevelt. He was only a little clearer on September 22 when he assured his superiors that if Japan were to "give up forceful aggressions, Japanese-American trade relations could be restored, and the United States would even go so far as to render economic assistance . . . ."[82] While this was also

[78] Memorandum by Grew, Sept. 6, 1941, *Foreign Relations: Japan, 1931-1941*, II, 604-606.
[79] Draft proposal presented by Nomura, Sept. 6, 1941, *ibid.*, pp. 608-609.
[80] Hull, *Memoirs*, II, 1029-1030.
[81] Nomura to Gaimudaijin, Sept. 17, 1941, *Pearl Harbor Hearings*, pt. 12, exhibit 1, p. 28.   [82] Nomura to Toyoda, Sept. 22, 1941, *ibid.*, p. 31.

true as a general proposition, it stated an issue that had to be worked out in highly specific terms, and the Japanese government had fully demonstrated its reluctance to be specific except where its own demands were concerned.

On September 22 Toyoda handed Grew another set of Japanese proposals for liquidating the China Incident. But these contained nothing new. Substantially a repetition of earlier offers, this memorandum was no more acceptable than any of its numerous forebears. Nevertheless, Toyoda took advantage of the opportunity to press again for a leaders' conference.[83] On September 25,[84] and again two days later,[85] Grew received further proddings on this subject. Although a preliminary agreement seemed as far distant as ever, reiteration had its effect; and on September 29, after another interview with Konoye, Grew sent Hull a long report urging serious consideration of the conference idea. The Ambassador also warned that the failure of a conference to materialize might cause the downfall of the Konoye government and the formation of a military dictatorship that would have no desire to avoid war with the United States.[86]

Grew, in truth, was seriously disappointed by Washington's attitude. In his view, the United States had everything to gain and nothing to lose at the proposed conference. He believed further that Konoye was sincere in his professed desire to find a basis for settlement, and it was the Ambassador's best opinion that the Konoye government, if given the chance it requested, would find the strength to control the dissatisfaction of the extremists and persuade the country's leading elements to accept a solution that would make war unnecessary. The demand for an advance commitment "wholly satisfactory to the United States" in principle and detail was, to Grew's mind, completely unrealistic.[87]

Because they were not given full details, Japan's European partners

---

[83] Memorandum by Grew, Sept. 22, 1941, *Foreign Relations: Japan, 1931–1941*, II, 631.

[84] Grew, *Ten Years*, p. 435.

[85] Memorandum by Grew, Sept. 27, 1941, *Foreign Relations: Japan, 1931–1941*, II, 642.

[86] Grew to Hull, Sept. 29, 1941, *ibid.*, pp. 649–650.

[87] Joseph C. Grew, *Turbulent Era; A Diplomatic Record of Forty Years, 1904–1945*, ed. Walter Johnson (Boston: Houghton Mifflin Co., 1952), II, 1313, 1350–1354. The Department of State's thoughtful and well-informed Economic Adviser, Herbert Feis, does not concur in this view of the leaders' conference proposal. Feis believes that the records made available since the war neither "confirm the opinion that Konoye was prepared, without reserve or trickery, to observe the rules set down by Hull" nor indicate "that he would have been able to do so, even though a respite was granted and he was allowed to grade the retreat gently." See Herbert Feis, *The Road to Pearl Harbor* (Princeton, N. J.: Princeton Univ. Press, 1950), p. 275.

took these negotiations quite seriously. As early as August 29, the German Ambassador in Tokyo asked Toyoda whether Konoye's overtures to Roosevelt implied any weakening of Japan's affection for the Tripartite Pact. On September 30 the Japanese Ambassador in Rome reported that Italy was suspicious.[88] The next day the Japanese Ambassador to Germany informed his government that a similar feeling existed in Berlin. German leaders no longer concealed their annoyance at Japan's independent negotiations with the United States. If Tokyo persisted in such a course, he warned, no one could tell "what steps Germany might take without consulting Japan." [89]

But Roosevelt and Hull were unimpressed by any part of the Japanese effort. Despite its concern over American military weakness in the Far East, at least a portion of the General Staff agreed with them. In a memorandum prepared on October 2 the Acting Assistant Chief of Staff, G–2, expressed the view that no useful purpose could be served by a leaders' conference unless Japan would commit itself in advance of such a meeting to withdraw from the Axis. Instead of recommending the acceptance of Konoye's proposal, therefore, this estimate advised the President to apply still greater pressure in the Far East.[90] The same day, Hull gave Nomura a blanket reply to the various statements and proposals which had dribbled in from Tokyo over the past month. Pointing out that Japan's attitude had hardened steadily since the beginning of September, he suggested that the two countries open a new series of conversations and a new effort to reach agreement; when agreement in principle was achieved, the leaders' conference could be held. He was particularly eager to have Japan manifest its good intentions by withdrawing its troops from China and Indo-China at once.[91]

Finally convinced that the limit had been reached, Nomura answered that he did not think his government could go any further at this time.[92]

[88] Memorandum by Amau, Aug. 29, 1941, *Pearl Harbor Hearings*, pt. 18, exhibit 132–A, p. 2949; and Japanese Embassy in Rome to the Japanese Foreign Office, Sept. 30, 1941, *ibid.*, pt. 12, exhibit 1, pp. 44–45.

[89] Japanese Embassy in Berlin to the Japanese Foreign Office, Oct. 1, 1941, *ibid.*, pp. 48–49.

[90] Memorandum by Kroner, Oct. 2, 1941, *ibid.*, pt. 14, exhibit 33–A, pp. 1385–1388.

[91] Oral statement by Hull, Oct. 2, 1941, *Foreign Relations: Japan, 1931–1941*, II, 659–661.

[92] Memorandum by Ballantine, Oct. 2, 1941, *ibid.*, p. 655.

VI

In the six weeks following the Atlantic Conference the United States moved perceptibly closer to war. Talks with Japan were resumed on a note of stern warning against further changes in the Far Eastern *status quo,* a warning which hinted clearly that new Japanese advances in the Orient might lead to military action by the United States. Once resumed, negotiations continued, but they were on topics remote from the basic issues in the controversy. Outwardly, at least, the main question now centered about procedure. Japan began and ended each exchange of views by emphasizing Konoye's desire for a conference with Roosevelt, while the United States adhered just as consistently to its demand for a preliminary agreement. From the first, Hull was inclined to view his work as little more than a delaying action, and it was plain by October 2 that this phase of discussion had worn itself out.

American relations with Spain tended to grow slightly better as the prospect of new economic discussions was revealed. The increasingly totalitarian aspect of the Vichy regime, on the other hand, threatened to complicate relations with France, but with respect to neither country did American policy undergo a definite change. Coöperation with Russia broadened rapidly, encouraged to some extent by the diplomatic pressure which Hull exerted against Rumania and Finland, but aided more directly by the speed and generosity of the Russian-aid program. Moscow's less than satisfactory response to Roosevelt's views on the religious question had no immediate bearing on larger policy, and Stalin's aggressive concern over postwar questions, while perfectly evident, was still only a small cloud on a distant horizon.

In its dealings with Japan and Russia the United States was merely preparing for action. In the Atlantic, however, the country grappled with action itself. The Navy's patrol area was enlarged to include Iceland. It assumed its full place in transatlantic convoy operations. Shooting orders were given and openly avowed. Definite plans were made for new revisions in the neutrality act.

Public opinion, moreover, seemed generally to approve these developments. By September 2 no less than 52 per cent of those interviewed by the American Institute of Public Opinion favored using the American Navy to convoy war materials to Britain. By the end of the month 46 per cent thought the provision relating to combat zones should be withdrawn from the neutrality act, while only 40 per cent definitely opposed such a change.[93] That the American people were not yet thoroughly acclimated to their new friendship with Russia was indicated by a *Fortune* poll taken in October, when those expressing opinions were almost equally divided on the question of whether the Soviet government was a more admirable institution than the German government.[94] Some confusion also existed with regard to Japan. In October, according to a *Fortune* survey, 43 per cent of the population was not greatly exercised by any direct threat Japan might offer to the United States.[95] But a month later 64 per cent of those approached by the Gallup organization thought the United States should take immediate steps to keep Japan from becoming any more powerful. Even though 79 per cent of those interviewed during October opposed an immediate declaration of war against any country,[96] it was quite evident that Roosevelt, on specific issues, was not dangerously ahead of public opinion. If the American people were not growing more belligerent, they at least seemed more resigned to the inevitable.

[93] *Public Opinion Quarterly*, V (Winter 1941), 680.
[94] *Ibid.*, VI (Spring 1942), 152.   [95] *Ibid.*, p. 150.   [96] *Ibid.*, pp. 163–164.

CHAPTER XI

Releasing the Stops

I

WHEN NOMURA TOLD HULL ON OCTOBER 2, 1941, THAT HE DID NOT THINK Japan would go beyond its latest proposal in an effort to obtain a settlement with the United States, he was being no more pessimistic than the situation warranted. For Prince Konoye was already seeking his colleagues' permission to better the Japanese offer of September 6, and his lack of success did not belie the ambassadorial prediction.

Fully aware that the time limit set by the Imperial Conference was nearing its end, Konoye had opened talks with various members of the Cabinet late in September. Blocked at every turn by earlier decisions, he apparently hoped to secure their agreement to some new concession which might satisfy Washington's demand for a preliminary understanding and dispose Roosevelt to accept his invitation to a conference.[1] Thus Hull's note of October 2 merely spurred him to fresh exertions, and the suggestion that Japan withdraw its troops from China and Indo-China as an earnest of good faith pointed the way to compromise.[2] Without delay, therefore, Konoye tried to set at least one foot upon the indicated path by arguing for a partial evacuation of China. He saw Emperor Hirohito on October 4, and then conferred with members of the Japanese High Command. The next day he talked with War Minister Tojo—who, as acknowledged leader of the militarists, represented the chief hurdle he needed to cross. But his efforts were not productive. On October 7 Tojo informed him that the Army would find it "difficult . . . to submit" to any kind of withdrawal from China. Confronted by this dictum, Konoye took refuge during the next three

---

[1] Konoye memoirs, United States, Congress, Joint Committee on Investigation of Pearl Harbor Attack, *Hearings Pursuant to S. Con. Res. 27, Authorizing Investigation of Attack on Pearl Harbor, Dec. 7, 1941, and Events and Circumstances Relating Thereto* (79th Cong., 1st and 2nd sess.) (Washington, D. C.: U. S. Govt. Printing Office, 1946), pt. 20, exhibit 173, p. 4008. Cited henceforth as *Pearl Harbor Hearings*.

[2] Nomura to Toyoda, Oct. 3, 1941, *ibid.,* pt. 12, exhibit 1, p. 53.

days in talks with the Navy Minister and the Foreign Minister on "methods of avoiding a crisis." [3]

But Konoye was held prisoner by the inflexible decisions of September 6 and could think of nothing better than to let Washington make the next move. Ignoring the scores of notes which already lay in his files, Toyoda thereupon asked Grew to obtain a statement of just what the American government wanted. He attempted to justify this surprising request with the assertion that Nomura had been unable to provide the desired information from his post in the American capital. Observing that Nomura seemed very fatigued, he also mentioned the possibility of sending an experienced diplomat to assist the Ambassador.[4]

Having created a temporary diversion, Konoye held a further series of conferences on October 12, 13, and 14 to discuss the general question of peace and war. The Premier made it clear to his associates that he wished to continue negotiations with the United States as long as possible, and he reëmphasized his desire to withdraw some troops from China. He was supported by Toyoda and, somewhat less vigorously, by the Navy Minister. But Tojo was adamant. To withdraw troops from China, he argued, would not only destroy the fighting spirit of the Army; it would invite further highhanded acts on the part of the United States. Such negotiations would lead nowhere, and Japan could pursue this forlorn hope only at the risk of losing its best military opportunities. The sole result of the talks was Tojo's suggestion on October 14 that the Cabinet resign en masse to clear the way for a thoroughgoing reëxamination of policy. He indicated that he thought Prince Higashikuni, Chief of the General Staff, would be a suitable choice to head the new government.[5]

Konoye offered no further argument. He saw the Emperor again on October 15 and explained Tojo's stand. Hirohito was generally noncommittal, and he did nothing to impede the course of events except to voice a doubt concerning Higashikuni's availability as Premier. With war in the offing, he did not think it was the proper time for a member of the Imperial Family to assume direct responsibility in the government. Konoye discussed the matter that evening with the Prince himself, but again he could obtain no immediate decision. Therefore, he

---

[3] Konoye memoirs, *Pearl Harbor Hearings*, pt. 20, exhibit 173, pp. 4008–4009.

[4] Grew to Hull, Oct. 10, 1941, United States, Department of State, *Papers Relating to the Foreign Relations of the United States: Japan, 1931–1941* (Washington, D. C.: U. S. Govt. Printing Office, 1943), II, 678–679.

[5] Konoye memoirs, *Pearl Harbor Hearings*, pt. 20, exhibit 173, pp. 4009–4010.

let events take their course. Together with every member of his Cabinet, he resigned the morning of October 16.[6] The next day General Tojo received the Emperor's command to form a new government. The significance of this change was immediately clear despite Japanese efforts to keep it hidden. Konoye hastened to assure Grew that the new Cabinet would not break off conversations with the United States; [7] and the Ambassador received additional enlightenment to the effect that Tojo had been appointed Premier because, as a general still on the active list, he would be able to quell the Army's discontent with the policy of peaceful negotiation to which the government was still committed.[8] Nomura, in Washington, expressed a similar view to Lord Halifax.[9] But messages then passing between the Japanese Foreign Office and himself belied this comfortable assessment. An intercepted cablegram from Toyoda, dated October 17, gave a full explanation of the disagreement leading to Konoye's resignation. Although Toyoda indicated that talks with the American government would continue,[10] Nomura's return message of October 18 (likewise intercepted) asking to be relieved of his Washington assignment on the ground that he felt unable to accomplish anything more in the United States did not indicate that the Ambassador himself placed much value on this assurance.[11] That the militarists were now in power could not be doubted, and the proposed leaders' conference, the trade-mark of Konoye's diplomacy since the early part of August, dropped immediately from sight.

There followed a lull of slightly more than two weeks while the Japanese government prepared its next move. Just what this might be was uncertain, but Grew lost no time before discounting the peaceful intentions of the new Cabinet. On November 3 he pointed out the "shortsightedness of underestimating Japan's obvious preparations to implement an alternative program in the event the peace program fails" and added that war might come on Japan's initiative "with dangerous and dramatic suddenness." [12]

The next day, November 4, Grew was apprised by the Japanese For-

[6] *Ibid.,* pp. 4010–4011.
[7] Konoye to Grew, Oct. 16, 1941, *Foreign Relations: Japan, 1931–1941,* II, 691.
[8] Memorandum by Grew, Oct. 25, 1941, *ibid.,* pp. 697–698.
[9] Memorandum by Halifax, Oct. 16, 1941, *Pearl Harbor Hearings,* pt. 19, exhibit 158, p. 3464.
[10] Toyoda to Nomura, Oct. 17, 1941, *ibid.,* pt. 12, exhibit 1, p. 76.
[11] Nomura to Togo, Oct. 18, 1941, *ibid.,* p. 79.
[12] Grew to Hull, Nov. 3, 1941, *Foreign Relations: Japan, 1931–1941,* II, 704.

eign Office that Saburu Kurusu, a career diplomat and former Ambassador to Germany, would join Nomura in Washington to assist with forthcoming negotiations. In this connection he was asked to have the departure of the Pan-American clipper from Hong Kong postponed two days in order that Kurusu might board her for the United States.[13] On November 5 Nomura finally yielded to the solicitations of the new Foreign Minister, Shigenori Togo, and agreed, somewhat reluctantly, to stay at his post.[14] Both cast and setting were now complete. Only a script was needed to open the final act.

Already the script was being prepared. Togo had informed Nomura on October 21 that Japan could do nothing more except urge the United States to reconsider its views as to what a settlement should contain. He asked the Ambassador to suggest at "an opportune moment" that Japan could not afford to spend much more time in these discussions, and told him to emphasize Tokyo's desire for a new American counterproposal, but he gave no other specific instructions.[15] When the counselor of the Japanese Embassy attempted to press these points with Welles on October 24, the Under Secretary merely stated that the American position had been made clear and that no further counterproposals were required.[16] On October 30 Togo approached Grew with a plea for coöperation in his efforts to bring Japanese-American conversations to a speedy and successful end.[17] But it was not until November 4 that anything definite emerged.

On that date Togo favored Nomura with another prolix survey of the dangerous relationship between Japan and the United States, reemphasized the importance of time, and gave him two sets of proposals for use in the new talks which he was to open as instructed later. One set, designated "Proposal A" and characterized in Togo's message as Japan's "revised ultimatum," had four main points: (1) Japan would offer to apply the principle of nondiscrimination in trade throughout the Pacific area, including China, if this principle were extended to the rest of the world by the United States; (2) with respect to the Tripartite Pact, Japan would merely state that it wished to "avoid the expansion of Eu-

[13] Joseph C. Grew, *Ten Years in Japan* (New York: Simon and Schuster, 1944), pp. 470–471.

[14] Nomura to Togo, Nov. 5, 1941, *Pearl Harbor Hearings*, pt. 12, exhibit 1, p. 100.

[15] Togo to Nomura, Oct. 21, 1941, *ibid.*, p. 81.

[16] Memorandum by Welles, Oct. 24, 1941, *Foreign Relations: Japan, 1931–1941*, II, 693–694.

[17] Memorandum by Grew, Oct. 30, 1941, *ibid.*, p. 699.

rope's war into the Pacific"; (3) all Japanese troops would be evacuated from China after the conclusion of peace with that country, save those in North China, Mongolian border regions, and the island of Hainan, where they might remain for twenty-five years; and (4) Japanese troops would be withdrawn from Indo-China as soon as the China Incident was terminated.[18]

The other set, "Proposal B," was for use only if "Proposal A" made no headway; then it could be advanced "with the idea of making a last effort to prevent something happening." In reality, however, "B" was nothing more than an elucidation of "A." It specified that neither country should invade any area in southeastern Asia or the southwestern Pacific, Indo-China excepted; that the two governments should co-operate in obtaining essential materials from the Dutch East Indies; that the United States should suspend its freezing order and resume oil shipments to Japan; and that Japan's efforts to establish peace in China should not be hampered in any way. If necessary, stipulations relating to equal commercial opportunity and the Tripartite Pact could be added.[19]

Having intercepted this material, the American government now was aware of the essence of Japan's "maximum" concessions and "minimum" demands. Diplomacy was about to enter its last phase.

II

Meanwhile, American preparations for war in the Far East continued. At least since the tacit adoption in late July or early August 1941 of the new and more optimistic plan for defending the Philippines, the primary objective of these efforts had been to prepare the islands, especially Luzon, for a more or less permanent resistance. But this question could never be separated from the larger one of concerting measures with the British, Dutch, and Australians to sustain their joint position in southeastern Asia and the southwestern Pacific.

As observed earlier, new plans for holding the Philippines were based on the assumption that two hundred thousand troops and a really effective force of B-17's could be made available to General MacArthur before the outbreak of war. After the Philippine Army was mustered into

[18] Togo to Nomura, Nov. 4, 1941, *Pearl Harbor Hearings*, pt. 12, exhibit 1, pp. 92–95. [19] *Ibid.*, pp. 96–97.

United States service on July 27 and thus added to the minuscule Regular Army units already on the ground, he had about half the required number of soldiers. Training camps in the United States were to make good the deficiency.[20] But considering the extreme scarcity of trained men available to military authorities, it was obvious that a troop movement of such dimensions would require several months, at best. Other shortages were hardly less exigent, and similar delays could be anticipated in building up American air power in the Philippines and in stocking the islands with adequate quantities of war materials. During the rest of the summer, therefore, MacArthur and his principal subordinates—Major General George Grunert, commanding the Philippine Department; Major General Jonathan M. Wainwright; and Brigadier General Henry B. Claggett, commanding the Air Force—could do little except make plans and proceed with training as rapidly as possible.[21] Not until fall did the situation improve greatly. But the extremely high priority of the Philippines in current supply operations began to yield results by the end of September.[22] On the sixth of October the Secretary of War was able to advise Hull that "we needed three months to secure our position" in this area.[23]

Military men themselves were both more and less optimistic than Stimson. Whatever their reasons for such a belief, they were proceeding on the assumption that hostilities with Japan would not commence before April 1, 1942. During the second week of October, when about to depart for the Philippines to relieve General Claggett of his command over the Far East Air Forces, Major General Lewis H. Brereton discussed war prospects with authorities in Washington. The view that peace in the Far East would not be ruptured until the following April was held so strongly by members of the General Staff that Brereton was prepared to share their conviction.[24] On his arrival in Manila he found that MacArthur entertained exactly the same opinion; the mo-

[20] Samuel Eliot Morison, *The Rising Sun in the Pacific, 1931—April 1942* (Boston: Little, Brown, and Co., 1948), p. 153.

[21] See Jonathan M. Wainwright, *General Wainwright's Story*, ed. Robert Considine (Garden City, N. Y.: Doubleday and Co., 1946), pp. 11–12; and Allison Ind, *Bataan: The Judgment Seat* (New York: Macmillan Co., 1944), pp. 17–19, 20–21, 30–33, 50–56.

[22] Cf. Ind, *Bataan*, pp. 58–61.

[23] Henry L. Stimson and McGeorge Bundy, *On Active Service: In Peace and War* (New York: Harper and Bros., 1948), p. 389.

[24] Lewis H. Brereton, *The Brereton Diaries: The War in the Air in the Pacific, Middle East, and Europe, 3 October 1941—8 May 1945* (New York: William Morrow and Co., 1946), p. 10.

bilization and training plans of the Philippine Department were geared to a schedule which did not contemplate battle readiness before spring.[25]

On the other hand, those who exercised direct command in the future battle areas disagreed with Stimson's estimate of the time needed to tighten the defense of the Philippines. They were pessimistically certain that, whatever might happen, the American positions could not be secured by the end of the year. Although he echoed MacArthur's guess as to the probable starting date of hostilities, General Wainwright believed "that even if the Japs held off that long it would still be a tight squeeze." [26] Others in the Philippines voiced similar apprehensions.[27] And even before he reached his new command and its multitudinous problems, Brereton himself grew critical on the basis of what he learned and observed. War Department plans for stocking Luzon with B-17's that would have to operate without much fighter escort did not fit his notion of sound Air Force doctrine, and General Marshall's dismissal of this procedure as a "calculated risk" failed to overcome his misgivings.[28] Brereton's worries increased as he flew to the Philippines near the end of October. At Oahu, for example, he was "surprised and somewhat disappointed to note the incomplete preparations against air attacks, particularly the lack of adequate air warning equipment." [29] Nor did he find the situation in Luzon much better. Brereton had scarcely alighted from the plane which brought him to Manila when he was confronted by a number of tasks which made it perfectly evident that the Far East Air Forces lacked a good deal of being ready for war. These tasks included such major items as reorganization of the command, improvement of airport facilities, and arrangements for a new transpacific air route with landing fields in remote parts of Australia and New Guinea.[30]

Time was less significant as far as naval preparations were concerned. The maritime defense of the Philippines was entrusted to the Asiatic Fleet as then constituted. Unlike MacArthur, Admiral Hart enjoyed no prospect of reinforcement in advance of hostilities. Such preliminary physical arrangements as could be made were about complete by the fall of 1941. The main strength of the Asiatic Fleet had been transferred to Manila from Shanghai the year before. During the summer, Manila

---

[25] *Ibid.*, pp. 19–20; cf. *General Wainwright's Story*, p. 13.
[26] *General Wainwright's Story*, p. 13.
[27] Ind, *Bataan*, p. 60.   [29] *Ibid.*, p. 12.
[28] *Brereton Diaries*, p. 8.   [30] *Ibid.*, pp. 21–24; and Ind, *Bataan*, p. 69.

Bay and Subic Bay had been mined, and other routine preparations had been made.[31] Since his battle force was already in being, moreover, Hart's training problem was much less serious than that of his Army colleagues. Only with regard to his plan of operations did he feel immediate uncertainty, and here he was uncertain indeed.

Under the former plan, the Asiatic Fleet was to play no direct part in the defense of the Philippines. Instead, as the land forces withdrew to Bataan, the Fleet was to retire southward and westward to carry on the war from less vulnerable positions in the Indian Ocean.[32] But the design had lost its original simplicity, for Rainbow No. 5, the Army-Navy basic war plan drawn up in May to implement the decisions of the Washington staff conference, had added a kind of paradox. While it assumed that the Asiatic Fleet would retire very early to the southwest in order to support Dutch and British positions in the East Indies and Malaya, it also stated that Hart's primary duty was to bolster the defense of the Philippines as long as that phase of resistance continued.[33] Since Rainbow No. 5 clearly intended that the Asiatic Fleet should be preserved as a force in being at all costs, the duty to the Philippines obviously had to be construed with some freedom, and the contradiction of telling Hart to fight and run at the same time was not serious so long as the general operations plan remained substantially unchanged. But the new defense concepts which took root during the summer transformed this section of Rainbow No. 5 into a special problem.

Both MacArthur and the General Staff seem to have been notably vague with respect to their changing views on the possibility of defending the islands, for Hart was apparently not informed of their new orientation until the autumn was well-advanced. But having learned what the Army now had in mind, Hart asked the Navy Department on October 27 to authorize a change in his own plans. Briefly, he wanted to concentrate the Fleet in Manila Bay instead of leading it southward. Supported by the growing Air Force, he believed it could aid materially in holding the islands. Until an answer came three weeks later, however, this question remained in suspense.[34]

At the same time, Hart was forced to consider another matter scarcely less perplexing. The second most weighty of his duties under Rainbow

---

[31] Morison, *The Rising Sun in the Pacific*, p. 155.   [32] *Ibid.*, p. 150.
[33] Sec. 1, chap. 3, pt. 3, WPL–46, Navy basic war plan, *Pearl Harbor Hearings*, pt. 18, exhibit 129, p. 2894.
[34] Morison, *The Rising Sun in the Pacific*, p. 154.

No. 5 involved support of the British and Dutch. He was authorized by this plan to shift his base to a British or a Dutch port at his own discretion, whereupon any forces thus transferred came under the strategic control of the British Commander-in-Chief, China, to be used with Dutch and British naval units in the defense of British and Dutch possessions.[35] Existing plans rested on the assumption that Hart would move soon after the fighting started, but owing to the rejection of the Singapore staff agreement by Marshall and Stark, there was as yet no real understanding as to the exact form which coöperation with the British and Dutch might take. In August, following the disapproval of the Singapore report, Great Britain had proposed a new agreement somewhat more in accord with American views. But negotiations lagged through September and October.[36] Finally, on November 11, Stark directed Hart to open new talks with Admiral Tom Phillips of the Royal Navy, who was about to take command at Singapore.[37] More than three additional weeks were to elapse, however, before this exchange of views got under way. In the meanwhile Hart waited—uncertain as to whether he should prepare to hold or prepare to withdraw, and equally uncertain as to what he should do if withdrawal became necessary.

Through late October and early November the weakness of American defenses in the Pacific had a marked influence over all deliberations on the closely related problems of future policy toward Japan and guarantees of aid to China.

In recent talks with Japan, particularly those carried on since the spring of 1941, the United States had evinced a determined solicitude for the interests of China; and this concern, diligently stimulated by promptings from the Chinese government, was mirrored in direct relations between Washington and Chungking. Stressing the importance of Chinese morale, Sumner Welles had urged Hopkins on July 7 to increase the flow of Lend-Lease supplies to China as rapidly as possible.[38] Professor Owen Lattimore, American political adviser to Chiang Kai-shek, had sounded a kindred note on August 12 in a message to presidential assistant Lauchlin Currie. The Generalissimo thought that his

[35] Sec. 3, chap. 1, pt. 3, WPL–46, Navy basic war plan, *Pearl Harbor Hearings*, pt. 18, exhibit 129, pp. 2894–2895.

[36] Turner's testimony, Dec. 20, 1945, *ibid.*, pt. 4, p. 1932.

[37] Stark's testimony, Jan. 4, 1946, *ibid.*, pt. 5, p. 2369.

[38] Robert E. Sherwood, *Roosevelt and Hopkins: An Intimate History* (New York: Harper and Bros., 1948), p. 403.

alignment with the democratic cause deserved a more explicit type of recognition than it currently enjoyed, and he wanted Roosevelt to persuade Great Britain and Russia to join China in a formal alliance. If this could not be done, he wanted the President at least to make arrangements for giving China a voice in Pacific defense conferences. Either expedient, Lattimore noted, would "safeguard China's equal status among the anti-Axis powers . . . remove the stigma of discrimination . . . and thereby strengthen Chinese morale." [39]

Neither of the moves outlined by Chiang was practicable just then. Before the end of the month, however, Roosevelt mollified the Chinese somewhat by appointing Major General John Magruder to head a military mission to Chungking.[40] Thus during the next few weeks the main complaints of the Chinese related to the slowness of Lend-Lease deliveries.[41] But by late October, when Magruder actually reached Chungking, the Generalissimo was occupied with new fears of imminent Japanese aggression in the south. Receiving Magruder for the first time on October 28, Chiang confronted him with a request that Roosevelt intercede with Great Britain to have the Singapore Air Force support his armies in resisting an anticipated drive on Kunming, capital of Yunnan province and a city with a commanding position on the Burma Road. He also wanted Britain and the United States, acting jointly, to warn Tokyo that any such move by Japan would be considered "inimical" to British and American interests.[42] The same request was presented in Washington two days later by T. V. Soong, who, though China's Foreign Minister, had been in the United States for some time trying to expedite Lend-Lease deliveries.[43]

Chiang's plea was referred to Hull, who saw its implications at once. Another warning to Japan might result in war, for it could not be effective unless the Army and Navy were prepared to support it with military and naval action. This threw the decision to Marshall and Stark. Accordingly, the Army–Navy Joint Board met on November 3 to ponder the situation. Marshall appears to have taken the lead in this conference,

[39] Quoted in Sherwood, *Roosevelt and Hopkins,* p. 404.

[40] Press release, Aug. 26, 1941, United States, Department of State, *Department of State Bulletin* (Washington, D. C.: U. S. Govt. Printing Office, 1939——), V (Aug. 30, 1941), 166.

[41] For some account of approaches made to Hopkins and others during this period, see Sherwood, *Roosevelt and Hopkins,* pp. 404–410.

[42] Magruder's telegram, Oct. 28, 1941, *Pearl Harbor Hearings,* pt. 15, exhibit 47, pp. 1480–1481.

[43] Message from Chiang Kai-shek, Oct. 30, 1941, *ibid.,* pt. 14, exhibit 16–A, pp. 1079–1080.

stating flatly that the United States was not ready for war in the Orient and expressing his conviction that, until the nation finished building up its Far Eastern forces, it should aim at avoiding war with Japan even at the cost of certain "minor concessions which the Japanese could use in saving face." He thought this objective might be achieved through some relaxation of economic pressure.[44] The other Board members signified their agreement with the Chief of Staff, and it was decided that his views should be embodied in a memorandum for the President and the State Department.[45]

Neither Hull nor the Joint Board had misread Chiang's thoughts; a simple warning, without force behind it, was not what he desired. The Generalissimo made this clear in a message which the President received the following day, November 4. This time he did not even mention the proposed warning. Instead, he revealed that he had asked Churchill for air support "with American coöperation" and went on to request the United States to "draw on its air arm in the Philippines to provide either an active unit or a reserve force in the combined operations."[46]

Chiang was obviously out of tune with Washington, but that he struck a more responsive chord in London was indicated by the cablegram which Roosevelt received from Churchill on November 5. The Prime Minister, although he declared his readiness to assist Chiang with both pilots and planes "if they could arrive in time," evidently thought more highly of the Generalissimo's other suggestion. In his view, the situation called for a "deterrent of the most general and formidable character," one that would keep Japan from any action leading immediately to war. Observing that Britain was unable to furnish such a deterrent by itself because of heavy engagements elsewhere, Churchill expressed the hope that Roosevelt could warn the Japanese against any move into the Chinese province of Yunnan. Great Britain, he said, would support whatever policy the President chose to follow.[47]

This was the climax of a vigorous and concerted effort to place China on a basis of equality with Malaya, the East Indies, and the Philippines in Anglo-American strategic calculations. But Marshall and Stark were convinced that China should be kept in a separate category, and on

[44] Minutes of the Army–Navy Joint Board, Nov. 3, 1941, *ibid.*, exhibit 16, pp. 1063–1064.

[45] *Ibid.*, p. 1065.

[46] Chiang Kai-shek to Roosevelt, Nov. 2, 1941 (delivered by Hu Shih on Nov. 4), *ibid.*, pt. 15, exhibit 47, pp. 1476–1478.

[47] Churchill to Roosevelt, Nov. 5, 1941, *ibid.*, pt. 14, exhibit 16, p. 1061.

November 5, the very day of Churchill's message, they handed Roosevelt the memorandum outlined in the meeting of the Army–Navy Joint Board two days earlier.

Brushing aside all quibbles, they said that the real question was whether the United States would be justified "in undertaking offensive military operations . . . against Japan, to prevent her from severing the Burma Road." Their basic premise was that "such operations, however well disguised, would lead to war." [48]   Founding their case on the strategic decisions made earlier in the year, they proceeded to examine the readiness of the United States for war in the Pacific. Temporarily, at least, Japanese naval strength in that ocean was greater than American naval strength. Only by withdrawing for all practical purposes from the Atlantic war could the United States give the Pacific Fleet enough reinforcement to undertake "an unlimited strategic offensive." As a result, planning had been restricted to defense of the Philippines and the East Indies in coöperation with the British and the Dutch, and even here defensive arrangements would not be complete until February or March 1942. By that time, United States air power in the Philippines would have reached a point where it might be able to discourage any attack against Malaya or the Indies, while the British position at Singapore would have been considerably strengthened by the addition of new air and naval units. Eventually, a more aggressive attitude could be assumed. For the present, however, they thought military action against Japan should be reserved for the contingencies envisioned by the defunct Singapore staff agreement: (1) a direct attack by Japanese forces on "the territory or mandated territory of the United States, the British Commonwealth, or the Netherlands East Indies" and (2) "the movement of Japanese forces into Thailand to the west of 100 degrees east or south of 10 degrees north; or into Portuguese Timor, New Caledonia, or the Loyalty Islands." A Japanese advance into Yunnan, Thailand (except as indicated), or Siberia obviously did not fall within the limits of this defensive outlook. In other words, Marshall and Stark favored no aid to China which called for gratuitous intervention against Japan, and they strongly advised the rejection of Chiang's plea for special assistance.[49]

Their views prevailed. Hull gave the memorandum strong support,[50] and Roosevelt appears to have done likewise. In his reply to

[48] Memorandum by Marshall and Stark, Nov. 5, 1941, *Pearl Harbor Hearings,* pt. 14, exhibit 16, p. 1061.

[49] *Ibid.,* p. 1062.   [50] Hull's testimony, Nov. 23, 1945, *ibid.,* pt. 2, p. 428.

Churchill on November 7 the President discounted the likelihood of an immediate Japanese advance against Yunnan, promised that Lend-Lease aid to China would be increased, spoke reassuringly of continued defense preparations in the Philippines, and expressed his doubt as to the advisability of confronting Japan with a new warning, since its effect might be the very opposite of what was desired.[51] A week later, on November 14, a similar message was sent to Chiang Kai-shek.[52]

While this action effectively disposed of the Chinese request, it did nothing to solve America's basic problem in the Far East. Although Japan's "final proposals" had not yet been brought into the open, the American government knew their substance as stated in the intercepted messages received by Nomura on November 4. That a crisis was fast approaching regardless of what was done in China could not be doubted, and a policy was needed for meeting it.

Roosevelt still seemed to be of two minds. On the one hand, he thought of delaying hostilities with minor concessions, as Marshall had suggested on November 3. Talking with Stimson on November 6, he discussed the possibility of a six-month truce with no troop movements on either side. The Secretary of War gave him little encouragement, objecting that such a course would not only tie the hands of the United States but would also leave China at a serious disadvantage. The next day, however, the President veered sharply and asked the members of his Cabinet whether they thought the American people would support a direct attack on Japan. All agreed that the country would accept such a development.[53] Roosevelt's formulation of the case seems to have been regarded as more or less hypothetical and was doubtless so intended. But since it raised the question of immediate war, it did point out the likeliest alternative to a *modus vivendi*. That the American government would soon have to grant concessions or restrain Japan with forceful countermeasures was now obvious.

III

Atlantic Conference plans regarding the Azores, the Canaries, and the Cape Verde Islands were not carried out in September as scheduled. For one thing, Hitler's continuing difficulties in Russia lessened the im-

[51] Roosevelt to Churchill, Nov. 7, 1941, *ibid.*, pt. 14, exhibit 16–B, pp. 1081–1082.

[52] Hull's testimony, Nov. 23, 1945, *ibid.*, pt. 2, p. 428; and Roosevelt to Chiang Kai-shek (undated), *ibid.*, pt. 14, exhibit 16, pp. 1072–1076.

[53] Statement by Henry L. Stimson, *ibid.*, pt. 11, pp. 5431–5432.

mediate probability of a German drive into the Iberian Peninsula and the consequent seizure of these outposts by German troops. The attitude of Portugal seems to have furnished another reason. In their discussions at Argentia, Roosevelt and Churchill evidently thought that the Portuguese government was ready to permit a British or American occupation of the Azores and the Cape Verde Islands. But the formal invitation which Churchill undertook to secure was not issued, and consequently, while returning to the United States from his September conversations at the Vatican, Myron C. Taylor stopped briefly in Lisbon for an exchange of views with Dr. Salazar. He found the dictator almost painfully cautious. Taylor gained an impression that Salazar believed any American intervention in the war would prolong the struggle indefinitely. In Salazar's opinion, Great Britain could serve European interests most effectively by reaching an agreement with Hitler. This, coupled with German annexation of the Ukraine, would establish a sort of Continental balance and keep Russia in check. He also appeared to think that British or American occupation of the Atlantic islands might precipitate a Nazi invasion of Spain and Portugal, and he knew very well that neither Great Britain nor the United States could do anything to hinder such a move.[54]

Roosevelt was unable to deny the logic of Salazar's position. When he lacked a compelling reason to do otherwise, moreover, he was inclined to be sympathetic toward the problems of lesser nations caught in a struggle among the great powers, and the occupation project did not seem to be overwhelmingly urgent as long as the Russo-German war continued in full course. As a result, these plans were slowly moved into the background of Anglo-American intentions. Here they remained until October 1943, when, in exchange for two corvettes, the British government unspectacularly acquired base rights in the Azores and permitted the American government to share its facilities.

The new cordiality which had begun to sweeten American relations with Spain in late September persisted, on the whole, through the next two months. Weddell's relatively favorable interview with Serrano Suñer on September 30, 1941, was followed, as Cárdenas had promised, by an invitation from the Caudillo himself. The Ambassador saw Franco on October 6. Betraying a marked concern for economic problems, the latter discussed Spain's shortages of oil, wheat, and cotton and enlarged upon the country's exchange difficulties. Weddell replied

[54] Sherwood, *Roosevelt and Hopkins*, p. 400.

that the necessary foreign exchange would have been supplied by American purchases of various Spanish commodities if Spain had been willing to sell. He added, with obvious reference to his long exclusion from direct contact with the Foreign Minister, that he had received no official statement of Spain's economic needs during the past year, and he thought it regrettable that his services had not been used. As for gasoline, the most important single item in trade between the United States and Spain, he explained that shipping delays were occasioned by "administrative adjustments" growing out of "restrictions on the exportation of gasoline for reasons of military defense." When Franco said that he wanted to examine the possibility of improving commercial relations with the United States, Weddell suggested the Ministry of Trade and Industry as the most appropriate agency to act on Spain's behalf. But the Caudillo answered, doubtless to the other's extreme disappointment, that such talks would be handled by the Foreign Ministry.[55]

It had become fairly clear that the Spanish government's attitude was improving, at least temporarily, even though the chronically pro-German Serrano Suñer had been left in charge of trade negotiations with the United States. But because he was in charge and because it was suspected that Spain was using American oil to fuel German submarines, the United States did not wish to proceed too rapidly. It was known, for example, that two German supply ships had been allowed to meet U-boats regularly in the outer harbor of Las Palmas until early October, when the Spanish government yielded to British demands and restricted the German vessels to the inner harbor.[56] This was not quite the same thing as permitting the Germans to draw oil from Spanish storage tanks, but neither was it calculated to engender great confidence.

Instead of acting immediately, therefore, Washington continued to study the situation. In a long memorandum, dated October 9, the State Department reviewed its program of oil deliveries to Spain. Noting that such deliveries were kept within narrow bounds by three different factors—the British navicert system, Spain's limited tanker capacity, and United States export-license control—it expressed the opinion that no significant stocks of oil would fall into German hands even if Spain were invaded by Axis troops. All available evidence pointed to the conclusion that Spanish authorities were not engaged in a systematic effort to

[55] Weddell to Hull, Oct. 6, 1941, MS Department of State (711.52/203).
[56] Herbert Feis, *The Spanish Story: Franco and the Nations at War* (New York: Alfred A. Knopf, 1948), pp. 141, 146.

supply the Axis with petroleum products. Therefore, it was believed that oil deliveries should be continued on the existing plan.[57]   Meanwhile, other aspects of a possible commercial agreement with Spain were brought under examination, special emphasis being given to America's increasing need for such Spanish commodities as cork, wolfram, zinc, and mercury. Everything considered, the United States government was not averse to trade negotiations with Spain, but it was growing more determined than ever to furnish nothing particularly scarce or essential until Franco was prepared to reciprocate in kind.[58]

To this extent, Washington's Spanish policy now forged ahead of London's; for Great Britain still concentrated on buying Franco's abstention from the war and, as a result, generally bargained for little else. Quite apparently, the State Department believed that it had Spain at a serious disadvantage.   Quite apparently, too, it did not anticipate any sudden change in the balance of forces on the Iberian Peninsula.   For it betrayed not the slightest disposition to hurry as week followed week, and the middle of November was well past before it finished drafting a new trade proposal for submission to Madrid.

The buffeting sustained by the administration's Vichy policy in August and September 1941 continued through October and into November without much change.   It is true that a number of more favorable signs could be discerned as the autumn advanced.   Hull became almost optimistic with regard to the general temper of the French people. It seemed to him that popular feeling reflected a growing dislike for all types of collaboration between France and Germany.   The Secretary attributed this development to the sense of outrage produced by the occupation authorities' wholesale shooting of French hostages during the month of October, to the growth of an organized resistance movement, and to the circumstance that Russia's failure to collapse was gradually destroying the myth of German invincibility.[59]

Admiral Leahy supplied corroborating evidence.   He noted on October 15 that Darlan and his cohorts were now leaning "toward our side of the question" and expressed the view that their final attitude was "dependent upon the outcome of the campaign in Russia." [60]   About the same time, another source revealed that one of Darlan's associates had

[57] Memorandum by the Department of State, Oct. 9, 1941, MS Roosevelt Papers (Official File, Box 422–A).   [58] Feis, *The Spanish Story,* p. 142.

[59] Cordell Hull, *The Memoirs of Cordell Hull* (New York: Macmillan Co., 1948), II, 1042.

[60] Leahy to Roosevelt, Oct. 15, 1941, in William D. Leahy, *I Was There* (New York: Whittlesey House, 1950), appendix 12, p. 465.

characterized the Vice Premier as "the most detested man in France," adding that Darlan was extremely sensitive about his unpopularity and that he had lost much of his former confidence in German victory.[61] But these auguries, however favorable, were still too nebulous for immediate profit, and they were more than offset by rumors of an entirely different sort. For Vichy, in October, once more came to life with talk of Weygand's impending dismissal.

According to information that was pieced out later, the Germans had been pressing for Weygand's removal since December 1940. Their campaign was intensified in September 1941 when Otto Abetz, Hitler's chief representative in occupied France, confronted Pétain with a written demand that the General be ousted from his post in Africa. This document went so far as to hold that Weygand's original appointment had been an act unfriendly to Germany.

Pétain was evasive from the outset. But Darlan, whatever change his views on collaboration were then undergoing, still had no use for Weygand—a dislike which was more than shared by the powerful and fascist-minded Banque Worms group—and it was common knowledge by late October that their influence stood behind the Germans. Amid foreboding rumors, Weygand came to Vichy on October 22. This brought no definite result. But when Abetz saw Pétain again in early November, and Weygand was hurriedly summoned for still another consultation, little hope remained. Even though Pétain assured the American chargé on November 11 that the General would return to Africa, it was clear by the middle of the month that Weygand's hold on office was tenuous in the extreme.[62]

Hull's efforts during October and November to secure Finland's retirement from its war with the Soviet Union resulted in a comparable frustration. As noted earlier, he had been well satisfied with the statement of war aims given by the Finnish Minister of Industry and Commerce in the early part of September. But as the Finnish Army continued its advance week after week, he lost patience. Returning to the attack on October 3, he addressed a number of sharp comments to Procopé, expressing his pleasure at Finland's recovery of lost territory but asking once more whether the Finnish government meant to press its advantage so far as to involve itself in the general war.[63] He got no

---

[61] William L. Langer, *Our Vichy Gamble* (New York: Alfred A. Knopf, 1947), p. 191.

[62] *Ibid.*, pp. 192–193; and Leahy, *I Was There*, pp. 56–58.

[63] Memorandum by Hull, Oct. 3, 1941, *Department of State Bulletin,* V (Nov. 8, 1941), 363.

answer, however, and subsequent endeavors by the United States Minister in Helsinki to obtain a clear statement of Finnish intentions elicited nothing but a refusal to make any promises.[64] Therefore, Hull addressed a pair of notes to the Finnish government—dated October 25 and October 27—which, in his own words, were "so strong that they fell just short of a breach of relations." [65]

This description is accurate enough. The first note stated categorically that Finland, if it wished to retain American friendship, would have to guarantee an immediate cessation of hostilities and undertake to withdraw its forces to the 1939 boundary. Moreover, the launching of any attacks from Finnish-controlled territory against shipments of American supplies bound for Russia would provoke an immediate crisis in Finnish-American relations. The second note argued that Finland's current operations against Russia were of marked service to Germany in its program of world aggression, and declared that they directly threatened the security of the United States without strengthening Finland's long-term position in any way.[66]

Hull's next move was to publicize the whole issue. In a press conference held November 3 he repeated much of this argument and dwelt at considerable length upon Helsinki's failure to use the intelligence communicated by Welles to Procopé on August 18 regarding Soviet willingness to make peace on the basis of territorial concessions.[67] But his words again fell on barren ground. In a long reply, submitted November 11, the Finnish government reviewed its dealings with the Soviet Union since 1939, denied that its policy had any relation to American security, stoutly maintained that Russia still threatened the security of Finland, and declined to withdraw its forces to the 1939 boundary. With respect to the peace feeler of August 18, the note pointed out that no concrete terms had ever been mentioned and observed, justly enough, that Welles's statement to Procopé had constituted neither a genuine peace offer nor a clear recommendation that a possible future offer be accepted. It had been nothing more than an item of information.[68]

[64] David J. Dallin, *Soviet Russia's Foreign Policy, 1939–1942,* tr. Leon Denman (New Haven: Yale Univ. Press, 1942), p. 402. [65] Hull, *Memoirs,* II, 980.

[66] John H. Wuorinen, ed., *Finland and World War II, 1939–1944* (New York: Ronald Press Co., 1948), pp. 136–137.

[67] *New York Times,* Nov. 4, 1941, p. 1, col. 1, and p. 10, col. 2.

[68] Memorandum presented by the Finnish Ministry of Foreign Affairs, Nov. 11, 1941, World Peace Foundation, *Documents on American Foreign Relations, 1941–1942,* ed. S. Shepard Jones and Denys P. Myers (Boston: World Peace Foundation, 1942), pp. 645–651.

This concluded, for the time being, Hull's efforts to stop the Russo-Finnish conflict. They were not resumed until long after the United States entered the war.

While the negotiations with Finland were in progress, the United States completed arrangements to carry out its supply agreement with Russia. On October 30, 1941, President Roosevelt informed Stalin that he had approved the Moscow protocol and that delivery of the articles specified was about to commence. To finance the program, he said, he had allocated $1 billion in Lend-Lease funds. If the Soviet government concurred, repayment could be made over a ten-year period, without interest charge, the first installment coming due five years after the end of the war.[69] On November 4 Stalin accepted this arrangement with many signs of appreciation,[70] and Roosevelt concluded the formalities three days later with a public announcement to the effect that Russia had been granted $1 billion in Lend-Lease assistance.[71] By various gradations, not all of them subtle, Russia had moved in a little more than four months from a position of psychological and diplomatic hostility into a relationship with the United States which, on the material side at least, bore a notable similarity to that occupied by Great Britain.

IV

Throughout October and November the Atlantic policy evolved by the American government since the spring of 1941 yielded a steady harvest of belligerent episode and informal expedient which continued to strain relations with Germany and which drew the United States ever closer to Great Britain. But the most significant development of all took shape in Washington, as the administration finally succeeded in changing the neutrality act of 1939.

Guided from start to finish by very restrained estimates of public and congressional opinion, the President thought it advisable to initiate this move by asking for less than he desired. Although the prohibition respecting combat zones was an even greater hindrance to the most effective use of America's maritime potential than was the clause which forbade the arming of the country's merchant ships, administration

[69] Roosevelt to Stalin, Oct. 30, 1941, *Department of State Bulletin*, V (Nov. 8, 1941), 365–366.
[70] Stalin to Roosevelt, Nov. 4, 1941, *ibid.*, p. 366.
[71] Press release, Nov. 7, 1941, *ibid.*

leaders had determined in late September that their first objective should cover only the arming of merchant ships. In this connection, Hull requested Admiral Stark to present his views. Stark, on October 8, declared himself strongly in favor of abolishing combat zones as well as the restriction on the arming of merchant vessels,[72] but the original strategy was not changed. Though Roosevelt alluded generally to several undesirable features of the act as he drove home the opening wedge in a special message to Congress on October 9, his main theme was the necessity of permitting United States merchant vessels to carry armament, and the only change he specifically recommended was the repeal of section 6.[73]

The House of Representatives acted quickly. An administration bill calling for abandonment of the offending provision was promptly introduced and referred to committee. Hearings were held October 13 and 14,[74] and on October 15 the bill was favorably reported despite a minority complaint that the measure would expose civilian crews to unnecessary dangers and that it was, in any event, part of a scheme to put the nation into war by subterfuge.[75] Two days later the bill received House approval. So far, the President's request had been met with considerable dispatch. But he had received nothing extra.

In the long run, however, events were with him. The number of American ships sunk or damaged by submarine action increased sharply after the middle of September, and added to sinkings of a more or less ordinary nature were a pair of attacks which recalled the *Greer* incident. The American vessel *Pink Star* was sent to the bottom on September 19. She was followed in rapid succession by the *I. C. White* on September 29, the *W. C. Teagle* and the *Bold Venture* on October 16, and the *Lehigh* three days later.[76] On October 17 the U.S.S. *Kearny*, one of five American destroyers sent from the neighborhood of Iceland to help

[72] Memorandum by Stark, Oct. 8, 1941, *Pearl Harbor Hearings*, pt. 16, exhibit 106, p. 2216.

[73] Message of the President to Congress, Oct. 9, 1941, *Department of State Bulletin*, V (Oct. 11, 1941), 257–259.

[74] United States, Congress, House of Representatives, Committee on Foreign Affairs, *Arming American Merchant Vessels: Hearings before the Committee on Foreign Affairs on H. J. Res. 237, Oct. 13 and 14, 1941* (77th Cong., 1st sess.) (Washington, D. C.: U. S. Govt. Printing Office, 1941).

[75] United States, Congress, House of Representatives, Committee on Foreign Affairs, *House Report No. 1267* (77th Cong., 1st sess.) (Washington, D. C.: U. S. Govt. Printing Office, 1941), p. 3.

[76] Data regarding attacks on American-owned merchant vessels, August–October 1941, *Documents on American Foreign Relations, 1941–1942*, pp. 86–87.

repel the assault of a German "wolf-pack" on a slow-moving convoy, was torpedoed. She made port badly damaged and with a loss of eleven men.[77] The naval tanker *Salinas* suffered an attack on October 30.[78] Then came the hardest blow of all. On the morning of October 31 the U.S.S. *Reuben James,* an American destroyer on convoy duty, was torpedoed and sunk about six hundred miles west of Ireland. Only forty-five men out of her crew of a hundred and sixty were rescued. This was the first United States warship to be lost in the Second World War.[79] Stark reported that the incident set naval recruiting back about 15 per cent.[80] And Count Ciano, from his vantage point in Rome, expressed an unqualified fear that it could not help but accelerate the crisis in German-American relations.[81]

While none of these incidents produced anything like a popular demand for war, they certainly gave Congress a new sense of urgency. As early as October 22, the President obtained a confidential opinion from Senator Josh Lee (Democrat, Oklahoma) that recent sinkings had so changed legislative sentiments that the time was ripe to strike for repeal of sections 2 and 3, which dealt with combat zones, as well as of section 6. If Roosevelt would let it be known that he wanted the additional changes, and if a few key men in the Senate and House would lend their help, Lee thought the entire matter could be disposed of at once. On October 27 Senator Tom Connally (Democrat, Texas) supported the abolition of combat zones on the ground that merchant ships could not be protected merely by restricting the area of their movements. And Senator W. Lee O'Daniel (Democrat, Texas), on October 31, tried to make the *Reuben James* incident the occasion for demanding an immediate vote on repeal.[82]

In the circumstances, Congress gave the President exactly the kind of revision he wanted. As disaster continued to strike in the Atlantic, the

[77] Samuel Eliot Morison, *The Battle of the Atlantic, 1939–1943* (Boston: Little, Brown, and Co., 1947), pp. 92–93.

[78] Walter Karig (with Earl Burton and Stephen L. Freeland), *Battle Report: The Atlantic War* (New York: Farrar and Rinehart, 1946), p. 77.

[79] Morison, *The Battle of the Atlantic,* p. 94.

[80] Stark to Kimmel, Nov. 25, 1941, *Pearl Harbor Hearings,* pt. 16, exhibit 106, p. 2224.

[81] Count Galeazzo Ciano, *The Ciano Diaries, 1939–1943,* ed. Hugh Gibson (Garden City, N. Y.: Doubleday and Co., 1946), p. 400.

[82] Memorandum by Edwin M. Watson, Oct. 22, 1941, MS Roosevelt Papers (Official File, Box 1561); and United States, Congress, *Congressional Record* (Washington, D. C.: U. S. Govt. Printing Office, 1874———), LXXXVII (77th Cong., 1st sess.), 8248, 8377.

House resolution went before the Senate and met an extremely friendly reception. On October 25 the Committee on Foreign Relations not only approved the arming of merchant vessels, but moved for the abolition of combat zones as well. It was unreasonable, the Committee said, to produce war materials at American expense without taking steps "necessary to insure their full utilization." Furthermore, sections 2 and 3 of the neutrality act were undesirable as voluntary restrictions imposed "in derogation of American rights under international law."[83] Thus amended, the resolution was approved on November 7. Senate changes gained acceptance in the House on November 13. Four days later the bill became law.[84] Every major aspect of the special neutrality legislation of the nineteen-thirties was now dead.

Meanwhile, the Atlantic partnership with Britain continued to grow. It was a phase without sweeping new agreements, expressed or implied —a development which reflected little save the momentum of established policy. But this was enough. As the mounting intensity of German attacks on United States vessels, merchantmen and warships alike, gave new emphasis to the similarity of their positions in the Atlantic war, the American and British navies tended more than ever to operate as a single unit.

By its very nature, escort and patrol duty necessitated a constantly growing sphere of activity, and the operations of United States naval forces expanded by almost insensible degrees to a point where they included virtual support of the Royal Navy's blockade of the European coastline. Toward the end of October, for example, Admiral King arrived at an informal understanding with British authorities which divided the responsibility of guarding the northern approaches to the transatlantic convoy route. Under this agreement the British Home Fleet was to observe and intercept Axis ships trying to enter the Atlantic between the Faeroe Islands and Iceland, while American units based on Iceland were to hold the line in Denmark Strait. If any hostile craft managed to evade this dual watch, it was agreed that ships of the Atlantic Fleet would be placed under temporary British command to assist in hunting them down.[85] That this was more intimately related to

---

[83] United States, Congress, Senate, Committee on Foreign Relations, *Senate Report No. 764* (77th Cong., 1st sess.) (Washington, D. C.: U. S. Govt. Printing Office, 1941), pp. 2–3.

[84] United States, Department of State, *United States Statutes at Large* (Washington, D. C.: U. S. Govt. Printing Office and others, 1845———), LV, 764–765.

[85] Morison, *The Battle of the Atlantic*, pp. 81–82.

North Atlantic patrol problems than to the blockade activities of the Royal Navy goes without saying, but the two endeavors were obviously beginning to overlap.

How easily and informally a United States patrol craft might serve as adjunct to the British blockade was demonstrated in the case of the *Odenwald*, a German blockade runner captured a few hundred miles off the coast of Brazil by the United States cruiser *Omaha* in the early part of November. Disguised as an American ship—the S.S. *Willmoto* of Philadelphia—the *Odenwald* was then heading for Germany with a cargo of rubber obtained in Japan. Since she was not a raider, the *Omaha's* captain lacked instructions for dealing with her. But he held the ship anyway, on the altogether remarkable allegation that she was suspected of being a slave trader, and took her into Port-of-Spain, Trinidad—a British harbor.[86]

It was also during this period that Roosevelt fulfilled the promise of aid he had given Churchill in connection with the projected movement of additional British forces to the Middle East. The original plan, as formulated in conference with the naval staff on September 5, apparently took it for granted that the transports assigned to this duty would pick up the troops in the British Isles and proceed to Iran from there. Being government-owned, these ships—like all regular naval vessels—were not barred from combat zones by the neutrality act. As a result, their voyage to British ports would have involved no legal transgression. But the likelihood of a German attack once they entered the combat zone could not be ignored, and the President soon realized that an incident of this type would furnish his congressional opponents with a new ground for accusing him of interventionist tendencies and perhaps spoil his opportunity to do away with the objectionable features of the neutrality act. So he reopened the question in early October, explained his misgivings to Churchill, and offered the Prime Minister a choice of two alternatives. The ships might be temporarily loaned to the British on a Lend-Lease arrangement, whereupon they could proceed with British officers, British crews, and British flags. Or the troops could be embarked at Halifax, Nova Scotia, after being sent to that port in British ships. This would allow the American convoy to remain in the Western Hemisphere until it reached the South Atlantic. Then it could swing east, sail round the Cape of Good Hope, and avoid the main submarine zones completely. Although Roosevelt indicated his preference for the

[86] *Ibid.*, p. 84.

first alternative, Churchill chose the second, and this arrangement was permitted to stand.[87]

By early November one British division (some twenty thousand men) had arrived at Halifax. The troops were quickly shifted to three American transports—U.S.S. *Mount Vernon,* U.S.S. *Wakefield,* and U.S.S. *West Point*—and the convoy left port on November 11 under strong United States naval escort, subsistence for the troops being furnished out of Lend-Lease funds.[88] Fortunately, this move had no special repercussions. (Indeed, the convoy was still two days out of Capetown when the Japanese attacked Pearl Harbor,[89] and the United States declared war on all three Axis countries within the next four days.) But this convoy action was one more proof of the government's increasing disregard for America's nonbelligerent status.

In terms of broad policy, Germany's response to this extension of naval warfare was extremely cautious. On September 17, following Roosevelt's public announcement of shooting orders, Admiral Raeder urged that his submarines be freed of a number of restrictions which hampered their ability to meet new conditions.[90] But Hitler demurred, insisting that it was still advisable to keep direct clashes with the United States at a minimum. While he agreed to permit a slight intensification of U-boat warfare, the operating directives of the Naval High Command remained unchanged.[91]

According to a summary of existing orders drawn up at this time, it was forbidden to attack American naval vessels that could be recognized as such even within the original German blockade area—which corresponded to the American combat zone extending from the European coast westward to the 20th meridian. Attacks within the extended zone of operations—which touched the three-mile limit of Greenland—were allowed only when such action became necessary in self-defense or when the vessels encountered were actually performing escort duty. United States merchantmen could be sunk in the original zone—from which they were barred by American law anyway—but attacks outside this area were not permitted even when the ships formed part of a convoy.

---

[87] Sherwood, *Roosevelt and Hopkins,* pp. 375–376.

[88] Morison, *The Battle of the Atlantic,* pp. 109–110. [89] *Ibid.,* p. 112.

[90] Report of the Commander-in-Chief, Navy, to the Fuehrer, Sept. 17, 1941, United States, Department of the Navy, *Fuehrer Conferences on Matters Dealing with the German Navy, 1939–1941* (Washington, D. C.: Issued in mimeographed form by the Office of Naval Intelligence, 1947), 1941, II, 38–39.

[91] *Ibid.,* p. 49.

German forces were under orders to engage in no warlike acts on their own initiative anywhere within the limits of the Pan-American safety zone.[92]

It becomes clear, on analysis, that Germany exercised no great forbearance. Wherever United States naval activity made a direct contribution to the task of supplying Hitler's enemies, German commanders were authorized to move with almost complete freedom. The same liberty existed whenever the safety of German naval units was directly menaced by American forces. That German submarines were not unduly hampered in their efforts to deal with United States patrol and escort vessels is proved by the *Greer, Kearny,* and *Reuben James* incidents, while a number of the merchant sinkings listed previously occurred in locations and under circumstances which made it perfectly evident that general restrictions were not always observed in specific cases. Nevertheless, German naval orders maintained a careful distinction between the treatment to be accorded the United States and that prescribed for full belligerents.

Viewed in the light of what is now known about German policy in the fall of 1941, this distinction still had one kind of substantial meaning, for it reflected Germany's continuing hope that immediate war with the United States could be avoided. Of course, Hitler's American policy had undergone many changes since 1939, and the probability of a final break was much more apparent now than it had been at that time. Submarine activity had been greatly intensified; the German press had cast off most of its restraint when commenting upon things American; and the Fuehrer had long since abandoned his hope of using the good offices of the United States to obtain a favorable peace by negotiation.[93]

Recently, moreover, the Tripartite Pact had been causing him no little anxiety. As long as it helped Japan maintain a position as counterweight to the United States in the Pacific, that treaty served its proper end. But the progress of the Hull-Nomura conversations over the past several months had emphasized the difficulty of keeping affairs in so static a condition. If the talks should produce a worth-while settlement, Japan's usefulness to Germany would be greatly reduced. Definite failure of these negotiations, however, would presumably involve the

---

[92] *Fuehrer Conferences,* 1941, II, 44–45. Outside the extended blockade area there was apparently no distinction between the treatment accorded American ships and that prescribed for the vessels of Spain and Japan, the "friendly neutrals."

[93] Hans L. Trefousse, *Germany and American Neutrality, 1939–1941* (New York: Bookman Associates, 1951), p. 135.

United States in war with all three Axis partners; this outcome now appeared much more likely.[94] By the end of October Hitler's thoughts on this problem must have been extremely complex, but he still hesitated to drop his last restrictions on activities affecting the United States. All the available evidence indicates that, as late as November 20, he was definitely committed to his old policy of keeping America out of the war.[95]

Hitler did feel venturesome enough on November 1 to authorize the deployment of submarines about Cape Race and in the Straits of Belle Isle, off the coast of Newfoundland.[96] According to German naval records, two U-boats were present in this area by November 10.[97] The High Command accepted its loss of the *Odenwald* in a philosophic mood, however, and decided that no formal protest should be offered in view of the fact that the ship had been flying the American flag when captured. By this time, November 13, German naval strategists were deeply concerned about the prospective revision of the American neutrality act and invited Hitler to say what measures he planned to take in the event of such a change in United States policy. But the Fuehrer would venture no predictions, and Raeder had to content himself with an elaboration of previous directives which emphasized the responsibility of German commanders to take offensive action against United States forces as soon as the safety of their own vessels was threatened in any manner.[98] Nor was there an immediate change in German naval policy four days later when the American government abolished its combat zones and authorized the arming of merchant ships.

While Hitler tried to resolve these contradictions of his own making, the United States added once more to the structure of hemispheric defense. Important for its bauxite mines—which furnished 60 per cent of the requirements of the American aluminum industry—and for its strategic location on the northern coast of South America, the inadequately defended colony of Dutch Guiana had offered a growing security problem for a number of months. At the very least, German groups working in the area threatened to minimize its economic usefulness; and considering its weak defenses, it was not even proof against German seizure. With the blessing of Queen Wilhelmina and the approval

[94] Trefousse, *Germany and American Neutrality*, pp. 102, 138.
[95] *Ibid.*, pp. 140–141. [96] Morison, *The Battle of the Atlantic*, p. 95.
[97] Report of the Commander-in-Chief, Navy, to the Fuehrer, Nov. 13, 1941, *Fuehrer Conferences*, 1941, II, 68.
[98] *Ibid.*, pp. 58–66.

of neighboring Brazil, therefore, Dutch Guiana was occupied by American troops on November 24.[99]

V

Between early October and mid-November 1941, the character of American-Japanese relations shifted from one of admitted strain to that of evident crisis. The tension created in July, August, and September by Tokyo's relentless designs on Indo-China, the breaking off of the Hull-Nomura conversations, the freezing orders, Roosevelt's warning of August 17, the Japanese decisions of September 6, and the bootless resumption of the Hull-Nomura talks was so exacerbated by the fall of Prince Konoye, misgivings in Chungking and London, and the new proposals communicated to Nomura on November 4 that the United States government now recognized the imminent danger of having to choose between concessions and war. Former strategic decisions were not changed, however. It had always been assumed that war, if it came, would have to be waged in the Atlantic and Pacific simultaneously, and it was still believed that the Atlantic constituted the more important theater.

While it kept American policy makers from losing sight of the main objective, this rigid adherence to the design of the Washington report did not simplify all decisions. Even though Marshall and Stark thought the *casus belli* would arise if Japan overstepped boundaries defined in the Singapore staff conversations, the inability of the United States to defend those limits before the spring of 1942 led them to advocate a partial abandonment of the "hard" diplomacy which had been adopted to restrain Japan from the very moves they feared. By the end of the first week in November, therefore, President Roosevelt was torn between concession and firmness—between a *modus vivendi* and a decision to let events take their course. Neither alternative offered much hope unless supported by a major transfer of United States naval power from the Atlantic to the Pacific.

On the other hand, the implementation of the supply agreement with Russia—as well as Washington's continued, if somewhat ineffectual, labors with the affairs of Spain, France, and Finland—demonstrated

---

[99] Hull, *Memoirs*, II, 1051; and press release, Nov. 24, 1941, *Department of State Bulletin*, V (Nov. 29, 1941), 425.

that nothing was left undone with respect to the European theater, and expanding naval operations in the Atlantic caused Admiral Stark to remark on November 7, in a private letter to Hart, that "whether the country knows it or not, we are at war." [100]   Ten days later, as the prospect for peace in the Orient grew more and more dubious, final revision of the neutrality act rounded out the nation's program of nonbelligerent activity on this side of the world, giving the American merchant marine a freedom which, in its own sphere, was roughly equivalent to that already enjoyed by the United States Navy.

[100] Stark to Hart, Nov. 7, 1941, *Pearl Harbor Hearings*, pt. 16, exhibit 109, p. 2456.

CHAPTER XII

The Last Phase

I

IN ITS ATTEMPT TO HOLD FAR EASTERN LINES BY ULTIMATUM AND ECONOMIC coercion, the United States had knowingly tempted fate since August 1941, and the dangers of such a policy could be ignored no longer. By November the chief threat of formal and unlimited hostilities lay in the problem of Japan. But America was committed to a world strategy which kept its strength oriented toward Europe throughout the final month of nonbelligerency. While the eastward thrust of American power maintained a steady pressure against the European Axis, a relatively unsupported diplomacy looked westward to the source of grimmer crisis.

The opening move in the last phase was Japan's. The third Imperial Conference since the beginning of July assembled in Tokyo on November 5 and straightway approved the proposals sent to Nomura the day before. Having obtained this ultimate sanction, Togo immediately directed Nomura to confront Hull with "Proposal A." He pointed out that Japan expected the United States to obtain the consent of Great Britain and the Netherlands to any terms needing their acquiescence, explained that "Proposal B" would be substituted for "A" if progress was slow, and emphasized the necessity of completing a settlement before November 25—although the Ambassador was to avoid giving Washington the impression that a time limit had been set.[1]

Likewise on November 5, Admiral Yamamoto, Commander-in-Chief of the Japanese Combined Fleet, issued a basic directive to fleet and task force commanders. Entitled "Combined Fleet Top Secret Operation

[1] Togo to Nomura, Nov. 5, 1941, United States, Congress, Joint Committee on Investigation of Pearl Harbor Attack, *Hearings Pursuant to S. Con. Res. 27, Authorizing Investigation of Attack on Pearl Harbor, Dec. 7, 1941, and Events and Circumstances Relating Thereto* (79th Cong., 1st and 2nd sess.) (Washington, D. C.: U. S. Govt. Printing Office, 1946), pt. 12, exhibit 1, p. 99. Cited henceforth as *Pearl Harbor Hearings.*

Order No. 1," it announced that war with the United States, Great Britain, and the Netherlands was expected.[2] It also gave plans for a tremendous initial offensive extending from the Hawaiian Islands to Malaya, and included arrangements for a surprise attack on Pearl Harbor.[3] Two days later Yamamoto made known that hostilities would probably begin about December 8.[4] These directives, of course, were preparatory. Like many operations plans issued by American military and naval chiefs, they depended for their full effect upon an order of execution. But if they had been revealed to United States authorities at that moment, they would have given the Foreign Minister's deadline an ominous significance.

Nomura addressed himself to his appointed task without delay, informing Hull on November 7 that he had been directed to resume conversations. According to his analysis, he said, the main points at issue between Japan and the United States were three: (1) the problem of ensuring equal opportunity in international trade, (2) Japan's obligations under the Tripartite Pact, and (3) the China question. He thought it would not be difficult to reach agreement on the first two, but he admitted that the third presented obstacles. With this, he handed the Secretary of State a document which contained the formulas of "Proposal A" regarding nondiscrimination in international trade and the withdrawal of troops from China. Observing that the memorandum offered nothing on the Tripartite Pact, Hull remarked that a definite statement concerning Japan's obligations to Germany was in order. But Nomura replied that he thought his government had said enough on this matter to render its position clear.[5] Since Hull did not press the point, the rest of the discussion was more or less general, consisting largely of Nomura's request for an interview with President Roosevelt and of the Secretary's reminder that the President would undertake no formal negotiation without first consulting Great Britain, China, and the Netherlands.[6]

[2] Japanese Combined Fleet Top Secret Operation Order No. 1, Nov. 5, 1941, *Pearl Harbor Hearings*, pt. 13, exhibit 8, p. 433.

[3] *Ibid.*, pp. 433–441; and U. S. Navy summary of Japanese submarine operations at the Pearl Harbor attack, *ibid.*, pp. 488–492.

[4] Japanese Combined Fleet Top Secret Operation Order No. 2, Nov. 7, 1941, *ibid.*, p. 486.

[5] Memorandum by Ballantine, Nov. 7, 1941, and document presented by Nomura, Nov. 7, 1941, United States, Department of State, *Papers Relating to the Foreign Relations of the United States: Japan, 1931–1941* (Washington, D. C.: U. S. Govt. Printing Office, 1943), II, 706–710.

[6] Memorandum by Ballantine, Nov. 7, 1941, *ibid.*, pp. 708–709.

Although its ignorance of Yamamoto's directives to the Japanese Fleet concealed the exact urgency of the situation from the American government, Togo's messages to Nomura had been regularly intercepted, and the significance of the November 25 time limit was not entirely lost on the State Department. In Cabinet meeting the same afternoon (November 7), Hull made it clear that a Japanese attack was to be expected any time,[7] while Roosevelt, as indicated in the last chapter, solicited the views of those present as to whether the American people would back him in an aggressive policy toward Japan. When Nomura saw the President on November 10, therefore, the atmosphere was one of mounting crisis.

Elaborating the proposals given to Hull three days earlier, the Ambassador explained that Japan was ready to accept the principle of equality in international trade for the whole of Asia, including China, if this principle were extended to the rest of the world. He repeated his government's statement of September 27 on the Tripartite Pact—that while its aim was peace, Japan had to be guided by considerations of self-defense and would undertake nothing except to reach an independent decision as to the proper interpretation of that treaty if the United States became involved in war with Germany. Regarding the third problem, Nomura said that most Japanese forces would be drawn out of China within two years of a Sino-Japanese peace settlement. However, troops stationed in certain parts of North China, in Inner Mongolia, and in Hainan would remain where they were "for a certain required duration." He warned that Japan viewed the American, British, and Dutch freezing orders as an economic blockade, and concluded by assuring his host that the proposals he had just submitted represented his government's "utmost effort" to reach an understanding with the United States.[8] The President's reply was general in the extreme. Although he expressed a hope that the new round of talks would have a favorable outcome, and remarked that Japan and the United States ought to seek a *modus vivendi,* he offered no concrete suggestions.[9]

As though he feared Nomura would not make the Japanese position clear enough, the Foreign Minister opened a secondary campaign in Tokyo at the same time. He informed Grew on November 10 that the new offer embraced Japan's "maximum possible concessions" and asserted that feeling in his country would "not tolerate further protracted

---

[7] Hull's testimony, Nov. 23, 1945, *Pearl Harbor Hearings,* pt. 2, p. 429.

[8] Memorandum by Hull, Nov. 10, 1941, *Foreign Relations: Japan, 1931–1941,* II, 715–717.   [9] *Ibid.,* pp. 718–719.

delay in arriving at some conclusion." He added a hope that Great Britain, in view of its Pacific interests, would settle its own differences with Japan simultaneously. Referring to Japan's well-known population problem, he stressed his country's need for raw materials, complained of the hardships which had arisen from the freezing orders, and noted that "continued economic pressure" might eventually force his government into "measures of self-defense." [10]

British Far Eastern policy, at this critical juncture, had little to offer. Tacitly since 1937, and expressly since mid-1940, Great Britain had left the initiative in that part of the world to the United States. The British government's vacillation during the past eighteen months, its habit of threatening to appease Japan while urging the American government to exert greater pressure in the Pacific, accurately reflected its sense of weakness and a realization that, ultimately, Britain could only follow where the United States led. Owing to the rejection of the Singapore staff agreement, moreover, British officials had no certain understanding as to what the American government would do in any given circumstance. These facts, plus Britain's heavy commitments elsewhere, doubtless explain London's want of clarity on Far Eastern issues and its tendency to view them with such an air of abstraction. As Churchill later explained, "the whole Japanese menace lay in a sinister twilight, compared with our other needs." He thought that the United States would come into the war if Japan attacked British possessions, but he could not be entirely sure. And if the American government decided otherwise, Britain would have no choice except to let the Far East go by default. [11] Churchill's actions in mid-November were fully compatible with this point of view.

Having failed at the beginning of the month to persuade Roosevelt that Japan should be confronted with a new warning, the Prime Minister now washed his hands of the whole matter. He rumbled defiance on November 10 in a public announcement that his government would declare war "within the hour" if hostilities should commence between Japan and the United States. [12] But he also extended the olive branch. Acting on instructions from London, the British Ambassador to Japan, Sir Robert Craigie, urged Togo on November 11 to make a supreme effort to reach an understanding with the United States. When Wash-

---

[10] Memorandum by Grew, Nov. 10, 1941, *Foreign Relations: Japan, 1931-1941,* II, 711-714.

[11] Winston S. Churchill, *The Grand Alliance* (Boston: Houghton Mifflin Co., 1950), p. 587.   [12] *New York Times,* Nov. 11, 1941, p. 1, col. 1

ington and Tokyo reached the point of actual negotiation, said Craigie, Great Britain would likewise be prepared to seek an agreement.[13] Everything, in effect, was still being left to Roosevelt and Hull.

In Washington, meanwhile, Nomura continued his efforts to fulfill the inflexible directives of his superiors. On November 12 he pressed Hull for an early decision regarding the latest Japanese proposals, but the Secretary put him off with a statement that they were being considered with all possible dispatch.[14] Nomura obviously deprecated the growing strain between his country and the United States. He was somewhat unnerved by the labor of trying to implement a policy of which he did not approve, and the future distressed him sorely. His agitation increased on November 14, when he received from Togo the English text of the note he was to use in submitting "Proposal B." [15] Although he was not to present this "final" offer until he received additional instructions, he was more than a little taken aback at the speed with which the Japanese Foreign Office was now moving. Nomura immediately cabled his strongest advice against hasty action and requested that the November 25 time limit be extended by one or two months.[16] But Togo answered this plea with a curt refusal to alter the deadline, adding a cryptic statement that the "fate of the Empire hangs by the slender thread of a few days." [17]

More dismayed than ever, Nomura tried again to hasten the responses of the State Department. He saw Hull on November 15 and endeavored to persuade him that their talks had reached a stage where formal negotiation might begin, but the Secretary replied that it was impossible to think in such terms until he had had an opportunity to discuss Japan's offer with the British, the Dutch, and the Chinese.[18] Another grim note was sounded the same day as instructions concerning "the order and method of destroying . . . code machines in the event of an emergency" were rushed to Japanese missions abroad.[19]

Saburo Kurusu, who had left Japan on November 5, reached Wash-

[13] Togo to Nomura, Nov. 11, 1941, *Pearl Harbor Hearings*, pt. 12, exhibit 1, pp. 117–118.

[14] Memorandum by Ballantine, Nov. 12, 1941, *Foreign Relations: Japan, 1931–1941*, II, 723.

[15] Togo to Nomura, Nov. 14, 1941, *Pearl Harbor Hearings*, pt. 12, exhibit 1, pp. 125–126.

[16] Nomura to Togo, Nov. 14, 1941, *ibid.*, pp. 127–129.

[17] Togo to Nomura, Nov. 16, 1941, *ibid.*, pp. 137–138.

[18] Memorandum by Ballantine, Nov. 15, 1941, *Foreign Relations: Japan, 1931–1941*, II, 731–732.

[19] Togo to Nomura, Nov. 15, 1941, *Pearl Harbor Hearings*, pt. 12, exhibit 1, p. 137.

ington at this point. As Togo had described it to Grew, Kurusu's mission was to help Nomura reach a settlement with the United States; but his real purpose, to all appearances, was to stiffen the latter's resolution and to see that he maintained a sufficiently uncompromising attitude throughout the final diplomatic exchanges. In Nomura's company, Kurusu was received by Hull on November 17. Here he stressed his government's desire for peace but mentioned no further offers,[20] and his initial interview at the White House later the same day was equally unproductive.[21]

That evening, however, the Japanese envoys "went to call on a certain Cabinet member." [22] Presumably their host was Postmaster General Walker,[23] who had been interested in the unofficial talks which Bishop Walsh and Father Drought had carried on with the Japanese Embassy early in the year. At all events, this personage suggested that the United States might be willing to moderate the freezing order if Japan withdrew its troops from Indo-China as a display of good intentions.[24]

Nomura was clutching at every straw which offered the least hope of peace; and when he and Kurusu saw Hull again the next morning, he repeated this as a tentative proposal. Even Kurusu seemed to think well of the idea. Indeed, he gave it explicit support, although he explained his attitude with the decidedly partial assertion that the embargo established by the freezing orders was chiefly responsible for the growth of a belligerent spirit in Japan. Needless to say, Hull was suspicious. While he did not reject Nomura's proposal out of hand, he obviously viewed it with distinct reservations. He emphasized the difficulty of changing American policy with respect to Japanese trade so long as Japan adhered to the Tripartite Pact and questioned his visitors as to just how much the Japanese government would alter its course in return for a relaxation of the freezing orders.[25] The subject was discussed again, however, on November 19; and after Nomura explained that he was

[20] Memorandum by Ballantine, Nov. 17, 1941, *Foreign Relations: Japan, 1931–1941*, II, 738–739.   [21] Cf. memorandum by Hull, Nov. 17, 1941, *ibid.*, pp. 740–743.

[22] Nomura to Togo, Nov. 18, 1941, *Pearl Harbor Hearings*, pt. 12, exhibit 1, p. 154.

[23] United States, Congress, Joint Committee on Investigation of Pearl Harbor Attack, *Investigation of Pearl Harbor Attack, Report Pursuant to S. Con. Res. 27, to Investigate Attack on Pearl Harbor on December 7, 1941, and Events and Circumstances Relating Thereto* (79th Cong., 2nd sess.), S. Doc. 244 (Washington, D. C.: U. S. Govt. Printing Office, 1946), p. 356. Cited henceforth as *Pearl Harbor Report*.

[24] Nomura to Togo, Nov. 18, 1941, *Pearl Harbor Hearings*, pt. 12, exhibit 1, p. 154.

[25] Memorandum by Ballantine, Nov. 18, 1941, *Foreign Relations: Japan, 1931–1941*, II, 749–750.

proposing nothing more than a temporary arrangement for use while they continued to seek a broader understanding, the Secretary appeared to be in a more receptive frame of mind.[26]

Although he was not averse to exploring the possibilities of a *modus vivendi,* Hull had ample reason for his coolness toward the arrangement here suggested. Thanks to "Magic," he knew perfectly well that Nomura and Kurusu were still acting on their own responsibility, and he soon learned that they had no chance of obtaining their government's approval. On November 18 both envoys sent cablegrams to the Japanese Foreign Office, urging that their solution be given the fullest consideration and stressing their belief that it represented the only alternative to war.[27] But the Japanese government was not interested in a compromise of this type. On November 19 Togo refused absolutely to entertain the project suggested by the two diplomats, and instructed Nomura to proceed at once with "Proposal B." [28] The same day, the Foreign Office added to the sense of crisis by acquainting its missions abroad with the signal that would be used to order the destruction of code materials if the emergency became crucial.[29]

Togo had again made it clear that he could accept no agreement which did not fit the program laid down by the Imperial Conference of November 5, and a settlement which harmonized with those decisions was so far out of the question that Nomura protested immediately. At the hazard of further rebuke he expressed his conviction that war was inevitable unless a temporary agreement could be patched together, and he added the thought that long years of fighting in China had not prepared Japan for a trial of strength with the United States.[30] But Togo's answer, received on November 20, was peremptory: "Proposal B" should be handed to the American government without delay.[31]

II

It was apparent that Tokyo had sounded the death knell of its envoys' scheme for a truce to keep hostilities at bay until a wider settlement could be achieved. They now had no choice but to comply with the

[26] Memorandum by Ballantine, Nov. 19, 1941, *ibid.,* pp. 751–752.

[27] Kurusu to Togo, Nov. 18, 1941, and Nomura to Togo, Nov. 18, 1941, *Pearl Harbor Hearings,* pt. 12, exhibit 1, pp. 151–152.

[28] Togo to Nomura, Nov. 19, 1941, *ibid.,* p. 155.

[29] Togo to Nomura, Nov. 19, 1941, *ibid.,* p. 154.

[30] Nomura to Togo, Nov. 19, 1941, *ibid.,* p. 158.

[31] Togo to Nomura, Nov. 20, 1941, *ibid.,* p. 160.

Foreign Minister's orders; and Kurusu, who seems to have been less reluctant than his colleague, submitted "Proposal B" to Hull later the same day.

As presented, this draft called for a mutual undertaking against further troop movements into any part of southeastern Asia or the southern Pacific area, except Indo-China. Although Japanese forces in southern Indo-China would be withdrawn to the northern part of the country, they would remain there until the "restoration of peace between Japan and China or the establishment of an equitable peace in the Pacific." In return, the American government should suspend its freezing order, furnish Japan a "required quantity of oil," and abstain from any activities which might hamper Japanese efforts to make peace with China. The United States should also agree to coöperate with Japan in obtaining from the Dutch East Indies the raw materials needed by both countries.[32] This version of "Proposal B" was even narrower than the one originally framed in Tokyo, and correspondingly further removed from American views, for it omitted the stipulations regarding the Tripartite Pact and equal commercial opportunity which had been mentioned for possible inclusion by Togo's cablegram of November 4. Nevertheless, it produced little immediate change in the trend of discussion. While it was completely unacceptable as it stood, it did envisage limited concessions in southeastern Asia. Thus it corresponded in a general way to Nomura's recent proposal for a temporary arrangement, and Hull told Kurusu that the new offer would be examined in a sympathetic spirit.[33]

Meanwhile, the American government continued to study the possibilities of a *modus vivendi*. The President himself furnished one basis for these deliberations. For at least two weeks he had been toying with the notion of proposing some kind of diplomatic armistice, and in an undated memorandum, apparently written about November 20, he outlined a suggestion for a six-month truce. It ran as follows: If Japan would agree not to invoke the Tripartite Pact even though the United States did enter the European war, and if Tokyo would undertake to send no more troops to the Manchurian border, Indo-China, or southward generally, the United States would resume limited economic relations and endeavor to pave the way for a broad settlement of Asiatic problems by encouraging China to open direct conversations with the

[32] Draft proposal presented by Kurusu, Nov. 20, 1941, *Foreign Relations: Japan, 1931–1941*, II, 755–756.

[33] Memorandum by Ballantine, Nov. 20, 1941, *ibid.*, p. 753.

Japanese government. After such a beginning, he ruminated, a definitive settlement of the questions at issue between Washington and Tokyo could be deferred for a time.[34] Combining these ideas with others supplied by the State Department's Far Eastern Division, Hull finished the initial draft of an American counterproposal on November 22. This document had two parts. The first and most crucial section offered terms for a possible *modus vivendi*. The second contained proposals which, in Hull's view, should underlie a permanent settlement.

The second section did little but reiterate principles which the United States had consistently upheld for years.[35] But the proposals relating to a *modus vivendi* were fairly concrete. Based upon a reciprocal agreement to outlaw military advances in southeastern and northeastern Asia, and in the northern and southern Pacific areas, they called for an immediate reduction of Japanese forces in Indo-China to a total of twenty-five thousand men. At the same time, American-Japanese trade would be restored to the extent made possible by the suspension of freezing orders in both countries, although other export controls deemed necessary for national defense in either country would be unaffected. The United States would also encourage similar action by Great Britain, the Netherlands, and Australia.[36]

The same afternoon, November 22, Hull discussed this program with Halifax, Loudon, Casey, and Hu Shih—the British Ambassador, Dutch Minister, Australian Minister, and Chinese Ambassador. While the first three raised no objections, Hu Shih was doubtful, especially when Hull made it clear that his proposal did not rule out further advances by Japan in China proper. But even the Chinese Ambassador's criticism appears to have been mild,[37] and nothing happened during this conference to suggest that Hull ought to relinquish the project. Until the four envoys had specific instructions from their governments, however, the Secretary could do little except study possible changes in his offer.

Still later the same day, Hull explained to Nomura and Kurusu that he was not yet able to reply to the proposal of November 20, but he hinted that a *modus vivendi* was not out of the question.[38] Since the

---

[34] Memorandum by Roosevelt (undated), *Pearl Harbor Hearings*, pt. 14, exhibit 18, p. 1109.

[35] Draft of "Proposed Basis for Agreement," Nov. 22, 1941, *ibid.*, pp. 1116–1121.

[36] Draft of proposed *modus vivendi*, Nov. 22, 1941, *ibid.*, pp. 1113–1115.

[37] Memorandum by Hull, Nov. 22, 1941, *ibid.*, pp. 1122–1123.

[38] Memorandum by Ballantine, Nov. 22, 1941, *Foreign Relations: Japan, 1931–1941*, II, 757.

two Japanese had in the meanwhile received word from Tokyo extending the November 25 time limit to November 29,[39] Nomura expressed their readiness to wait a short while longer.[40]

Hull had no further contact with the Japanese representatives until November 26; but his discussions with Halifax, Loudon, Casey, and Hu Shih were resumed on November 24, when he handed them a slightly revised draft of his proposal. Although the only noteworthy change was the inclusion of more detailed arrangements for the resumption of American-Japanese trade,[41] the Chinese Ambassador expressed a much more determined opposition than he had indicated two days earlier. Hull dwelt at length on General Marshall's view that the presence of twenty-five thousand Japanese troops in Indo-China would constitute no threat to Chiang Kai-shek, but Hu objected strenuously to the retention of more than five thousand troops in that country. The others seemed merely apathetic about the *modus vivendi*. Though every one of them appeared to accept Hull's argument that all interested governments stood to gain by a three-month truce, they did not seem to evaluate the situation from quite his point of view. The Secretary was annoyed by his impression that all were thinking "of the advantages to be derived without any particular thought of what we should pay for them . . . ." His irritation increased when he discovered that the Dutch government alone had registered its formal approval of the *modus vivendi*. Hull felt keenly that he was not receiving the coöperation he had a right to expect. Considering the trouble he had encountered learning the views of the several governments, he said, he was not sure he would present the offer to Japan after all.[42] But there appeared to be some comfort in the thought that Churchill had not yet spoken, for that evening, at Hull's suggestion, Roosevelt sent the Prime Minister a personal message urging that the proposed truce be given sympathetic study.[43]

A third draft of the *modus vivendi* was ready by the following day, November 25. Here the section which placed a limit of twenty-five thousand on the number of troops to remain in Indo-China was altered to provide that the Japanese forces in that country should be reduced

[39] Togo to Nomura, Nov. 22, 1941, *Pearl Harbor Hearings*, pt. 12, exhibit 1, p. 165.
[40] Memorandum by Ballantine, Nov. 22, 1941, *Foreign Relations: Japan, 1931–1941*, II, 761.
[41] Draft of proposed *modus vivendi*, Nov. 24, 1941, *Pearl Harbor Hearings*, pt. 14, exhibit 18, pp. 1127–1131.
[42] Memorandum by Hull, Nov. 24, 1941, *ibid.*, pp. 1143–1146.
[43] Roosevelt to Churchill, Nov. 24, 1941, *ibid.*, pp. 1139–1141.

to the total present on July 26, 1941, when full-scale occupation had begun.[44] However, both Roosevelt and Hull were fast losing confidence in the idea. The President's message to Churchill the previous evening had stated his belief that Japan would decline the *modus vivendi* anyway, and this pessimism grew rapidly. At a meeting with Stimson, Knox, Marshall, and Stark on November 25 Hull expressed the opinion that an agreement with Japan had become virtually impossible,[45] while the President—according to Stimson—thought that the Japanese might attack as early as the following Monday. Therefore, the real question was "how we should maneuver them into the position of firing the first shot without allowing too much danger to ourselves." [46]

These misgivings were quickly stimulated by advices from London and Chungking. In a memorandum which reached Washington the same day, British Foreign Secretary Anthony Eden treated the *modus vivendi* with unconcealed hostility. Though he gave Hull leave to do as he thought best, Eden thought that the Japanese proposal of November 20 should be looked upon "as the opening move in a process of bargaining." He suggested that any American counterproposal ought to demand total Japanese withdrawal from Indo-China and immediate suspension of advances in China itself, as well as assurances covering the rest of Asia and the southern Pacific area. He also believed that the proposed resumption of American-Japanese trade should not go too far; certainly it should include no commerce in oil.[47]

Hu Shih's statements had afforded ample reason to suppose that China's official reaction would be even less favorable, and this expectation was more than borne out. A somewhat violent message from Chiang Kai-shek, delivered on November 25 by T. V. Soong, stated in the most unqualified terms that any relaxation of American freezing orders which was not preceded by an agreement calling for the withdrawal of Japanese armies from China would convince the Chinese people that they had been abandoned, would ruin morale, and would bring about the collapse of Chinese resistance.[48] Hu Shih visited Hull that evening in an effort to explain this cablegram; and despite his own waning affec-

[44] Draft of proposed *modus vivendi*, Nov. 25, 1941, *ibid.*, pp. 1150–1154.

[45] Hull to Roberts, Dec. 30, 1941, *ibid.*, pt. 20, exhibit 174, p. 4113.

[46] Stimson's notes, Nov. 25, 1941, *ibid.*, pt. 11, p. 5433.

[47] Memorandum presented by Halifax, Nov. 25, 1941, *ibid.*, pt. 14, exhibit 18, pp. 1164–1167.

[48] Copy of message from Chiang Kai-shek to T. V. Soong, delivered to Stimson on Nov. 25, 1941, *ibid.*, p. 1161.

tion for the *modus vivendi,* the Secretary made no attempt to conceal his irritation. In a placatory tone the Ambassador explained that the Generalissimo did not comprehend the full relationship between Japanese policy and the world situation, and he undertook to secure some modification of his government's point of view.[49]   But Eden's note had made it clear that Chiang was not alone in his worries, and Churchill now voiced much the same fears in his answer to Roosevelt's message of November 24.[50]   It was evident by the morning of November 26 that the projected truce had scarcely a friend left.

By his own statement, Hull decided to abandon the *modus vivendi* on the night of November 25, even before the message from Churchill was received. As he later explained, "The slight prospect of Japan's agreeing to the *modus vivendi* . . . did not warrant assuming the risks involved in proceeding with it, especially the risk of collapse of Chinese morale and resistance, and even of disintegration in China."[51]   The major factors in his decision, therefore, were the attitudes of Japan and China. While he may have given Chiang's fulminations too much weight, the Secretary's belief that Japan would not accept his terms was solidly based in knowledge derived from messages intercepted in transmission between the Foreign Office in Tokyo and the Japanese Embassy in Washington. Thanks to these intercepts, the American government never had much reason to doubt the ultimate nature of "Proposal B," and another bit of instruction received by Nomura on November 24 was enough to turn belief into certainty. For Togo in this message warned his underling that the United States could satisfy Japan only by accepting every point contained in his offer of November 20, and he emphasized the fact that one of these points called for a cessation of American aid to China—[52] a guarantee which Hull's project did not offer even indirectly.

Having concluded that a *modus vivendi* was not feasible, Hull approached Roosevelt on November 26 with a recommendation that it be dropped altogether. He wanted to use only the second section of the draft counterproposal in his reply to Japan.[53]   Being thoroughly familiar with the unpromising status of the *modus vivendi* and rather irritated

[49] Memorandum by Hull, Nov. 25, 1941, *Pearl Harbor Hearings,* pt. 14, exhibit 18, pp. 1167–1169.

[50] Churchill to Roosevelt, Nov. 26, 1941, *ibid.,* exhibit 23, p. 1300.

[51] Cordell Hull, *The Memoirs of Cordell Hull* (New York: Macmillan Co., 1948), II, 1081.

[52] Togo to Nomura, Nov. 24, 1941, *Pearl Harbor Hearings,* pt. 12, exhibit 1, p. 172.

[53] Memorandum by Hull, Nov. 26, 1941, *ibid.,* pt. 14, exhibit 18, pp. 1176–1177.

by new reports that a large Japanese convoy was heading south from Shanghai, the President seems to have yielded without much argument.[54] Late that afternoon, in consequence, Hull received Nomura and Kurusu at the State Department and handed them the note for which they had waited six days. As a first step, it proposed the formation of a multilateral nonaggression pact including the United States, Japan, the British Empire, China, the Netherlands, Russia, and Thailand. Next, all interested governments should guarantee the integrity of Indo-China. Thirdly, Japan should withdraw all its forces from both China and Indo-China. In the fourth place, Japan and the United States should agree to support no Chinese regime except the Nationalist government, give up their extraterritorial rights in China, and endeavor to persuade other countries to do likewise. With regard to each other, they should suspend their freezing orders, negotiate a new commercial treaty, and enter an agreement for stabilization of the dollar-yen rate. It' was also provided, in obvious reference to the Tripartite Pact, that neither government should be a party to any agreement with a third power which conflicted in any way with the establishment of peace in the Pacific.[55] The Japanese envoys received this document with long faces and said they would transmit its contents to Tokyo.[56]

The session had been quiet. But it was obviously the calm of resignation, not of agreement. Nomura and Kurusu had abandoned hope, while the Secretary of State regarded his proposal as little more than a gesture. The next morning, November 27, Hull informed Stimson that negotiations had, in effect, been broken off. "I have washed my hands of it," he added, "and it is now in the hands of you and Knox—the Army and the Navy." [57] Nor did military and naval leaders think differently. Marshall dispatched a message to Manila the same day, telling MacArthur that he was to let Japan make the first move, but was to guide his actions by the fact that negotiations appeared to be terminated.[58] Stark put the situation in even stronger terms. By a dispatch frankly characterized as a "war warning," the Chief of Naval Operations

[54] Hull, *Memoirs*, II, 1082.
[55] Document presented to Nomura, Nov. 26, 1941, *Foreign Relations: Japan, 1931–1941*, II, 768–770.
[56] Memorandum by Ballantine, Nov. 26, 1941, *ibid.*, pp. 764–767. For Nomura's comments in regard to the negotiations described here, see Kichisaburo Nomura, "Stepping Stones to War," United States Naval Institute, *Proceedings*, LXXVII (Sept. 1951), 927–930.
[57] Stimson's notes, Nov. 27, 1941, *Pearl Harbor Hearings*, pt. 11, pp. 5434–5435.
[58] Marshall to MacArthur, Nov. 27, 1941, *ibid.*, pt. 14, exhibit 32, p. 1329.

apprised Kimmel at Pearl Harbor that an aggressive move against the Philippines, Thailand, the Isthmus of Kra, or Borneo could be expected within the next few days, and ordered him to begin defensive deployment of his forces in accordance with Rainbow No. 5.[59]

III

The Japanese problem was not the only burden carried by the Department of State in those fateful days. If other concerns grew relatively smaller as the Far Eastern question took over the center of the stage, they were by no means lost to sight. Whatever happened in the Pacific, most of America's European policies still needed daily study, and these received their final prewar adjustments in late November and early December.

The review of a possible commercial agreement with Spain, an undertaking which had engaged the attention of the State Department since early October, had always moved at an extremely deliberate pace. Before the end of that month, President Roosevelt indicated his concurrence with the recommendation of October 9 that petroleum exports to Spain be allowed to continue within the established limitations.[60] But other aspects of United States trade relations with that country were not to be determined so readily, and a definite commercial proposal was not completed until the end of November.

The passage of time had not done much to soften American policy in this connection, for the terms of the offer reflected a very close-fisted attitude toward Spain. While the proposed agreement resembled the Murphy-Weygand accord in some ways, it was much more rigorous in others. So far as oil was concerned, the United States was prepared to supply just enough "to meet Spain's requirements for transportation and other essentials." To ensure that it would not be employed "in any manner useful to Italy or Germany, directly or indirectly," its distribution was to be supervised by American agents with free access to all facilities for receiving, shipping, storing, and refining oil. Spain might buy other commodities that were plentiful in the American market, as well as enough goods in the scarce and essential category to maintain

[59] Stark to Kimmel, Nov. 27, 1941, *Pearl Harbor Hearings,* pt. 14, exhibit 37, p. 1406.

[60] See Welles to Roosevelt, Oct. 31, 1941, MS Roosevelt Papers (Official File, Box 422–A).

economic activity at a restricted level—but only if Madrid could furnish satisfactory assurances against their reëxport, except from one Spanish destination to another, and against their being used "in any manner to benefit, directly or indirectly, the interests of Germany or Italy or countries occupied by Germany or Italy." The proposal also expressed the hope that the admission to Spain of such American articles as printed matter, current publications, motion-picture films, office equipment, and radio receiving sets would be facilitated. In return, Spain was to supply the United States with quantities of wolfram, cork, mercury, zinc, tin, lead, fluor spar, and various roots and drugs. So far as possible, moreover, Spain was to deliver these products in its own ships.[61]

The proposal was handed to Cárdenas, in Washington, on November 29. Although he managed to obtain certain changes in phraseology, the Spanish Ambassador was unable to secure alterations in substance; and as week followed week without bringing a reply from Madrid, it became evident that Franco was not yet prepared to do business on such terms. Nevertheless, Washington stood firm. While the State Department concentrated on other things, Spanish tankers were permitted to lie in American ports waiting for oil that did not come, and general commerce with Spain declined steadily. Since Great Britain favored a less exacting attitude on the part of the United States, this policy was somewhat relaxed in January 1942.[62] But the exchange of goods with Spain was kept at a low level even then, and Washington seemed as far as ever from a permanent, wartime understanding with the Franco government.

The crisis which had been brewing at Vichy in late October and early November finally broke on November 18, when Pétain informed Leahy that Weygand had been dismissed from his post in North Africa. The following day Welles told Henry-Haye, Vichy's Ambassador in Washington, that the General's removal was evaluated by the American government as a promise of growing Nazi influence in North Africa, and that it presented the United States with the necessity of a complete change of policy toward France.[63] In consequence, it was announced

---

[61] *Aide-mémoire* presented to the Spanish Ambassador, Nov. 29, 1941, MS Department of State (852.6363/249A).

[62] Herbert Feis, *The Spanish Story: Franco and the Nations at War* (New York: Alfred A. Knopf, 1948), pp. 151–153.

[63] William D. Leahy, *I Was There* (New York: Whittlesey House, 1950), pp. 58–59; Hull, *Memoirs,* II, 1043; and William L. Langer, *Our Vichy Gamble* (New York: Alfred A. Knopf, 1947), p. 196.

on November 20 that the North African aid program would cease while the entire French policy of the United States underwent review.[64] But second thoughts were already making their appearance. From his post in Algiers Murphy urged that all action be deferred until the significance of this development could be more thoroughly understood.[65] Even Leahy, who was personally disappointed in Pétain for his surrender, advised no positive break.[66] On November 21 Weygand wrote Murphy a message of assurance that French policy had not been altered by his own departure from the scene. "Just suppose that I have passed to the other world," he begged, and added his fervent hope that the "union" between France and the United States would continue.[67] These points of view found their echo in a memorandum prepared on November 28 by the State Department's Division of European Affairs. Pointing out that the winter stabilization of the Russian front and the new British advance into Libya augmented the likelihood of a German move against French North Africa, this document argued that the Murphy-Weygand accord had already been the means of placing a good deal of valuable intelligence before the American government, and advised that relations with Vichy, barring an overt act which clearly nullified Pétain's assurances of good behavior, should not be broken.[68]

The matter was kept under consideration for another week. By that time it was evident that nothing could be gained from hasty action, and Leahy was instructed on December 6 to tell Pétain that the United States might resume its North African program if he would give new assurances concerning the French Fleet and colonies, and offer a verbal guarantee that Weygand's dismissal heralded no change in his North African policy. This message was handed to the Marshal and Darlan on December 11; the required promises were made one day later; and the Murphy-Weygand Agreement went back into effect at once.[69]

As a matter of fact, the real crisis was already several days past. Accompanied by Darlan—and by General Alphonse Juin, the man selected by the Germans to take Weygand's place in North Africa—Pétain had met Goering at St. Florentin on December 1. Not very friendly at any point, and even tempestuous in spots, the ensuing interview had largely

[64] Press release, Nov. 20, 1941, United States, Department of State, *Department of State Bulletin* (Washington, D. C.: U. S. Govt. Printing Office, 1939——), V (Nov. 22, 1941), 407.   [65] Langer, *Our Vichy Gamble*, p. 195.
[66] *Ibid.;* and Leahy, *I Was There*, p. 58.
[67] Langer, *Our Vichy Gamble*, p. 195.
[68] *Ibid.*, pp. 196–197.   [69] *Ibid.*, pp. 200–201.

dissipated whatever plans for new collaboration Darlan might have cherished on the eve of Weygand's dismissal.[70] In the sequel, moreover, General Juin followed his predecessor's course so faithfully that Washington had little reason to complain.[71]

Although Finland's November 11 reply to his peremptory communication of October 27 ended Hull's direct efforts to secure that country's withdrawal from the Russian war, it did nothing to soften the asperity of his views concerning Finnish policy, and he continued to give Finnish activities a good deal of attention. At ceremonies held in Berlin on November 25, Finland—along with Bulgaria, Croatia, Denmark, Rumania, Slovakia, and the Wang Ching-wei government of China—was admitted to the Anti-Comintern bloc.[72] Hull drew unfavorable notice to this event at a press conference held three days later. At the same time, he made his first public statement regarding the Finnish note of November 11, observing that this communication did not make clear to just what extent Finnish participation in the war grew out of a joint Finnish-German military policy "intended to inflict damage on Great Britain and her Allies," or just how far this threatened the interests of the United States. Moreover, he declared, Finland's every act since dispatching the note had tended to make him believe that it had entered a phase of complete military coöperation with the Nazi government.[73]

Only a severance of diplomatic relations could have gone much further than this, and no such step was taken. But Hull apparently made no effort to keep the peace between Finland and Great Britain. The two countries had not maintained diplomatic relations since August, and Halifax told Hull in late October that Russia wanted Britain to go the whole distance by declaring war. Asked for an opinion, the Secretary of State declined to offer any guidance.[74] There was no action for another month, although British impatience grew steadily. Then, on November 28, Great Britain transmitted an ultimatum to Finland through the United States Minister in Helsinki. It said that the British government would have no alternative but a declaration of war unless the Finnish government ceased its military operations by December 5. The next day Churchill forwarded a personal letter of explanation to Marshal Karl Mannerheim, the Finnish Commander-in-Chief. Man-

[70] *Ibid.*, pp. 198–199. [71] See Hull, *Memoirs*, II, 1045.

[72] John H. Wuorinen, ed., *Finland and World War II, 1939–1944* (New York: Ronald Press Co., 1948), p. 118.

[73] Report of press conference, Nov. 28, 1941, *Department of State Bulletin*, V (Nov. 29, 1941), 434–435. [74] Hull, *Memoirs*, II, 980.

nerheim's reply to Churchill was delivered on December 2, that of the Foreign Office on December 4. While both notes indicated that Finland had nearly reached its objectives and was about to halt its advance, neither constituted an unequivocal acceptance of the British demand. Branding the Finnish attitude as unsatisfactory, Great Britain declared war on December 6.[75]

In the meanwhile, both London and Washington had been subject to nagging doubts as to future relations with the Soviet Union. Neither the German war nor Anglo-American guarantees of aid had moved the Kremlin to abandon its self-assertive diplomacy, and Soviet complaints were again falling thick and fast. Among the issues which now produced difficulty were Russia's dissatisfaction with British and American refusal to recognize its annexation of the Baltic states, its desire for a second front, its demand for more generous supply commitments, and its irritation with unavoidable delays in meeting delivery schedules on supplies already promised. Most disturbing of all, however, was Stalin's flagrantly self-centered preoccupation with the European settlement which would follow Germany's eventual downfall.

As long as the advance of Hitler's armies continued unchecked and the all-important supply arrangements were being worked out, British and American representatives had managed to evade any serious consideration of the last issue. But when the German attack began to slow down, Russia grew more insistent. Stalin made it clear that he desired agreements covering such matters as the future status of Latvia, Lithuania, and Estonia; the postwar boundaries of Finland, Poland, and Rumania; and the restoration of the Sudetenland to Czechoslovakia. When the Red Army recaptured the important city of Rostov on November 29, and Soviet demands could be ignored no longer, Great Britain took the initiative in attempting to moderate this program. With no more delay, Anthony Eden decided to visit Moscow "to smooth out our relations in general, to explore the possibility of some kind of political agreement, and to discuss certain postwar problems." [76]

Roosevelt and Hull considered this an appropriate moment to take a position regarding Soviet policy. Accordingly, Winant was instructed

[75] *Finland and World War II*, pp. 134–135; and Churchill, *The Grand Alliance*, pp. 533–535.

[76] Memorandum of the Soviet Embassy, Nov. 25, 1941, MS Roosevelt Papers (Secretary's File, Box 71); Churchill, *The Grand Alliance*, pp. 457–458, 528–530; Robert E. Sherwood, *Roosevelt and Hopkins: An Intimate History* (New York: Harper and Bros., 1948), p. 401; and Hull, *Memoirs*, II, 1165.

on December 5 to give Eden the following verbal explanation for use in his talks at Moscow: In the view of the American government, the speed with which it had concluded supply agreements for the benefit of the Soviet Union gave ample proof of its sincere devotion to the Russian cause. It would remain faithful to these commitments until victory was won. So far as the postwar situation was concerned, however, United States policy was set forth in the Atlantic Charter. To endeavor to reach a more specific understanding at this time would be "unfortunate." Above all, the United States could enter no secret accords.[77]

Eden received this statement the morning of December 6 and left for Russia the next day, after hearing the first reports of the Japanese attack on Pearl Harbor.[78] Since the United States was now a belligerent, he apparently cited Roosevelt's position with considerable freedom at Moscow. But nothing did much good. Although Eden declined on behalf of the British government to recognize the annexation of eastern Poland and the Baltic states, Stalin would abandon neither these demands nor any of a dozen others. By the end of the month, when the British Foreign Minister returned to London, he had more than sufficient evidence that coöperation with Russia, even in wartime, would entail admitted disagreement as well as the expected nervous strain.[79]

IV

Although the Australian Minister and the British Ambassador had given little support to the *modus vivendi* to be offered to Japan while it was still under consideration, both revealed strong misgivings as soon as they learned of its abandonment. Casey saw Hull on November 27 to inquire whether the idea had been permanently discarded. On being informed that there were no current plans for reviving it, he wanted to know the reasons for this decision. He was told that the studious reserve of Eden and Churchill, added to the grim opposition of Chiang Kai-shek, had convinced the American government that the plan was not feasible.[80] With a similar purpose, Halifax called on Welles the same

[77] Hull to Winant, Dec. 5, 1941, *Pearl Harbor Hearings*, pt. 19, exhibit 166, pp. 3648–3651.

[78] Sherwood, *Roosevelt and Hopkins*, pp. 439, 402; cf. Churchill, *The Grand Alliance*, pp. 628–631, 695.

[79] Sherwood, *Roosevelt and Hopkins*, p. 451; and Hull, *Memoirs*, II, 1166–1167.

[80] Memorandum by Hull, Nov. 27, 1941, *Pearl Harbor Hearings*, pt. 14, exhibit 18, pp. 1182–1183.

day and received an almost identical answer.[81]   When he took the matter up with Hull on November 29, the response was even more blunt.
The Secretary told him, in effect, that Churchill's seemingly careless adherence to the views of Chungking had greatly weakened the American
position and made it almost impossible to deal with Chinese objections.[82]
Loudon, whose government had supported the *modus vivendi,* enjoyed a
much friendlier reception.[83]

But Hull showed no sign of retreating from the decision which had
been made. On November 29 he declined an Australian proposal of
mediation;[84] and when Casey and Halifax urged him jointly on
November 30 to do his best to postpone a break with Japan, he gave them
no encouragement.[85] Nor did the British government itself seem to
favor a softer policy on the part of the United States. Despite the implications of Halifax's attitude, Churchill took advantage of the moment
to resurrect the advice he had already offered, first at the Atlantic Conference in August 1941 and again on November 5. What he wanted
was an American ultimatum. In a message dispatched on November
30 he urged the President to issue a clear warning that any further act of
Japanese aggression would lead "immediately to the gravest consequences." He expressed the willingness of the British government
either to participate in such a declaration or to make a similar one of its
own.[86]

Nomura and Kurusu saw Hull on December 1 to assure him that a
reply to his proposals of November 26 would be delivered in a few days.
They also reminded him that Japan's offer to withdraw its troops from
southern Indo-China was still open. But the Secretary confronted his
visitors with reports of new troop movements into that country and expressed scant optimism as to the future course of American-Japanese relations. He was even more pessimistic than he sounded, for a succession
of Japanese diplomatic messages intercepted over the past three days
pointed unmistakably to war. Among them was a cablegram received
by Nomura on November 28. Here Togo reported that the American
note of November 26 could not be accepted; negotiations would there-

[81] Memorandum by Welles, Nov. 27, 1941, *Pearl Harbor Hearings,* pt. 14, exhibit 18,
p. 1180.
[82] Memorandum by Hull, Nov. 29, 1941, *ibid.,* pp. 1194–1196.
[83] Memorandum by Hull, Nov. 27, 1941, *ibid.,* pt. 4, p. 1694.
[84] Memorandum by Hull, Nov. 29, 1941, *ibid.,* pt. 19, exhibit 168, p. 3689.
[85] Memorandum by Hull, Nov. 30, 1941, *ibid.,* p. 3690.
[86] Churchill to Roosevelt, Nov. 30, 1941, *ibid.,* pt. 14, exhibit 24, p. 1301.

fore be *"de facto* ruptured" when he sent more complete instructions in two or three days.[87] Messages picked up in transmission between Berlin and Tokyo led to the same grim conclusion, for these indicated that Ribbentrop was now telling Oshima that a Japanese decision to fight the United States would be of advantage to both their countries.[88]

Although the American government had no way of knowing the details, German policy had undergone a marked change since mid-November. The inherent contradiction between keeping America at peace and continuing to support Japan under terms like those of the Tripartite Pact could be ignored no longer. It is certain that many high German officials had recognized this contradiction much earlier, but Hitler and Ribbentrop apparently refused to see it clearly until the last ten days of November. Even then, Hitler did not cease vacillation.

To Japan, which had long been all too familiar with the Fuehrer's determination to keep the United States nonbelligerent, this was a dramatic reversal indeed. Wishing to make sure that it represented a steadfast decision, Japan immediately began to press for absolutely concrete assurances of German and Italian aid. Without revealing exactly when, or where, hostilities might be expected to start, the Japanese Foreign Office demanded specific pledges from both governments that they would meet their full obligations under the Tripartite Pact, and that neither would conclude a separate peace with Great Britain or the United States. Mussolini consented without much hesitation. But Hitler still had trouble reaching a final decision, and not until the early morning of December 5 was Ribbentrop able to give Oshima the guarantee Japan desired.[89] From the end of November, however, it seemed reasonably clear that this would be the outcome.

Meanwhile, the intercepted messages continued to reveal a part of what was transpiring. On November 30 Togo informed Oshima that Japan's conversations with the United States "now stand ruptured," and he directed the Ambassador to warn the German government of the "extreme danger" that war might "break out between the Anglo-Saxon nations and Japan through some clash of arms . . . quicker than anyone dreams." He even hinted at the direction of attack by observing that it

---

[87] Memorandum by Ballantine, Dec. 1, 1941, *Foreign Relations: Japan, 1931–1941,* II, 772–773; and Togo to Nomura, Nov. 28, 1941, *Pearl Harbor Hearings,* pt. 12, exhibit 1, p. 195.

[88] Oshima to Togo, Nov. 29, 1941, *Pearl Harbor Hearings,* pt. 12, exhibit 1, p. 200.

[89] Hans L. Trefousse, *Germany and American Neutrality, 1939–1941* (New York: Bookman Associates, 1951), pp. 142–147.

was to his country's advantage to "stress the south" for the time being.[90]

Need as well as opportunity beckoned Japan toward the poorly de-fended riches of southeastern Asia and the Indies, and all available data on Japanese preparations indicated the likelihood of a major drive against these areas. But another "clash of arms" was even nearer reali-zation, for the warlike orders issued to the Japanese Combined Fleet on November 5 and 7 had led to speedy action. A few days later Fleet units assigned to the Pearl Harbor striking force were ordered to assemble in Hitokappu Bay, a remote anchorage off Etorofu, largest of the Kurile Islands. The rendezvous was completed in great secrecy by November 22. An advance force consisting of twenty large submarines, five midget submarines, and eight supply vessels had already left for Hawaiian waters on November 18 and 20, proceeding directly from Kure and Yokosuka on the Inland Sea. Then, after final preparations, the main task force of six carriers, two battleships, two cruisers, nine destroyers, three submarines, and a supply train—the whole commanded by Vice Admiral Chuichi Nagumo—steamed out of Hitokappu Bay on the morning of November 26 (November 25, American time) and headed east.[91]

This was the significance of the initial time limit which Foreign Minister Togo, at the behest of military and naval authorities, had placed upon the final negotiations in Washington. The extension of this limit to November 29 seems to have been prompted by the belief that orders could be countermanded and the task force brought back to Japan with no harm done if the United States, contrary to expectations, should accept "Proposal B" in advance of that date. But even the ultimate deadline was now past. On December 1 the Japanese Cabinet approved Tojo's decision to begin hostilities one week later, thus con-firming the date mentioned in Yamamoto's order of November 7. As a result, Nagumo was directed, by radio, to proceed with his attack plans and strike the United States Pacific Fleet at its Pearl Harbor anchorage on the morning of December 8 (December 7, American time).[92]

The secret was kept perfectly. Few persons not in high naval com-mand, including responsible officials of the Japanese government, had any kind of advance knowledge; indeed, there is reason to believe that

[90] Togo to Oshima, Nov. 30, 1941, *Pearl Harbor Hearings,* pt. 12, exhibit 1, p. 204.
[91] *Pearl Harbor Report,* pp. 56–57. See also Samuel Eliot Morison, *The Rising Sun in the Pacific, 1931—April 1942* (Boston: Little, Brown, and Co., 1948), pp. 88–89, 95.
[92] Report from MacArthur, in Tokyo, on Japanese plans for the Pearl Harbor attack, Dec. 13, 1945, *Pearl Harbor Hearings,* pt. 13, exhibit 8–D, p. 426.

even Tojo, the Premier, did not learn about the Pearl Harbor plan until November 30. American intelligence activities failed to uncover the move, and since no hint of it was entrusted to the Japanese diplomatic code, even the usually fruitful interceptions gave no warning. Moderately heavy weather and a good deal of fog also helped the Japanese escape detection, while Kimmel's unaccountable failure to maintain distant air reconnaissance north and west of the Hawaiian Islands guaranteed a surprise.[93]

On the other hand, Washington continued to receive news of specific Japanese preparations for large-scale activities in the south. The effect of this was augmented by persuasions growing out of what might be termed the psychological atmosphere. The administration was still acutely sensitive to American public opinion and feared that even new aggressions might not render it easy to secure a declaration of war against Japan unless these involved a direct attack upon United States territory. Believing that Japan would open its drive in the manner best calculated to avoid provoking intervention by the United States, American policy makers—civilian and military alike—were convinced that Tokyo's first overt move would be directed against southeastern Asia and the Indies; for there Japan, without invading a single American possession, could obtain the raw materials needed to consolidate its position for a long war. This concept was so firmly established in late November and early December that it ruled out any serious thought of an earlier or simultaneous attack elsewhere.[94]

Immediate strategic planning with reference to Japan, therefore, was confined almost entirely to the Far East, and little attempt was made to look beyond the Marshall-Stark memorandum of November 5. On November 27 the two repeated their advice in somewhat different form. They recommended that until the Philippines could be completely reinforced military action should be considered "only if Japan attacks or directly threatens United States, British or Dutch territory," and they urged that arrangements with the British and Dutch be made to issue a joint warning against any threatened invasion of Thailand.[95] Handed

[93] Morison, *The Rising Sun in the Pacific*, p. 92; *Pearl Harbor Report*, pp. 114–117; and Robert E. Ward, "The Inside Story of the Pearl Harbor Plan," United States Naval Institute, *Proceedings*, LXXVII (Dec. 1951), 1278.

[94] *Pearl Harbor Report*, p. 198; and Henry L. Stimson and McGeorge Bundy, *On Active Service: In Peace and War* (New York: Harper and Bros., 1948), p. 390.

[95] Memorandum by Marshall and Stark, Nov. 27, 1941, *Pearl Harbor Hearings*, pt. 14, exhibit 17, p. 1083.

to the President on November 28—just nine days before the Japanese attack—the memorandum gave prevailing calculations further support.

This preoccupation with the Far East was still not allowed to change the basic war plan, however. Under Rainbow No. 5 the Pacific Fleet was to confine its efforts to a zone which did not extend westward of 140 degrees east longitude except in the neighborhood of Japan. Considering this and the multitude of tasks assigned to Kimmel's command in its own area, its support of United States forces in Asia would have to be more or less indirect for a good while.[96]   However America became involved in hostilities—whether through voluntary aid to the British and Dutch or through the stark necessity of resisting an attack on the Philippines—the Far Eastern establishment was expected to carry the brunt of the war during its initial stages. Thus it was doubly necessary to complete defensive arrangements for that area as quickly as possible.

On November 20 Admiral Hart finally received an answer to his suggestion of October 27 that the Asiatic Fleet be concentrated in Manila Bay to assist the Army's defense of Luzon. Since the answer was a brusque refusal, Hart immediately started his deployment southward.[97] This rendered the question of Anglo-American naval coöperation more urgent than ever, but he still had to wait another two weeks before conferring with Admiral Phillips, the new British commander at Singapore. When Phillips finally reached Manila on December 5, time was running short. In a series of talks which lasted a bare twenty-four hours, the two concluded that Singapore was indefensible and that Manila would constitute a much more useful base for offensive operations against a Japanese drive into the southwestern Pacific. But Manila's port facilities admittedly required expansion; and since Phillips, in any event, lacked the necessary air power to cover a shift of his larger units from Malaya to the Philippines, it was decided that the transfer should be postponed until April 1942. As a result, Hart and Phillips did not change the initial disposition of their main forces. Their only agreement for immediate action was an undertaking by Hart to send four destroyers to join Phillips' command.[98]

---

[96] Sec. 5, chap. 1, pt. 5, WPL–46, Navy basic war plan, *Pearl Harbor Hearings*, pt. 18, exhibit 129, p. 2912; and sec. 1, chap. 2, pt. 3, *ibid.*, pp. 2889–2890.

[97] Morison, *The Rising Sun in the Pacific*, p. 154.

[98] Morison, *The Rising Sun in the Pacific*, p. 157; and Hart to Stark, Dec. 7, 1941 (Dec. 6, Washington time), *Pearl Harbor Hearings*, pt. 3, pp. 1933–1935. The four destroyers involved had already joined the southward movement and were then at Balikpapan, Borneo.

Meanwhile, the Army did what it could. Still far short of the two hundred thousand total envisaged when defense concepts had been changed in late July, MacArthur's force was in a pitiable condition for war. Substantial reinforcements were on the way. One group was at sea as Japan struck, and twenty-one thousand more troops were about to leave the United States.[99] But that was not the same as being in the Philippines. When General Wainwright, having completed his duties with the Philippine Division, left Fort McKinley and journeyed north to take command of four new divisions mobilizing in central Luzon, land preparations for defending the islands had advanced about as far as they were destined to advance. This was November 28.[100]

Likewise on November 28 that group known unofficially as the "War Council"—Roosevelt, Hull, Stimson, Knox, Marshall, and Stark—met for further study of military policy and possible diplomatic action. Going now somewhat beyond the question of a warning to Japan on behalf of Thailand, they agreed that the United States would have to join Great Britain in resisting any Japanese move against the Isthmus of Kra (southern Thailand). It was also decided that Roosevelt should endeavor to postpone hostilities by sending a personal appeal to Emperor Hirohito and by delivering a public warning to Japan in the form of a message to Congress.[101] Drafts of both statements were prepared at once and submitted to Roosevelt the following day. But as Hull had suggested that the message to Congress be postponed until "the last stage of our relations . . . has been reached," action was deferred on both counts.[102]

Diplomatic efforts did not cease entirely. Intelligence reports left no doubt that Japan was increasing its forces in southern Indo-China,[103] and Welles, following the President's instructions, asked Kurusu on December 2 to explain this activity. But Kurusu claimed ignorance.[104]

[99] Morison, *The Rising Sun in the Pacific*, p. 74.

[100] Jonathan M. Wainwright, *General Wainwright's Story*, ed. Robert Considine (Garden City, N. Y.: Doubleday and Co., 1946), pp. 13–14.

[101] Stimson's notes, Nov. 28, 1941, *Pearl Harbor Hearings*, pt. 11, p. 5436.

[102] Memorandum by Hull, Nov. 29, 1941, *ibid.*, pt. 14, exhibit 19, p. 1203. See also attached drafts of proposed message to Congress and proposed message to the Emperor of Japan, *ibid.*, pp. 1204–1228.

[103] See memorandum by Stimson, Nov. 26, 1941, *ibid.*, pt. 16, exhibit 98, p. 2014; memorandum presented by Halifax, Nov. 30, 1941, *ibid.*, pt. 14, exhibit 21, pp. 1251–1252; and message sent from Bangkok to Tokyo, Nov. 29, 1941, *ibid.*, pt. 12, exhibit 1, p. 203.

[104] Memorandum by Ballantine, Dec. 2, 1941, *Foreign Relations: Japan, 1931–1941*, II, 779.

Although Welles's inquiry was duly referred to Tokyo, the Foreign Office's reply, which reached Washington on December 5, told little more. Blandly ignoring the question of southern Indo-China, the Japanese government merely stated that it was reinforcing its troops in the northern part of that country to counteract certain Chinese troop movements on the other side of the border.[105]

Much less difficult to assess were a number of intercepted Japanese messages which became available at about the same time. One of these was a dispatch to Togo from the Japanese Ambassador in Rome, dated December 3, revealing that the latter had asked Mussolini whether Italy would join Japan in the event of a declaration of war against the United States and Great Britain. To this question Mussolini had replied: "Of course. She is obligated to do so under the terms of the Tripartite Pact." [106] On December 4 American monitors picked up a message from Togo which indicated that the Japanese Embassy in Washington was about to destroy its code machines and other code material.[107] When reading this message, President Roosevelt agreed with his naval aid, Admiral Beardall, that it was a meaningful sign of approaching war.[108] The State Department took a similar view, ordered Grew the next day to prepare for an emergency, and sent him instructions for destroying codes, confidential files, and related materials as soon as the emergency arose.[109] By the afternoon of December 6, when the Japanese Embassy was alerted to await transmission of a fourteen-part reply to the American note of November 26,[110] both governments were prepared for an immediate breach of relations.

Earlier in the day the State Department had received information from London that two large Japanese task forces had passed Cambodia Point and were then nearing the coast of Thailand with the apparent intention of striking either at Bangkok or the Isthmus of Kra.[111] If the American government needed anything more to round out its picture of Japanese designs, this information was it. The final stage mentioned

---

[105] Statement presented by Nomura, Dec. 5, 1941, *Foreign Relations: Japan, 1931–1941*, II, 784.

[106] Japanese Embassy in Rome to the Japanese Foreign Office, Dec. 3, 1941, *Pearl Harbor Hearings*, pt. 12, exhibit 1, p. 229.

[107] Togo to Nomura, Dec. 4, 1941, *ibid.*, p. 231.

[108] Beardall's testimony, Apr. 11, 1946, *ibid.*, pt. 11, p. 5284.

[109] Hull to Grew and others, Dec. 5, 1941, *ibid.*, pt. 2, p. 745.

[110] Togo to Nomura, Dec. 6, 1941, *ibid.*, pt. 12, exhibit 1, pp. 238–239.

[111] Two messages, Winant to Hull, Dec. 6, 1941, *ibid.*, pt. 14, exhibit 21, pp. 1246–1248.

by Hull appeared to have begun, and some time on December 6—the record does not establish the exact hour, but it seems to have been mid-afternoon at the latest—Roosevelt decided to send his message to Emperor Hirohito.[112] The draft which had been prepared several days earlier was subjected to final revision, and the dispatch left Washington at 9:00 that evening.[113]

The President's telegram to the Japanese Emperor represented the last attempt on either side to avert hostilities. Certainly no one in the American government expected it to be successful. In essence it was another reiteration of what Hull and Roosevelt had been saying for months. It reviewed Japanese policy in China, Indo-China, and southeastern Asia generally. It emphasized the American desire for peace. It carried the assurance that withdrawal of Japanese forces from Indo-China would stabilize relations between the United States and Japan. And it expressed the President's "fervent hope" that the Emperor would "give thought in this . . . emergency to ways of dispelling the dark clouds." [114]

Of course, it did no good whatever. Since Roosevelt yielded nothing, the gesture was futile from its very inception. Besides, it arrived too late. Apparently owing to slow delivery by Japanese postal authorities after it reached Tokyo, the message was delayed in reaching Grew; its progress was slowed again in the Foreign Office; and it was not placed in the Emperor's hands until 3:00 A.M., December 8 (Tokyo time), about twenty minutes before the attack on Pearl Harbor started.[115]

Meanwhile, Japan's lengthy reply to the American note of November 26 began to reach Washington. By 9:00 in the evening of Saturday, December 6, the first thirteen parts of the fourteen-part message were decoded and ready for distribution. Some of the persons who ordinarily received copies of the intercepted messages were no longer in their offices and were not readily available elsewhere, so only a partial distribution was made that night. Copies were delivered to President Roosevelt and Secretary Knox by a Naval Intelligence officer, while Stimson and

[112] Memorandum by Hull, Dec. 6, 1941, and notation by Roosevelt, *ibid.*, pt. 14, exhibit 20, p. 1239.
[113] See *ibid.*; and *Foreign Relations: Japan, 1931–1941*, II, 784 n.
[114] Roosevelt to Emperor Hirohito, Dec. 6, 1941, *Foreign Relations: Japan, 1931–1941*, II, 784–786.
[115] Grew's testimony, Nov. 26, 1945, *Pearl Harbor Hearings*, pt. 2, pp. 569–570; and Joseph C. Grew, *Ten Years in Japan* (New York: Simon and Schuster, 1944), pp. 486–487.

Hull—who were on the Army's distribution list—apparently received nothing until the following day.[116]

The initial reactions of most of the officials who saw the dispatch that evening are obscure; but there is no doubt that Roosevelt, for one, immediately interpreted it as evidence that war was very near.[117]   On the other hand, the thirteen available parts of the Japanese reply were not especially informative.   The first twelve parts gave a rather tedious survey of Japanese-American relations since the preceding April, and the thirteenth stated clearly that the American proposals of November 26 were unacceptable.[118]   But it had been known for over a week that this would be the outcome, and since the message contained neither a declaration of war nor a positive sign of a break in diplomatic relations, nothing was greatly changed.   As a result, there was no effort to call a meeting of the "War Council" or to take any other action until the next day.

The fourteenth and final part of the Japanese memorandum was received and decoded during the night.[119]   Summing up what had gone before, it accused the United States of conspiring with Great Britain and other countries "to obstruct Japan's efforts toward the establishment of peace through the creation of a New Order in East Asia, and especially to preserve Anglo-American rights and interests by keeping Japan and China at war."   Its conclusion ran as follows: "The Japanese Government regrets to have to notify . . . the American Government that in view of the attitude of the American Government it cannot but consider that it is impossible to reach an agreement through further negotiations."[120]   In the light of what was already known, this indicated clearly that a breach of diplomatic relations was to be expected almost at once.

Hull, Stimson, and Knox had previously made arrangements to confer at the State Department on Sunday morning.   The complete text of the Japanese memorandum was in their hands by the time they assembled.[121]   That an attack could be expected they all agreed.   But since

---

[116] For a summary of the evidence as to which officials received translations of the first thirteen parts of this message the evening of December 6, see *Pearl Harbor Report,* pp. 433–434.

[117] Schulz's testimony, Feb. 15, 1946, *Pearl Harbor Hearings,* pt. 10, pp. 4662–4663.

[118] Togo to Nomura, Dec. 6, 1941, *ibid.,* pt. 12, exhibit 1, pp. 239–245.

[119] *Pearl Harbor Report,* p. 434 n.

[120] Togo to Nomura, Dec. 6, 1941, *Pearl Harbor Hearings,* pt. 12, exhibit 1, p. 245.

[121] Kramer's testimony, Feb. 6, 1946, *ibid.,* pt. 8, p. 3907.

the message did not challenge their established ideas regarding its probable location, they seem to have discussed nothing but the likeliest points of attack in southeastern Asia and the problem of future coöperation in that area with the British, the Dutch, the Australians, and the Chinese.[122]

While this conversation progressed, two later messages from the Japanese Foreign Office were distributed. One ordered the immediate destruction of all code machines and code materials remaining in the Japanese Embassy.[123] The other directed Nomura and Kurusu to present the fourteen-part memorandum to the Secretary of State at 1:00 P.M. that day.[124] When General Marshall reached his office between 11:15 and 11:30 A.M., he read both of these dispatches, as well as the long memorandum, and immediately perceived the likelihood of a relationship between the hour stated and the Japanese plan of attack.[125] The fact that 1:00 P.M., Washington time, nearly coincided with the hour of sunrise in Hawaii apparently escaped him, but he did call Stark and suggest that all theater commanders be alerted at once.[126] Stark demurred at first. "War warning" messages had been sent to Manila and Pearl Harbor as long ago as November 27. MacArthur was as nearly ready as he was likely to be; Lieutenant General Walter C. Short, Army commander in Hawaii, had been maintaining a special alert against sabotage and subversive activities since November 29;[127] and the Admiral thought further warnings might produce confusion. He soon changed his mind, however, and urged Marshall to go ahead.[128] So Marshall drafted the following message to the Western Defense Command, the Hawaiian Command, the Panama Command, and the Philippine Command: "The Japanese are presenting at 1 P.M. Eastern Standard Time, today, what amounts to an ultimatum. Also they are under orders to destroy their code machines immediately. Just what significance the hour set may have we do not know, but be on the alert accordingly."[129]

This dispatch was filed at the Army signal center at 11:50, and Mar-

---

[122] Hull's testimony, Nov. 27, 1945, *ibid.*, pt. 2, p. 611.

[123] Togo to Nomura, Dec. 7, 1941, *ibid.*, pt. 12, exhibit 1, p. 249.

[124] *Pearl Harbor Report*, p. 437; and Togo to Nomura, Dec. 7, 1941, *Pearl Harbor Hearings*, pt. 12, exhibit 1, p. 248.   [125] *Pearl Harbor Report*, pp. 223–224.

[126] List of telephone calls made from outside through the White House switchboard, Dec. 7, 1941, *Pearl Harbor Hearings*, pt. 15, exhibit 58, p. 1633; and Stark's testimony, Dec. 31, 1945, *ibid.*, pt. 5, p. 2132.

[127] Short to Marshall, Nov. 29, 1941, *ibid.*, pt. 14, exhibit 32, p. 1331.

[128] Stark's testimony, Dec. 31, 1945, *ibid.*, pt. 5, pp. 2132–2133.

[129] Marshall to Short, Dec. 7, 1941, *ibid.*, pt. 14, exhibit 32, p. 1334.

shall was assured that it would reach the designated commanders by 1:00 P.M.[130]   But the copy intended for Short, who needed it most, ran afoul of unexpected delays in transmission and was not placed in his hands until the Japanese had come and gone.[131]   Thus the intelligence collected from Japanese messages during the night of December 6 and the morning of December 7 was used to no effect whatever so far as the attack on Pearl Harbor was concerned.

About noon, the Japanese Embassy made an appointment for Nomura and Kurusu to see Hull at 1:00 P.M.   A little later, however, the interview was postponed until 1:45 at the Embassy's request, and the pair did not actually arrive at the State Department until nearly 2:00.[132] In the meanwhile, the first report that Pearl Harbor was being attacked reached Washington.   At 1:50 P.M. the Navy Department received a dispatch from Kimmel: "Air raid on Pearl Harbor. This is not drill." [133]

President Roosevelt was informed at once, and he relayed the news to Hull by telephone without delay.[134]   Thus, when the Secretary of State received Nomura and Kurusu a few minutes later, he was not only familiar with the contents of the note they were about to present but also had a report which, though unconfirmed, offered a reasonably sure indication that war had started.   With grim control Hull listened to Nomura's explanation that he had not been able to present his government's memorandum at 1:00 P.M., as instructed, owing to difficulties in decoding.   But after pretending to read the document which Nomura then gave him, Hull abandoned much of his restraint.   Using language which he subsequently admitted would not be considered "diplomatic . . . in ordinary times," [135] he gave the Japanese his unvarnished opinion of the faithless and generally devious behavior which had marked Japan's course in recent months—whereupon Nomura and Kurusu, according to the official record, "took their leave without making any comment." [136]   It was the last in a long series of talks.

[130] *Pearl Harbor Report*, p. 225.

[131] For a summary of these delays, see Report of Army Pearl Harbor Board, *Pearl Harbor Hearings*, pt. 39, exhibit 157, pp. 94–96.

[132] Memorandum by Ballantine, Dec. 7, 1941, *Foreign Relations: Japan, 1931–1941*, II, 786.

[133] Baecher to Richardson, Apr. 8, 1946, *Pearl Harbor Hearings*, pt. 11, p. 5351.

[134] Hull's testimony, Nov. 27, 1945, *ibid.*, pt. 2, p. 607.

[135] Hull, *Memoirs*, II, 1096.

[136] Memorandum by Ballantine, Dec. 7, 1941, *Foreign Relations: Japan, 1931–1941*, II, 787.

A few hours later an equivalent scene was enacted in Tokyo. At about 7:30 A.M., December 8 (Japan time), the Japanese Foreign Office summoned Grew to receive its answer to Roosevelt's message of the preceding day. This consisted of the memorandum already presented in Washington. After reading it, Grew returned to the Embassy, still ignorant of what had befallen Pearl Harbor. He did not have much longer to wait, however. Before noon, he received a note from Togo announcing that a state of war existed.[137]

The blow at Oahu had taken American strategists by surprise. In the long run, nevertheless, their judgment was substantially vindicated. The task force which struck at Pearl Harbor withdrew as quickly as it had come, and Japan's permanent thrust was southward. Japanese forces were attacking Guam, Wake, Midway, Hong Kong, Malaya, and the Philippines in less than twenty-four hours. This was the situation faced by the United States when President Roosevelt delivered his war message to Congress and the nation shortly after noon on December 8.[138]

Reactions among Japan's allies, while speedy, were not entirely unanimous. For on the day after Pearl Harbor Count Ciano placed the following record in his diary: "A night call from Ribbentrop; he is joyful over the Japanese attack on the United States. He is so happy, in fact, that I can't but congratulate him, even though I am not so sure about the advantage." [139] But the forebodings of Mussolini's son-in-law, even had they not been private, could not have stemmed the surge of events. Confidence was high in Axis capitals, and on December 11 Germany and Italy fulfilled their destinies under the Tripartite Pact by joining in the war against America.

V

The American government consciously faced grim reality throughout the month directly preceding its official entry into the war, for the ultimate implications of a political program which outran existing military capacity were by this time clearly understood. Nevertheless, it

[137] Grew, *Ten Years*, p. 493.
[138] Message of the President to Congress, Dec. 8, 1941, *Foreign Relations: Japan, 1931–1941*, II, 794.
[139] Count Galeazzo Ciano, *The Ciano Diaries, 1939–1943*, ed. Hugh Gibson (Garden City, N. Y.: Doubleday and Co., 1946), p. 416.

adhered to its basic concept of the world situation with a persistence that was almost dogged. Despite the threat of imminent hostilities with Japan, it continued to prosecute the Atlantic war with vigor and to maintain an active diplomacy in Europe generally. Viewed in retrospect, this course was sound; Germany was unquestionably a greater threat to America than was Japan. But United States policy embraced immediate as well as long-range objectives during those final weeks of nonbelligerency, and judged by the attainment of immediate goals, it was not very successful.

The United States retained its initiative in the Atlantic, to be sure. In Europe, however, it barely held its own. Although Spain was now actively seeking economic favors, Washington drew no closer to a trade agreement with Madrid, and its influence with the Franco government continued to be a negative rather than a positive quantity. At the same time, its Vichy policy received another blow in Weygand's dismissal. Though the North African economic program was reinstated by the middle of December, the French situation still gave rise to serious misgivings. Nor was there much ground for complacency with respect to northern and eastern Europe. The United States made no direct effort to change Finland's course after receiving the Finnish memorandum of November 11, but that country's retirement from hostilities was still an American objective. With Britain's declaration of war against Finland on December 6, however, the Russo-Finnish conflict became an integral part of the general struggle. And despite the growing momentum of the Russian-aid program, Stalin's desire for immediate concessions in regard to the postwar territorial settlements again promised a multitude of future difficulties.

The greatest immediate aim was to gain time in the Far East. Although the hope for permanent peace no longer existed, the American government wanted to delay the outbreak of war in this area until its defensive preparations were considerably improved. To achieve this end a *modus vivendi* was kept under consideration the greater part of November. But Roosevelt and Hull knew that Japan would refuse any truce which prevented it from moving ahead, and to allow the Japanese any real advance would be to violate a principle to which the United States had been committed since August. This was the fundamental reason why the *modus vivendi* was abandoned.

Indeed, it is rather surprising that it was considered at all. No one doubted that the new round of conversations opened on November 7 was largely a façade. The American government was aware that Japan planned to take action if the United States did not consent to what was known to be an impossible settlement within a specified time. It was obvious that neither side believed in the likelihood of a compromise, because it was clear that neither side was prepared to accept a compromise. Nevertheless, an appearance of negotiation was maintained until November 26.

After that, the whole initiative rested with Japan.

Conclusion

I

Viewed in the broad setting of its relationship to the world crisis
of 1937–1941, American foreign policy was neither independent nor dy-
namic. Its forms were largely determined by the prior actions of other
governments, and it remained essentially defensive from beginning to
end. That it finally seized a worth-while initiative in certain limited
areas cannot be denied, but its commoner problem was to minimize dangers in situations which it had not been able to forestall. Instead of
guiding events, it was, on the whole, guided by them; and sometimes its
reactions were hazardously slow. Nevertheless, American policy in
1941 differed greatly from American policy in 1937 and 1938. Judged
by range of activity, firmness of purpose, and willingness to assume responsibility, it went through two distinct phases in the four and one-half
years leading up to the Japanese attack on Pearl Harbor and the entry
of the United States into the war.

Until France collapsed and Hitler's armies stood victorious on Europe's Atlantic coast, the efforts of the American government to influence
the world situation did not extend beyond the use of moral force, legal
argument, and economic measures—all so contrived as to avoid military
and political guarantees of any kind whatever. Even the coming of
war in Europe had produced no fundamental change. While it was
never impartial in the strict sense of the word, the United States adhered
generally to its concept of formal neutrality from September 1939 until
June 1940. Once Germany threatened to invade England, seize control
of the eastern Atlantic, and deprive the democratic cause of its last foothold in the European theater, however, the American government
quickly abandoned a part of its underlying caution. Justifying its acts
on grounds of national defense, it now began to give the British significant material aid and diplomatic support and to lay plans for a possibly
deeper involvement in the future. The ultimate effect of thus identi-

fying the British cause with the security of the Western Hemisphere was to bring the United States and Great Britain as close together as they could have been brought by a formal treaty of alliance. While localized differences continued to mar the singleness of Anglo-American endeavors, this tight and active association with the British Commonwealth remained the dominant theme.

II

The extremely isolationist neutrality act which became law on May 1, 1937, was responsible to some degree for the weakness in the next twenty-eight months of American efforts to dissuade Germany from going to war. More indirectly, it hampered the effective conduct of relations with Japan for an even longer period. That it restricted the President's freedom to issue threats and make promises cannot be denied, but the powerful national sentiment which lay behind the law was a much greater obstacle to decisive action. For the American people, long after the act was substantially modified, remained strongly opposed to any commitments which might draw the United States into a European or an Asiatic war. The President's reluctance to affront this sentiment made him extremely—perhaps unduly—cautious about using the wide authority over the conduct of foreign relations that he still enjoyed.

The deeply rooted conviction that the United States should have nothing to do with armed conflict arising outside the Western Hemisphere was partly the fruit of American tradition and partly the result of a special disillusionment with the First World War. But the more extravagant attempts to revise the Versailles war-guilt thesis, a certain misreading of the lessons of American intervention in 1917, and such parallel influences as those which grew from the work of the Nye Committee helped give isolationism the peculiarly virulent form it assumed in the middle nineteen-thirties and largely determined the content of the early neutrality acts.

Because it gradually changed with the advance of time, the external policy of the Roosevelt administration between 1933 and the summer of 1940 cannot be dismissed with any single judgment. Although the principles of internationalism gained some recognition at the theoretical level in 1933, American foreign policy until 1937 was tentative, shapeless, and wholly secondary to the treatment of domestic problems. By and large, the administration deprecated the growth of isolationism in the

United States. But it was internationalist more by precept than by example. In part, this weakness grew out of the President's resolve to deal
gently with public opinion. And some of it was inherent in the nature
of his own early objectives, for his domestic rehabilitation program called
for a wide degree of economic nationalism.

Not until 1937 did the American government look consistently beyond the isolationism of the American people. From early 1937 to the
outbreak of war in September 1939, however, its caution was tempered
by a growing sense of responsibility and a sincere wish to control international tension so far as that could be done without political or military
commitment. Its use of the embargo in support of the nonintervention
committee's efforts to keep the Spanish civil war from overflowing the
boundaries of Spain was one evidence of this desire. Roosevelt's "quarantine" speech was another. His simultaneous espousal of Welles's
scheme to create a kind of world peace front was a third. But appeasement was now a definite policy in Europe; and it soon became clear that
the United States, if it wished to coöperate with other governments at
all, had to support Chamberlain's efforts to deal amicably with Hitler
and Mussolini. After some delay, the President did exactly that. When
the Anglo-Italian Mediterranean pact was signed in April 1938, he gave
the principle of economic appeasement his formal, if somewhat reluctant, benediction. And his clearly implied endorsement of Chamberlain's objectives during the Munich crisis apparently helped the Prime
Minister overcome a threatened division in his own Cabinet, while
Welles, if his public statement can be accepted, viewed the resulting
settlement with gratification.

The appeasement philosophy was based on the hope that patience,
open-mindedness, and a willingness to compromise would bring aggressor nations to their senses, persuading them that negotiation was more
profitable than war and affording moderate elements in such states an
opportunity to gain control. While the United States never paraded
its acceptance of this thesis as openly as Chamberlain did, it played a
substantial role in American foreign policy from 1937 onward, appearing in many different connections and under various guises. Nor was
appeasement always a mistake. Despite its unsavory name following the
collapse of the Munich settlement, it provided a sound approach to
worth-while objectives on more than one occasion.

Since Roosevelt had little hope of converting Germany after 1937,
the United States never became deeply involved in this phase of appease-

ment. But both he and Welles thought Italy would prove more amenable, and this conviction remained the basis of their Italian policy until the late spring of 1940. Hull thought it was futile to make concessions to Hitler and Mussolini, and events proved him right. Yet the Secretary of State relied on a similar hope in a number of other situations. This was especially evident in relations with Japan, Hull's own preserve. Although the revival of Japanese aggression in China during the summer of 1937 struck directly at American interests and responsibilities, the Far Eastern policy of the United States was soon reduced to a series of formal protests, accompanied by periodic reassertion of the principles of international virtue. This type of appeasement was not wholly discontinued until the summer of 1941.

The remaining aspects of American policy before September 1939 can be summed up quickly. While he made it clear that the United States assumed no responsibility for what happened in Europe, Roosevelt brought his personal counsels of restraint to bear in all major European crises from the summer of 1938 to the outbreak of the war. He also supplemented the nonrecognition doctrine with various economic measures which, if not very effective in themselves, expressed strong disapproval: the withholding of tariff reductions from aggressor nations, the discriminatory loan, the moral embargo, and the countervailing duty. A concurrent effort to improve the defenses of the United States and of the Western Hemisphere generally was reflected in the adoption of a more ambitious naval program and in the numerous agreements for cooperation with the other American republics.

Though the United States persisted until June 1940 in its refusal to accept new obligations, American policy underwent a subtle change soon after the European conflict began. As the war strengthened the nation's sympathies, confirmed its dislikes, and sharpened its fears, the administration tried to find means of preventing a complete German victory. This problem was attacked in four different ways. First, Roosevelt demanded and secured repeal of the arms embargo, thereby giving Britain and France permanent access to American war supplies on a cash-and-carry basis. Second, the State Department religiously avoided a complete break with Russia; as long as it could be regarded as a potential ally, Russia was not to be driven further into Hitler's camp. The Soviet dictatorship was not appeased entirely. But the neutrality acts were never invoked against it; diplomatic relations were not broken; and access to the Kremlin was maintained. Third, Roosevelt considered the possibility of a negotiated peace before the war should reach a more decisive phase. It was decided that nothing should be done to encourage German peace feelers in October 1939, but the President did open this question through the Welles and Mooney missions in February and March 1940. Fourth, he kept Germany from gaining control of new funds in the United States by freezing the American assets of Denmark, Norway, the Netherlands, and Belgium as those nations were occupied during the spring.

Although neutrality remained its official text, every major aspect of United States policy was thus oriented toward Great Britain and France. At the same time, the Allied cause rose steadily in public opinion. Neither then nor later did the American people display any eagerness for intervention. But they had always distrusted the consequences of German victory, and their fear of one side made them think more charitably of projects for helping the other. These fears reached a climax in May and June, as Hitler's armies moved from victory to victory in western Europe. American security was now confronted by a definite threat.

III

Amid the disasters of May, Winston Churchill began showering Roosevelt with specific requests for aid. When it became obvious that French resistance was nearing an end, the President waited no longer. With the arms transfer of early June, consummated by executive action, the United States moved from neutrality to nonbelligerency. The revival of naval talks with Great Britain in August confirmed this decision. And when the destroyer transfer was announced at the beginning of September it was clear that the American government had made a definite and permanent choice of sides. At the same time, the national defense program gained significant speed. The building of a two-ocean Navy was authorized in July, and the Selective Service Act became law on September 16.

The Japanese problem had assumed much larger proportions in the meanwhile. Notwithstanding their gravity, Far Eastern affairs had played a subordinate role in American policy since 1937. This was doubly true after the beginning of the European war; for if Japan's New Order constituted a direct threat to the American position in China, Germany endangered the Western Hemisphere itself. The denunciation of the commercial treaty with Japan had suggested an intent to use economic reprisals of a fairly drastic character. But the lapsing of the treaty in January 1940 brought no further action. Except for basing the Pacific Fleet at Pearl Harbor in May, Washington did not go beyond its established procedure of uniting general statements of principle with detailed complaints regarding Japanese violations of American rights.

When Japan began to move into Indo-China after the fall of France, however, the United States quickly took umbrage. In September Roosevelt used his new powers of export control to place scrap iron and steel under the licensing system. This struck a heavy blow at one aspect of Japan's precarious war economy, but it was as far as the United States went for some time. Japan again moved closer to Germany and Italy with the conclusion of the Tripartite Pact, an agreement which made it clear that European and Asiatic problems could no longer be separated, even in theory. This helped confirm old trends, and subsequent American planning was decisively founded on the principle that Germany should be stopped first. The building up of its own defenses and the widening of its coöperation with Britain remained the dominant objectives of the United States through the next twelve months.

Extensive progress was made between the autumn of 1940 and the late summer of 1941. The Lend-Lease Act solved the monumental economic problems of such a relationship, and the Washington staff report laid out the basic strategy of wartime collaboration. As a parallel to these developments, the United States assumed vast new responsibilities in the actual conduct of the war. It established a protectorate over Greenland, sent troops to occupy Iceland, and on at least two occasions during this period contemplated seizing the Azores. The patrol activities of the Atlantic Fleet were pushed eastward to the 26th meridian generally, and beyond it in the latitude of Iceland; American ships relieved the British Navy of escort duty over the western half of the transatlantic convoy route; and additional forces were moved from the Pacific to ensure an adequate performance of this demanding role. By September 1941 the American and German navies were openly engaged in a shooting war.

Meanwhile, every other aspect of United States policy was aimed at keeping international balances as static as possible: to maintain speaking, if not cordial, relations with Russia, whose good will often seemed a dubious quantity; to avoid a break with Japan, which grew no less restive as time went on; and to keep Germany from seizing any new strategic advantage in the Atlantic, southern Europe, the Mediterranean, or French Africa.

With respect to these goals, American diplomacy was cautious and slow-moving. Policy toward Russia followed the course which had been set in 1939. By playing upon the economic needs of France and of Spain, the United States strove to keep those countries from any damaging coöperation with Germany. There was also a last-minute effort, verbal in nature, to combat Nazi penetration of the Balkans. At the same time, policy toward Japan remained conservative. As the Japanese continued their advance in Indo-China and extended their influence in Thailand, Roosevelt gradually built up economic pressure against them by placing additional exports under licensing control. There was no drastic action, however. In his conversations with Nomura Hull clung firmly to his principles, but he drew no lines which Japan was forbidden to cross. Japan's avowed desire for a peaceful settlement even gave the Secretary a faint hope that its adherence to the Tripartite Pact might be loosened. This, together with an acceptable solution for the China Incident, became his principal objective in the talks which ran from April to July.

Such containment procedures were remarkably successful, on the whole, down to the summer of 1941. Although the American government was conscious of having fought a rear-guard action, it had suffered no very tangible reverses in the Far East, and it could count a number of definite gains so far as Europe was concerned. Germany had achieved little in either France or Spain; the *status quo* in French Africa and the western Mediterranean had not been disturbed; both the United Kingdom itself and Anglo-American control of the Atlantic were much more secure than they had been a year earlier. Only in the Balkans had Germany obtained a significant new advantage, and from the standpoint of grand strategy this was more than offset by the results of the Nazi attack on Russia.

This last development helped stabilize the affairs of western Europe immediately. But it also hastened Japan's decision to move south in force and placed the Far East in a state of growing crisis. As Japan took over the remainder of Indo-China and set itself for still greater expansion in the area beyond, the United States broke off the Hull-Nomura conversations, stopped all exports to Japan by impounding that country's American funds, and issued what amounted to an ultimatum against further advances at any point. This ended the administration's attempt to win Japan over by a kind of appeasement and signalized a total reversal of American policy in the Far East.

It was a dangerous, if nearly inevitable, decision. Anything less forceful would have had no chance of deterring Japan and would, in effect, have sanctioned the course Tokyo had chosen. But the action taken was drastic indeed. Japan had already been made to feel a distinct economic pinch, and the total embargo produced by the freezing order of July 26 cut off at one stroke its vital supply of American oil. Japan had to make a choice, and quickly: it could accept terms satisfactory to the United States, or it could seize new petroleum supplies where they were most readily available—that is, in southeastern Asia and the Indies. The freezing order, taken in conjunction with the warning of August 17, reduced the Japanese government, for all practical purposes, to a choice between surrender and war.

If the United States had been ready for war in the Pacific, this simultaneous application of economic and political pressure might have achieved its end. But the United States was not ready, nor could it devote its full attention to getting ready. Although Germany's war with the Soviet Union somewhat lightened the tasks of American diplomacy in Europe, it tended to increase the total demand on the nation's resources. Growing responsibilities in the Atlantic forbade any diversion of strength from that theater; Britain's needs were as great as ever, and added to these were the burdens of the Russian-aid program. Only by changing the over-all strategic plan, slighting Great Britain and Russia, and withdrawing some naval forces from the Atlantic could the American potential for taking decisive action in the Far East have been altered as quickly as Washington's diplomatic mien, and the arguments against such a course were overwhelming. Immediate political objectives now reached far beyond the military preparation needed to sustain them. From this moment forward it was a question of how long the disparity could be maintained without a breakdown.

Japan, of course, still wanted to get as much as possible by peaceful means. And the American government, although it had forsaken the real basis of its delaying tactics, still wanted to postpone a rupture as long as it could. Hence the reopening of conversations in the latter part of August, the fruitless and somewhat farcical negotiations concerning a leaders' conference, and the study of a possible *modus vivendi*. But the advantage never rested with Hull and Roosevelt. Japan was prepared to act, the United States was not; and both sides understood these facts perfectly.

IV

Considering their multitudinous problems, domestic and foreign, the authors of American policy accomplished a great deal from 1937 onward. Their deeds sometimes failed to bear out their words, and they did not always choose the best among possible alternatives. Nevertheless, their part in the general failure to halt aggression before it led to war was a small one. Much could be said about the potentialities of the years before 1937, but there was little chance of creating a genuine peace front after that time.

The American government's generalized support of Chamberlain's program in 1938 had little practical importance. It was a rather detached support in any event, and Chamberlain was obviously determined to give his hopes a trial whether the United States shared them or not. American efforts to deal gently with totalitarian governments after the war started were not undertaken primarily to avoid responsibility. They grew out of a prudent desire to keep such nations from adopting expedients which would make a bad situation even worse. That the policy of the United States toward Russia, Vichy France, and Spain was justified in each instance by the results up to the end of 1941 can hardly be denied. One might ask, indeed, whether a more sympathetic appreciation of Japan's economic troubles would not have yielded valuable dividends at certain points in relations with that country.

Sometimes American policy was confused by internal divisions. This was especially true in the relations with France and with Spain. On larger issues Welles and Hull repeatedly disagreed. The Under Secretary was fertile with expedients, some of which were not very practical, while Hull now and then carried his misgivings to the point of utter inaction. Stimson, too, was critical of certain policy trends, for he thought the administration lacked courage in its dealings with public opinion. But Roosevelt was, in final analysis, the real maker of policy, and the external effect of such differences was never grave. Far Eastern policy was badly muddled in the autumn of 1941, but attendant circumstances rather than confused thinking lay at the root of this difficulty.

Otherwise, the American government followed a clear set of objectives with persistence and skill from the fall of France to the attack on Pearl Harbor. This did not avert war, nor did it postpone war as long as had been hoped. But the alternative—to do nothing—might have resulted in disaster. As it was, the United States entered the conflict with a basic plan and a corresponding, if partial, deployment of forces which led to ultimate victory.

Bibliography

MANUSCRIPT SOURCES

Papers of the Department of State, Washington, D. C.:

File Numbers

121.840 Welles, Sumner	761.94
124.61	762.9411
700.00116—M.E.	793.94
711.52	852.00
711.61	852.51
711.94	852.6363
740.0011 European War 1939	860D.51
740.0011 Pacific War	860D.61
741.61	893.24
760D.61	894.00

Franklin D. Roosevelt Papers, Franklin D. Roosevelt Memorial Library, Hyde Park, New York.

PRINTED SOURCES

1. *Official Documents*

FRANCE

Foreign Office

Le Livre jaune français: Documents diplomatiques, 1938–1939. Paris: Imprimerie Nationale, 1939.

High Court of Justice

Le Procès du Maréchal Pétain, Vol. I. Paris: Éditions Albin Michel, 1945. 2 vols.

GERMANY

Foreign Office

Documents on Events Preceding the Outbreak of the War. New York: German Library of Information, 1940.

Roosevelts Weg in den Krieg: Geheimdokumente zur Kriegspolitik des Präsidenten der Vereinigten Staaten. Berlin: Im Deutschen Verlag, 1943.

GREAT BRITAIN

Foreign Office

Agreement between His Majesty's Government in the United Kingdom and the Government of the Union of Soviet Socialist Republics Providing for Joint Action in the War against Germany (with Protocol), Moscow, July 12, 1941, Cmd. 6304 (1941). London: H. M. Stationery Office, 1941.

Agreement between the United Kingdom and Italy, Consisting of a Protocol with Annexes and Exchanges of Notes, April 16, 1938, Cmd. 5726 (1938). London: H. M. Stationery Office, 1938.

Documents concerning German-Polish Relations and the Outbreak of Hostilities between Great Britain and Germany on September 3rd, 1939. New York: Farrar and Rinehart, 1939.

Parliament

House of Commons

The Parliamentary Debates: Official Report, 5th series, Vols. CCCXXX, CCCXLV–CCCXLVII, CCCL, CCCLVIII, CCCLXII-CCCLXV, CCCLXX. London: H. M. Stationery Office, 1909——.

House of Lords

The Parliamentary Debates: Official Report, 5th series, Vol. CVI. London: H. M. Stationery Office, 1909——.

INTERNATIONAL MILITARY TRIBUNAL

Nazi Conspiracy and Aggression, Vols. IV, VI. Washington, D. C.: U. S. Govt. Printing Office, 1946–1947. 11 vols.

The Trial of German Major War Criminals: Proceedings of the International Military Tribunal Sitting at Nuremberg, Germany, pt. 13. London: H. M. Stationery Office, 1947–1949. 21 parts.

POLAND

Foreign Office

Official Documents concerning Polish-German and Polish-Soviet Relations, 1933-1939. London: Hutchinson and Co., 1939.

UNITED STATES

Congress

A Compilation of the Messages and Papers of the Presidents, 1789-1902, ed. James D. Richardson, Vols. I, II. New York: Bureau of National Literature and Art, 1903. 10 vols.

Congressional Record, Vols. LXX, LXXVI, LXXXI, LXXXIII–LXXXVII. Washington, D. C.: U. S. Govt. Printing Office, 1874——.

House of Representatives

Committee on Foreign Affairs

Arming American Merchant Vessels: Hearings before the Committee on Foreign Affairs on H. J. Res. 237, Oct. 13 and 14, 1941 (77th Cong., 1st sess.). Washington, D. C.: U. S. Govt. Printing Office, 1941.

House Report No. 2040 (72nd Cong., 2nd sess.). Washington, D. C.: U. S. Govt. Printing Office, 1933.

House Report No. 1727 (73rd Cong., 2nd sess.). Washington, D. C.: U. S. Govt. Printing Office, 1934.

House Report No. 1267 (77th Cong., 1st sess.). Washington, D. C.: U. S. Govt. Printing Office, 1941.

Journal of the House of Representatives of the United States of America. Washington, D. C.: U. S. Govt. Printing Office and others, 1814——.

Joint Committee on Investigation of Pearl Harbor Attack

Hearings Pursuant to S. Con. Res. 27, Authorizing Investigation of Attack on Pearl Harbor, Dec. 7, 1941, and Events and Circumstances Relating Thereto (79th Cong., 1st and 2nd sess.). Washington, D. C.: U. S. Govt. Printing Office, 1946. 39 parts.

Investigation of Pearl Harbor Attack, Report Pursuant to S. Con. Res. 27, to Investigate Attack on Pearl Harbor on December 7, 1941, and Events and Circumstances Relating Thereto (79th Cong., 2nd sess.), S. Doc. 244. Washington, D. C.: U. S. Govt. Printing Office, 1946.

Senate

Committee on Foreign Relations

Senate Report No. 1155 (76th Cong., 2nd sess.). Washington, D. C.: U. S. Govt. Printing Office, 1939.

Senate Report No. 764 (77th Cong., 1st sess.). Washington, D. C.: U. S. Govt. Printing Office, 1941.

Committee on Naval Affairs

Senate Report No. 617 (77th Cong., 1st sess.). Washington, D. C.: U. S. Govt. Printing Office, 1941.

Journal of the Senate of the United States of America. Washington, D. C.: U. S. Govt. Printing Office and others, 1814——.

Special Committee to Investigate the Munitions Industry

Senate Report No. 944 (74th Cong., 2nd sess.), pt. 5. Washington, D. C.: U. S. Govt. Printing Office, 1936. 40 parts.

Department of the Navy

Fuehrer Conferences on Matters Dealing with the German Navy, 1939–1941. Washington, D. C.: Issued in mimeographed form by the Office of Naval Intelligence, 1947. 5 vols.

Department of State

Department of State Bulletin. Washington, D. C.: U. S. Govt. Printing Office, 1939——.

Department of State Press Releases. Washington, D. C.: U. S. Govt. Printing Office, 1929–1939.

Digest of International Law, by Green H. Hackworth, Vol. IV. Washington, D. C.: U. S. Govt. Printing Office, 1940–1944. 8 vols.

Documents on German Foreign Policy, 1918–1945, Series D, Vols. I, II. Washington, D. C.: U. S. Govt. Printing Office, 1949——.

"German Documents on Sumner Welles Mission, 1940," *Department of State Bulletin,* XIV (Mar. 24, 1946), 459–466.

Nazi-Soviet Relations, 1939–1941. Washington, D. C.: U. S. Govt. Printing Office, 1948.

Papers Relating to the Foreign Relations of the United States—1911, 1917 Supplement, 1927, 1928, 1932. Washington, D. C.: U. S. Govt. Printing Office, 1862——.

Papers Relating to the Foreign Relations of the United States: Japan, 1931–1941. Washington, D. C.: U. S. Govt. Printing Office, 1943. 2 vols.

Peace and War: United States Foreign Policy, 1931–1941. Washington, D. C.: U. S. Govt. Printing Office, 1943.

Soviet Supply Protocols. Washington, D. C.: U. S. Govt. Printing Office, 1948.

The Spanish Government and the Axis: Official German Documents. Washington, D. C.: U. S. Govt. Printing Office, 1946.

United States and Italy, 1936–1946: Documentary Record. Washington, D. C.: U. S. Govt. Printing Office, 1946.

United States Statutes at Large, Vols. XLIX, L, LII, LIV, LV. Washington, D. C.: U. S. Govt. Printing Office and others, 1845——.

National Archives

Federal Register, Vols. IV–VI. Washington, D. C.: U. S. Govt. Printing Office, 1936——.

Office of Lend-Lease Administration

Third Report on Lend-Lease Operations. Washington, D. C.: U. S. Govt. Printing Office, 1941.

Strategic Bombing Survey

The Effects of Bombing on Japan's War Economy. Washington, D. C.: U. S. Govt. Printing Office, 1946.

URUGUAY

Foreign Office

The Uruguayan Blue Book: Outline of Events Prior to the Sinking of the "Admiral Graf Spee" and the Internment of the Merchant Vessel "Tacoma." London: Hutchinson and Co., 1940.

2. Unofficial Documentary Collections

BASSETT, JOHN SPENCER, ed., *Selections from "The Federalist."* New York: Charles Scribner's Sons, 1921.

CHAMBERLAIN, NEVILLE, *In Search of Peace.* New York: G. P. Putnam's Sons, 1939.

CHURCHILL, WINSTON S., *The Unrelenting Struggle,* comp. Charles Eade. Boston: Little, Brown, and Co., 1942.

ROOSEVELT, FRANKLIN D., *The Public Papers and Addresses of Franklin D. Roosevelt—1937, 1938, 1939, 1940,* comp. S. I. Rosenman. New York: Random House, Macmillan Co., Harper and Bros., 1938–1950. 13 vols.

ROYAL INSTITUTE OF INTERNATIONAL AFFAIRS, *Documents on International Affairs, 1937,* ed. J. W. Wheeler-Bennett. London: Oxford Univ. Press, 1938.

—— *The American Speeches of Lord Lothian, July 1939 to December 1940.* London: Oxford Univ. Press, 1941.

WILSON, WOODROW, *President Wilson's Foreign Policy: Messages, Addresses, Papers,* ed. James Brown Scott. New York: Oxford Univ. Press, 1918.

WORLD PEACE FOUNDATION, *Documents on American Foreign Relations—1938–1939, 1939–1940, 1940–1941, 1941–1942,* ed. S. Shepard Jones and Denys P. Myers. Boston: World Peace Foundation, 1939——.

3. Personal Papers, Letters, Diaries, Memoirs

ADAMS, JOHN, *The Works of John Adams,* ed. Charles Francis Adams, Vols. II, VIII, IX. Boston: Little, Brown, and Co., 1850–1856. 10 vols.

BRERETON, LEWIS H., *The Brereton Diaries: The War in the Air in the Pacific, Middle East, and Europe, 3 October 1941—8 May 1945.* New York: William Morrow and Co., 1946.

BULLITT, WILLIAM C., "How We Won the War and Lost the Peace," *Life,* XXV (Aug. 30, 1948), 83–97.

CASSIDY, HENRY C., *Moscow Dateline, 1941–1943.* Boston: Houghton Mifflin Co., 1943.

CECIL, VISCOUNT ROBERT, *A Great Experiment: An Autobiography.* New York: Oxford Univ. Press, 1941.

CHURCHILL, WINSTON S., *Step by Step, 1936–1939.* New York: G. P. Putnam's Sons, 1939.

—— *The Gathering Storm.* Boston: Houghton Mifflin Co., 1948.

—— *The Grand Alliance.* Boston: Houghton Mifflin Co., 1950.

—— *Their Finest Hour.* Boston: Houghton Mifflin Co., 1949.

CIANFARRA, CAMILLE M., *The Vatican and the War.* New York: E. P. Dutton and Co., 1944.

CIANO, COUNT GALEAZZO, *The Ciano Diaries, 1939–1943,* ed. Hugh Gibson. Garden City, N. Y.: Doubleday and Co., 1946.

DAVIES, JOSEPH E., *Mission to Moscow.* New York: Simon and Schuster, 1941.

DEANE, JOHN R., *The Strange Alliance: The Story of Our Efforts at Wartime Coöperation with Russia.* New York: Viking Press, 1947.

DODD, WILLIAM E., *Ambassador Dodd's Diary, 1933–1938,* ed. W. E. Dodd, Jr., and Martha Dodd. New York: Harcourt, Brace, and Co., 1941.

EDDIS, WILLIAM, *Letters from America.* London, 1792.

FARLEY, JAMES A., *Jim Farley's Story: The Roosevelt Years.* New York: Whittlesey House, 1948.

FISCHER, LOUIS, *Men and Politics.* New York: Duell, Sloan, and Pearce, 1941.

FRANKLIN, BENJAMIN, *The Works of Benjamin Franklin,* ed. John Bigelow, Vol. X. New York: G. P. Putnam's Sons, 1904. 12 vols.

GAFENCU, GRIGORE, *Last Days of Europe: A Diplomatic Journey in 1939,* tr. E. Fletcher-Allen. New Haven: Yale Univ. Press, 1948.

—— *Prelude to the Russian Campaign: From the Moscow Pact (August 21st 1939) to the Opening of Hostilities in Russia (June 22nd 1941),* tr. E. Fletcher-Allen. London: Frederick Muller, 1945.

GREW, JOSEPH C., *Ten Years in Japan.* New York: Simon and Schuster, 1944.

—— *Turbulent Era; A Diplomatic Record of Forty Years, 1904–1945,* ed. Walter Johnson, Vol. II. Boston: Houghton Mifflin Co., 1952. 2 vols.

HAYES, CARLTON J. H., *Wartime Mission in Spain, 1942–1945.* New York: Macmillan Co., 1946.

HENDERSON, SIR NEVILE, *Failure of a Mission: Berlin, 1937–1939.* New York: G. P. Putnam's Sons, 1940.

HIGGINSON, FRANCIS, *New-England's Plantation.* London, 1630.

HITLER, ADOLF, AND MUSSOLINI, BENITO, *Les Lettres secrètes échangées par Hitler et Mussolini,* with introd. by André François-Poncet. Paris: Éditions du Pavois, 1946.

HOARE, SIR SAMUEL (VISCOUNT TEMPLEWOOD), *Complacent Dictator.* New York: Alfred A. Knopf, 1947.

HULL, CORDELL, *The Memoirs of Cordell Hull.* New York: Macmillan Co., 1948. 2 vols.

ICKES, HAROLD L., "My Twelve Years with F. D. R.," *Saturday Evening Post,* CCXX (June 5–26, 1948), and CCXXI (July 3–24, 1948).

IND, ALLISON, *Bataan: The Judgment Seat.* New York: Macmillan Co., 1944.

JEFFERSON, THOMAS, *The Works of Thomas Jefferson,* ed. Paul Leicester Ford, Vols. IV, V. New York: G. P. Putnam's Sons, 1904–1905. 12 vols.

LANSING, ROBERT, *War Memoirs of Robert Lansing.* Indianapolis, Ind.: Bobbs-Merrill Co., 1935.

LEAHY, WILLIAM D., *I Was There.* New York: Whittlesey House, 1950.

MCINTIRE, ROSS T. (WITH GEORGE CREEL), *White House Physician.* New York: G. P. Putnam's Sons, 1946.

MOLEY, RAYMOND, *After Seven Years.* New York: Harper and Bros., 1939.

MORGENTHAU, HENRY, JR., "The Morgenthau Diaries," *Collier's Magazine,* CXX (Sept. 27—Nov. 1, 1947).

MYERS, ALBERT C., ed., *Narratives of Early Pennsylvania, West New Jersey, and Delaware, 1603–1707.* New York: Charles Scribner's Sons, 1912.

NOMURA, KICHISABURO, "Stepping Stones to War," United States Naval Institute, *Proceedings,* LXXVII (Sept. 1951), 927–931.

PAINE, THOMAS, *The Writings of Thomas Paine,* ed. Moncure D. Conway, Vol. I. New York: G. P. Putnam's Sons, 1906. 4 vols.

PERKINS, FRANCES, *The Roosevelt I Knew.* New York: Viking Press, 1946.

ROOSEVELT, ELLIOTT, *As He Saw It.* New York: Duell, Sloan, and Pearce, 1946.

ROOSEVELT, FRANKLIN D., *F. D. R.: His Personal Letters, 1928–1945,* ed. Elliott Roosevelt, Vol. II. New York: Duell, Sloan, and Pearce, 1950. 2 vols.

SERRANO SUÑER, RAMÓN, *Entre les Pyrénées et Gibraltar.* Geneva: Les Éditions du Cheval Ailé, 1948.

SHOTWELL, JAMES T., *On the Rim of the Abyss.* New York: Macmillan Co., 1936.

SMITH, JOHN, *Travels and Works of Captain John Smith, 1580–1631,* ed. Edward Arber, Vol. I. Edinburgh: John Grant, 1910. 2 vols.

STETTINIUS, EDWARD R., JR., *Lend-Lease: Weapon for Victory.* New York: Macmillan Co., 1944.

STIMSON, HENRY L., *The Far Eastern Crisis; Recollections and Observations.* New York: Harper and Bros., for the Council on Foreign Relations, 1936.

STIMSON, HENRY L., AND BUNDY, MCGEORGE, *On Active Service: In Peace and War.* New York: Harper and Bros., 1948.

TAYLOR, MYRON C., ed., *Wartime Correspondence between President Roosevelt and Pope Pius XII.* New York: Macmillan Co., 1947.

TOLISCHUS, OTTO D., *Tokyo Record.* New York: Reynal and Hitchcock, 1943.

TULLY, GRACE, *F. D. R., My Boss.* New York: Charles Scribner's Sons, 1949.

WAINWRIGHT, JONATHAN M., *General Wainwright's Story,* ed. Robert Considine. Garden City, N. Y.: Doubleday and Co., 1946.

WASHINGTON, GEORGE, *The Writings of George Washington,* ed. John C. Fitzpatrick, Vol. XXXI. Washington, D. C.: U. S. Govt. Printing Office, 1931–1944. 39 vols.

WASSON, THOMAS C., "The Mystery of Dakar," *American Foreign Service Journal,* XX (Apr. 1943), 169–174 ff.

WELLES, SUMNER, *Seven Decisions That Shaped History.* New York: Harper and Bros., 1950.

—— *The Time for Decision,* 9th ed. New York: Harper and Bros., 1944.

—— *Where Are We Heading?* New York: Harper and Bros., 1946.

WINANT, JOHN G., *Letter from Grosvenor Square: An Account of a Stewardship.* Boston: Houghton Mifflin Co., 1947.

ZACHARIAS, ELLIS M., *Secret Missions: The Story of an Intelligence Officer.* New York: G. P. Putnam's Sons, 1946.

4. Biographies, Histories, Monographs, Articles

ALSOP, JOSEPH, AND KINTNER, ROBERT, *American White Paper: The Story of American Diplomacy and the Second World War.* New York: Simon and Schuster, 1940.

ANDREWS, CHARLES M., *The Colonial Background of the American Revolution.* New Haven: Yale Univ. Press, 1924.

"Arms and the Men," *Fortune,* IX (Mar. 1934), 53–57 ff. [An article by the editors.]

BAILEY, THOMAS A., *The Man in the Street: The Impact of American Public Opinion on Foreign Policy.* New York: Macmillan Co., 1948.

—— *Woodrow Wilson and the Great Betrayal.* New York: Macmillan Co., 1945.

BALLANTINE, JOSEPH W., "Mukden to Pearl Harbor: The Foreign Policies of Japan," *Foreign Affairs,* XXVII (July 1949), 651–664.

BARNARD, ELLSWORTH, "War and the Verities," *Harper's Magazine,* CLXXX (Jan. 1940), 113–128.

BARNES, HARRY ELMER, "Assessing the Blame for the World War," *Current History,* XX (May 1924), 171–195.

—— Review of *Europe since 1870,* by E. R. Turner, *New Republic,* XXIX (Jan. 18, 1922), 228–230.

—— "Seven Books of History against the Germans," *New Republic,* XXXVIII (Mar. 19, 1924), 10–15.

—— *The Genesis of the World War: An Introduction to the Problem of War Guilt.* New York: Alfred A. Knopf, 1926.

BEARD, CHARLES A., *American Foreign Policy in the Making, 1932–1940: A Study in Responsibilities.* New Haven: Yale Univ. Press, 1946.

—— *President Roosevelt and the Coming of the War, 1941: A Study in Appearances and Realities.* New Haven: Yale Univ. Press, 1948.

—— *The Devil Theory of War.* New York: Vanguard Press, 1936.

BEMIS, SAMUEL FLAGG, *Jay's Treaty.* New York: Macmillan Co., 1923.

—— *The Diplomacy of the American Revolution.* New York: D. Appleton-Century Co., 1935.

BENDINER, ROBERT, *The Riddle of the State Department.* New York: Farrar and Rinehart, 1942.

BORCHARD, EDWIN M., "The Attorney General's Opinion on the Exchange of Destroyers for Naval Bases," *American Journal of International Law,* XXXIV (Oct. 1940), 690–699.

—— AND LAGE, WILLIAM P., *Neutrality for the United States.* New Haven: Yale Univ. Press, 1937.

BRIGGS, HERBERT W., "Neglected Aspects of the Destroyer Deal," *American Journal of International Law,* XXXIV (Oct. 1940), 569–587.

BRUNER, JEROME S., *Mandate from the People.* New York: Duell, Sloan, and Pearce, 1944.

CANTRIL, HADLEY, "America Faces the War: A Study in Public Opinion," *Public Opinion Quarterly,* IV (Sept. 1940), 387–407.

CORWIN, EDWARD S., *The President: Office and Powers,* 2nd ed. New York: New York Univ. Press, 1941.

CURTI, MERLE E., *The American Peace Crusade, 1815–1860.* Durham, N. C.: Duke Univ. Press, 1929.

—— *The Roots of American Loyalty.* New York: Columbia Univ. Press, 1946.

DALLIN, DAVID J., *Soviet Russia's Foreign Policy, 1939–1942,* tr. Leon Denman. New Haven: Yale Univ. Press, 1942.

DAVIS, FORREST, AND LINDLEY, ERNEST K., *How War Came.* New York: Simon and Schuster, 1942.

DEAK, FRANCIS, "The United States Neutrality Acts: Theory and Practice," *International Conciliation,* No. 358 (Mar. 1940), pp. 71–128.

DeWilde, John C., "The War and American Shipping," *Foreign Policy Reports,* XVI (Apr. 1, 1940), 18–28.

Dulles, Allen W., and Armstrong, Hamilton Fish, *Can We Be Neutral?* New York: Harper and Bros., for the Council on Foreign Relations, 1936.

Eagleton, Clyde, "The Duty of Impartiality on the Part of a Neutral," *American Journal of International Law,* XXXIV (Jan. 1940), 99–104.

Engelbrecht, Helmuth C., and Hanighen, F. C., *Merchants of Death: A Study of the International Armaments Industry.* New York: Dodd, Mead, and Co., 1934.

Fay, Sidney B., "New Light on the Origins of the World War," *American Historical Review,* XXV (July 1920), 616–639; XXVI (Oct. 1920), 37–53; XXVI (Jan. 1921), 225–254.

—— *The Origins of the World War.* New York: Macmillan Co., 1928. 2 vols.

Feiling, Keith G., *The Life of Neville Chamberlain.* London: Macmillan and Co., 1946.

Feis, Herbert, *The Road to Pearl Harbor.* Princeton, N. J.: Princeton Univ. Press, 1950.

—— *The Spanish Story: Franco and the Nations at War.* New York: Alfred A. Knopf, 1948.

Fenwick, Charles G., "Neutrality on the Defensive," *American Journal of International Law,* XXXIV (Oct. 1940), 697–699.

—— "The 'Implication of Consultation' in the Pact of Paris," *American Journal of International Law,* XXVI (Oct. 1932), 787–789.

Fleming, Denna F., *The United States and the League of Nations, 1918–1920.* New York: G. P. Putnam's Sons, 1932.

—— *The United States and World Organization, 1920–1933.* New York: Columbia Univ. Press, 1938.

Gabriel, Ralph H., *Main Currents in American History.* New York: D. Appleton–Century Co., 1942.

Garner, James W., "Non-Recognition of Illegal Territorial Annexations and Claims to Sovereignty," *American Journal of International Law,* XXX (Oct. 1936), 679–688.

Goodman, Warren H., "The Origins of the War of 1812: A Survey of Changing Interpretations," *Mississippi Valley Historical Review,* XXVIII (Sept. 1941), 171–186.

Gordon, Margaret S., *Barriers to World Trade: A Study of Recent Commercial Policy.* New York: Macmillan Co., 1941.

Grattan, C. Hartley, *Why We Fought.* New York: Vanguard Press, 1929.

Griswold, A. Whitney, *The Far Eastern Policy of the United States.* New York: Harcourt, Brace, and Co., 1938.

HART, ALBERT BUSHNELL, "A Dissent from the Conclusions of Professor Barnes," *Current History*, XX (May 1924), 195–196.

HILL, CHESNEY, "Recent Policies of Non-Recognition," *International Conciliation*, No. 293 (Oct. 1933), pp. 357–477.

HINTON, HAROLD B., *Cordell Hull: A Biography*. Garden City, N. Y.: Doubleday, Doran, and Co., 1942.

HYDE, CHARLES CHENEY, "The City of Flint," *American Journal of International Law*, XXXIV (Jan. 1940), 89–95.

JACOB, PHILIP E., "Influences of World Events on U. S. 'Neutrality' Opinion," *Public Opinion Quarterly*, IV (Mar. 1940), 48–65.

JOHNSON, ALAN CAMPBELL, *Viscount Halifax: A Biography*. New York: Ives Washburn, 1941.

JOHNSON, WALTER, *The Battle Against Isolation*. Chicago: Univ. Chicago Press, 1944.

JOHNSTONE, WILLIAM C., *The United States and Japan's New Order*, rev. ed. New York: Oxford Univ. Press, 1941.

KARIG, WALTER (with Earl Burton and Stephen L. Freeland), *Battle Report: The Atlantic War*. New York: Farrar and Rinehart, 1946.

KOENIG, LOUIS W., *The Presidency and the Crisis: Powers of the Office from the Invasion of Poland to Pearl Harbor*. New York: King's Crown Press, 1944.

LANGER, ROBERT, *Seizure of Territory: The Stimson Doctrine and Related Principles in Legal Theory and Diplomatic Practice*. Princeton, N. J.: Princeton Univ. Press, 1947.

LANGER, WILLIAM L., *Our Vichy Gamble*. New York: Alfred A. Knopf, 1947.

—— AND GLEASON, S. EVERETT, *The Challenge to Isolation, 1937–1940*. New York: Harper and Bros., for the Council on Foreign Relations, 1952.

LASSWELL, HAROLD D., *Propaganda Technique in the World War*. New York: Alfred A. Knopf, 1927.

LAUTERPACHT, HERSH, *Recognition in International Law*. Cambridge, Eng.: Cambridge Univ. Press, 1947.

LAVINE, HAROLD, AND WECHSLER, JAMES, *War Propaganda and the United States*. New Haven: Yale Univ. Press, 1940.

McCLURE, WALLACE M., *International Executive Agreements*. New York: Columbia Univ. Press, 1941.

McNAIR, ARNOLD D., "The Stimson Doctrine of Non-Recognition," *British Yearbook of International Law*, XIV (1933), 65–74.

MASLAND, JOHN W., "Pressure Groups and American Foreign Policy," *Public Opinion Quarterly*, VI (Spring 1942), 115–122.

—— "The 'Peace' Groups Join Battle," *Public Opinion Quarterly*, IV (Dec. 1940), 664–673.

MILLIS, WALTER, *The Road to War; America, 1914–1917.* Boston: Houghton Mifflin Co., 1935.

MORISON, SAMUEL ELIOT, *The Battle of the Atlantic, 1939–1943.* Boston: Little, Brown, and Co., 1947.

—— *The Rising Sun in the Pacific, 1931—April 1942.* Boston: Little, Brown, and Co., 1948.

MORRISSEY, ALICE M., *The American Defense of Neutral Rights, 1914–1917.* Cambridge, Mass.: Harvard Univ. Press, 1939.

NAMIER, LOUIS B., *Diplomatic Prelude, 1938–1939.* London: Macmillan and Co., 1948.

NEVINS, ALLAN, *America in World Affairs.* New York: Oxford Univ. Press, 1942.

PEARSON, DREW, AND BROWN, CONSTANTINE, *The American Diplomatic Game.* Garden City, N. Y.: Doubleday, Doran, and Co., 1935.

PERKINS, DEXTER, *Hands Off: A History of the Monroe Doctrine.* Boston: Little, Brown, and Co., 1945.

PETERSON, HORACE C., *Propaganda for War: The Campaign against American Neutrality, 1914–1917.* Norman, Okla.: Univ. Oklahoma Press, 1939.

PONSONBY, SIR ARTHUR, *Falsehood in War-Time.* London: G. Allen and Unwin, 1928.

PREUSS, LAWRENCE, "Some Effects of Governmental Controls on Neutral Duties," American Society of International Law, *Proceedings, 1937,* pp. 108–119.

—— "The Concepts of Neutrality and Non-Belligerency," *Annals of the American Academy of Political and Social Science,* CCXVIII (Nov. 1941), 97–109.

PRINGLE, HENRY F., *Theodore Roosevelt: A Biography.* New York: Harcourt, Brace, and Co., 1931.

RAUCH, BASIL, *Roosevelt: From Munich to Pearl Harbor.* New York: Creative Age Press, 1950.

RIPPY, J. FRED, *America and the Strife of Europe.* Chicago: Univ. Chicago Press, 1938.

—— AND DEBO, ANGIE, "The Historical Background of the A ierican Policy of Isolation," *Smith College Studies in History,* IX (April–June 1934), 66–165.

ROBINSON, EDGAR E., *They Voted for Roosevelt: The Presidential Vote, 1932–1944.* Stanford University, Calif.: Stanford Univ. Press, 1947.

ROYAL INSTITUTE OF INTERNATIONAL AFFAIRS, *Survey of International Affairs—1937, 1938,* by Arnold J. Toynbee and others. London: Oxford Univ. Press, 1938, 1939.

SAVELLE, MAX H., "The Appearance of an American Attitude toward External Affairs, 1750–1775," *American Historical Review,* LII (July 1947), 655–666.

SCHMITT, BERNADOTTE E., *The Coming of the War*. New York: Charles Scribner's Sons, 1930. 2 vols.

SEYMOUR, CHARLES, *American Diplomacy during the World War*. Baltimore: Johns Hopkins Press, 1934.

—— *American Neutrality, 1914–1917*. New Haven: Yale Univ. Press, 1935.

—— *Woodrow Wilson and the World War*. New Haven: Yale Univ. Press, 1921.

—— BUELL, RAYMOND LESLIE, BECKER, CARL, AND OTHERS, "Assessing the Blame for the World War: A Symposium," *Current History*, XX (June 1924), 452–462.

SHERWOOD, ROBERT E., *Roosevelt and Hopkins: An Intimate History*. New York: Harper and Bros., 1948.

SHOTWELL, JAMES T., "Plans and Protocols to End War: Historical Outline and Guide," *International Conciliation*, No. 208 (Mar. 1925), pp. 79–109.

—— *What Germany Forgot*. New York: Macmillan Co., 1940.

SQUIRES, JAMES D., *British Propaganda at Home and in the United States from 1914 to 1917*. Cambridge, Mass.: Harvard Univ. Press, 1935.

STONER, JOHN E., *S. O. Levinson and the Pact of Paris: A Study in the Techniques of Influence*. Chicago: Univ. Chicago Press, 1942.

TANSILL, CHARLES C., *America Goes to War*. Boston: Little, Brown, and Co., 1938.

—— *Back Door to War: Roosevelt Foreign Policy, 1933–1941*. Chicago: Henry Regnery Co., 1952.

THOMPSON, VIRGINIA, "The Japan-Indochina Trade Pact," *Far Eastern Survey*, X (June 2, 1941), 116–118.

TREFOUSSE, HANS L., *Germany and American Neutrality, 1939–1941*. New York: Bookman Associates, 1951.

TYLER, MOSES COIT, *A History of American Literature*, Vol. II. New York: G. P. Putnam's Sons, 1878. 2 vols.

VAN ALSTYNE, RICHARD W., *American Diplomacy in Action: A Series of Case Studies*. Stanford University, Calif.: Stanford Univ. Press, 1944.

WARD, ROBERT E., "The Inside Story of the Pearl Harbor Plan," United States Naval Institute, *Proceedings*, LXXVII (Dec. 1951), 1271–1283.

WARREN, CHARLES, "The Troubles of a Neutral," *Foreign Affairs*, XII (Apr. 1934), 377–394.

WILLIAMS, BENJAMIN H., *Foreign Loan Policy of the United States since 1933*. New York: Council on Foreign Relations, 1939.

—— "The Coming of Economic Sanctions into American Practice," *American Journal of International Law*, XXXVII (July 1943), 386–396.

WRIGHT, QUINCY, "The Future of Neutrality," *International Conciliation*, No. 242 (Sept. 1928), pp. 353–442.

—— "The Meaning of the Pact of Paris," *American Journal of International Law*, XXVII (Jan. 1933), 39–61.

—— "The Stimson Note of Jan. 7, 1932," *American Journal of International Law*, XXVI (Apr. 1932), 342–349.

—— "The Transfer of Destroyers to Great Britain," *American Journal of International Law*, XXXIV (Oct. 1940), 680–689.

—— AND NELSON, CARL J., "American Attitudes toward Japan and China, 1937–1938," *Public Opinion Quarterly*, III (Jan. 1939), 46–62.

WUORINEN, JOHN H., ed., *Finland and World War II, 1939–1944*. New York: Ronald Press Co., 1948.

Index